Praise for *The Universal Tone*

'Santana's journey from obscurity and abject poverty to affluence and superstardom is expressed eloquently via an informal conversational style that captures the cadences of his speaking voice ... there's plenty of humour – and tales of rock 'n' roll excess – to offset any overriding sense of sobriety'
Charles Waring, *Mojo*

'A testament to [Santana's] geniality'
New Statesman

'Once you start to explore his life, you will not be able to put the book down'
The Beat Magazine

'In this frank and impassioned memoir, iconic, influential musician Santana ... weaves together the rhythmic, domestic and spiritual dimensions of his career. Generously reflective and well-balanced ... Charismatic and soulful ... An appreciative and unpretentious chronicle, this is required reading for Santana fans and devotees of classic rock legends'
Kirkus Reviews

About the Authors

CARLOS SANTANA was born in Autlán de Navarro, Mexico, in 1947. He is a guitarist, songwriter, and founding member of Santana. He has recorded or appeared on more than ninety albums. He lives in Las Vegas with his wife, the drummer Cindy Blackman.

ASHLEY KAHN was born in the Bronx, New York, in 1960. He is an author, journalist, educator, and production manager who has been in the music business since the 1980s. His books include *A Love Supreme: The Story of John Coltrane's Signature Album*. He lives in Fort Lee, New Jersey.

HAL MILLER was born in the Bronx, New York, in 1941. He is a jazz drummer, a writer, a frequent lecturer at music institutions, and one of the world's foremost collectors of jazz videos. He has been a close friend of Carlos Santana for almost thirty years. He lives in Albany, New York.

THE UNIVERSAL TONE

BRINGING MY STORY TO LIGHT

WITH ASHLEY KAHN
AND HAL MILLER

WEIDENFELD & NICOLSON

First published in Great Britain in 2014 by Orion Books
This paperback edition first published in 2017
by Weidenfeld & Nicolson
An imprint of the Orion Publishing Group Ltd
Carmelite House, 50 Victoria Embankment,
London, EC4Y 0DZ

An Hachette UK Company

1 3 5 7 9 10 8 6 4 2

A CIP catalogue record for this book
is available from the British Library.

ISBN (paperback)   978 1 409 15655 0
ISBN (ebook)   978 1 409 15656 7

Printed in Great Britain by
CPI Group (UK) Ltd, Croydon, CR0 4YY

The Orion Publishing Group's policy is to use papers that
are natural, renewable and recyclable and made from wood
grown in sustainable forests. The logging and manufacturing
processes are expected to conform to environmental
regulations of the country of origin.

www.orionbooks.co.uk

This book is dedicated to my dearest mother, Josefina B. Santana, for her power, patience, tenacity, unshakable faith, and total conviction. She was a lover of truth, and I feel her energy now more than ever. Thank you, Mom — I love you eternally. Your prayers worked.

Contents

CONTENTS

The Universal Tone

INTRODUCTION

Conviction and Charisma

Josefina Barragán   José Santana

Mi historia comienza con un desfile.

My story starts with a parade.

But really, we could start at any point in my life, and that would be cool. It's like the set list for a Santana concert. You could just rip it up, throw it in the air, then put it back together. Anything you start or end with can work, really. It's all the same circle, and it all connects.

There are a lot of chapters to my story. There are a lot in anyone's life. But my life has three parts. There's my musical journey; there's my being a son, brother, husband, and father—what I call domestic rhythm; and there's the spiritual dimension, the invisible realm. They are woven together tightly—the physical and the spiritual, the seriousness and the humor, the sacred and the earthy. So is this book.

I know you want to hear about the Fillmore and Woodstock, and you will. And about the '60s, the '70s, and of course about *Supernatural* and the awards shows and everything that's happened since then. I will give it all the correct, complete hug: my past teachers, my divorce, my new marriage, my being molested as a boy—all of it.

There is my childhood in Mexico and the trip we made from Autlán to Tijuana with my mom, sisters, and brothers. My dad teaching me violin and sending me my first electric guitar from San Francisco. My sisters sitting on top of me, forcing me to listen to Elvis. The family moving from Tijuana to San Francisco, where I learned English and began my life in a new country as a dishwasher.

This book is not a discography or a year-by-year chronicle of the rock group Santana's every show. All that is for another time and another book. This book is not *his*-tory, it's my story. In telling my story, I know that what I remember is a choice I have. There is such a thing as divine rationale: I call it celestial memory. In fact it's anyone's choice to look back and see the past as beauty and blessings. I think ice cream can taste sweeter when I look back on tasting it, and even the air can feel better in the lungs. I also celebrate honesty and the details that tell the stories of my life.

My goal was to make this book multisensory, to make it read the way my mother's home cooking tasted. Interesting but also delicious. Not crass, and not boring.

The food I love from Mexico, the clothes and the colors and the music, it's all still alive for me. I still smell the inside of the strip clubs in Tijuana and backstage at the Fillmore Auditorium in San Francisco. I see the people, I smell the weed. I feel the guitars I played in my hands and can hear the sounds each of them made. I'm so grateful for all these memories.

That parade I mentioned? That is *not* one of my memories. I don't remember it because I wasn't there. The day of the parade was when my father and mother met for the first time as adults. That's when it all began for me.

My mom would tell me that it was five in the afternoon—the sun was getting low, and everything looked golden, as it does at that time of day. All of a sudden she heard this commotion out on the street. This was in her hometown—Cihuatlán, in the Jalisco province in Mexico, on the Pacific coast. It was around 1938, when Mom was still living with her family. Her name was Josefina Barragán.

My grandfather—her dad—was complaining, "Oh, it's that *diablo* Farol." They called my dad El Farol. It literally means "lantern" and was a nickname they gave him because of a song he used to sing and play.

"What are you talking about?" she said. "It's him—José Santana." My mom had run into him once when she was a little kid and he was a teenager. Her ball landed between my dad's feet, and she ran over to get it. "Boo!" he said. "Hey, little blond girl, your hair is straight, like corn silk." And she ran away.

More than ten years later, my mom parted the window curtains and saw a group of people walking down the middle of the street with José in the lead—and all the town's prostitutes following him. Everyone was laughing, making music, and singing. The man who would become my father was holding up his violin bow like it was a flagpole, and a pair of panties and a brassiere were hanging from it. The mayor was next to my dad, and there were other musicians, too. The town priest, who was really pissed off, was following them and trying to throw holy water on everyone. They're all making this incredible *barulla*, this racket. The way my mom told it, I got the feeling that these guys had been carrying on all night and through the day and were just so full of themselves, drunk and wasted, that they decided to take the party into town. It was such a small town, anyway. Everybody was looking at this spectacle and shaking their heads.

The mayor just adored my dad. He loved musicians and their

lifestyle, so who's going to tell them they can't sing and play in the streets? Most people liked my dad—he was charismatic. He was born in Cuautla, a small town around three hours inland, and, like his father, he had become a musician. He had moved to Cihuatlán for the work—playing in symphonies and in bands that played popular Mexican songs. Don José, they called him.

In 1983, after my son, Salvador, was born, I visited that part of Mexico with my dad. I met a lady there who told me, "Carlos, I grew up with Don José. We were from the same generation. I want you to know that you might be recognized around the world. But here Don José is the Santana that counts." My dad just looked at me. I smiled and said, "Hey, that's fine with me."

Not everybody felt that way in Cihuatlán—not the priest, and definitely not my mom's dad. He didn't like José because he was a musician and especially because he was a real Mexican, a Mexican mestizo. You could see the Indian blood in him. He was dark in complexion and proud of it. But his name—Santana, or Santa Anna—came from Europe. Saint Anne was Mary's mother, Joseph's mother-in-law. Jesus's grandma. Can't get much more Catholic than that.

My mom's family was lighter-skinned, European. I once saw my family tree, and there's some Hebrew on that side of the family—there were many Jews who came over from Spain to the New World after 1492. We Santanas ate pork, but my mom had some strange rules about food—what we could and couldn't eat and when; foods that couldn't be eaten at the same time. Some of that could have been handed-down kosher stuff.

The Barragáns lived on a hacienda. They owned horses and stables and had people working for them. All my dad had was his violin.

That didn't stop my mom. She used to tell me, "When I saw your father at the front of that crazy parade I knew that would be the man I would marry and leave this little town with. I had to leave. I didn't like the smell of the ranch; I didn't like men who smelled like horses and leather. But your father did not smell like that."

José and Josefina met up and fell in love. She did not get any blessings from her father. They eloped on a horse; Dad just stole her away. Her family came looking for them, and a friend helped hide them in Cihuatlán. Then they ran off to Autlán, where they started our family. Mom was eighteen, and Dad was twenty-six. I was born a few years later, the middle child of seven.

I never found out exactly what the parade was about, what unholy event they were celebrating. My father never spoke about his younger days. He never spoke much about anything, really. It doesn't matter. I love all parts of their story: the sex and the religion and the humor. It shows Dad's supreme sense of charisma and mom's supreme conviction. It shows them coming together, and it shows what they gave to me.

From my mom I have this rage and fury to make things right. In all the pictures I've seen of my mom as a little girl, she has an intensity of focus about her, almost like she's angry—between angry and committed. At a very young age she questioned everything. She even questioned the Bible. "I need to know: I don't just accept something," she used to say. Her character was definitely made out of steel.

My dad was strong, too, but he was romantic. He loved playing music. I can remember how he would put his chin on the violin, slowly, as if it were the shoulder of a woman. Then he would put the bow on the strings with his eyes closed. All women belonged to him at that moment. He played from the center of his heart.

Dad lived to play, and he played to live. That's what musicians are meant to do. He played what was asked of him for work—polkas, boleros, mariachi music. But he was a pure melody guy at home. His favorites were the songs of Agustín Lara, who was the Cole Porter of Mexico—many of his songs were in the films of the time. He wrote the song "Farolito," which my dad loved to sing and was how he got the nickname El Farol. Since he played Lara's music for himself at home, that's the first music I heard. That and "Ave Maria."

This book was written to honor my dad and all the other musical heroes who left their fingerprints on me—my "Who's your daddy?" list. Lightnin' Hopkins, Jimmy Reed, and John Lee Hooker. B. B. King, Albert King, and Otis Rush. Buddy Guy, Jimi Hendrix, and Stevie Ray Vaughan. Gábor Szabó, Bola Sete, and Wes Montgomery. Miles Davis, John and Alice Coltrane, and many, many more.

I'm proud to say that I met almost all of them and was able to shine in their light and feel a connection with them through the music they shared with the world. I looked straight into their souls and I saw me, and because I love them, I love me. A lot of people spend their lives in such a hurry that when they die, life's going to seem like one big blur. But the times I spent with Stevie Ray or Otis or Miles Davis—I can just freeze that moment right now in my brain and get in it and tell you what they were wearing, what we said to each other. Every moment is still very clear—they're some of the memories that you'll find in this book.

When I started creating this book, it wasn't easy. It was like looking in the mirror first thing in the morning before you get a chance to get yourself right. I told myself I'd have to give myself another mantra: "I'm not afraid to dance in my own light." And I'm not.

I used to be a very intense, compulsive person. I was always angry because my ego had convinced me that I was hopeless and worthless. I was playing hide-and-seek with myself. I remember a long time ago in Mexico someone asked me, "What are you most afraid of?" I told him, "Disappointing God." Now I realize there's no way I could disappoint God because this isn't an issue to him. It's only an issue for my ego. What is an ego except something that thinks it's separate from God?

When I could understand that, I was like a snake shedding its skin. The old skin was guilt, shame, judgment, condemnation, fear. The new skin is beauty, elegance, excellence, grace, dignity. More and more I'm learning to bless my contradictions and my fears and transform them. More and more I want to use my guitar and my music to invite people to recognize the divinity and light that is in their DNA.

That's the story behind the stories, the music inside the music. John Coltrane called it A Love Supreme. I call it the Universal Tone, and with it ego disappears and energy takes over. You realize that you are not one alone; you are connected to everyone. Everybody's born with a way to receive the Universal Tone, but very few allow it to give birth to itself. Most people abort it with things that are more important to them, such as money or fame or power. The Universal Tone is outside of me, and it's through me. I don't create it. I just make sure I don't get in its way.

Marvin Gaye was once asked, about his album *What's Going On,* "How did you create such a masterpiece?" He said, "I just did my best to get out of the way and let it happen." My wife, Cindy, tells me that Art Blakey used to talk to her about drumming and tell her that the music comes "straight from the Creator to you." He used to say that a lot, and his music felt that way. Real musicians know that real music arrives like that. It doesn't go to you—it goes through you.

It's the same thing with John Coltrane, Mahalia Jackson, Bob Marley, Dr. Martin Luther King—all the message givers. I'm really grateful that I was able to hear so many of their sounds live. Some people are put on this planet to help elevate consciousness, and through them come the sound and words and vibrations and music. It has nothing to do with show business or entertainment. It's not elevator music—it's *elevating* music.

That's the Universal Tone doing what it does. Suddenly the music compels people to go against what they thought was aesthetically solid for themselves, and what used to fit so well then feels really uncomfortable, like shoes that have become too tight and can't be worn anymore. It raises people's consciousness and stops the static so they can hear the forgotten song within. Their molecules are changed so they can stand outside the realm of themselves and outside of time. They can stand in a forever now.

I have been fortunate to see how universal the Universal Tone really is. It's such an incredible thing to be known worldwide, to be a point of connection between so many people. I accept being a conduit. I accept that grace has chosen to work through me as it wants to, and I also accept the gifts and awards and accolades and royalties that come with it.

I didn't always feel that way—I didn't have the confidence that would make me feel comfortable carrying the Universal Tone. I had to learn that from being around other musical shamans and spirit givers, people like Herbie Hancock and Tito Puente, B. B. King and Wayne Shorter. Watching how they rise above the fame-and-stardom thing while their feet never leave the ground. How they accept the nice hotels and first-class seating and awards shows along with the late hours and fast food and early wake-up calls and sound problems. How they serve the music and carry the Universal Tone.

I met a beautiful couple in Saint Louis not long ago who had given away a lot of money to help people who badly needed it. The wife said something that knocked me out: "It's a blessing to be a blessing." Those words were perfect. They said what's been inside me for so many years, even when ego, shame, and guilt have gotten in the way.

I'm just one man. I have feet of clay, like everyone else. I like ecstasy and orgasm and freedoms and all the kinds of things I can afford now, but I am very, very guarded with myself. I keep my darkness in check. Most of the time I try to get the best out of myself by being gracious and consistent and humble, not obnoxious or rude or cruel or vulgar.

Then suddenly: damn it, I blew it again. I had a temper tantrum. I got knocked out by my own ego and said or did things without thinking. Said something wrong to somebody I care for. Before, I did not know that anger is just fear with a mask. Now I know that, and I know I have to move on. Take a deep breath, forgive myself— get back to the Universal Tone.

People know me as much for being a spiritual seeker as for my music. "Cosmic Carlos," "Crazy Carlos"—I know what people say, and I have no problem with that. I'm the guy who talks about light and luminosity and always wears dead people on his shirts and jackets. Many people put people on their clothes. In my eyes John Coltrane, Bob Marley, Billie Holiday, Miles Davis—they are inspirers and igniters, finders of blessings and miracles. They are all immortals, still alive in an eternal now. And they make me look good—try them on for yourself.

"Cosmic" to me means being connected. From the place where I am, where I am blessed to be, I have been able to see how we're all connected. When people call me cosmic or crazy I take it as a compliment and say, "Well—behold. My craziness is working. How's your sanity doing?"

If people really want to know me, they shouldn't stop there. They should know that I'm always going to become better and that it took me a long time to realize it's time to stop seeking and start being. The spiritual goal I was looking for wasn't something that was far away, at the top of some mountain—or even a few feet above that. It is always right here, in the here and now, in my spirit and music and intentions and energy. I'm constantly hoping to use my energy and blessings for the highest good, to do things and say things and play music that all resonates on the same frequency— the Universal Tone.

When you put out a certain music and energy, you never know whom it will hit and who will be shining with it. Sometimes I'm sitting down to eat and just about to put a fork in my mouth, and someone says, "I'm sorry to disturb you..." and they have a story to tell me. Or they want me to sign something or have a photo taken with them. At that point, food really is not important.

Friends will be eating with me sometimes when this happens, and they'll ask me how I deal with it. I'll say, "Look, man, where are we right now?"

"Uh...in a restaurant."

"Okay. And you know who's paying for this food? They are. And that nice car outside that's waiting for us? They helped me get that, and they're paying for the gasoline, and the house I'll be driving to after I eat, and I wouldn't be here eating if it weren't for them. So if they want to take a picture, hell, take two."

I put the fork down, I make eye contact with the people who come up to me, and I listen to them. I'll give them a hug if it's appropriate.

It's about accepting a role that I have been chosen for and learning when to make myself available—and when not to. One time in Philadelphia I was stopped on the street by this guy who started hustling me. "Hey, 'Tana! Is that you? No, you ain't 'Tana, are you? Wait: yes, you are! Well, now, looka here, now—that's you, right, 'Tana? Man, I got all your shit, 'Tana—the records and the CDs, the eight-tracks, the cassettes, and I just got some DVDs." This was definitely before iPods. "I know you're going to help a brother out with the rent now, right 'Tana?"

I told him that my name is *San*tana, not Santa Claus, and that maybe he should have paid his rent first. I walked away, but that name followed me—to this day there's a few friends who still call me 'Tana. I'm cool with it. We talk about how some things are "'Tana stuff" and some stories are "'Tana stories." My assistant, Chad, calls me 'Tana, and my friend Hal asks for the Tanaman when he calls the house.

Sometimes it's about knowing when to leave, like the time a guy came up to me with his wife after a show at Madison Square Garden wanting me to stand next to her for a photo. "Come on, honey, get close to Carlos. Closer! Okay, now kiss him." I was like, "Hey!" and got away.

That's a little too close, thank you. Once in Paris, a hotel doorman was telling me how each of his children had been conceived to Santana music and started to run down a list of all the kids and all the songs. I thanked him before he went too far. That's all a little too much connection for me — I'm not that universal.

I told myself that this book should be healthful, healing, elevating, informative, raw, honest, and elegant. It should absolutely be entertaining, in a form that anyone, especially my children and family, can read and enjoy, laugh with and understand. There's so many funny things I've experienced that I feel I have to share — experiences that prove God has a sense of humor.

I like to laugh, and I love stories, and I wanted all that in this book, too. One of my favorite stories is about a man who is so successful at business that all he can do is make money, and everything he does or touches keeps making more money, but the more money he makes the more depressed he gets, and he can't figure out why. A friend tells him about this one special guru who has the secret to happiness and lives in a cave at the top of a mountain way across the ocean — where they always live, right? It was a long, long, expensive trip — on a plane, then a boat, a taxi, a horse, and then on foot. He spends weeks and weeks and finally finds the right mountain and climbs to the cave and goes in. Slowly his eyes adjust to the darkness, and he sees an old man with a long beard meditating — deep, deep, deep. Like, just buzzing. He waits and waits for the guru, and finally the old man opens his eyes and looks at him. "O Wise One, I've come a long way," the pilgrim says. "What is the meaning of all this, of existence?"

The old man just smiles and tilts his head toward a sign by his feet. The pilgrim looks at it — it's hard to see in the cave. The sign says HOKEY POKEY. He's thinking, "What? Huh?" He looks back at the guru and says, "Hokey pokey?"

"Yup. That's what it's all about."

The lesson is a simple one: you have to have fun with your

existence. At some point you have to stop taking things seriously and personally and getting all stiff, which only paralyzes your creativity and vitality.

I can tell you what I didn't want this book to be about—I didn't want it filled with any regrets, remorse, or guilt. You can read other books for that. A friend told me something I kept in mind in writing this: when you go through hell—your own darkest night of the soul—don't take pictures to show to your friends. Someone else said, "Don't cry when you see your own movie." It all makes sense to me.

When somebody would ask me how I want to be remembered, I used to just shrug that off and say, *"Me importa madre"*—I don't give a damn. But now I say, as someone who consciously and unconsciously is doing things to inspire people to aspire, this book is about accepting the responsibility to raise consciousness in others and to express my supreme gratitude to everyone, every spirit who has guided my life and given me the chance to acknowledge these gifts and share them. It's through them that I'd like to be remembered.

And as for what I've learned: be an instrument of peace. Be a gentleman at all costs. Enjoy yourself—have fun with your existence. Learn to listen to your inner voice and don't overdose on yourself. Keep your darkness in check. Let music be a healing force. Be a real musician: once you start counting money before notes, you're a full-time wannabe. Put your guitar down and go outside and take a long drink of light with your eyes. Go walk in the park and take off your shoes and socks and feel the grass under your feet and mud between your toes. Go see a baby smiling, go see a wino crawling, go see life. *Feel* life—all of it, as much as possible. Find a human melody, then write a song about it. Make it all come through your music.

Welcome to my story—welcome to the Universal Tone. *Vamos a empezar.*

CHAPTER 1

(Clockwise from top left) Irma, Laura, Tony, me, Lety, and Jorge in Autlán, 1952.

Maria, 1959.

I believe I grew up with angels. I believe in the invisible realm. Even when I've been by myself, I've never been alone. My life has been blessed that way. There was always someone near me, watching me or talking to me—doing something at the right time. I had teachers and guides, some who helped me get from one place to another. Some saved my life. When I look at the whole vortex of things that happened in my life, it's amazing how many times angelic intervention came through various people. This book is because of them and is written to acknowledge them. It's about angels who came into my life at the point where I needed them the most.

Bill Graham, Clive Davis, and my high school art teacher, Mr. Knudsen. Yvonne and Linda — two friends in junior high school who accepted me and helped me with my English. Stan and Ron — two friends who gave up their day jobs to help me get a band together. The bus driver in San Francisco who saw me carrying my guitar and made me sit near him to keep me safe when his route went through a very rough part of town. Musicians I played with who were my mentors — Armando, Gábor, and many, many more. My sisters and brothers, who helped me grow up. My three beautiful children, who are so wise and are now my teachers. My mom and my dad. My beautiful wife, Cindy.

I believe the world of the angels can come through anyone at any time, or at just the right time, if you allow yourself to move the dial on your spiritual radio just a little bit and hold it at the right frequency. For that to happen, I have to avoid making my own static, avoid ego rationalization.

People can change the way they see things by the way they think. I think we are at our best when we get out of our own way. People get stuck in their stories. My advice is to end your story and begin your life.

When I was just a kid, there were two Josefinas in our home. One was my mom, and the other was Josefina Cesena — we called her Chepa. She was a mestiza, mostly Indian. Chepa was our housekeeper, but she was more like one of the family. She cooked, sewed, and helped my mom raise all us kids. She was there before I was born. She changed my diapers. When my mom would try to spank me, I'd run behind Chepa and try to hide in her skirt.

When moms are pregnant, they spank harder and more often. When I was little, it seemed like my mom was always pregnant, and Chepa protected me from a lot of whippings. She was also the first angel to intervene on my behalf.

Things were already hard for my family. Dad and Mom had been married ten years, and he was traveling more and more to play his music and make money. Autlán did not have enough opportunities for a professional musician, so he started to travel for work and was gone for months at a time. You can tell his travel schedule by looking at his children's birthdays. Starting in 1941, every two years another child was born. My three older siblings were all born in late October. The other four of us have our birthdays in June, July, and August.

When my turn came, Dad decided another child was one too many. The family was struggling financially. "Go over there and cook the tea," my dad had said to Chepa when he found out my mom was pregnant again. He had gone out and come back with this bag of tea that was toxic and meant to induce an abortion. I'm not sure how many times that happened before I came along, but I know that in total my mom was pregnant eleven times and lost four of her babies. After Antonio—Tony—then Laura and Irma, I was the fourth to come along.

"Boil this thing, and I want to see her drink all of it," my father told Chepa. But she knew my mother did not want to lose the child. When he wasn't looking Chepa pulled a three-card monte— substituted one tea for another. She saved my life before I was even born.

It was my mom who told me this story—twice, in fact. The second time, she forgot she had told me and was totally surprised when I told her I knew. It could not have been an easy thing for her to do. Can you imagine telling your child that he was almost aborted? Or that he was almost called Geronimo?

I was born on July 20, 1947. My dad wanted to name me Geronimo. I would have loved it, personally. It was because of his Indian heritage—he was proud of that. I think it was the first and only time my mom put her foot down about our names and said, "No, he's not Geronimo. He's Carlos." She picked the name because of Carlos Barragán Orozco, who had just died. He was a distant cousin who had been shot in Autlán. I had light skin and full lips, so as a child Chepa used to say, *"Que trompa tan bonita"*—what beautiful lips. Or they would just call me Trompudo.

I've seen my birth name listed in some places as Carlos Augusto Alvez Santana—who the hell came up with that? My given name was Carlos Umberto Santana until I dropped the middle name Umberto. I mean, Hubert? Please. My full name now is simply Carlos Santana.

Many years later my mom told me that she had a premonition of what kind of person I would be. "I knew you were going to be different from your sisters and brothers. All babies grab and hold on to the blanket when the mother covers them. They pull on it until they have a tiny ball of lint in their little hands. All my other babies would rather bleed than open up their fists and give it to me. They'd scratch themselves first. But every time I would open your hand, you let it go so easily. So I knew that you had a very generous spirit."

There was another premonition. My mom's aunt, Nina Matilda, had a head of hair that was totally white, white as white can be. She would go from town to town selling jewelry like some people sell Avon products. She was good at it, too—a very unassuming old lady who would show up on people's doorsteps and open up a bunch of handkerchiefs containing all this jewelry. Anyway, Nina Matilda said to my mom after I was born, "This one is destined to go far. *El es cristalino*—he is the crystal one. He has a star in him, and thousands of people are going to follow him." My mom thought I was going be a priest or maybe a cardinal or something. Little did she know.

People ask me about Autlán: what was it like? Was it city or country? I tell them, "You know that scene in the movie *The Treasure of the Sierra Madre* when Humphrey Bogart is in a shootout in the hills with banditos who claim to be Federales? And one of the banditos says, 'Badges? We don't need no stinkin' badges!' "

That's Autlán—a small town in a green valley surrounded by

big, rugged hills. It's actually very pretty. When I lived there in the early '50s, the population was around thirty-five thousand. Now it's around sixty thousand. Only recently did they get paved roads and traffic lights. But it was more together than Cihuatlán, and that's what my mom wanted.

My memories of Autlán are those of a child. I was only there for my first eight years. At first we lived in a nice place in the middle of the busy town. To me, Autlán was the sound of people passing by with donkeys, carts — street sounds like that. It was the smell of tacos, enchiladas, pozole, and carne asada. There were chicharrónes and pitayas — cactus fruit — and jicamas, which are like turnips, big and juicy. Biznagas — sweets made from cactus and other plants — and alfajor, a kind of gingerbread that's made with coconut. Yum.

I remember the taste of the peanuts that my dad would bring home, still warm from being roasted — a whole big bag of them. My brothers and sisters and I would grab them and crack them open, and he'd say, "Okay, who wants to hear the story of the tiger?"

"We do!" We'd get together in the living room, and he'd tell us a great story about El Tigre that he would make up on the spot. "Now he's hiding in the bushes, and he's growling because he's really hungry." We would start huddling close together. "His eyes are getting brighter until you can hear him go... *roar!!*"

It was better than television. My dad was a great storyteller — he had a voice that triggered our imaginations and got us involved with what he was saying. I was lucky: from as early as I can remember I learned the value of telling a good story, of making it come alive for others. It permeated me and I think later helped me in thinking about performing music and playing guitar. I think the best musicians know how to tell a story and make sure that their music is not just a bunch of notes.

We lived in a few different houses in Autlán, depending on how Dad was doing bringing in the money. There was one that was on a little run-down parcel of land in between other houses — my dad probably got a deal on that because he had friends. The best one was more like a house with a number of rooms and a big yard with a working well. There was no electricity or plumbing—just candles and an outhouse. I remember this house was closer to the ice warehouse than the others. The ice was stored in sawdust to keep it from melting, and we could go get it anytime and bring it home.

From Autlán to Tijuana and even San Francisco, it seemed like we never had much space. We usually had just two bedrooms, a kitchen, and a living room. Mom and Dad always got their room, and the girls got theirs, so we boys would sleep on the couches or in our own room if things were going well with Dad and the money.

I guess my dad must have been doing pretty good when we started in Autlán. Tony and I, and later Jorge, shared a room. But there were compromises. The roof was a little rotten, and I remember getting ready to fall asleep one night when suddenly there was a thud. My brother Tony said, "Don't move—a scorpion just fell, and it's next to you." Next thing I heard was the creature skittering across the floor, running away. Man, that was a creepy feeling.

A sound that is really beautiful is the *plop* of mangos falling down when they're ripe. They're big, red, and they smell really beautiful. I would play in the yard, which had mango and mesquite trees, and there were these chachalacas—little birds that are a cross between a pigeon and a peacock. They'd wake us up in the morning because they can be so loud.

That yard had a dried-up well, and for some reason when nobody was looking I decided to throw some little baby chicks down there. Tony saw me and said, "Hey, what are you doing?" and I started climbing down to go get them, and he grabbed me before I hurt myself. "Hey! Don't go in there, stupid. It's really deep." We covered up the hole later on to make sure nothing bad happened.

I don't think I was a troublemaker—I was just a normal, curious kid. I knew right from wrong. The yard had this old wall that I didn't know was starting to fall apart. It had all these vines on it, and one day I started pulling on them to get at the seed pods. I'd open them so the seeds, which each had little parachutes, could go *whoosh* and fly away. I was really enthralled with them, so I kept pulling on the vines until suddenly part of the wall collapsed and landed right on my feet, tearing up my huaraches and smashing my toes.

My feet were bleeding, and I was scared to death that my mom was going to beat me because the huaraches were brand new and I had destroyed the wall. Everybody was looking for me for a long time. Chepa finally found me hiding under my bed. "*Mijo*, what are you doing there?" She saw my feet and gasped. She told my mom, who felt really bad that I was so afraid of her that my first reaction was to run and hide. She didn't spank me — that time.

Life at home was about living by Mom's rules. She was the disciplinarian, the enforcer. It was her house, and she was in charge. Dad was gone most of the time, so it was just us kids and our mother, and she could be real intense. My mom and dad were not really good at showing affection and demonstrating their love — to us or to each other. Of course we honored our mom, but she was not the huggy-bunny kind.

Looking back, I realize that she was learning to be a mom while doing all the mom stuff and Dad was learning to be a father — and a husband. My parents did the best with what they had and who they were. They didn't have any formal education. I don't even know how they learned to read or write. They taught us, by example, that you make your own way. "Maybe we don't have much in the way of education or money, but we're not going to be ignorant or dirty or lazy."

Mom had a modest beauty about her. She was tall, and her style was elegant but not lavish. She didn't like extravagant stuff — but she never wore anything that made her look cheap or desperate. We kids saw how she carried herself — she walked differently from the way most other women walked. Even when we were very poor, you could tell she came from a certain kind of upbringing, some kind of privilege.

My mom had a system with us kids. We all had roles, starting from an early age. "Today you two will clean the beds and the floor, and you two will do the dishes and get the pots and pans clean.

Tomorrow you guys'll switch. And when you sweep I want you to straighten up and make your back look like that broom—straight. Put your spine behind it, and don't just move that dirt around; get rid of it. When you wipe the dinner table don't just smear it, clean it up. Get a hot, hot towel so the steam can wipe out the germs. I don't want any *mugre,* any filth. We're poor, but we're not filthy poor. No one is going to embarrass the family or embarrass the name Santana."

It was amazing. She could tell if we were putting our backbones into it, and if we didn't—*pow!* We would get it. Now we appreciate what she did, because she created a certain thing that all my sisters and brothers and I have—a pride in what we do and in our family. But back then it was tough. My mom was really intense to live with. We were both the same kind of intense. She questioned everything, and so did I.

I remember one time she was angry at me for some reason, and I just took off. I must have been all of five or six years old. I left the house, pulling this little toy crocodile on wheels behind me. I wasn't crying or sad, I was just exploring and getting away from Mom, thinking about avoiding the rocks with my crocodile and not hitting certain lines in the pavement. I got involved with people in the market and the horses passing by. I was also thinking, "This is really cool—I can put a distance between my angry mom and myself for a little bit."

When my sisters found me, they ran up to me. "Weren't you afraid, being by yourself? Didn't you get lonely or scared?" Truth is, I didn't have time to think about it. I think I was born living in the now, not being concerned with what's up ahead. I think that experience planted a seed in me so that in years to come I wouldn't limit myself or be so self-absorbed with fear. I would feel welcome walking into new and strange places, like, "Oh, I'm in Japan!"—and my eyes would get bigger as I would start noticing the beautiful temples. Or, "Oh, I'm in Rome; look at this street; look at that one!" and I'd be off exploring.

When you're a child everything seems new and wonderful—even the scary stuff. I first saw a fire when the local supermarket burned. Apparently even back then somebody wanted to collect insurance, so he burned down his own store. I had never seen flames so big. The sky looked red and everything.

Another time I saw a man almost die when he was badly gored by a bull. I must have been five or six. I remember a bunch of men walking through town with posters announcing a bullfight. That weekend my mom dressed me up, and we went to the Plaza del Toros, which was on the other side of town from our house. I walked in the parade at the start of the event—marching to the *pasodoble* next to this little girl who was also dressed up. Years later I was able to tell Miles Davis that he and Gil Evans got it right when he did "Saeta" on *Sketches of Spain*. That's the tempo and feel at the start, when everyone walks around the ring.

You only have to see a few bullfights to know that when most bulls enter the ring they run to the center and look around, snorting and angry. But that day a bull came in and just looked at the toreadors. He was cool, like a fighter sizing up his opponent—like Mike Tyson before he had money. Then he ran. But he jumped over the fence, and people were leaping out of their seats and running for their lives!

They somehow got the bull, opened the gate, and led him back into the ring. He went running into the middle again and stopped and just stood there, still saying, "Okay—who's got the guts to come and deal with me?" One bullfighter stepped up with his red cape, but this was no idiot bull—he wasn't going for the color. He was going for the guy. The bullfighter got too close, and one of the bull's horns got him right in the side. They had to distract the bull so they could rescue the man. The guy lived. I don't know what happened to the poor bull.

I remember when I started going to Autlán's public primary school, the Escuela Central. There were paintings of all the Mexican heroes on the walls—Padre Miguel Hidalgo, Benito Juárez,

Emiliano Zapata—and we began to learn about them. I liked the stories about Juarez best because he was the only Mexican president who had worked in the fields as a peasant and was a "real Mexican"—that is, part Indian, like my dad. My favorite teachers were the best storytellers: they would read from a book and make it all come alive—the Romans and Julius Caesar, Hernán Cortés and Montezuma, the conquistadors and the whole conquest of Mexico.

Mexican history is a hard subject to talk about now, because as I grew up I quickly learned that it's pretty much been a merry-go-round of everybody taking turns raping the country: the pope, the Spanish, then the French and the Americans. The Spanish couldn't beat the Aztec warriors with their muskets, so they spread germs to kill them off. I could never swallow that one. The history I was taught was definitely from a Mexican perspective, so I was curious about this country up north that was founded by Europeans who took it away from American Indians and then from us Mexicans. To us, Davy Crockett got killed for being in a place he shouldn't have been to begin with. The next thing you know, Mexico lost all its territory, from west Texas all the way up to Oregon. All that originally belonged to Mexico. From our perspective, we never crossed the border. The border crossed us.

Our awareness of America was through its culture. My mom wanted to get away from her hometown because she saw a world of elegance and sophistication in the movies of Fred Astaire and Cary Grant. I learned about America from Hopalong Cassidy, Roy Rogers, and Gene Autry. And *Howdy Doody*. I would learn a lot more later through the music, but first it was through the movies. In Autlán there wasn't a proper theater, so the people used to wait until nighttime and hang a big sheet across the middle of a street and project the movies on it, like a drive-in without the cars.

I've always been conflicted about America. I would come to love America and especially American music, but I don't like the way America justifies taking what didn't belong to it. On the one hand, I have a lot of gratitude. On the other hand, it can piss me off when it puffs up its chest and has to say, "We're number one in the world, and you're not!" I've traveled the world and seen many other places. In many ways, America's not even in the top five.

I was not a great student. I didn't enjoy the classes. I got bored very quickly and had trouble sitting still. As a child I never wanted to sit and learn things that didn't mean anything to me. At recess time, I was allowed to go home for lunch. It was a long walk, and I liked doing that, though one time I remember going back home to find that my mom had prepared some chicken soup, even though it was hot outside. I said, "I don't want to eat soup." Of course, like any mom, she said, "Eat it; you're going to need it."

When she turned her back, I grabbed a whole wad of red chili powder that was on the table and dumped it in the soup. "Mom, I made a mistake. I wanted a little bit of chili, but the whole thing went in there!" She saw right through that. "Eat all of it."

"But Mom..." So I ate it. Man, I got back to school fast after that!

I was young and could be foolish, but I was always learning, especially out in the world. In Autlán, I was old enough to understand that my father was a musician, that he made a living playing the violin and singing. My dad played music that was about functions. It was music to celebrate by—we need some happy music, music to raise our glasses to. Can't have a party without some polkas to dance to. Music to help someone serenade his girl, to get her back after he messed up. Music to feel sorry for yourself—cry-in-your-beer music. I could never stand that last kind of music—there's way too much of that in Mexico. I love real emotion and feeling—I guess you call it pathos—in music. I mean, I love the blues! But I don't like it when the music is about whining or feeling sorry for yourself.

I got to know the kind of music Dad liked—Mexican popular music of the 1930s and '40s was his bag. Love songs that everyone would hear in the movies, and the ballads of Pedro Vargas, a Cuban singer who was really big in Mexico—"Solamente una Vez," "Piel Canela." He'd play those melodies with such conviction, slow them down, either by himself at home or with a band in front of an audience. It didn't matter. But he knew a wide repertoire of Mexican music—he had to. Mexican music is basically European music: German polkas—oompah, oompah—and French waltzes.

By the late 1940s, around the time I was born, *corridos*—history songs and all that macho cowboy stuff, including mariachi music—started to push away all the other music. My dad had no problem with that. He would play the mariachi standards that everyone knew. He would get dressed up in those costumes and the wide-brimmed hats. That's what people wanted to hear; that's the music that got you paid to play. It's like so many fathers and sons—he had his music, and I had to have mine.

But that came later. In Autlán I was too young to really appreciate what my dad's being a musician meant for us. Later on I found out that he was supporting not only our family but also his mother and a few of my aunts—his sisters—with his music. His father, Antonino, was also a musician, as was Antonino's father before him. They called them *músicos municipal*—municipal musicians—and they played in parades, at civil functions, and were paid by the local government. Antonino played brass instruments. But he developed a drinking problem and could no longer function. Then he dropped out of the picture. I never met him—the only thing I ever saw of my dad's father is in a painting. There he looked like a real, *real* Mexican Indian: he had a large nose, his hair is all messed up, and he was standing with a band and playing a *córneo*, a small French horn. That's the look of Mexico for me, the real Mexico.

My father never talked about those things—not then, not really ever. He was one of ten children, and they grew up in El Grullo, a small town halfway between Autlán and Cuautla, where he was born. We only visited a few times, when my mom wanted to appease my dad. I remember my grandma frightened me—her silhouetted shadow on the wall, cast by the candlelight, scared the hell out of me. She was sweet as pie with my dad, but with us and my mom she was a little guarded.

That's where we met our cousins—my aunt's kids. My siblings and I may have been from a small town, but we were city kids compared to them. They were country, country, country—which meant that we got a real education. They would say, "Come here; see that chicken? Look in her eyes."

"Why? What's wrong with her eyes?"

"She's going to lay an egg!"

"What?"

I didn't even know chickens laid eggs. Sure enough, the chicken's eyes got wide, it started clucking, and all of a sudden—*pop!* Out came this steaming egg. I was like, *"Wow!"* Not until we visited my grandparents did I experience that or the sound and smell of cow's milk when it hits the bucket. There's nothing like it.

It came to a point one afternoon when nature was taking its course and I had to go to the bathroom. I was used to toilets or an outhouse, but I didn't see any around. So I asked my cousins. "See those bushes?" they said. "Do it right there."

"No—outside? Really?"

"Yeah, right there beside those bushes. Where else?"

"And how do you clean yourself?"

"Leaves, of course."

I was like, "Uh...okay."

So I was over there doing my business. The next thing I knew I felt this wet, hairy thing touching my booty. I turned around and got the fright of my life—it was a pig's snout, and he was snorting and trying to eat my stuff! I was like, *"Aaaah!!"* I ran out of there with my pants still around my knees, trying to get away from that hungry pig, and all my cousins and brothers and sisters were laughing so hard they were falling over. They didn't warn me to be careful of the pigs and do your business fast, because that's what pigs love to eat. It was enough to make me stop eating bacon.

When I was seven years old, our family was as big as it was going to get, and things began to get really tough. We were seven kids—from thirteen-year-old Tony down to baby Maria, plus Chepa and a small dog that looked like a white mop and had no name. Some guy had asked my mom to hold it for him and never returned to get it back. My dad was working harder than ever, trying to keep money coming in for food, and he started to leave for longer periods. I missed him all the time; everyone did. When he would come back home, we all wanted to be with him, especially my mother. But they would fight—about money and about women.

Through the eyes of a child, I saw only the fighting. They would yell at each other, and I hated that, because I loved my dad and my mom. I didn't understand the reasons behind the behavior, and I didn't know words like *discipline* and *self-control*. Hearing them fight when I was a child was like looking at a book with words and pictures, and you get a general idea from the pictures but you can't read what's written to get the full meaning.

All I knew is that they would go at it, and then my dad would leave and come back at four in the morning with a bunch of musicians, and he'd serenade my mom from the street outside. You could hear them coming, and all of us would wake up. My dad would stand right in front of our window and play the violin and start singing "Vereda Tropical." It was their make-up anthem. Like B. B. King, my dad never sang and played at the same time, ever. He'd sing the lines—"Why did she leave? You let her go, tropical path / Make her return to me"—and then to bring it home he'd embellish the melody with the violin.

We'd watch my mom, and if she went to the window and opened the curtains, we said to ourselves, "They're going to be all right, thank God." It was beautiful, and we kids felt relieved. "Okay, they're going to keep it together." That happened a number of times.

Some of their loyalty to each other I think came from experience, from learning to get past the rough stuff. When they were first married my mother couldn't cook at all. She'd been raised on a ranch with servants and cooks. When she first tried to bring him food, my dad was rough. "I work really hard. Don't waste any more money, and don't ever bring me this crap again. Go next door and ask the neighbor to teach you how to cook. Go ask somebody."

My mom did that. "I swallowed my pride," she told me. The

neighbors said, "Don't worry, Josefina, we'll teach you. You put grease in here and then a little piece of tortilla, and when it turns a certain color, then you can put the chicken in." My mom eventually became one of the greatest cooks ever.

Still, in the first years of their marriage, sometimes my mom would take her babies and go back to Cihuatlán. This happened a few times, until my grandfather said, "Look, this is the last time. If I'm going to take you in, you need to stay here. But if you're going to go back with him I don't want to hear about him mistreating you. You need to make a choice."

My mom made her choice—she stayed in Autlán.

After a few years my dad was in better graces with my grandfather, who invited the whole family to come to his ranch. At one point, my mom told me, her father asked my dad to join him and his workers in a big room, and they all gathered around.

My grandfather was going to play a joke on my dad. "José, would you like a coconut?"

"Sí, gracias, Don Refugio." Don Refugio was what they called my grandfather.

He gave my dad a big machete and a coconut. "Okay, go ahead," he said. My dad didn't know how to hold the knife, so he started hacking at the thing, making a mess, and everybody started laughing. My mom immediately saw what her father was doing. She stepped up and said, "Don't do that, José. You're going to cut your fingers. You're a musician." Then she opened my father's instrument case, grabbed the violin, and handed it to my grandfather. "Okay, now you play a song," which of course he couldn't do.

Everybody was stunned, you know? In that culture at that time, you never questioned your parents. But she didn't like what her father was doing and wanted to make a point. My mom was really different.

It was years before we kids could piece together the story of her family. My mom would open up now and again and give us a little information, such as the fact that she was one of eight kids and that she grew up with her grandparents. It was common in Mexico:

some children were sent to live with their grandparents for a while, then they'd come back home. She never told us why she was the one in her family who was sent away, but from an early age my mother was strong-willed and would speak her mind. I think her grandmother enjoyed hearing her opinions and allowed her to say things and spoiled her a little, so that when she came back home and tried to do that she'd get into trouble. Plus she wasn't the center of attention anymore.

My mom did mention that her father was well-off, and that after her mother died—this was in the early '50s, when I was still very small, so I don't remember my grandmother at all—my grandfather didn't know how to keep things together. He started lending money to people who couldn't pay him back, which was something his wife would never have allowed. She had been in charge of the family's finances. That's what I heard from my mom. What I heard from other people is that my grandmother died from some intestinal problem that developed because she found out that her husband had a child with one of their maids. From then on, everything went downhill, and my mom was at war with her dad and his new lady.

Later I learned from my mom that my dad was not an easy person to live with, either. He was very old-school in his way of being a husband. My mom told me what he said to her when they decided to get married: "You're never going to get a ring, or a postcard, or flowers, or something special on birthdays or Christmas." He pointed to himself and said, "I'm your present. As long as I come home to you, that's what you get." I was like, "Damn, Mom! That's a little intense. Would you still do it all over again?"

"In a breath. I always wanted a real man. He's a real man."

My mom never rolled with any man other than my dad. She only danced with him maybe seven times, if that. But she never danced with another man, either. And he never got her a ring. I don't understand that, and I'm sure a lot of women today would scratch their heads. But most women I know didn't grow up in that generation or in that culture or experience what she did.

My sister Laura told me years later, when she had a beauty shop in San Francisco, that my mother was there having her hair and nails done, and the women were talking. This one lady is going on about her rings: "See? I got this from my first husband, and I got this from my second husband." Someone said, "Hey, Josefina, we notice you don't have a ring." She looked at them and said, "I may not have a ring, but I still got my man."

In Autlán, it seemed my dad could not help but play around—he just loved women, and women loved my dad. He was a charismatic man, and he had a way with women. He knew his music had an effect on them—any good musician knows that and can see it. I notice it. If you play from your heart, as my dad would, it can sweep women off their feet. You don't even have to be good-looking, man: just play from the right part of your heart, and women are transported to a place where they feel like they're beautiful, too. He was part of a very macho generation. You showed how much of a man you were by how many women you had.

Of course that didn't square with my mom. She did not buy into that excuse, and it caused problems between them. She took the fight outside the house, and she didn't care who knew it.

One evening around six or seven my mom yelled, "Carlos, come here!" She started cleaning me up, combing my hair. "Where are we going?" I asked.

"We're going to church."

"But it's not Sunday."

"Don't talk back."

Okay, we're going to church.

So she's ready, I'm ready, and we headed out of the house like it was on fire. My feet were barely touching the ground she was walking so fast. We passed the church and kept going. "Mom, the church is over there."

"I know."

Okay.

Two or three blocks later we suddenly stopped outside of a store. We waited outside until the last customer left and the lady behind the counter was by herself. My mom went in and said, "My name is Josefina Santana, and I know you're messing with my husband." Then she grabbed the long, beautiful braids this woman had, pulled her right over the counter, got her on the floor, put her knee on her neck, and started beating the crap out of her.

You know, when you go to a boxing match it sounds so different from hearing people getting beat up on TV. It's so different when it's happening right in front of you—you never forget it. Then when it was over Mom walked out, grabbed my hand, and we walked back just as quickly. My mom was strong. Of course my dad heard about what happened and came home and they fought. I mean really fought—he shut the door to their room, and it was terrible. We kids were all scared. We could hear everything and couldn't do anything about it.

Years later my mom told me stories that were kind of brutal. She didn't need to tell me—I remembered hearing those sounds and not being able to do anything about them. I'd say, "I don't know why you stayed with him so long." From what I learned later, there were mainly two things that set things off for my dad—my mom getting jealous and her getting between him and his family. My dad loved his mom and his sisters and provided for them when he could. But my mom felt he had his own family to take care of, and sometimes when a letter would come to my dad from them my mom would open it and start arguing with him. He'd get angry because she was opening his mail and getting into his stuff, and *bam!* That door would slam shut again and we'd hear the fighting.

One time after we moved to Tijuana, Tony came home for something that he forgot and witnessed the whole thing going on. But by that time he was old enough to do something. He kicked in the door and picked up my dad from the floor so that his legs were dangling in the air. They were looking at each other eye to eye. Our dad was tight in his arms, and Tony said, "Don't you *ever* touch my mom like that again." Then he put my dad down slowly and walked out. It got really quiet in there. That was my brother Tony.

The last time any of that happened was in San Francisco. Dad came near Mom, and she grabbed a big black frying pan. "No, José. We're in America now," she said. "You try it and you're going to get hurt."

I think the cycle of violence has to stop, and it's up to each of us to do all we can to stop it. So much violence comes from fear and ignorance, and from that word I truly hate: *macho*. Because macho is fear—fear of being too "feminine" and not being man enough, fear of being seen as weak. It can be like the worst virus, an infection that starts in the family and goes out into the street and spreads through the world. Violence has to be stopped where it starts—at home.

To be honest, I once hit a woman.

When I left home for the first time I moved in with a woman who had two children, and we got into it one night. She got a little crazy, then I did too, and I tried to avoid the argument but the next thing you know we're throwing punches at each other.

To this day I ask myself why I didn't just walk away. It wasn't complicated. I had four sisters and my mom at the time. Now I have an ex-wife, a new wife, and two daughters—I would not want *anyone* to treat any of them like that. In fact, I don't want anyone to treat anyone like that, male or female. As men, we are given power, but with that power comes responsibility. I think that's something that should be part of the curriculum in schools—how to treat yourself and others.

For me it happened that one time, never again. That was enough for me to see what was happening, how I was going down a path of false, macho bullshit. Knowing it happened in front of my girlfriend's two children made me sick to my stomach. It made me think back to when I was a child in Autlán and the way I felt when I would hear my dad hitting my mom.

I still wonder how much of my dad spilled into me. In so many ways I can thank my dad for being an example of what I should and should *not* do.

My mom never stopped getting upset when she thought about women messing around with my dad. I remember another time when she was boiling water to throw on this lady. Chepa wrestled it away from her and made sure she didn't end up in jail. With my mom, when jealousy took over, she didn't have the benefit of thinking about her children. She just wanted to beat the crap out of any woman who came between her and her man. I'm sure when we left Autlán, the whole town breathed a sigh of relief—definitely the women.

The end result was that my dad stayed away from Autlán more. He was making less and less money in the towns around Jalisco, and he didn't like Mexico City, so he started to travel farther away, as far north as Tijuana, on the border of the United States. It was the mid-1950s, and Tijuana was a big party town with lots of work for musicians. He'd be gone, and then we'd get a letter with some money and sometimes a photo. One he sent showed him standing next to Roy Rogers and Gilbert Rolland—a Mexican actor who was making it big in Hollywood back then. I used to carry that picture of him in my back pocket all the time. I'd be riding around on a bike, take it out and look at it, and show it to everybody. "Just look at it," I'd say. "Don't touch it; you're going to rip it, man."

Dad's career was not stable. Sometimes he got together a group, and they would travel caravan-style to a hotel gig for a few weeks— a large group of eight or nine. Many times he was on his own. He'd take a bus into a new place, find the musicians, arrange a trio or quartet, and play in the town square. They would go to various restaurants and ask if they could play inside or outside or go from table to table. Or they might find the best hotel in town and ask if it was okay to come in. "No, sorry—we already have a band playing tonight." Or, "Yeah, okay, no one else is here; come on in."

That's how they did it back then. No posters or advance promotion, no ticket sales, no box office. All the business was done on the spot—asking the tourists for fifty cents or a dollar per song, asking the restaurant to feed the band if everyone was happy. Then it was back to a couch at one of the musician's homes or back on the bus.

"This place seems to be a little slow. Should we try Tecate? Maybe Nogales?" Then it was back on the bus again.

That's how my dad made his money—he asked to play. I really admire the fact that he was able to build a career that way, to bring in the money and feed us. It wasn't easy.

After a while it seemed like he was always gone. When we were in Autlán, it got to the point that my dad would be gone for months and months at a time. Years later, when I'd hit the road with Santana and people would say something about the time I was gone away from my family, I'd say, "Nah, it's not so crazy." I would go on the road for four or five weeks at a time when my kids were growing up, but that would be the most that I would do. I learned from what I experienced in Mexico. I think I was pretty balanced compared to what my dad did.

At one point a year had gone by, and suddenly my dad had come back, and I was so happy and proud. He'd take me with him when he went riding through town on his bicycle, and he let me ride on the back, grabbing hold of his belt—he'd wear this thin golden belt, very fashionable at the time. I loved the way he smelled. He'd use this Spanish soap called Maja. I can still remember that scent to this day.

I was so proud—he'd be waving at people, and they would greet him like he was a returning hero. "Oh, Don José!"

"Hey, how you doing?"

Every few minutes someone would stop us. "Do you remember me? You played my *quinceañera!*" Or someone would say, "You played my baptism!"

"Oh, yes, of course. Please give my best to the family."

"Oh, Don José, thank you. Can we take a picture?"

I learned early on that I had to share my dad—with my family, his work, and his fans. All us kids knew this. My sister Maria told me that after someone would stop to say hello, she would ask my father, "Do you know that person?" His answer was, "No, but saying that makes them feel good." I always remembered that about my dad. It was part of the eulogy I read at his funeral in 1997.

*　　*　　*

When I was eight, we hadn't seen my dad in almost a year, and we had gone from living in the middle of Autlán to living in the worst neighborhood in the area, just a few blocks from the edge of town. It was a small two-room place filled with cooties—that's lice. It also had *chinches*—bedbugs—and *pulgas,* or fleas. When a letter containing a big check came from my dad, my mom had had it. It was time to leave Autlán.

It was almost like Dad was trying to get rid of us: "Here's some money for rent and maybe buy a stove or something." My mom took the letter to the middle of town, where all the cab drivers hung around. She knew a guy named Barranquilla, who was close to my dad. She told him that she had received a letter from José telling her to give Barranquilla some money to drive the family up to Tijuana. "He told me to pay you half and that he'll pay you the rest and more when you get us there. Take this money and pick us up on Sunday, okay?"

Of course, Barranquilla thought this was weird, since my dad never said anything to him. He asked to read the letter. My mom acted as if he were out of his mind. "No! You can't read this—you crazy? There's personal stuff in here!"

So this is Thursday or Friday. My mom started selling off everything she could—furniture, whatever we had. She got together a little bit of food and money for the trip, enough to pay for the gasoline. On Sunday, she got us all up and made sure we were washed, dressed, and looking good. Barranquilla brought the car around, and it was like a big tank—one of those big American sedans you smelled before you saw. My sisters, brothers, and I—our eyes were really big, wondering. "Where are we going, Mom?"

"We're going to your dad," she said. I think only Tony and Laura knew before that morning that we were leaving.

My mother put my four sisters, my brothers, Chepa, the dog, and me in the car, got in, and said, *"Nos vamos."* It was five thirty in the morning. We were heading for a man we hadn't seen in a year. We had enough money for a one-way trip and no guarantee we would find him. I remember looking out the back window and watching the town get smaller. We headed east out of town. West would have taken us to the coast, and the east road went for a while and then forked. One way went to Guadalajara, and the other way went left, toward El Norte. That was the road that led to all sorts of possibilities, the promise of a good life—El Norte. Tijuana? Who cared that it was on the Mexican side of the border? To my mom, Tijuana *was* America. We were going to join Dad, and we were going to America. That was the road we took.

CHAPTER 2

Me in grade school, 1954.

In Tijuana, very early in the morning, when the sun was just coming up, I would walk to school. Just outside of town I would see a line of people — Indios, mestizos — walking like they were in some religious procession, going up into the hills, where they could get red clay. They'd take chunks of clay home, where they'd mix it with water and shape it into two-feet-high figurines, about as tall as from your elbow to the end of your fingers. They'd let them dry, then paint them white and add other details, and there! You'd have the Virgin of Guadalupe — the patron saint of all Mexicans. She would look really beautiful by the time they were done.

They'd take the statues into town to sell to tourists or anyone near the cathedral in downtown Tijuana — Our Lady of Guadalupe. Or they'd walk between the cars in the middle of the road, the way they sell oranges and stuff like that. People would buy the statues, take them home, put flowers or candles on them, and start praying from the heart to these little figures. Who's to say whether their prayers were answered? Just days before, they had been nothing more than some red clay up in those hills.

When I arrived in Tijuana, I was a Mexican kid like so many others. I was just raw material, man. I didn't have much hope to go anywhere or get any higher than I was. Everything that I became began to crystallize in that border town — becoming a musician and becoming a man. Miles Davis used to compliment me in a way he understood. "You're not the little Mexican who walks around with his tail between his legs apologizing for being Mexican and asking permission to get a driver's license." That kind of validation and approval has meant more to me than anything.

Here's something else Miles told me: "I'm more than just a little guy playing some blues." I feel the same way. I'm all the animals in the zoo, not just the penguins. I'm all the races, not just Mexican. The more I develop spiritually, the less nationalistic I am about Mexico, the United States, or anywhere else.

I am sure a lot of people get pissed off. "You're forgetting your roots. You're not a Mexican anymore." But I am still working out my own identity, crystallizing my existence, so that I can be more consistent in saying I am proud to be a human being on this planet, no matter what language I am speaking or what country is collecting taxes from me. I came from the light, and I'm going to return to the light.

Those statues of the Virgin had a very special look to them — you could recognize them right away. After Santana hit it big and we began to tour the world, I would come across those Virgins in America and in Europe — even once in Japan. Somebody had been to Tijuana and bought one and brought it home. It was like seeing an old friend again.

CARLOS SANTANA

The trip from Autlán to Tijuana took place in August of 1955, just after my birthday, and we traveled for almost five days. It took a long time to get there because not all the roads were paved. I remember that each of those days felt like a week. It was hot, and we were cramped against each other in the car, and it didn't get much better when we stopped. Barranquilla was crabby and grumpy, complaining the whole time. My mom would say, "I ain't got time for that, you know? Take it up with José."

There weren't any hotels or motels along the way, and even if there had been, we didn't have money for anything but gas. We slept in the desert under the stars, worried about scorpions and snakes. The food ran out. So every time we stopped somewhere, Mom would try to buy something that we could eat. We had to eat at truck stops, where the food was horrible. I have never smelled or tasted beans that were so rancid. How can somebody screw up beans? I still can't understand that—it's like messing up granola. There were these ugly frijoles, and we kids were getting sick left and right. So we drank a lot of Kern's canned juices. I can still taste that sandpaperlike sap. To this day I don't want to see another one of those juices ever again.

I can still hear the music from the radio on that trip—especially Pedro Vargas. He had the baddest trumpet players at the time—they could play high and clean, like Mexicans. All his songs were romantic. What they were really about was sex.

We came to a big river, and we had to put the car on a raft that was just a bunch of planks. Then people would pull the rope from the other shore to get us across. I remember Barranquilla told us there had been rain upriver the night before and that the river was going to swell up, so if we didn't leave right then it'd be another three days before we could even think of getting across. Man, it was scary. The water was already starting to get rough, but my mom decided we had to go.

We got into Tijuana around two thirty in the afternoon. Mom had the return address on my dad's letter. The car pulled up, and my brother Tony remembers that he and my mom got out of the car alone and told us to wait. My memory is that we all stumbled out of the car, tired, hungry, and cranky. Either way, I know we all needed baths badly. Mom knocked on the door, and nobody answered. She knocked again, and a woman answered. It was pretty clear, as I look back on it, that she was a prostitute.

To be honest I didn't know what a prostitute was, or a floozy, or anything like that. I didn't even know the words yet. Later on I would figure it out. But she looked like something the cat dragged in, and I knew enough to know that she wasn't someone like my mom. My mom carried herself very differently.

This woman started screaming at my mom. "What do you want?" My mom stood up to her: "I want to talk to my husband, José. These are his children."

"Ain't no José here."

Bam! She slammed the door. My mom just broke down crying. I still feel it in my gut. Mom was crying and getting ready to leave and give up, and we were all wondering what would happen to us. We could see it in each other's eyes.

It was time for another angel to appear—someone in the right place at the right time, guiding us and saying, "Don't quit." This time it came in the form of a wino who was lying next to the building, asleep. He woke up because of all the commotion and asked, "What's going on?"

"I'm looking for my husband, José, and this is the only address I have," my mom said.

"You got a picture of him?"

She showed him a photo, and he said, "Oh, yes. He's inside."

So Mom knocked on the door again. The lady came out again, screaming. And this time all the screaming woke up my dad. He came out, and I was the first thing he saw. Then he saw everyone else, and I saw his face starting to look like a bowl of M&M's. I mean, all the colors in the rainbow: red, blue, yellow, green. His face went through all the emotions and all the colors.

Dad grabbed my mom by the arm and asked, "Woman, what are you doing here?"

"Don't grab me like that!" And they started into it.

I'm amazed every time I think about the pure, steel-like conviction my mom had. She would not be deterred, even when her friends and family told her that she was crazy to do this, that she didn't know what was going on in Tijuana. "You're crazy—what if he doesn't take you back?"

"Oh, he's going to take me back. If he's not, he's got to look me in the eye and say that—and look in his children's eyes."

Dad got hold of somebody he knew and found a place for us to stay. They were building a house that didn't have any windows or doors yet, and it was way up in the worst part of town, Colonia Libertad—ghetto, ghetto, ghetto. That neighborhood is still there. We had gone from the ghetto in Autlán to the ghetto in Tijuana. At first my dad wasn't staying with us. My mom was pissed. He would come and visit us and bring a bag of groceries, but he would only stay for a short time.

Eventually Dad left the other woman, and we were all together again. Later on we started moving up, living in better places with electricity and plumbing, but I remember that the summer of 1955 was so hot we couldn't even sleep. We were tired and cranky all the time. We had no money at all. We were hungry. There were fields nearby filled with big tomatoes and watermelons, and at night we kids would go and gorge ourselves. I think the owners looked the other way because they knew we were hungry.

My mom and all the other ladies in that part of Colonia Libertad did their washing using water from one particular well. They would haul these big *cubas*—laundry tubs filled with dirty clothes—and work those washboards. The well was so deep that the water had a sulfuric smell to it. One time I suddenly realized something: we didn't have plumbing—we *should* have plumbing. If we did, Mom wouldn't be washing clothes outside, using dirty water. I said, "Mom, someday when I grow up I'm going to get you your own house and a refrigerator and a washing machine." She just kept washing and patted me on the head. "That's nice, *mijo*, that's really nice."

"Hey! Don't dismiss me like that," I was thinking. "I *am* going to do it." Of course I didn't know then how I was going to do it; I was still just eight years old. But I made a promise—to my mom and to myself. As it turned out, it only took fifteen years. It felt so good when it came to be in 1970. I did it with my very first royalty check from the first Santana album. Even after everybody took a cut—the accountants, managers, lawyers—there was enough to keep my promise. I know it made her and my dad really happy. That was the first time they started looking at me like I wasn't so crazy after all. They thought I had lost it after smoking all that weed and hanging around the hippies. To this day I can't think of them in their own house in San Francisco without thinking about that disgusting well. It still feels good that I was able to come through.

Despite the circumstances, it was actually a nice transition from small-town Autlán to Tijuana. It was new, exciting, and different. I have great memories of learning to play marbles. My brother Tony taught me; he was really good with them. They looked like diamonds to me—I used to hold them up to the sun and look at them sparkle.

The tastes of Tijuana were a change from those of Autlán, because as I started to grow up my tastes were changing, too—from sweet to savory. There was pozole, a stew that my mom always ate when she was pregnant—that and tamales. There was mole sauce—which is like chocolate, just not sweet—and pipián sauce, more orangey and made from pumpkin seeds. Man, she could stretch the chicken with those sauces. She was great with shrimp and chiles rellenos, which are fried with cheese inside and batter outside—very few people know how to make it so it doesn't get soggy and weird. My mom had that down, and she was an expert with machaca—shredded beef with eggs and so much spice that you'd get a good heat going. Wash it down with agua de Jamaica, which is made out of hibiscus petals and tastes like cranberry juice, only better.

I also remember that I started hearing more music than I had ever heard before. Right across the street was a restaurant with a very loud jukebox. It sounded like we were just one room over. That was the summer of Pérez Prado—"Cherry Pink and Apple Blossom White." He was Cuban but moved to Mexico. A lot of Cubans came over, and they'd record and get big in Mexico City, then humongous all over. Those mambos sounded so good. It was like an ocean of trumpets.

In the middle of the 1950s, Tijuana was a city with two sides to it—depending on which way you came into town. If you were American and drove south, it was Fun City, another Las Vegas. It had nightclubs and racetracks, late nights and gambling. It's where the soldiers and sailors from San Diego and all the actors from Hollywood went to party. Tijuana had nice hotels and five-star restaurants—like the one in the Hotel Caesar, where they invented the Caesar salad.

For those of us heading north into town, Tijuana might as well have been the United States. It didn't matter that we hadn't crossed the border. There was a flavor of America, and a lot of Americans were always there, walking down our streets in nice suits and new shoes, making us think of what it was like just across the border.

The streets of Tijuana were not like those of Autlán. Autlán was the country as far as the ways people thought and treated each other were concerned. Tijuana was the city, and you could immediately feel a difference. People were drunk, angry, or upset about something at all times of the day. I soon started to learn that there was a way to walk those streets—a different kind of walk. Without disturbing anybody, you could project an attitude of "Don't mess with me." You don't want anybody to mess with you there. When I got older and people would tell me about tough neighborhoods in Philadelphia or the Bronx, I would say, fuck that. That ain't nothing compared to Tijuana. There's a code of survival there that you learn very quickly.

You realize it's true what they say—don't mess with the quiet ones. They were the most dangerous. The ones that shot off their mouths—I'm going to do this or do that—they didn't do shit. I also learned you didn't want to mess with the Indians or mestizos. The cholos and pachucos might pull a switchblade. But those Indians would whip out a machete and could chop up a body like it was a banana.

I saw it almost happen one time just after we got to Tijuana, right outside of church. The machete hit the ground when one guy missed chopping another guy's leg off. Sparks flew off the street when the blade hit it. You don't forget stuff like that—the sound or the sparks. It was scary. Next thing, the police came over and started shooting in the air to break up the fight before the men did some damage. I realized that this was not a movie. This was real life, man. I also learned that very seldom was the fight about money; it was almost always about a woman.

I don't remember being hassled at all in Autlán. We kids had to fight more in Tijuana. The good thing was that it was more about bullies than gangs. The gangs would come later, after I left. Bullies used to pick on me, and looking back on it I see that it wasn't personal. It was just that ignorance is ignorance, and the hood was nasty. I had to be able to know when to walk away and know when to hold my ground so they didn't keep piling up on me. I learned that if they thought I was crazier than they were, they would rather go around me. A few times I had to do that—fight and act crazy. It got to the point where I would find a rock that was the size and shape of an egg, and if things got weird I would put it in between my fingers and get ready to punch.

At the time I looked a lot different from the way I look now. I had fair hair and was light-skinned, and my mom dressed me like I was a little sailor kid. I mean, come on—of course I was going to get into fights. One time I got to school—Escuela Miguel F. Martinez—just after my mom had spanked me for some reason, and I had a lot of anger in me. Sure enough, some guy said something like, "Look at this guy! You can tell his mama dresses him." I had the rock in my hand, and I nailed him hard! Everybody was standing around, waiting to see what he was going to do. I was looking at him like, "I hope you try to do something, because I'm ready to die." There's two kinds of desperation: one is born of fear and one is born of anger, and in the one born of anger you just don't want to take it anymore. I forget his name, and I didn't realize then that he was one of the street bullies. He never bothered me again.

The thing is, he was right—my mom was dressing me. I used to tell her, "I'm getting beat up in school; you got me in short blue pants and stuff. This is like saying, 'Come and get me.'"

"Oh, you look so nice," she'd say.

"Nice? You're dressing me like a choirboy. Mom, you don't understand."

"Shut up!"

Once my mother wanted me to wear some pants I didn't like. She got angry and said, "You're like a crab. You're trying to straighten everybody else out, but you're the one who always walks crooked." That stayed with me. I said to myself, "I'm no crab, and now there's no way I am going to wear those pants."

It took a while to convince my mom, and I talked to my dad to help me out. Slowly they came around. They were so involved in trying to make it to the next day, so concerned with food and getting the washing done—it wasn't like we sat down to break bread and talk about these things. All of us kids had stuff like that to deal with, and we just had to get through it.

It was toughest on Tony. He was a teenager and new to town. And he was dark-skinned, but I was fair-skinned and had light hair back then. When we would go out together, they really picked on him a lot. "Hey, Tony, how much do they pay you?" He didn't know yet to ignore them. He'd say, "Who pays me for what?"

"Aren't you babysitting that kid?"

"No. He's my brother."

"No, he ain't—look at you. He doesn't look like he's part of you!" They'd start laughing, and he had to answer them somehow, and the fists would start flying.

The worst that happened was a few years after that, when Tony got hit in the head with a hammer in some street brawl. He told us that he could have avoided it, but his friend wanted to come home the same way they had gone into town, back on the same street where they had gotten into an argument with some guys. He survived, but that was what it was like. Welcome to Tijuana.

I'm glad I'm not the oldest in my family. The ground was tested by Tony, Laura, and Irma before I came along, and whatever was going on with Mom and Dad, Toño—that's what we called him—got the brunt of it. He got the main bruises because my mom and dad didn't know yet how best to deal with kids. He was like my buffer and second father and has always been in my corner—my first defender and my first hero. I'll always be so proud of him.

I love my family, man. They're all so different, each one of my sisters and brothers. Laura, she was in charge when my mom and Tony weren't around, since she was the oldest girl. She was like the scout and would be the first to check things out when we moved into a new place—very curious and mischievous. She was an instigator, too, like, "Let's cut school and go get some jicamas!" Or "Let's go pull some carrots out of the ground and eat them!" Like I needed convincing. "Sure, okay—sounds good to me."

I remember one time Laura decided to get some candy on credit from a store, and she shared it with all of us. When my mother found out about it, there was hell to pay—for all of us. I wasn't even there when all this went down, but when I got home there was another beating waiting for me. That was what Laura was like—a troublemaker and fearless! Irma was more introverted than Tony and Laura, more on her own planet, and she also was the first of us kids to get into music. She told me that she used to peek into the room where our dad would be practicing his violin until he said, "Venga"—come here. He started teaching her songs and some piano, how to read music. She was a natural.

In Tijuana, the rest of my sisters and brothers were all small and growing up—Leticia, Jorge, and Maria. I didn't get as much of a chance to babysit or take care of them, as Tony and Laura had done for me. I feel especially bad for Jorge that I wasn't as much a big brother for him as Tony was for me. He would have to figure out a lot of things on his own. After we left Autlán, I was either out on the streets or hanging with Dad.

From the moment we got to Tijuana, we started to learn to survive another way, too—it was time for all of us to go to work, to start supporting the family. All hands on deck, you know? I give the credit to my mom and my dad for all that. They implanted in us some really no-nonsense, hard-core values and morals. You never borrow or beg. What doesn't belong to you, you don't take. What's yours, you fight to the death for it.

One day when my father woke us up, he had with him a couple of boxes of Wrigley's spearmint gum and a shoe-shine box. He gave half the gum to Tony and half to me, and he gave the shoe-shine box to Tony. "Go down to Avenida Revolución, and don't come back till you sell all of it," he said.

Avenida Revolución was our Broadway, the center of downtown Tijuana, where the bars and nightclubs were and where all the tourists went—American and Mexican. Tony and I would go up to them, selling gum and shining shoes. That was really the beginning of my introduction to American culture. It was the first time I saw a black man—a really tall dude with big feet. I just stared at the size of his shoes while polishing them. I began to learn a few words in English, and I learned to count. "Candy, mister?" "Ten cents." "A quarter." Fifty cents, if I was lucky.

We would get just enough money to take the bus, so we had to make enough money to pay for our inventory and supplies plus enough to ride home and get there the next day. Sometimes we ended up walking because we had no bus fare—like the time Tony got a huge fifty-cent tip on a shoeshine and we decided to take the rest of the day off. We were rich for an afternoon, watching a movie and eating candy, but we forgot to save something for the ride home. The next day, it was back to the same schedule—wake up early, help out at home, go to school, take the bus downtown, and sell, sell, sell—help Mom and Dad with the rent.

I think I did miss out on a certain part of my childhood, as many kids do. In the first ten years I was with my first wife, Deborah, I would sneak into toy stores and buy little figurines, action figures. Thing is, a few years after that, in 1986, I was hanging out with Miles's drummer, Tony Williams. He started his career as a teenager, and I saw that his house was full of toys that he got from Japan—the first Transformers and all that. He saw me looking at them, and I said, "It's okay; I do the same thing."

"You do?"

"Yeah. What's this one do?" Suddenly it was not the same guy who played at Slug's with Larry Young and John McLaughlin or who drove Miles's band in the '60s. It was, "Oh, man, look at this!"

I'll tell you, that was a revelation to me. I think Michael Jackson was like that also. There was part of us that missed out on being a kid, and we didn't wean it out of our systems till much later. After a while, you grow up and put the toys away, but for a while that child needed to be expressed. I'm sure Deborah must have thought I was a peculiar dude.

What I went through was what all we Santanas went through. Everybody worked. After we were old enough to take care of ourselves, Chepa left (plus we couldn't afford her anymore), and Mom needed help to run the house, clean, and cook. So Laura and Irma helped Mom at home. All of us did whatever we needed to do to make the rent and get the food on the table. That part of my childhood I'm really proud of—nobody ever complained or asked, "Why do I have to do this?" or anything like that. It was just understood.

We moved a lot during those first two years—it felt like almost every three months we moved to another place in Colonia Libertad. Then we moved across the Tijuana River, which runs right through the middle of the ghetto and into the United States, to a small place on Calle Coahuila, in Zona Norte, a neighborhood that was a little better. Two years after we came to Tijuana, we moved to Calle H. These were bungalows, almost like a trailer park. I was ten years old, and I noticed people around us had little black-and-white TVs. We kids used to sneak around to the neighbors' houses and stand on our tippy-toes, peeking in their windows until—*snap!*—they closed the curtains. That's how I discovered boxing. It was funny— I remember every few months there was a matchup between Sugar Ray Robinson and Rocky Graziano—on TV, in the headlines. And there was my first *hero* hero: Gaspar "El Indio" Ortega.

Ortega was a welterweight and was the first boxer to come out of Mexico and go all the way up. His hometown was Tijuana, so as you can imagine the whole place talked about him and supported him. We followed every one of his fights, especially the one in '61, when he fought Emile Griffith and lost. It didn't matter—he was *our* hero.

Ortega was one of the first boxers to be very evasive in his fighting. He knew how to bob and weave. Years later I got my chance to meet him—he was living in Connecticut then and had to be in his eighties. He was proud of his fights, but he was proudest of one thing. "You know what, Carlos?" he told me. "I still got all my teeth. They never knocked them out."

I can still remember those fights, watching them and getting down on my knees and praying for Ortega and for Sugar Ray. "Don't let them beat him," I would say and squeeze my eyes shut. That's when I really learned to pray from the gut—when I first began to realize that God might be listening.

If it had been up to my mom I would have been doing my praying in a different place. As usual, my mom was diligent and relentless—"You're going to do this and you're going to do that." One time she decided I had to go to church and learn to be a *mona-guillo*, an altar boy. It's all about ritual and regalia, learning where to be at the right time, grabbing the book when you're supposed to. The very first time I was in a mass, there was this other boy who was training me—he had done it, like, five or six times—and I remember he was a jokester.

THE UNIVERSAL TONE

At one point this guy started cracking up. Then I started cracking up, and the more we got to laughing the angrier the priest got.
Then the next thing I know, all the people in the church started
laughing, too. I didn't know what was so funny—I was just trying
to keep it together. Then the priest picked up the chalice, and I tried
to pass him the book at the same time—"Okay, here it is; now read
it." The boy didn't tell me exactly what I needed to do—I didn't
know you're not supposed to give it directly to him. You're supposed
to put it in a certain place, and he'll pick it up.

After the mass, the priest gave me a smack in the head. Of
course that put a damper on my wanting to go to church ever again.
I was thinking, "If you're going to be with God, aren't you supposed
to be merciful and nice?" That priest single-handedly separated me
from the church right there and then. I mean, what's wrong with
smiling and laughing in church? Are these not the things that God
wants us to be doing—enjoying ourselves? I remember the Bible
stories—the Flood; God asking someone to sacrifice his son. "Your
God is an angry God; he's a jealous God," things like that. Come
on, that's not God—that's Godzilla. I think God has a sense of
humor. He has to.

I learned a few things in church—just the other day I made the
gesture of a blessing onstage, like the one a priest would make over
his sacred chalice, before I took a sip of wine. We were in Italy, so I
figured everyone there would get what I was doing—the sign of
the cross, hands like they're praying, look up to heaven before raising the glass, which these days is usually Silver Oak Cabernet. I
didn't think it was sacrilege. I think any kind of spiritual path
should have some humor.

Still, my mom persisted and persisted—two years after I got
smacked in the head for laughing in church she was still trying to
get me to go back there. She dragged me to confession at five in the
afternoon. "We're going there, and you're going to tell the priest
your sins." I was twelve at that point. "What sins, Mom?"

"You know what I'm talking about!" She wouldn't let go of me,
and she had a strong grip. I'm young and I'm pissed, and I'm

feeling guilty because you're not supposed to be angry at your mother—that's enough sins right there!

So we went to the church, and the little door opened, and I went in. I heard this voice on the other side of the wall say, "Go ahead, tell me your sins...go ahead...*go ahead!*" I didn't know what to say, so I finally thought, "The hell with this," and I ran out. My mom was so pissed. I told her the story of being smacked as a choirboy and reminded her that she didn't want to hear about that. I told her that if God can hear me, I'll talk with him directly, and that's it. "You can make me do a lot of things, but you can't make me do this, because I won't do it."

Nothing infuriated my mom more than her children standing up to her. That really pissed her off, and for some reason I was the only one who would argue with her. Everybody else just tucked in and took it. I was getting bigger, but she still would try to beat me. She was right-handed, and by then I had figured out that when she grabbed the belt—or extension cord or anything she could find—to swing at me, if I ran toward the left she would hit nothing but air. My sisters and brothers would start cracking up, which only made her angrier. I would get out of her grip and get out the door like a jackrabbit.

I would run away—I did it three times in Autlán and at least seven times in Tijuana. Then my brother Tony would have to come find me and bring me back. "When are you going to stop doing this?" he would say.

"When she stops hitting me."

"You just don't know the stuff she's going through."

"Yeah, but she doesn't have to take it out on me!"

I remember wandering around Tijuana after one fight. It was Christmastime, and I was looking at window displays—little trains and toys and puppets, all that stuff. For years after that, every time I saw Christmas decorations those feelings would come up. All that anger and frustration I had toward my mom stayed with me.

My mom had her own special relationship with God, her own

way of getting him on her side. When she needed something for the family, or when she thought something needed to happen, she would sit in a chair, cross her legs, fold her arms, and put all her focus on something far away. You could feel the determination. As kids, we got to know that look of supreme conviction. It was like, "Uh-oh, get out of the way—Mom's doing that thing." If we got close, we could hear her saying to herself, "God is going to give me this." It was like she was willing a miracle to happen. "I *know* this will happen. God will make it happen."

They weren't big things: money for food, a better home for the family, health stuff. One time my youngest sister, Maria, was having trouble conceiving a baby. She had polio as a child, and her husband had just undergone an operation for testicular cancer. It looked like it was just not going to happen. Every time we would visit, my mom would be in her chair, folded in on herself, with that look of 100 percent determination, talking to God, until she told my sister, "You should adopt a baby, and as soon as you do you're going to get pregnant."

"Mom, what is wrong with you?" my sister said. "I can't get pregnant—a bunch of doctors told me."

"Yeah? What do they know? They're not God. Do what I tell you." Maria went ahead and adopted a baby boy, Erik, from a Mexican mother and German father.

A year later I was in Dallas at a festival with Buddy Guy and Miles Davis. We were all in the hotel lobby, and a phone call came in—"Paging Mr. Santana!" It was my wife, Deborah. "You're not going to believe this, but your sister is pregnant."

"Which one?"

"Maria!" She called her baby Adam—we all called him the miracle baby.

My mom would go to church in the middle of the week, when everybody was making confession, and bring a couple of big bottles of water. She patiently waited for the last person to finish, then she would go up to the confessional, and the priest would say, "Yes? Would you like to confess?"

"No, Padre, I'm all right now, but can you bless these bottles of water?"

"The holy water's over there."

My mom would say, "I'm sorry, Padre, I don't want that water for my kids. *Está mugre*—that's dirty. It's filled with everybody's germs and sins. No. Bless this for me. It's for my kids."

Then she would bring those blessed bottles home, and suddenly she was like, "*Mijo,* how you doing?" Touching us, running her hands over us. "Hey, Mom, you're getting me all wet!" That's the way she approached her beliefs and how she went through life. She did things that made sense to her, for the family, with no sense of doubt or shame. When she decided on something, we knew not to get in her way—we didn't expect her to explain herself, and we didn't expect her to get lovey-dovey.

I think my mom went through her life hiding a lot of pain. She had my dad to deal with, and she lost four babies. She rarely opened up, and I'm not sure she ever addressed those things consciously. In her solitude, when nobody was looking, she might have licked her wounds and cried for the children who died. But she never shared her suffering with us. She knew the difference between self-pity and its opposite—healing herself and moving on, restoring herself by looking at her suffering in the right light.

The last time my mom got pregnant in Tijuana she got really ill. I remember I was around eleven. We were living in a place where we used a packing crate as a front step to get into the house, and my mom slipped on that, fell down, and lost the baby. The ambulance came and took her away.

My mom told us later that when she woke up in the clinic there, she got the feeling that this was not a place to get better but a place to die. Nobody was paying attention to her or the other patients. People were dying to the left and right, and she could feel life leaving her. So she pulled out the lines and tubes and whatever they had in her, got up, walked home in her robe, and fucking fought for her life. She was not going to die in that place. She was not going to die at all.

My mom was alone through a lot of this. Because of the culture and who my dad was, she could not lean on him for help. In Spanish we say, *"Ser acomedido"*—be accommodating, make yourself useful. Don't be a bump on a log. If you see that you can pitch in and help, do it. Even if you're a man, it's okay to wash your own dishes—you're not gimped, you can help your partner. But that never happened. She was on her own.

It made her strong and independent. But I think it also made her harder than she needed to be. I remember not long after she lost the baby, she was outside talking to a neighbor, and I heard her mention my name. You know how you hear your name in the middle of someone else's conversation and your ears prick up? I heard my mom say, *"Carlos es diferente."* She saw me looking and told me to come to her.

She told me, *"Sentarte,"* so I sat down on her knee as she wanted me to. Suddenly—*pow!*—she smacked me right across the side of my head. She did it so hard my ear was going *eeeeee*, just ringing! I jumped up and was glaring at her with my mouth open. I just looked at her and she looked at me, and she said, "If you could, you would, huh?" Which meant, "If you could slug me, you would, right?" I just looked at her like, "Don't ever do that again." Then she looked at the neighbor. "See? The other ones don't do that."

That was cruel *and* that was ignorant. I wasn't a toddler anymore. Why would she do that? Just to make a point with the neighbor—am I a guinea pig or something? I think part of the reason for it may have been her anger against my dad, and she took it out on me. He showed a blatant favoritism toward me. Maybe she was jealous; I don't know.

The ringing in my ear was still going on minutes later. Something had broken between my mom and me that would take years to heal. She and I became rivals. I would buy her a house, but I would not invite her to my wedding. Not until Salvador was born did I start letting my mom back inside my heart and my psyche.

Yes, I was hardheaded. Just as she was. I guess "hardheaded" is the best way to describe it, or you can call it conviction. I've read that a person's cells continue a pattern of emotion from one generation to another, that you can inherit a pattern of resentment or remorse. You can try to stop yourself from doing certain things, but you wind up asking yourself, "Why did I just say that? Why did I do that? Why can't I stop myself?" That's one reason I read spiritual books—to get answers that can help me separate the light, compassion, and wisdom from behavior patterns. It can be scary—it's like letting go of something that is ugly, but it's who you think you are.

When I became a dad, I let my kids know I loved them all the time. I still tell them, "You don't need to audition for me. You passed the audition when you were born. I was there when you came out, all three of you, and you opened your eyes. You passed the audition." The rest—how you're going to use what has been given to you—is up to you. And I'm not afraid to say, "Come here, man, I need a big old juicy kiss and a hug. I need a second hug because the first one is just courtesy and the second one is long and *ahh*..." It can get mushy.

Everything changed with my mother when Salvador was born. All of a sudden, she was hugging him as a mother does. It surprised all of us. It changed me, too, and started to give me a stability that I didn't know I had lost. I could be anywhere in the world at any time, and I would pick up the phone and call Mom: "Hey, how you doing? I've been thinking about you all day."

"Yeah, I know," she would say. "Because I was asking you to call me."

Validating my parents was not easy, and it took a lot of work. Part of it is constantly correcting the psyche, freeing myself from what has been put upon me by other people, including my parents. There's nothing like being in a moment of clarity to let all that stuff fall way. But the worst thing you can say is, "Hey, I forgive you." I made that mistake just one time. My mom looked at me with this expression and said, "What do you have to forgive me about?"

"Oh, nothing," I replied, and I changed the subject. In that one look I got her point of view. I didn't have anything to forgive her for. Not when I had so many things to thank her for.

Around 1956, just as my dad's father did with him, my father decided it was time for me to learn an instrument. He never really told me what motivated him to get me started, but I knew. Part of it was a family tradition, and part of it was to have something else that could put food on the table. Also he loved keeping me busy. I know he had tried to get Tony to play an instrument, but it just wasn't part of my brother's constitution. Tony had a mechanical mind and was really good with numbers. Laura was not inclined that way, either. Irma liked to sing, and Dad was already teaching her songs. Now it was my turn.

I remember the first time my father pulled me away from my brothers and sisters to show me something about music. *"Ven aquí,"* he said, and he took me out to the backyard. The sun was setting, and everything looked golden. He very carefully opened his violin case, took the instrument out, and put it underneath his chin. *"Hijo, quiero mostrarte algo"*—I want to show you something. *"Estás viendo?"*—Are you watching?

"Sí, Papa."

Then he started pulling the bow across the violin very slowly, playing these little sounds, and out of nowhere a bird flew down and landed on a branch right next to us. It was looking at my dad, twisting its head, and then it started singing with the violin!

I was thinking, "Damn!"—or whatever word I had in my head when I was nine years old. He kept playing and looking at me, watching my reaction, not looking at the bird. They traded some licks for a while, then he stopped, and the bird flew away. My mouth was just hanging open. It was as if I suddenly found out my father was a great wizard like Merlin, and now he was going to teach his son how to communicate with nature. Only this wasn't magic—it was music.

"Si puedo hacer que un pájaro, puede hacerlo con la gente, sí?"—If
I can do this with a bird, you can do this with people—got it?

"Sí, Papa."

I was nine when my dad put me in a music school that I went to
every day after regular school. Originally I wanted to play
saxophone—but I would have had to learn clarinet for a year first,
and I was young and wanted to shout and scream! My dad tried to
teach me to play violin, but it was too difficult. Then he tried to get
me to learn the *córneo,* the same instrument my grandfather had
played. I hated the taste of brass on my lips, but at the same time it
was my dad. I couldn't say no, so I tried to stick with it—I really
did. After he finished teaching me what to do with my lips and the
fingering, and how to clean the instrument with brass cleaner,
eventually he realized that I didn't have a love for the horn, so we
went back to a small violin—three-quarter size.

My dad was my primary teacher. He would show me a melody
and have me play it over and over. "Slow it down!" he would say.
"Again, slower!" That used to drive me bananas, but it not only
made me remember the mechanics, it also imprinted the music in
me. I was learning tunes such as the *William Tell* overture,
Beethoven's Minuet in G, von Suppé's *Poet and Peasant* overture,
Hungarian gypsy music, Mozart, Brahms—all with sheet music. I
was a clever fool. I learned to memorize a melody and pretend I was
reading it. My dad would be busy shaving or doing something and
see me looking at the paper. Years later I was in the studio, and Joe
Zawinul saw me figuring out some music—"Do, re, mi, fa, so, la,
ti..." He laughed. "Oh, you're one of those!"

I would say to myself that I would show my dad how good I
could be and practice a song so I knew it cold. "I'm going to learn
this." Stroke, stroke, stroke. Again—stroke, stroke. "Got it, here he
comes..." I'd play it for him, and he'd say, *"Bueno, campeón."* He'd
call me "champion." "You really know this one. Now here's one for
tomorrow." Man. I thought I was going to get a reprieve, maybe
some time to go play with the other kids, hang out with Tony, or
play hide-and-seek with Rosa from down the street because I heard

she was okay with kissing and stuff like that. But I couldn't get ahead of him. By the time I finished the lesson everyone had gone home.

My dad knew how to be effective with music, how to own it — and that was maybe the most valuable thing he taught me. It helped to realize on my own that the violin could be a very demonstrative instrument, very emotional. I realized how to put my finger on the string and how much pressure to put on the bow so it had personality — stroke, stroke — then add a little more tension, like you're nudging somebody awake. "Mmm..." Nobody can teach you how to develop a personal expression. The only way is to work it out with yourself in your room. The most my parents were able to do was ask me to please just close the door.

My dad was a good teacher, but he wasn't necessarily gentle. He would push me, and then the shouting would come, and I would start crying. I don't mean to be melodramatic, but the salt from all those tears started discoloring part of the violin. I just wanted to try to please my dad, and in my mind it all went together — the way the wood smelled, the way the strings sounded, the feeling of frustration.

It wasn't long before my mom stepped in. "You're breaking his heart, José. He shouldn't learn music like that — it's just too brutal." She had seen Tony run away from playing music for the same reason. "We don't have too much money, but why don't you take a break from teaching Carlos and have somebody else do it?" My dad acceded to my mom's request and found me a teacher — actually two guys. One was big, like linebacker big, and the other was older. I started going to their houses, which were nearby, to get tips on holding the bow and other things. They were both really good at showing me stuff, helping me build my character, and reaffirming the good things I was doing, which was the opposite of what Dad was doing.

Here's a story about one of those violin lessons. One time I was at the older guy's house, and he and his wife were arguing about something in the kitchen, and I was bored sitting there on the sofa.

My hands started to go between the cushions and I started feeling coins in there! Sure enough, I found almost two dollars—which was a lot of money for a nine-year-old in 1956. I quickly put the coins in my pocket, I did my lesson, and when I got half a block away I ran right to the store and spent all the money on M&M's. The guy looked at me as if I were crazy. When I got home, my mom was hanging clothes on the line to dry, so I had the house to myself. I went inside, spread them all out on the bed, and separated them all by color. Then I ate them—first the green ones, then red, then yellow, then brown. I couldn't stop.

It took me a while to like chocolate again after that. And when my mom found out what I did, of course she scolded me. "We don't have any money, and you spent it on M&M's? And you didn't even share them with your brothers and sisters?" She didn't spank me that time, but it was clear that she was less angry about my wasting money on candy than she was about my not giving any to my siblings. For her, it was always about sharing what you have with the whole family. That was the lesson that chocolate and money taught me—I think it freed me from thinking only about myself at a very young age.

Feeling the music was the first lesson, but money was a big part of it for my dad. He persuaded me to join up with two brothers who both played acoustic guitars, go out on the street, and make some money. I can't remember their names, and we didn't have a name for ourselves, but they were good. They knew the right chords, the right rhythms, and I had to really pay attention to keep up with them. I remember we had a big repertoire and could get the attention of the tourists. We would walk up and down Avenida Revolución, or take a bus to Tecate or Ensenada, and approach people. "Song, mister? Fifty cents a song."

They would look at us, and we looked young. "Can you actually play those things?"

"*Sí, señor.*"

"Okay, play something."

We'd play the obvious favorites, like "La Cucaracha" and "Bésame Mucho."

We were good, and it was a good experience—my first band. Every experience has its lessons. For me, this one began with learning to deal with band members. They were brothers, but they couldn't have been more different, and they were always arguing. I think they must have had different fathers. I also learned about eating other people's cooking, because a lot of places where we played would feed us—chicken tacos, enchiladas. It was good, and it was different from my mother's cooking.

But one of the best lessons I learned from working with those two was how to carry a melody—how important that is on any instrument, an absolute must. It was like learning how to walk with a glass of water, carefully, without spilling a drop, from way over there to this point here. I would find out later that a lot of guys really can't carry a melody, and if you can't do that I think you should just find something else to do. Every musician I love can do that, no problem. When a musician can do that one simple thing, he's going to nourish people's hearts and not tax their brains.

The other thing I got from playing with the brothers was confidence. I started to feel good about my playing and about doing it in public.

My father saw this and started to enter me into little music contests around Tijuana—at street fairs and radio stations—and I started to win prizes such as food baskets, big bottles of Coca-Cola, and some fancy buttons, all of which I would immediately give to my mom. "Fascination" was the tune that I would kill with—all the ladies loved that one. Most of the time I competed with mariachi singers—but one time when I must have been thirteen or fourteen it ended up that my sister Irma and I were the only ones not eliminated at the end of a contest. She sang a doo-wop song, like "Angel Baby," and I played my song and I got the bigger applause. "I don't think your sister took it so well," I remember my mom told me.

It was around this time that I started to feel very uncomfortable with favoritism, embarrassed by the amount of attention my dad would give me. I could feel the distance that it put between me and my siblings. It was something I came to resent and another pattern that followed me through the years—an uncomfortable feeling that would come over me when certain people, including Clive Davis, Miles Davis, and Sri Chinmoy, would show an obvious favoritism toward me. I would come to see Bill Graham in his office, and he'd ignore other people. "Tell him I'll call him back—Carlos, how you doing?" Even my mom would do it—she'd hang huge pictures of Deborah, the kids, and me in her house, but there would be smaller—or no—pictures of my sisters, brothers, and their families. I tried to explain it to her. "Mom, this makes me uncomfortable, and it's not fair."

"Why? This is my house and my choice."

I had to say, "Well, actually, it's my house, Mom—I'm paying for it. Please either take down those big pictures or put up the same number of the rest of the family—please." Finally she understood what I was telling her and took them down.

The more music I played, the more I could appreciate my father's talent for doing it day in and out. He was a natural-born leader and kept things together—a no-nonsense kind of guy. He had stature in Tijuana. They knew him and associated him with Agustín Lara's "Farolito," so much so that it became a signature song. When he performed, people expected it, like people later expected Santana to play "Oye Como Va."

Years later, I was working with my son, writing the song for my dad—"El Farol"—that we put on *Supernatural*. What else could we call it? That's when I got a call from Deborah saying that I needed to call my family right away—somebody had left. "Who? Where'd they go?" I could tell from her voice what she meant. My dad died just as we finished putting that song together. I was equal parts proud and sad when it got a Grammy the next year.

My dad commanded respect without saying a word. I never saw him reprimand or correct or get upset with the musicians he worked with—but he wanted them to respect themselves, too. My dad would look the musicians up and down to see how they were dressed. If he saw someone wearing dirty shoes or a wrinkled shirt, he'd say, "Go home and come back, because you've got to be presentable, *hermano.*" He wanted them to want to look their best.

A lot of it was simply being willing to trust the other musicians, and they paid him the same compliment. He could walk into a room, and people would greet him. "*Hola,* Don José. How are you?" One time we walked in together when someone was telling a dirty joke, and they stopped immediately.

My dad knew his position, how to work hard. He's the one who first told me, "Never pay or feed musicians before they play."

"Really? Okay, Dad."

In the early days, he would bring me with him to a place where he was playing and put a quarter in my hand so that I could get some candy or grapes—grapes were my favorite. Then he'd tell me where to sit. Soon he had me playing with his band on some shows.

There's a photo from around this time of my dad and me with a bunch of musicians, all dressed up—we look like Don Corleone's henchmen, you know? You can tell by the way we're dressed that we were playing for somebody who had a lot of money, real hoity-toity, a high-society kind of gig for Tijuana. I remember that the occasion was something like a twenty-fifth anniversary, a one-time thing, not a regular band gig. We were playing waltzes and Italian ballads—no polkas or any kind of *norteño* music for that crowd.

It was during this time, around 1957, that I went to hear my father play one day and met an American tourist who became friendly with my parents. I think the best way to describe him is that he was a cowboy from Burlington, Vermont. He got close to me while my dad played, talking to me and keeping me company. He was a character, and as a youth I was fascinated with him and didn't know better. Neither did my mom and dad. They couldn't figure him out. At first they were suspicious of this gringo, but slowly he gained their trust. He showed up a few times after that and started buying me stuff like toy guns and holsters. Then he offered to take me with him across the border to visit San Diego.

What kid wouldn't want to go? It would be my first time to America. My siblings and I were poor kids—we talked about America with wonderment, wondering what it would be like to cross the border and see the country. We knew about it from TV— *Howdy Doody,* the Little Rascals, and *The Mickey Mouse Club.* We could see America from our neighborhood in Tijuana—bright lights and nice buildings. San Ysidro was really just minutes across the border. It *smelled* different, I knew it. I wasn't eleven yet, but I was ready to go.

My memories of what exactly happened are very sketchy, like old photographs more than a movie. Everything was going fine, then all of a sudden the man started molesting me. I'm not sure how many times it happened. I remember it sometimes happened in a car and sometimes in a motel room. It was just so sudden— there was the surprise of it happening and an intense feeling of pleasure mixed with confusion, shame, and guilt for letting it happen.

It was like not knowing the words to describe the prostitute who answered the door when we arrived in Tijuana. I didn't know what to call what was happening to me when it happened—I didn't even know that there were words for what the guy was doing. I could understand that there was an exchange happening—I do something for you, like buying you candy or toys, and you let me do something for my gratification.

But I had the feeling that something about it was very wrong. Then it was over until the next time. More candy, more toys. Later, when I learned what the word *molest* meant, I was able to describe it with the vocabulary of a grown man. But I wanted not to think about it—it was painful to remember. I was numb to it for many,

many years, until I finally realized where a lot of my anger and negative energy were coming from.

The molesting ended for two reasons—first, my mom heard about his reputation from a friend, and she confronted me. She did it in front of the whole family, in a way that made me feel like I was on trial, as if it were my fault. Man, we didn't have the wisdom to know how to talk about it. "Carlos, get over here! Did something happen to you? Did he do something?" I was just standing there with everyone looking at me. I didn't know what to say. I didn't know the words! I was so ashamed and angry at the same time.

My father was silent about it, which I think was for the better, because there was no sense in attacking or killing the guy and then going off to jail with the rest of the family wondering, "What are we going to do now?"

That was the worst part of it—being angrier at my mom than at the guy who molested me, which only created more distance between her and me. It was a negative emotional pattern that took a long time to shed. One of the things I still regret is that I didn't have someone at that time to sit me down and help me transform my anger, because it put a lot of distance between my mom and me. It was the reason I did not invite her to my wedding in 1973. I explained it to my in-laws by saying that she was a control freak and the event would be better without her. I would keep my distance from her for another ten years after that.

I know it hurt my mom a lot, too. Despite all those bad feelings, she turned out to be my best friend when it came to music, helping me in ways I didn't even know about till years later.

The second reason the molesting stopped was that the cowboy found someone younger than I was and moved on. That was cool with me. A little while later he was driving in the car with some other kid, and the two of them were doing whatever they were doing, and they ended up crashing into a ditch. He became an invalid, collected some insurance, and moved out of Tijuana. That's what I heard, anyway.

The whole thing had me growing up really fast, because I was thinking that this is not for me, this is a mistake, and I was starting to pay attention to a Chinese girl, Linda Wong, who lived near us. Her family owned a grocery store where we shopped, and I was totally fixated on her. So it all ended, and in my mind it was like it never happened.

Back in Tijuana I had to go to school; I had to go make money. I had to keep practicing the violin. By 1958 I had sold my last pack of gum and shined my last pair of shoes and started earning money exclusively from making music. I stayed with the violin for almost six years, on and off, from 1955 to 1961. During that time I was turning into a teenager. I was twelve when I saw Linda and had my first crush. She was thirteen but had the body of a twenty-year-old. She even smelled like an adult. I felt like I was eight when I was around her.

I was beginning to develop my own taste in music. There was a lot to choose from around me—the classical and dance music from Europe that my father taught me and the mariachi and other Mexican music that the tourists always asked for. There were *rancheras* from the country, *cumbias* from Colombia, and Afro-Caribbean clave music, which they called salsa and we called *música tropical*. There was the heavily orchestrated big band music that I first heard when I was trying to learn the *córneo*—music that I thought of when I heard the word *jazz*—which I associated with a dinner club in Tijuana called the Shangri-La. I called jazz Shangri-La music until Santana drummer Michael Shrieve introduced me to people like Miles Davis, John Coltrane, and Thelonious Monk and turned my head around. Then there was American pop music and doo-wop songs on the radio and TV and singers like Paul Anka and Elvis Presley, whom my sisters loved and I hated.

I was still working out what I liked, but I knew what I didn't like, and a lot of it was stuff I heard at home. My mother liked big bands such as Duke Ellington's—she *really* liked Duke, I later found out—and guys like Lawrence Welk. When she played that at home, I'd say, "I'll be outside, Mom." When she finished with the record player, then Elvis Presley ruled. My sisters would jump on the turntable with their Elvis records, then jump on me when I tried to leave. They would tackle me like they were football players and pin me to the floor, all four of them. The more I struggled, the more they'd tease me and scratch me. Part of me would be in agony, and the other part would be laughing, and my mom would hear us and come in. *"Qué pasó?" Whoosh*—they got off me. "What do you mean, 'Nothing'? What happened to your neck, Carlos?"

Of course none of my sisters remembers anything about this at all. But to this day you won't find any Elvis Presley records in my house.

It wasn't that I didn't like Elvis. I was just starting to know the music that Elvis liked—Ray Charles, Little Richard. Later on, after I started on guitar, I would discover B. B. King, Jimmy Reed, Muddy Waters—all the string benders. But back then, I was just opening the door for the first time, checking out this *Americano* music, and leaning in the direction of early rock and roll and rhythm and blues. I didn't know enough to have a name for it yet—but my dad did.

"You want to play that freakin' pachuco shit?" Calling it pachuco was like calling it delinquent music, and my dad was not happy about it. I was around twelve at the time. He had made me play with him at a bar in the worst part of Tijuana—it was like tourist hell. The tables were all black from cigarette burns and who knows what else; there were no ashtrays. There was a cop who was putting his hands all over a woman, and I could see that she couldn't protest because she'd end up in jail. The whole place smelled like piss and puke—worse than Bourbon Street in New Orleans. They expected us to play *norteño* music—Mexican *rancheras* with polka beats that they play in border towns and across the border.

Back then I thought that this type of music was meant to drink beer and tequila to, to feel sorry for yourself to. I just never connected with it. It felt like wearing somebody else's shoes. It wouldn't go inside my body. Years later I would look back and say I hated mariachi music, but it really wasn't about that—it was about my feelings. It was because this kind of music reminded me of painful, hard times with Mom and Dad, and it took me a while to look at it differently.

There's so much that comes from Mexico that I love now that I know more about it—like those big mariachi orchestras with one hundred strings. Incredible. Or *son jarocho,* which is like flamenco but much funkier—just amazing. Ritchie Valens's "La Bamba" is a *jarocho* rhythm brought into a rock-and-roll format. Then there are groups like Los Muñequitos de Matanzas—the little dolls. They're Cuban, but their lyrics could be totally Mexican: "I'm in the corner at this cantina / Reminiscing about the one that got away / And I wait impatiently for my tequila." Those guys are still around and huge in Mexico.

I was too young to pick up any of this at the time. I was more focused on practicing my violin lessons for my dad. But I learned later to be proud of all the great music that came from Mexico, or that came through it. There's so much cross-pollination of music there—from Europe, Cuba, even Africa. But Cuba especially: the *son, danzóns,* boleros, rumbas. Back in the 1950s Mexico City was like Miami is today: the city where musicians from Central America and South America came to record and go viral. The Havana connection was tight—we had Toña La Negra, the singer Pedro Vargas, and Pérez Prado, of course, who was the most popular one. Mexico City had the studios and radio stations, and they had movies that needed sound tracks, and it was all on the doorstep to the United States.

I was just ten when I first saw the influence of Mexico north of the border. I remember my dad rented me a mariachi suit—size small, but still too big. Then he took me with his band to play in Pasadena, which was around a three-hour drive from Tijuana back in 1957. This was the night before the Rose Parade, so the whole town felt like it was ready for a party. We performed for Leo Carillo, the Mexican American actor who played Pancho in *The Cisco Kid* on TV. He had this big, lavish house—it was the first time I had been in a place like that. It felt like we were in a Doris Day movie!

Leo was very proud of his heritage—in fact, all Mexican people are really proud of their mariachi and their food and the tequila. I remember Leo was a very happy and gracious person. He had all this Mexican food spread out, and we played all night for his American friends. The whole thing felt good—Dad was proud of me.

But this joint on the other side of Tijuana was something else. It wasn't just the music—it was the whole scene, because in fact we were playing in a place where the style of music didn't even matter. Nobody was listening anyway. Most of the people were too drunk or too busy working their own hustle.

I had to answer my dad straight right then, man to man, when he started picking on my taste in music. "Look at where we are and what we're playing. Could the music I like be worse?" He looked at me and didn't try to hit or spank me. But he got really angry. "Leave. Go. You always have to have the last word. You are just like your mother."

He wasn't wrong. I've got my mom's fire, and it still gets me in trouble. Sometimes I don't know how to hold my tongue or my temper. Poor Mom—I'm blaming her. My dad was completely the opposite. I never really saw my dad lose it with me—get really angry or anything like that. Later on I realized my dad was an example of what I could work toward—catching myself if I felt I was going to snap. From him I tried to learn to be more considerate and more understanding and trusting. I can tell you for me it's still an every-day thing. I think one of the truest things I ever heard was Archbishop Desmond Tutu's observation that we are all a work in progress, a masterpiece of joy still being created.

My dad was the one with taste *and* practicality. He loved his Agustín Lara and European music, but he played mariachi music to feed us. He never said he didn't like mariachi or *norteño* music, but I don't think he could afford to, and I don't think Tijuana was meeting our needs anyway. My mother was pushing him to find better opportunities—pushing him north again, just as she had done in Autlán. The next thing I knew he began to go to San Francisco to play. I remember going with him when he went to catch a bus across the border and saying good-bye.

Then he was gone, and I stopped playing the violin. I figured, "My dad's not here to torture me, to make me play music that I don't like." I also never really liked the tone I got on the thing — it sounded corny, like some Jack Benny stuff. Many years later I was walking in Philadelphia, checking out a street festival with my friend Hal Miller, and I heard this young violinist. She could not have been older than fifteen, and she had the most amazing tone. Just lovely. I couldn't move. I remember thinking if I had been able to get that kind of sound out of that instrument, there'd be one less electric guitarist playing today.

So I decided to give music a rest and play hide-and-seek with Rosa and just be normal with the rest of the kids. Of course my mother was not going to let that happen. She always had ideas — making plans, doing something. She was about to do something that would change my life.

CHAPTER 3

The Strangers, with me third from right, 1962.

Music is a force that can divide generations, fathers and sons. It can also bring them together. My son, Salvador, was sixteen, and we were in the car—he was already in that mode when parents are the most uncool people, and so is their music. I was listening to John Coltrane's Live in Seattle, *recorded in 1965 with Pharoah Sanders—very challenging music. Salvador was looking out the window, real quiet. That's one thing Sal and my little brother, Jorge, have in common—you can tell they chew on things for a while before they open their mouths. They think and are considerate of other people's feelings. I could still learn from that. I say what comes into my mind, and sometimes I'll read an interview in which I've gone and said something about another musician,* and I'll say, "Damn, that was a little harsh." Later on I'll have to apologize to someone.

The music started to get real far-out, and suddenly Sal turned to me and said, "Hey, Coltrane's playing Stravinsky right now. You know, Dad, you can't just bug out and play like that. You got to know what you're doing." I was chuckling inside, but I kept cool. I know that music is not easy to listen to. But he was listening hard, and he had an opinion about what he heard. I respected that.

Not long after that, we were in the car and listening to—what else?—Coltrane, and again Salvador got quiet. Then he said, "You know, for a long time I thought that you and your friends Hal Miller, Tony Kilbert, and Gary Rashid were all a bunch of music snobs."

"Really?"

"Yeah. I thought you guys were overly opinionated about music. But I was in the car with my sisters, and they started playing their music, and I felt just like you guys. I was thinking, "Oh, my God, do we have to listen to the Spice Girls over and over?"

I had to smile again—that made me think right away about my sisters and their Elvis records. It gave me great delight that Sal was thirsty for something more everlasting, and then it made me think of how we don't connect with certain music when we're young. Then we grow up and think again about the music we used to turn our noses up at. Like me and Mexican music.

I remember around the time I was disengaging from my dad and mariachi music, American singers were coming down to Mexico for material. Big stars such as Frank Sinatra and Nat King Cole did whole albums based on Mexican music—even Charlie Parker did that South of the Border album. I can remember when everybody was singing "Quizás, Quizás, Quizás"—which is a song written by Osvaldo Farrés, who's Cuban, but it was made famous in Mexico. And of course "Bésame Mucho," which could be the most recorded song of all time next to "La Bamba." A few years later, the Champs did "Tequila," and after that, Herb Alpert did "The Lonely Bull" with the Tijuana Brass.

It's funny, because at the time all those guys were crossing the border and coming south, I was starting to go the other way. It all started with *the songs I heard on the radio. It didn't matter if I was Mexican or American, black, white, or purple. I could only hear one thing—the blues.*

I n the summer of 1961 my dad had been up in San Francisco for almost a year, and my mom could see I had lost interest in playing music. She also knew she couldn't talk me back into it. But she was smart, and she wasn't going to let all those lessons and all that playing go to waste. One afternoon she grabbed me and said, "*Mijo*, come here—we're going to the park."

"What? Where?"

"You'll see." Oh, okay. Here we go again.

I could hear the music even before we got there. It was a boogie kind of beat and echo, echo, echo—just bouncing off the buildings and trees. We walked into the park, and I saw a band doing its thing with funky amplifiers and electric guitars and a booming bass sound. They were playing a riff-blues number like "Last Night," and then this one guitarist stepped up, and he's wearing khakis, pressed sharp as a knife, and his hair was piled up in a big mop and cut close on the sides, like Little Richard's. Real pachuco style, just like my dad hated. The guy starts soloing, and he's got a very distinctive twang on his guitar that was popular back then—like Duane Eddy or Lonnie Mack.

It was like a UFO had landed in my backyard. I had seen guitarists on TV before, but not like this—hearing it live made the hair on my arms go straight up. This was so different—to see it happening in front of me, to see someone snapping the strings and feel the sound going through you. To see how the music was made. I'm sure my mom could see the effect on me just by looking at my eyes and my body. I stood there and listened and couldn't move.

It was Javier Bátiz. He was one of the few guys playing that early style of rock and roll in Mexico at the time. He had come up playing with a black American singer and piano player from New Orleans named Gene Ross, who lived in Tijuana. Now he was leading his own group called Los TJs—short for "Tijuanenses." And it was pronounced "Tee-Jays," not "Tay-hotas," because we all wanted to be in with the in crowd, as American as possible. That group had some of the best players in Tijuana, including Javier's sister. They called her Baby Bátiz because she sang "Angel Baby" so well.

Javier himself was one of Tijuana's baddest guitarists, and his home gig was at El Convoy—a dance and strip club on Avenida Revolución. He was an amalgam of the three people he loved most: B. B. King, Little Richard, and Ray Charles. He had it down. But he didn't sound like a parrot. He had really invested a lot of his own energy and passion into it.

Of course I didn't know all this about Javier or the other musicians and their styles and fingerprints then. I didn't even know Javier's name. Not yet. All this made it more mysterious and attractive to me. What I could see was that it was not just the sound or the look of the band or the way they presented themselves. It was all that together. And I knew that this was not the kind of music that happened in that park too often. I'm not sure how they got the permit to play that loud outdoors, but there they were.

I remember thinking, with all my teenage conviction, "This is what I want to be. This is what I want to do for the rest of my life."

Two things happened right away because of what happened in the park that day. First, I started following Javier around—I became his shadow. I was thirteen at the time; he was only three or four years older than I was, but in my eyes he might as well have been in his early twenties. He wasn't overly friendly or anything to me, but he let me come and hang out at his place. He lived with his mother, and the first time I went to his place I noticed that everything smelled like glue because he was into model cars. His piano was covered with them! Wow. It was cars and records and guitars and music, and that was this guy's life—which made him the coolest guy around.

Another thing about Javier was that his mannerisms were so different from anything I had ever seen—it was definitely not mariachi, and it wasn't pachuco, either. There was nothing Mexican about his thing. It was a black American kind of charisma. He was a slick dresser, and he had swagger and confidence, even in the way he grabbed the guitar. It all fit with the music he played and the way his guitar sounded. It made a huge impression on this little Mexican kid—I was even wondering what kind of water he was drinking.

But there was a price to pay to be around Javier. Two of the TJs didn't like me and would try to shoo me away, punch me in the stomach, and pull my hair and my ears, just being bully assholes, and Javier did nothing to stop it. The worst was a saxophone player named Brachi. But he wasn't going to stop me. In my thirteen-year-old mind, getting my ass kicked by this bully was worth it in order to get the goods. I was the youngest kid there with these older guys. One day I came home all red-eyed from crying, and my mom told Javier that Carlos had an older brother who would kick their asses if the mistreatment didn't stop. It stopped. I heard years later they found Brachi's body somewhere on the outskirts of Tijuana—that he made the wrong deal with the wrong people.

Javier's bass player was nice—he looked like Jughead in the Archie comics—and the guy could really play the instrument, and he turned me on to Jimmy Reed. I remember going to his place, where he had a room with a bed, a dirt floor, and a phonograph. He would smoke a joint, lie on the bed, and put on a Jimmy Reed record, and that voice and harmonica had all the elegance and emotion of Duke Ellington's music as far as I was concerned. I still feel that way.

The second thing that happened after I heard Javier in the park was that my mom immediately sent a letter to my dad telling him that Carlos found this music that he loves, that he's following around this musician like a puppy dog, and he wants to learn electric guitar. She asked him to get one for me if he could afford it. I forget if he brought it with him the next time he got back to Tijuana or if he had someone else bring it. It was a big, fat Gibson—a beat-up hollow-body like the ones the jazz guys would play, black with a little yellow in it. I didn't have a clue what to do. First thing I did was to go out and buy strings for it—nylon strings!

I learned fast after that—that you need steel strings, and that you have to play through an amplifier. I learned what a pickup was. My ears were already trained from playing violin, and I knew how to hold strings against a neck, but this was totally different. Different feel on my fingers; different tuning. I learned a few chords from watching Javier, but it was mostly my dad at the start—and listening to records and the radio, just trying to pick up what I could.

The thing is, I hung out with Javier, but Javier was not really a teacher. It's been reported that he gave me lessons, but he was not someone who would say, "No; you're doing that wrong. Play with this finger here and that finger there." He let me hang around, he turned me on to different songs and the people I needed to know: B. B. King, Ray Charles. He had the albums, and he had the knowledge. But when it came to guitar technique, what he showed me mostly was his back. Really—that's how he would play, so I couldn't see what his hands were doing.

Of course years later I found out that making someone learn on his own is a big part of the blues tradition. You don't want to make it too easy or too accessible. Even my future father-in-law, Saunders King, one of the best R & B guitarists of his generation, didn't like to show me anything. My chops are my chops—go get your own!

I have been supportive of Javier and have acknowledged him accordingly. He has been a guest in my house. We have hung out together and played together—like when we jammed in Tijuana in 1993. I presented him with a Boogie amplifier and gave him one of my guitars. He now plays a Paul Reed Smith.

But I feel like I have to be careful now not to do things that will perpetuate the idea that some sort of debt is still unpaid. I owe Javier gratitude for turning me on to the electric guitar but not necessarily for showing me how to do it. What I learned about the guitar and about the music I would start out with—the blues—came from a whole school of teachers, some of whom I played with as a teenager and some of whom I got to know from listening to their records over and over.

*   *   *

Once I got turned on to the electric guitar, my whole world started to shift and change. It was like all the energy and conviction that had been spread out among boxing and girls and toys and candy was suddenly focused on just one thing: the electric guitar. It didn't matter at first if it was just blues or R & B—what mattered was whether there was a guitar.

I started to pick up on guitar music everywhere—on the radio, on the records at Javier's place—and I began to hear the melodies that went with guitars. Groups like the Ventures caught my ear, though I thought a lot of their stuff sounded like corny surfer music. But they were great players. Also Los Indios Tabajaras, who were as big as Elvis in Mexico. They were this bad two-guitar band from Brazil, and their shtick was posing as Brazilian *Indios*. They sounded like Santo & Johnny unplugged, smooth and precise. I'm sure Santo & Johnny grew from their style—that's how it sounds to me.

As I said, I was mostly on my own after the few chords my dad showed me. I learned how to dissect a song by playing the record three or four times with the guitar in my hand, going up and down the neck of the guitar till I grabbed the right chord. It was easy after a while—I would focus on one part and then another. First the guitar, then the horns, then the bass. One of the first songs I learned all the parts to was James Brown's "Night Train."

I was teaching myself to listen, to figure out how to take a song apart and put it back together, like a mechanic. This is what the piano player, the guitar, the bass, the saxophone is doing. Being a kid, dissecting a song, I could do it for hours. It's still fun for me. Just the other day I was dissecting the horn parts to Bob Marley's "Iron Lion Zion."

The first melody I learned to play all the way through was "Apache," an instrumental by the Shadows, an English group. I really got that one down and loved it—so much so that it became my nickname for a while. *"Ahí viene El Apache,"* they'd say—here comes El Apache. When I found out there was this western called *Apache* with Burt Lancaster, that made me even prouder.

Funny thing is that years later—around the time of *Supernatural*—I discovered a tune from that movie called "Love Song from *Apache*," and it was performed by Coleman Hawkins. So another song called "Apache" got under my skin. I had the honor to play that tune with Wayne Shorter a number of times, and on one special occasion at the Montreux Jazz Festival I played it with the great saxophonist Joe Henderson. The festival director, Claude Nobs, had the idea to have us play together, but the choice of song was mine. *"Ahí viene El Apache"* still applies.

After "Apache" I learned "Rumble" by Link Wray and tunes by Duane Eddy, including "Red River Valley"—we called that rebel music. "Love Is Strange" by Mickey & Sylvia—one of my first songs with a string bend. I remember telling myself, "I *got* to learn that lick, man!" I got into Freddie King—the king of the instrumentals—with "San-Ho-Zay," "Tidal Wave," and of course "Hide Away."

There was Billy Butler's guitar solo on Bill Doggett's "Honky Tonk"—every guitar player had to know that. No exceptions. Javier turned me on to Bobby "Blue" Bland, and I picked up on everything his guitarist, Wayne Bennett, was doing. Later I came to know how much of that was T-Bone Walker's creation, almost note for note.

Playing any instrument is learning by doing, training your mind and fingers to do things. Getting frustrated but doing it again and again. I was hungry to keep learning—any tune anyone wanted to put in front of me—anything—I could figure it out on my own. I began to sit in with whoever would let me. Long before I played in any club, I had a chance to sit in and watch the TJs' rehearsals. I started picking up things, little by little.

Of course I wanted to play in the TJs—who wouldn't? At that time, Javier's band was more together than any other band doing that kind of music in Tijuana. They were the band to beat. They were winning all the contests in Tijuana and other cities—Juárez, Mexicali. They had their regular gig at El Convoy, on the main strip. But they were already a unit. I hung out and sometimes sat in with them, but mostly it was just hanging.

I remember one time I got to go in the car with them to a battle of the bands in Mexicali, which is as far from Tijuana as San Francisco is from San Jose. The TJs went up against a band called the Kings and lost. I thought they were ripped off. But I started to see that other bands were invested in this same sort of blues sound and that other guys could play guitar really well, too. It was all eye-opening.

Tony used to get pissed off about it. "When are they going to let you play, man?"

"At least they let me go with them in the car to the dances and gigs that they do," I'd say.

"Javier should invite you to play."

"Well, it's his band, and they only have so much time to play." I made excuses for him because I wanted to hang around and learn as much as I could—plus I was getting to know the scene. Hanging with Javier opened a door to parts of Tijuana that I had never seen with my dad.

Tijuana was not Mexico City. Mexico City was international, and everyone there spoke Spanish. The music there came from Mexico, Central America, and South America—lots of it from Cuba. Tijuana was more about American influences, and everyone spoke some English or at least Spanglish. At the start of the 1960s, Tijuana was a rock-and-roll town.

You could find it all on Avenida Revolución. On the north end, close to the border, were the hoity-toity clubs, like the Oasis and the Shangri-La. That's where you went for dinner and a sophisticated, Modern Jazz Quartet feel with piano and vibes, that sort of thing. Or Mike's Bar, which had dancing to live music. The bands there had to know how to play all the latest dances, including "Peppermint Twist," which was pretty killer. I remember when that came out in '61. They called it a twist but it was really a shuffle, and man, Joey Dee & the Starliters could play the hell out of shuffles.

Further south on Revolución things got grungier. That's where the strip clubs were, like the Aloha Club and El Convoy, where the TJs and other bands played and where I ended up playing. It was a little place with a bar to the right when you enter, a place for tables and chairs in the middle of the floor and under a small balcony, and a stage all the way in the back, where the band played. The girls danced right in front of the stage, then circulated among the customers, trying to get them to buy drinks and get drunk. It was dingy and dark and a bit smelly, but it was better than that joint with the *norteño* music that I couldn't stand.

It would be one hour of music, an hour of strippers—like that, all night long, but it was never really about the music. The customers were there to get laid, and they were too busy doing that to pay much attention to the band and make any stupid requests. It was the band's job to keep the party going and the customers drinking.

People began to hear that I could play. I sat in a few times with Javier and the TJs at El Convoy and started to meet other musicians and bands who played there, like the Strangers.

The leader of the Strangers was Manuel Delgadillo—he owned all the band's instruments, so he would decide who played what, and of course he was playing lead. At one point he needed a bass player, and he asked me if I wanted to give it a try. I already knew how to play violin, which also has four strings, so I was ready to do that. It was this cheap Kay bass, but I enjoyed it and was getting good at it. Then we had our first gig—it was either the Aloha Club or Mike's Bar—but we never got paid. My first real professional gig, and we got ripped off!

I continued to rehearse with the Strangers anyway, but every time we did someone would tell me that I played too many notes for a bass player—I was beating up Manuel! He decided to let me start playing guitar, and we kept rehearsing. Meanwhile, I was sitting in more at El Convoy, playing with their house band—not the TJs—and I started to get good at it. The first few times I got up to play, I was so nervous. I was so concerned with playing everything right that I couldn't look at the people or anything else, really. My eyes couldn't leave my fingers; I was busy making sure they were in the right position and on the right portion of the neck. I still do that a lot—focus more on what I'm doing than on the audience.

I wish I could tell you exactly when I played my first full gig on guitar, what I played, and how I felt — the one thing I remember is that I was allowed to play the club's guitar, which was some kind of solid electric, which was better than the big hollow-body my dad had gotten me.

I also do remember clearly that not long after that I ran into Javier on the street. He told me he was leaving El Convoy, moving to a better gig at the Club Latino Americano, and did I want to go with him and play bass? What could I say? The TJs were the first band I wanted to play with, so I said okay. I showed up and went back to bass and was doing well.

The next thing I knew, the manager of El Convoy, whom we called Manolete, found me on the street. (The original Manolete, the John Coltrane of bullfighters, was gored to death by a bull. He had a big hooked nose, and so did the manager.) Manolete said, "You need to get off that bandstand and get back to the Strangers right now or you'll never work on Avenida Revolución again."

Whoa. He was a big guy, and I was this scrawny little thing, fourteen years old. He also didn't like Javier all that much. Did I want to be part of that? Also, Javier's band had its own thing going on. They were the TJs wherever they played. Being in the house band at El Convoy meant you had one place you *would* play — which also meant you had a home.

I thought about it for a minute. Javier's gig was once a week, and El Convoy was almost every day. The job with Javier didn't pay as much — and I wanted to play guitar. So I put down the bass, left Javier, and went back to El Convoy. I was already making my own career decisions — not that it felt that way at the time. For me, it was just practical and it made sense. I needed the work, and I needed to eat. My loyalty to friends was not going to feed me. But man, Javier was disappointed. He didn't yell or anything; he just fixed me with a look, as if I were Benedict Arnold. That was it for Javier and me for a long, long time.

The El Convoy house band was basically a shuffle band, playing blues changes and three-chord songs like "Green Onions," "Hide

Away," and "Think" by the Royals — not the later James Brown version. And *definitely* "La Bamba." At that time, Ritchie Valens in Tijuana was like Bob Marley was later in Jamaica. He was the dude — a cholo Mexican. He was the only hero we had at the time — everyone knew Valens was short for Valenzuela.

Within months I could tell I was getting better, and I started to get confidence. I could tell because I'd see other kids my age who were also picking up the guitar, and they didn't know how to make heads or tails out of it. I also started to figure out the different things you can do on the instrument. You can play the melody, which is the lead; the chords — the rhythm; and the bass line. Once you get all that down, that's all you really need to know. Then you have to just work at it again and again until it becomes part of you. Maybe it was because I could do so many things with the guitar that I never felt like singing. But even when I was playing violin, singing was never my thing.

I could hear I was getting better, but I wasn't getting any words of encouragement from anyone, really — not in those places in Tijuana where I was playing. Everybody was more into chicks or drinking or whatever they were into. I just had to say those words to myself. I would take a break from my gigs and walk around to some of the other places to hear them playing — sometimes they'd let me in, and sometimes I had to just stand outside and listen and pick up stuff. I got really good, because that's all I did. That was my schooling.

All these clubs had some bands with some badass guitar players. There was one guy who was a terror: we called him Liebre Chica — Little Jackrabbit. He played with a ring pick on his thumb, like a country and western player, and had an incredible vocabulary, somewhere between B. B. King and a more jazzy sound. He would have had no problem dealing with Javier, and there was a lot of rivalry going on then! There was another guy, a Filipino, who would come around on a motorcycle with his Stratocaster strapped to his back. He was dealing speed and kept his stuff in the headlamp, which didn't work — he'd just unscrew that thing and put all the drugs in there when he had to cross the border. He could really play, and I remember he was a little bit more giving than other guitarists. He taught me the chords to "Georgia on My Mind," "Summertime," tunes like that.

I'll never forget the first strip club I went into. I was just fourteen and hanging with Jaime—he was a drummer who had these gorgeous sisters who had been in movies in Mexico City. I had done a gig with him, and he owed me money, so he said, "Come on; I need to pick up some money at the Aloha, and I can pay you." This was at three in the afternoon, so I went from bright sunshine into what seemed like pitch-black. While my eyes slowly adjusted, I heard the drums going *Bah-ba-bah, bah-ba-bah* and the saxophone doing that snake-dance thing—I'm telling you, to this day, when I hear Thelonious Monk or anyone doing "Bye-Ya" I think about the music they played in those strip clubs in Tijuana. I'm sure Monk was thinking about that kind of beat when he wrote it.

Then I saw the stripper onstage. This was the first time I had seen a woman totally naked. She had tassels on her nipples, and she was making them twirl—first one direction, then the other, then in opposite directions, clockwise *and* counterclockwise. That was talent—four different ways! I'm thinking, "How does she do that?" and I just stood there. She saw me and how young I was, and she started laughing, then everybody saw me and started laughing, too. She grabbed one of her breasts and pointed it at me. "Come here, little boy. You look like you need some milk; you're just so skinny." Can you imagine? My first time in a strip joint, and I was being called out for staring.

I learned a lot from watching strippers and listening to how the drummers would support them—do a roll when she swings those tassels. Crash the cymbal when she throws a hip or does a kick. You had to have it together, because some of those strippers were straight from the country and they needed help, otherwise they'd look stupid. If they didn't get a steady beat to dance to, they'd pick up a shoe and throw it—and they didn't miss.

These were tough women. Not all of them were dancers, but

many were *ficheras*, hookers. They didn't do the deed at El Convoy, though—there were no rooms there for that. They would try to take the guy home or to a hotel and make some cash that way, and they were there to make money any way they could. While the band would play, the strippers would wander through the club, go up to some guy who just walked in, and say, "Want to buy me a drink?"

"Sure," he'd say. She would ask for a drink and a Coke, then pour the drink into the Coke while he wasn't looking and order another one, and another. Keep milking it till the customer had to pay the big tab. If you drank that Coke, you'd pass out after one sip! Every time she ordered another drink, she got a *ficha*, a little chit—which is kind of funny, because *fichera* is the word for "prostitute." Anyway, she'd cash them all in at the end of the night and get paid a little extra. Sometimes that's all the money they made.

People think I played behind the strippers, but I never did when they stripped. That was mostly the job of the drummers, to do a rhythm thing that worked with their moves. I played when everyone would get up and dance together.

But playing in that kind of environment...I remember some guys would bring their girlfriends there, start to drink, and get distracted by these beautiful strippers. Then their dates would get jealous. We could tell from the stage what was going on—the tension, the emotion. We'd decide to have a little fun and start playing a tune with just the right breaks and heavy rhythm—*ba-da-bum, ba-da-bum*—and next thing you know the girlfriend would be up and taking off her shirt, then her brassiere. Two or three times we were able to make that happen—actually strip someone who wasn't a stripper. That's when I realized that a guitar could talk to a woman.

I can't tell you exactly when my perception changed from rock and roll to the blues, but it was like a laser when it happened. Over time you start to learn about it—you learn to understand that the blues is a very sacred language. It really has to be played by musicians who know and feel its history and respect its power. When you have people who do honor and respect the music like that—man, they are able to captivate. If they don't, they have to play at it, they cuss and swear, and it's like listening to a comedian who's not funny. Nothing sounds worse than mediocre blues. If you don't know how to play it, you have no business doing it. When you go to an altar at the Vatican you don't start putting up graffiti and shit.

The blues is a very, very no-nonsense thing. It's easy to learn the structure of the songs, the words and the riffs, but it's not like some other styles of music—you can't hide behind it. Even if you are a great musician, if you want to really play the blues you have to be willing to go to a deeper place in your heart and do some digging. You have to reveal yourself. If you can't make it personal and show an individual fingerprint, it's not going to work. That's really where you find the magnificence in the simple three-chord blues, in the fingerprints of blues guitarists like T-Bone Walker, B. B. King, Albert King, Freddie King, Buddy Guy, and all the cats from Chicago—Otis Rush, Hubert Sumlin.

There's a lot of misunderstanding about the blues. Maybe it's because the word means so many things. The blues is a musical form—twelve bars, three chords—but it's also a musical feeling expressed in what notes you play and how you play each note. The blues can also be an emotion or a color. Sometimes the difference is not so clear. You can be talking about the music, then the feeling, then what's in the words of a song. John Lee Hooker singing, "Mmm, mmm, mmm—Big legs, tight skirt / 'Bout to drive me out of my mind..." It's all the blues.

To me, jazz is like the ocean—wider than the eye can see, with many places to go to and explore. I see the blues as a lake—you can look across it, travel around it, get to know it quickly. But you have to really dive into it, because it can be very, very deep.

A lot of musicians put down the blues—it's too simple; it's too limited. They criticize it because they can't do it, and they have no interest in figuring out how to imprint so much feeling and emotion onto just three chords. Or a good blues shuffle? Just because someone plays jazz doesn't mean he should dismiss a rhythm like that. I'm not going to name names, because I don't want to get in trouble, but I am here to tell you that I've heard a few jazz drummers who do not know how to play a shuffle. Great jazz drummers. Again, some things are made of gold and should be respected that way. A good blues shuffle is pure gold.

The blues is nothing if not deep and emotional. The blues can be about joy and celebration, and of course imploring and lamenting—but the real blues is not whiny. Whiny is like a baby who's not really hungry, but he's still crying and maybe just wants to be picked up. That's the trouble with a lot of guitar players trying to play the blues: they whine a lot.

Imploring means, "I need a hug from the celestial arms, from the supreme. I need an absolute hug." That can happen to anybody. You can be rich or poor or healthy or sick. When a woman that you love more than your next breath leaves you, or when your own mom turns her back on you, that's the blues. The things of the earth are things of the earth, and things of the spirit are things of the spirit—and the spirit has to have what it needs. When they talk about the healing power of the blues, that's what they mean.

In Tijuana I would hear all sorts of music, Mexican and American, but for some reason it was the blues that felt most natural to me. I listened to the blues 24-7 and studied it as I had never studied anything before. In San Francisco we were the Santana Blues Band and played blues exclusively at the start. Then our music changed. We became Santana, but the blues was always part of the feel in the music. If you look at all the Santana albums now, you'll see that there are a few tunes you could call blues—"Blues for Salvador," obviously, and the beginning of "Practice What You Preach." The jam with Eric Clapton on *Supernatural*. They aren't strictly blues numbers, but that feeling will always come through my music.

I've been hanging around the lake for a long time now. Like jazz, the blues knows its own history. It has rituals and rules that must be respected. Everyone knows them, and everyone knows everyone—the guitar heroes and what they sound like. Who did you listen to, and where did you get your style? Who influenced whom, and who's your daddy? It's easy to hear that. I'll put it this way—B. B. King has a lot of children.

There's a story that Stevie Ray Vaughan told me. He had been playing in Texas for years before he got big in 1983, playing with David Bowie on "Let's Dance" and sounding that nasty, stinging tone like Albert King. Then he was playing blues and rock festivals— the big leagues. The first time he ran into Albert after that, Stevie was so happy to see him. Albert was backstage, sitting down and working on his pipe. He didn't get up, didn't shake Stevie's hand. He just looked at Stevie. "You owe me fifty thousand dollars."

That was the price for copping his style. You know what Stevie told me? He paid it.

When I started out in Tijuana, I played funky three-chord blues changes. After a while, I started to get into songs like "Georgia on My Mind" and "Misty" a little bit. As time went by, I got more and more into the blues—*black* blues. And more and more, the guys I hung out with were into nothing but the hard-core blues—black American music. Other groups in Tijuana would want to play Elvis Presley or Fabian or Bobby Rydell, that Dick Clark kind of stuff. Yuck. Even when songs by Pat Boone and Paul Anka, songs like "Volare," were popular and played on the radio, we didn't want to touch that. We had a badge of honor.

Once I started going down that road, there was no turning back. The blacker the sound, the rootsier the guitar, the more I wanted it. That meant I wanted to hear black singers whenever I could. Tijuana had its resident R & B star, Gene Ross—he sort of looked like Joe Frazier. Don Lauro Saaveda, who ran El Convoy, had brought him down from New Orleans. Gene had a falsetto voice like Aaron Neville's, with power, and he could play the hell out of the piano. He had a big repertoire of songs—many I didn't know till he sang them: "Summertime," "Georgia on My Mind," "Let the Good Times Roll," "Something's Got a Hold on Me." He'd sing "I Loves You, Porgy," and man, it just gave you chills.

Playing in the house band at El Convoy meant I eventually played as support for Gene and also behind these other weekend musicians, black Americans who came down from San Diego to play, like this one guy who called himself Mr. T and looked like he was Albert King's brother. He would hit Tijuana, score some grass and some uppers, get up some courage, and sing "Stormy Monday Blues." That was his one song, and he would kill it every time. Other musicians would come down from as far away as San Jose for a long weekend, spend all their money in their first night, then sing at El Convoy to make enough money to get back home on Sunday.

Gene and these black weekenders became my teachers—they took my blues training to another level. After a while I couldn't learn anything else from the radio or records—I had to really, really get in it live. The only way was if these blues guys were right next to me like that, close enough for me to feel the way the singer would stomp his foot, and the way he'd be getting on that piano. I would learn by the dirty looks they gave me if I messed up the changes or the time. It was all extremely educational because I learned the ingredients—the rhythms and the flow, the sound symmetry—of that music.

I remember Gene would be at the piano, and the bartender would line up between five and seven shots of tequila, and that's how many songs would be in the set. He'd finish one song and knock back a shot. The cat was blacker than black; his lips were purple, his eyes were yellower than yellow, and he had the prettiest voice I had ever heard. He also had the prettiest white girlfriend I had ever seen, like Elizabeth Taylor beautiful.

Gene was a rough dude—I remember one time his brother was visiting, and they started roughhousing with each other, just brothers messing around, and they almost tore the whole place down! Gene had served in Korea and could get real angry sometimes. Just a year after I left Tijuana for the last time I heard he got into a fight with some Mexican guy. He brought a knife to a machete fight, and that was the end of Gene Ross. It's too bad he never recorded, because that cat had the most gorgeous voice.

Later on I got to know that Tijuana was a kind of Casablanca for black Americans—neutral territory away from the race war of America. Let's face it: racism was very active then and still is, especially in San Diego, where you had a lot of white kids in the military who were raised thinking that way—angry, hating blacks and browns, looking for a fight. In Mexico everyone was on more even ground, and the Mexican police were just waiting for those racist kind of guys to get out of hand and give them some back-alley justice.

I want to say that it's a cliché about the drunk American tourists acting ignorant and getting derogatory, but I witnessed that many times—drinking and getting a little too loud with their feelings about Mexicans. "You're not in America now," the cops would say and whale away at them with nightsticks. Then they would throw the tourists in jail and "lose" their passports for a few days. There were so many stories about Tijuana jails—they could be brutal. You did not want to mess with the police there. You were not going to win that fight.

The first time I experienced racism directed at me I had just started to get into the guitar. I was still a little light-haired, and the border was a lot more open then. A friend had taught me how to pronounce "American citizen" like an American would, and he told me that all I had to do was walk across the border and say "American citizen" at the checkpoint and just keep walking. And it worked! Then I would take a bus to San Diego and go to a place Javier told me about—Apex Music. They had the best guitars—Gibsons, Gretsches, Epiphones. I wasn't so much a Fender guy, not even then. I found that you had to crank Fenders up really, really loud to get something out of them, or you would sound like the guys playing with Lawrence Welk.

I had just enough money with me to take the bus to Apex and

back, so I never went inside. I was too intimidated. One time I was standing there just salivating, looking in the store window at these most gorgeous freaking guitars and amplifiers with tweed covers. I wanted to smell and know what they felt like in my hands! Suddenly I heard a voice behind me. "Hey, you fucking chili-bean eater, fucking Mexican, Pancho Villa!" I froze. "Hey, I'm talking to you!" I slowly turned around and realized that there were two sailors screaming at me. "You fucking little Pancho Villa chili-bean eater!" What? Who? My mind filled with questions, but I just started walking away—quickly.

I was thinking that this was just like a bullfight—don't get in the bullring, and you'll be all right. Just keep walking and ignore them. I don't know if they were drunk, but it was around four in the afternoon. They followed me for a little bit, screaming like idiots. Then they got bored and went to drink some more, I guess. That was the first time I actually heard the sound of pure hate directed toward me simply because of the way I looked. That wasn't my first time across the border, but it made me think twice about going back.

By the beginning of 1962, I was playing all the time and learning fast. I had the steady gig at the Convoy, and it was a real high watching the music taking shape, doing songs by Etta James, Freddie King, Ray Charles—really getting to know that style of music. I loved it. When I started I only played weekdays—I would get there after school at 5:00 p.m. and play until 11:00 p.m., three sets a night. Then I got to play weekends on top of that, starting at eight and playing until five or six in the morning!

I was also back to playing my first instrument. Part of my deal with my mom when I first got the guitar was that I would get out my violin again and play as part of the church service every Sunday. I played "Ave Maria" and some classical pieces like Bach's Minuet in G Major with this one accordion player. I don't think they had enough money for an organ or a bigger band. I did that for almost half a year to appease my mom while I was getting stuck on the guitar.

I would get so high—on the music, on not getting enough sleep, and on playing all through the night. When I say high, I also mean dizzy—from forgetting to eat. It was funny, but I used to love getting out of the club in the morning, seeing the sunrise, and feeling light-headed from having played all night with no meal. If it was Sunday, I'd go straight from El Convoy to church and play "Ave Maria" on the violin and all that. I didn't have really good eating habits, but my friends turned me on to going to the street corner and getting juices. I mean, carrot juice, celery, and raw eggs, and then they blend it and you drink it. Man, that would get me so high it would take me to the next level. I never smoked any pot then, though everybody around me did, but I got stoned just being in that environment, and then I started drinking and soon realized that was going the wrong way when I woke up one day passed out on the street.

The freedom I had during that year and a half was heaven. I was like a sponge. I was learning how to take care of myself in the music business, learning lessons such as the more steady the gig, the more likely I was to get paid. I had been naive, playing my first gigs and not getting paid at all; getting burned because of all the bullshit they'd tell kids—"We can't pay you because you're not in the union"; "Come back next week and we'll pay you after the next show." Yeah, sure. Some things my father could tell me about being a musician, but I had to learn most things on my own and to build myself up.

By the time I was the featured guitarist at El Convoy, I was making nine dollars a week. I had no idea about the other musicians, but once a week the manager called me upstairs to the office. I'd get my money in cash, put it in my pocket, and take it home to Mom—she got all of it. I didn't question any part of this or try to negotiate. I was happy to be playing and to be part of the scene.

The education I was getting was a street education—I can see now that my view of people and of spirituality began from that experience. I started at the lowest level and learned to always watch out, because people would try to make me less than they were if I let them, try to shame me or guilt-trip me, then pay me less or not at all. I started to see that people put each other on different levels, looking down on someone or looking up to someone, and take advantage of that situation. It was the beginning of the way I look at things today — I don't allow anyone to have superiority over me and try not to let anyone have inferiority under me. I was talking with another musician one night, explaining that I did not want to have to look up to anybody. "Not even God?" he asked. I was ready for that. By then I had been thinking a lot about God — my answer had the kind of conviction my mom had about religion.

"God doesn't like to look down on anyone. Why should we?" I said. Even then in Tijuana I felt that was true and that it was important to realize it on a spiritual level and implement it on a street level.

I was in Tijuana for just seven years. For everyone, the years from eight to fifteen are when we grow up the most, when we become aware of the world around us. We start asking questions we will be asking again and again the rest of our lives. It was at that age when I first began to work and to play music. It was also when I went from G.I. Joe to "Where's Rosa?"

First there was Linda Wong, from my neighborhood. She was like a teenage Sophia Loren, and she was my first big crush, but nothing happened. I was still figuring out how to talk to girls, but that started me thinking. There was a party one time with all the musicians and girls from El Convoy at Rosarito Beach, which is between Tijuana and Ensenada. We had drinks and the radio on, and Ray Charles was singing, "One of these days and it won't be long..." Everyone paired up, and I could tell the girl I was with was disappointed she had to hang with this little kid. Still, she let me sneak a kiss. Then there was Rosa, who lived next door and would let me kiss her while we were hiding in the bushes. She didn't let me go any further.

Having these experiences as a teenager got me to thinking

about women, especially when I saw the girls who were stripping for money showing up at the church where I was playing the violin. It would be Sunday morning, and four or five of the women I just saw naked a few hours earlier were there. They had on nice, modest dresses and were with their small children, the girls dressed in little white socks and ribbons in their hair, the boys in their little suits. I began to realize that they had to do what they did to feed their kids, that they had little choice, and how hard it was for them in a culture that looked down on women for doing those kinds of things. I would talk to them, and they would tell me that they couldn't go home because their parents for whatever reason would not let them back in.

I began to look at women with a different eye. I had a conversation with one of the bouncers at El Convoy—this big thug who was always teasing me and pulling my hair. We were eating at the back of the joint in the place they had for employees, and this guy was pissed off at something. Or at everything. He was talking and talking about this and that, and he finally made some hateful comment about women in general—"They're all fucking whores!"

I don't know why, but I had to ask, "You mean all of them?"

"Yeah, to me, all of them!"

I kept going. "Does that mean your mother, too?" Silence. "And your sister?" He slowly turned to me. "Man, I could kill you." The only other person in the room was the woman who was cooking, and she looked at me as if I were crazy.

I had heard that kind of talk before from men. I've heard women speak about men the same way—"All men are dogs"—and that's not right, either.

But what the bouncer dude said was so negative and filled with so much anger that I couldn't just accept it. I had to say something. He threatened me, and I played it innocent. "Hey, I just wanted to know if you really meant all of them." He looked straight ahead and finished his food.

That left a tone in my head—not to judge women but to appreciate them. Not to judge people because of what they do in order to live and survive. As I grew up I tried to approach the sexual drive with dignity and grace. Years later, when we moved to San Francisco, I would be up early walking to work at a diner and there'd be a line of guys trying to pick me up in the Castro. And I'd say, "No; I don't do that, man." I got to understand how women feel when they walk through the streets and a bunch of guys are looking at their bodies and saying whatever. You feel like prey.

Since then my perception has been that the relationship between men and women is always a work in progress.

One day at El Convoy I ran into one of the substitute teachers from my school. He looked a lot like Barack Obama, now that I think about it, and he was a great storyteller. He told us a tale about a poor woman who had found some burning embers in her stove to keep herself warm during the night, and the glowing coals turned out to be the eyes of a big cat. Not sure what lesson we were supposed to learn from that, but I liked the story and I liked him, so when I saw him at the club with his arms wrapped around one of the girls there, I said, "Hey, Teach!" He jumped away from the girl like she was one of those hot coals. "Carlos, what are you doing here?"

"I work here, man. What are *you* doing here?"

By summer of 1962, those two parts of my life just didn't balance out anymore. It had not been easy playing music and going to school at the same time, so I eventually dropped out. My life with my family wasn't balancing, either. My hours were getting longer at El Convoy—from 4:00 p.m. to midnight on weeknights, and on weekends from opening time till the customers left. Meanwhile my dad was back in San Francisco again and had Jorge with him. Tony had found migrant work up in Stockton—an hour east of the Bay Area—picking artichokes and peaches. Soon my sisters would follow, too. As my mom had done in Autlán, she was still thinking El Norte—and as before, it was her decision to go. There was no discussion. But I was older by then, and I wasn't ready.

CHAPTER 4

Avenida Revolución, Tijuana, looking north toward the US border, 1964.

As soon as you left Tijuana and crossed the border, you would see humongous color billboards on which happy, smiling faces were selling houses and cars. Then you could drive to nice, clean supermarkets that had freezers, and everything was sparkling—no flies or funky smells, as there were back in Mexico. My mom and I used to talk about how good it would be to live in America. For her and the rest of my family, it was about a better way of life, like the one those billboards advertised. But what eventually made me want to go north was the sound of black America—blues and R & B. I wanted to be closer to that, marinate my spirit in that music.

CARLOS SANTANA

When we finally moved north, my family and I discovered that in the middle of all this affluence there were these intense pockets of conflict. Between rich and poor, between black, white, and brown. You had to watch out when you went two blocks in this or that direction, because there were ignorant, angry people living there who didn't like your kind, the way you talked, or the way you dressed. It can start in high school, but it really shouldn't even make it to that point.

I love being in the United States because it gives me a chance to say what I want to say. I realize in many places in the world that's not possible. The reason I speak my mind is because I see what's wrong and what can be better in this country. I think life is hard enough, and most people don't get that much unless they fight for it or get lucky or are born lucky. That's the true picture of America—not the idea of foreigners coming in and taking away this and that from Americans. My family moved here for a better life, because America is the land of opportunity—which means not only the opportunity to make something of yourself but also the opportunity to give back. I would never take anything from America that I wouldn't want to put back a hundred times. The majority of foreigners who come to this country, I believe, are like that.

I think the main problem is that people are afraid that other people will take away what is their fair share. You know that line of Billie Holiday's—"You can help yourself / But don't take too much"? That song, "God Bless the Child," should be up there with the national anthem and sung just as often. Those two songs next to each other would be perfect—the dream of America and the truth of America.

You want to talk about taking more than a fair share? Look at America and the world today. No country has ever been richer or more powerful than America is now. That's a fact. No country gives away more than America does, and at the same time no country demands more from the rest of the world. What Rome was in the time of Jesus, America is today. As it says in the Bible, render unto Caesar what is Caesar's and unto God what is God's. America takes what it wants, and it says that this is the right thing to do, without looking at the consequences.

y father was the advance scout for the family—he was the first to check out San Francisco around 1960, playing for a few months, then coming back. By the following year, he found steady work at the Latin American Club in the city's Mission District—not connected to the Club Latino Americano in Tijuana. With the help of the club's owner, Tony Mares, he put together one of San Francisco's first serious mariachi bands, recruiting from the Bay Area and Tijuana if necessary. Like they had done in Mexico, my dad's group played weddings and other important functions and got real busy. The Mexican community in San Francisco was growing fast at that point. He got tight with Tony and his wife, and they eventually became our sponsors, helping us come to America.

My mom's decision to move was a gradual thing, with lots of steps involved in preparation—my sister Irma remembers my father getting us English lessons from a private instructor in Tijuana. My mom went to San Francisco at one point to babysit the Mares's children for a few months and to help take care of their house—to be their Chepa, in other words.

I'm sure that's when my mom made up her mind. San Francisco can get in your veins, because it's beautiful in a way that San Diego and Los Angeles are not. She saw Golden Gate Park and got to visit other places in the city. To my mom, Los Angeles looked like Tijuana, only more crowded. San Francisco had the bridge and the bay and the hills. It had neighborhoods next door to each other with international people and flavors—Chinatown, Japantown, the Italian section. In some ways it was the world, not just America.

Tony was next to start crossing the border, around 1961. He went from being a mechanic in Mexico to working on a farm in California. He told me it was the hardest work he'd ever done in his life—up at dawn, bending over for the whole day until he collapsed every night from exhaustion, doing it again the next day, and sending what little money he got to Mom.

My mom and dad had a plan for the whole family, and in 1962

they started to put it into action—there was no stopping them. They saved up as much money as they could, and my dad started to work on finding a place for us in San Francisco. My mom told us what was happening, and my sisters complained—they were teenagers, young adults. Some had boyfriends by then. For me, it was like I had already joined the circus. I had already checked out of the family stuff—doing chores and going to school and being a normal kid. I was out every night, playing the blues and watching women take off their clothes.

My mom's attitude was, you can come with me to San Francisco or stay, but I'm going. Except for me, no one would choose to stay. The pull of the family was strong—stronger than any of the boyfriends were.

Meanwhile my mom started to work on the immigration papers to get us to the United States. She found a blind woman in Tijuana who had a typewriter and set up shop in the plaza near the Our Lady of Guadalupe cathedral. She had done the same thing for many Mexican families, so she had the routine down—being blind didn't matter. "What's your father's name?...Mother's name?... How many children?...Sponsor?" I remember it was my money from El Convoy that went directly to that woman to get the forms done.

My mother signed the documents and delivered them to the American government office. First my dad and Jorge went up north in the middle of the summer in 1962, staying in a small room above the Latin American Club. Jorge told me that one day Mr. Mares came to the door and told him he had to come downstairs and clean the place. He'd sweep and wax the floors, and at night he'd cry himself to sleep listening to our dad's violin and not knowing where his family was. He was just ten at the time! Around the end of spring, Tony joined them, then Laura and Irma came up from Tijuana, and finally my mom came with Leticia and Maria— closing down our last house in Mexico, on Calle Quinta, and everyone together in that little flat above the nightclub in San Francisco.

I held out till the end of summer, playing at El Convoy. I stayed at a place close to downtown with a cousin of my mom's. I gave them money for food and for washing my clothes, and I wasn't really there that much. It was basically just room and board, and I didn't want to go anywhere. I liked what I had in Tijuana—the music, the gig, playing blues and R & B; getting it together on guitar.

Then my mom came back from San Francisco with Tony to get me, and that was that—no argument or discussion. I had to go. As before, my birthday marked a major move in my life. I had just turned fifteen, and there I was in a car, crossing the border into San Diego, then making the long, straight drive up I-5 to San Francisco. The trip was much shorter than the one from Autlán—it was only a ten-hour drive back then, one long day. The roads in the United States were so much better than they were in Mexico, too—smooth and fast. I remember eating ketchup and Ritz crackers so we had enough gas money to make it.

There was not much in San Francisco in 1962 to change the fact that I wasn't happy. Not at first, anyway. I went from working as a full-time musician on the street to being a full-time student in the local junior high school—James Lick Junior High on Noe Street. Plus they held me back a year because I didn't speak English well enough, so I was in classes with thirteen- and fourteen-year-olds. I had been hanging around with dudes who were in their twenties and thirties, playing songs like "Stormy Monday Blues." Suddenly it was back to kiddie shit, and the music of the day was Jan and Dean and the Beach Boys, all this surf music, and I didn't even swim.

As we had in Tijuana, we started moving from one place to another almost immediately. We went from living above the club where my dad was playing to a funky little apartment on 3rd Street and Bryant in what was essentially the black ghetto, next to the American Can Company—an area they call China Basin.

We all had it tough at the start—lots and lots of tears. When the '62 school year started, suddenly all us kids had to learn how to get to school, how to make new friends, and we had to do it all in

English. My dad sat down with each of us, gave us just enough money for the bus, and explained the bus routes. "I'm only telling you once—you take this number bus and get off at that street, and take this other bus and change to this other bus." We were all scared and confused. Irma and Leticia got totally lost on their first day. Jorge and Maria only had to go down the block, since they were in elementary school—but they got teased for being Mexican. They didn't understand: the last time they were in school, everyone was Mexican! Jorge, who had never really seen a black kid's hair before, made the mistake of touching one boy's head. Man, he paid for that mistake again and again.

It didn't help that there was a language and culture gap between us and our neighbors and that there was a new set of street rules to learn. If three or four guys surrounded me on the way to school and wanted my lunch money, I emptied my pockets.

On my first day at James Lick, my pockets were empty anyway, because my mom and I didn't know that you had to bring money to buy a lunch or that you had to bring food. Come lunchtime, everybody went to the cafeteria. I wasn't going to ask anyone for food, so I went outside to watch people playing basketball or whatever they were doing. So there I was again—hungry, angry, upset.

A little later, just before we went back to classes, this guy Bruce came strolling by with his two flunkies. They knew I was new, and they started in on me with that "What are you looking at?" stuff. I didn't need to know English all that well to know what to do. "You want to meet after school?" I said, "*Sí, por qué?* Let's do this now!" His friend was saying, "Go ahead, Bruce, kick his ass," like they're trying to build up the energy or something, and I'm thinking, "What the hell is it with this waiting?"

So I just grabbed him and threw him against the lockers— *bam!* I yelled at him, "Man, I'm going to kick your ass, then I'm going to kick his ass." Everybody stepped back, going, "Whoa." Then the teachers came out and separated us, and we went back to class. But right away my reputation was, "That crazy Mexican—

don't mess with him." Being grumpy and hungry and angry about being there—that all helped.

We had sized each other up, and the next day Bruce came over and we started talking, and we got to music and he said, "You play?" I told him I played the blues on guitar, and he told me he was into doo-wop. "Oh? What's that?"

"You know, shoo-be-doo kind of music, like 'In the Still of the Night.' "

I went over to his house to listen to some records, and we became friends. Music got me through all kinds of circumstances.

There were some other good things that happened in those first days in junior high. On the day I stood up to the bully, a girl came up to me and said, "Hi. You're new here, right? Are you still going to fight Bruce?" Her name was Linda Houston. The boys and girls had different places for recess, and she had heard that this was going to happen. "He's the biggest bully in school, you know." So she was warning me a little. A few days before, I had met another girl in the morning assembly—Yvonne Christian—and she turned out to be Linda's best friend. "So what's your name?" she asked. I told her.

"Car Antenna?"

"No—Carlos Santana."

"Oh."

Linda and Yvonne were around thirteen years old when I met them, and I was fifteen, and that's a big difference at that age. They were two of the angels who stepped into my life at just the right time to guide me when I needed help. We would become friends for life—not so much in junior high, but in high school we became very tight, and they ended up helping me get more confident with my English and to feel more comfortable in a strange new place.

We're close friends to this day—it's amazing how things work out. Their friendship and loyalty has meant more to me than I can really explain without getting sentimental and sloppy. Even when we don't speak for a few years, when we get back together it's like we just hung up the phone an hour ago. Linda's now married to my old friend Michael Carabello, the original conga player in Santana, and Yvonne doesn't know it, but a while ago I wrote a song with her in mind that I still have to finish—"Confidential Friend." Now I guess I'll have to.

It was during these two months in '62 that I also met two Mexican American guys who lived in the Mission District and were into some good music. One was Sergio Rodriguez, who played bass— we called him Gus. He worked in his father's grocery store cutting meat in the butcher section. The other was Danny Haro, who played drums. Tony had found a job in Danny's family's tortilla factory and became good friends with Danny's cousin Lalo—Danny's father also owned a restaurant and some other businesses. Tony had been bragging about my guitar playing and introduced me to Danny. I remember going to the Haros' house—his family had money, so he had a nice drum kit and records by musicians like the Royals, Little Willie John—the baddest black music. I'd say, "Hey, Danny, can I borrow your records?"

"Sure, just don't scratch 'em." Most of his friends were black, too. He even conked his hair.

But man, they were playing some corny-ass songs, like Elvis Presley music. They also had a lead guitarist who was pretty good, but he was no match for me. We got together a few times to jam, and they were freaking out because I knew all these songs and I could play chords and a lot of lead. I'll be honest—I resisted showing them anything, mainly because I resented having to play on their level. I think we did two gigs together, but it didn't feel anything like the gigs I was used to playing on Avenida Revolución.

I couldn't get over being away from Tijuana—what was I doing in this school with these little teenagers when I could be making music, staying up late, and dealing with real life? It was a confusing time, but there was a lot of energy around, too. I won't forget those few weeks in October when the New York Yankees beat the San Francisco Giants in the World Series at Candlestick Park, just a few blocks away from where we were living. It was one of the longest-running World Series in history because of all the rain. Then we moved to Juri Street, right near the Mission District—it was bigger than the place on 3rd and had a small storage room that I'd hide in and practice guitar.

I had already started to study various guitar styles when I was in Tijuana. I wanted to cop the feel of Otis Rush, the feel of John Lee Hooker. Later I realized how blessed I was to find out early about three people—Lightnin' Hopkins, Jimmy Reed, and John Lee Hooker. They were the foundation of my blues education. I had a few blues records, and so did my friends, and we'd listen to them over and over. I marinated myself in that sound. How did he get that sustain? How did he hammer *and* get that sustain? What about that vibrato? My father played violin with vibrato, but I picked my vibrato up from B. B. and Otis Rush, and I'm still trying to get it right.

That storage room on Juri Street was the only quiet place in our house—I'd go and work on the guitar in the dark. No distraction to my ears or eyes. I'd figure out a riff and try to match the tone. I'd try it seven times in a row—nope, can't get it. It was dark in there, so you learned to trust your fingers. Eight, nine, ten—that's not it. Damn.

Figuring out different blues styles was like taking inventory of 777 groups of bees around the world and tasting the honey that each one made. This one is more creamy; this one's a little darker. What about this golden one? I had a taste for funky, raunchy guitar styles like the ones I heard on the records of Elmore James and Muddy Waters. I learned they call it gutbucket, or cut and shoot. John Lee Hooker was the king of that cut-and-shoot style. How come cut and shoot? Because in the places where they played that music, if they didn't like what you played, that's what happened to you. Some people didn't want to hear any sophisticated blues: "Don't put no fancy, freaking chords in there, man. Give me the shit."

I learned there are guitarists who never bend a string—like Freddie Green, who played with Count Basie, and his comping was un-freaking-believable. Later I learned about Wes Montgomery and Grant Green, and then Kenny Burrell. Those three for me would come to represent a kind of class and funky intelligence. People who don't bend strings can move faster. To me, the players who did bend strings claimed a different place in my heart because they had access to immediate emotion that went beyond superlatives. They shaped notes like the people who shape glass—they do it with fire.

I kept at it, learning songs like "Let the Good Times Roll"—the way B. B. King did it—"I'm Blue," by Ike Turner and the Ikettes, and "Something's Got a Hold on Me," by Etta James. I'd get frustrated. I would stop, go out and walk around, look at people in the park, come back to that little room, and try again. Stop, take another walk, go back. I knew that I couldn't be 100 percent like them even if I wanted to, because I was not who they were. But I wanted to know what it was they were accessing. I got the idea that it wasn't just the guitar technique or which guitar or amp they used. I started to think it was who they were, what they were thinking of when they played. Whoever it was—B. B., Buddy, Freddie— something happened in that person's life that hadn't happened to me. That's what made it their sound alone.

Charlie Parker said, "If you don't live it, it won't come out of your horn." I began to live my life, and my own sound began to come out of that closet and out of my guitar. It took a while—lots of gigs in Tijuana and in San Francisco. Lots of life experiences— growing up, leaving home, and coming back. Then, ultimately, leaving home for good.

When you take your time and listen to the real blues guys, you discover that each one has his own sound and you can recognize them by things they do, all while realizing that they don't repeat themselves. When you really dig into a blues it's like riding a horse bareback in the night under full moonlight. The horse takes off, and he doesn't throw you off. You go up and down and flow with the rhythm of the ride, go through all these changes, and never repeat yourself.

Too many guitarists never get past a limited vocabulary, and I can tell you that learning the blues never stops. Every time I play "Black Magic Woman" I'm thinking of Otis Rush, and at the same time my own sound is still developing. To my ears, just before he died Stevie Ray amalgamated all his influences—Albert King, Albert Collins, Lightnin' Hopkins—to the point where he finally sounded like Stevie Ray. It took him a while. He had to get there, because he had supreme dedication. He lived the blues life.

Two months into that first school year in the United States, I really got into it with my mom. It came down to this: I had been giving my mom all the money I had been making at El Convoy long before the family split for San Francisco. That's a year and half, nine dollars a week. It was a lot of money—she kept it all hidden away in a shopping bag. I knew a lot of it had to go to the family, most of it, but I also was planning on using some of the money to buy a new guitar for myself. I would remind her of that again and again. I told her, "Mom, you can have all the money, but save me a little bit so that when I see a guitar I want, I can get it."

"Yeah, yeah. Okay."

We had a deal, I thought.

A few days after the World Series ended, I saw a Stratocaster that I actually liked, and I asked my mom for the money. There was a record store on Market Street that had a few guitars in the back. I saw it, and I knew that was the one! I had to have it.

For the longest time I had been playing this black Gibson Melody Maker that I had bought used for just thirty-five dollars. It had no case, and it was having trouble staying in tune. It was a good instrument, but it was what you would call a starter guitar.

My mom told me she had spent all the money. But she didn't just tell me, she snapped at me—like, how could I even ask? No sense of graciousness and definitely no apology. Just, "We needed to eat and I needed to pay the rent and I spent the money." I mean, at least present it to me in a way that was civil. She didn't have the diplomacy, and I didn't have the wisdom that I now have, so we both just got pissed off.

That's when I said, "Forget it. You broke a promise to me. I'm going back." I was pissed and I said stuff that teenagers say and that I regret to this day, like, "I don't even want to see you—I don't want to live here, I don't want to eat your food, even if you force me to. I'm going to make life miserable here."

What could she do—argue? She knew I was serious. So she just raised the ante. She opened the door.

"Okay, you can go. Your father's friends are leaving tomorrow for Tijuana for a two-week break. Here's twenty dollars. Go with them." My dad was silent about it at the time—his feeling was that I was old enough to make my own decisions. I was making money and able to support myself.

So I took the twenty dollars, packed my stuff, and left with those friends of my dad. It's like I couldn't get out of there fast enough— I was still so angry. Did I have a place to stay? Did I have a gig lined up? Did the guys at El Convoy know I was coming back? No, no, and no.

We drove all the way to Tijuana and pulled into town in the middle of the evening. It was dark, and everyone was dressed up as demons and skeletons. It was Halloween time back in the United States—in Mexico it was the middle of Day of the Dead celebrations. I had gotten out of the car and was standing there in the middle of downtown Tijuana. It was spooky and weird, and that's when it hit me. For the first time in my life, I was alone, without a safety net. No going home to Mama. It was just me, and I was feeling it— I was scared.

Part of me noticed how small everything looked after being in San Francisco for just two months. Tijuana's tallest building was only six or seven stories high, and it seemed like a shack.

I did something I never expected I'd do on my own—I went to church. I went straight to Our Lady of Guadalupe, the big cathedral downtown. I walked in at seven at night, went all the way to the front of the altar, knelt down, and said, "The last time I was here, it was a few years ago with my brother Tony. We walked on our knees from the front door all the way to the altar because he was having some serious toothaches and needed to get his teeth fixed. I did some penance that time, but I didn't ask you for anything then, so I figure you owe me one."

I kept looking up at her. "What I'm going to ask for now is that I want you to help my mom and dad and my sisters and brothers be safe where they are. And help me get a job tonight. That's all I want."

I did not go to the priest or anyone else. I went straight to the Virgin — that's something I believe in to this day, that the relationship with one's highest power should be a direct one. There are times when we all need a spiritual hug, when we need to feel comfort from fear and be reminded of the oneness we share with all that is around us. I also learned about the power of prayer from my mom, and that prayer is not a one-way thing. What I was looking for was a conversation.

It was not the first or last time I would speak with the Virgin. In 2003 I was on tour, and the day we played Mexico City there was a press conference. They asked me what I had been up to while being back home in Mexico. I told them, "Yesterday I was in Autlán, where I was born, and I went to the chapel where I used to go with my mom when I was a baby. I kneeled down before this big picture of the Virgin of Guadalupe and said thank you, again. Then I heard this voice that said, 'I'm really proud of you.'"

There was a long pause. "Wait a minute: the Virgin of Guadalupe talked to you?" they asked. I think they were as surprised that I had gone into a church as they were that I had heard back from the Virgin. I answered their question with one of my own. "What kind of relationship do you have with God if you only talk and God don't talk back?"

On that night I went straight from the church to El Convoy. It was the middle of the week, and they were busy as usual. Everyone was there — the bouncers, the strippers, the musicians. Man, they were surprised. Once I had crossed the border, that was it. Goodbye, Carlos. They looked at me as if I were a ghost. "Man, what are you doing here?" The manager came down to talk to me. "You can't be here. Your mom told us you were going with her to San Francisco. You need your parents' permission because you're underage."

This is the part of the story that's really tricky. I had a letter with me, which I gave to the club manager. It came from my mom, and it said that I could return to El Convoy and play there. But my mom swore till the day she died that she never wrote that letter! In fact she'd get pissed if I brought up the subject, and I can't remember how I got it or who gave it to me! But I do remember pulling it out of my pocket and giving it to the manager, and I remember the manager opening it up and reading it. "Okay," he said and shrugged his shoulders. "Welcome back." Then he told the other guitarist to go home. "Go ahead — get up there," he said to me.

My luck didn't stop there. I played all through that night, but I still needed a place to stay. The drummer was a guy we called Tarzan. His aunt owned a motel, and he was staying in an extra room there — with only a mattress on the floor, a shower, and a toilet.

I moved in, and after a while we got a small black-and-white TV. I remember sitting there after a long night of playing at El Convoy, fermenting my brain on anything we could find on TV. We would watch and watch, and in a single three-hour stretch we might see Mahalia Jackson singing, Liberace playing piano, Rocky and Bullwinkle cartoons, and then *You Bet Your Life* with Groucho Marx.

I remember that TV to this day because it helped my English get better — I especially liked *Rawhide,* with Clint Eastwood. Soon my English was perfect — that is, perfect if I was going to go on a cattle drive. I can't tell you how weird it felt in 2011 when I was inducted into the California Hall of Fame along with a bunch of other people — including the Beach Boys, Amy Tan, Magic Johnson, and Buzz Aldrin. Guess who came out to induct me? Rowdy Yates himself — Clint Eastwood! He said some nice things about me and shook my hand.

I was the last one inducted, and I thanked them for the honor. Then with Clint and Governor Jerry Brown standing near me, I told them what I thought about California's governors when I was growing up. My exact words were, "I grew up here in California when Brown and Reagan were here, not necessarily being nice to the campesinos. Not necessarily being in harmony with Dolores Huerta and Cesar Chavez. I don't approve of creating airports and libraries for Ronald Reagan and people like that—because they were not nice."

Nobody said anything—you could hear the food falling off the forks of all the rich people sitting there. Jerry was not happy about my talking about his father, Pat, that way. Knowing Clint's politics, I don't think he would have wanted to hang with me that night.

Huerta and Chavez were the union organizers who led the Mexican migrant workers—people like my brother Tony. They formed the United Farm Workers and fought for their rights in the 1960s and got no support from Pat Brown or from Reagan. In the '70s Jerry Brown supported Chavez and Huerta, so the UFW helped him get elected. Jerry Brown was back as governor, but he had recently vetoed an important UFW bill—just as Schwarzenegger had done four times before!

In 1962, when I was playing in Tijuana on my own, Tony was breaking his back in Stockton—exploited and underpaid. Almost fifty years later, I was standing in Sacramento, just an hour north of those fields, getting an award for being a great Californian. But the struggle was still going on. That's why I said *"Sí se puede"* that night, which technically means "Yes, I can"—and basically means "We shall overcome." Huerta came up with that, and Chavez used to say it all the time. I had to say something.

The Day of the Dead in 1962 was the first night of a long year on my own playing blues and R & B at El Convoy. By then the club had bought its own Stratocaster, so I could play that, and I had my Melody Maker. They were still calling me El Apache. I could tell I was getting better on the guitar night by night.

I learned many things during my year alone in Tijuana—songs, solos, chord changes. I learned what I had to do to stay in tune, because I don't want to have to worry about that when I'm playing. I learned how to pull and stretch the strings before I put them on the guitar—one, two, three, four, five, six times. Then tune them, then do it again, for three or four rounds. You have to bend them until there's nothing to bend anymore. You have to tell them who's boss.

I started to learn about phrasing, mainly from singers. Even today, as much as I love T-Bone or Charlie or Wes or Jimi, it's singers more than other guitar players that I like to hang with. If I want to practice or just get reacquainted with my instrument, I think it's best to hang with a singer. I don't sing, but I will put on music by Michael Jackson and I'll be right there with his phrasing, like a guided missile—I'll do the same thing with Marvin Gaye and Aretha Franklin. Or Dionne Warwick's first records—my God. So many great guitarists play a lot of chords and have great rhythm chops, and I can do that. But instead of worrying about chords or harmony, I'll just try matching Dionne's vocal lines, note for note.

I began to really learn about soloing and respecting the song and the melody. I think too many guitar players forget that and get stuck in the guitar itself, playing lots of notes—"noodling," I call it. It's like they're playing too fast to pay attention. Some people thrive on that, but sooner or later the bird's got to land in the mist and you got to play the melody. Imagine if the song was a woman—what would she say? Did you forget me? Are you mad at me?

I still hear what Miles Davis used to say about musicians who play too much: "You know, the less you play the more you get paid for each note."

A few months after I got there, Tarzan and I got kicked out of the motel room, and I moved back to our old neighborhood to live with a friend of my mother's who didn't mind me coming home in the mornings. My mom had left some furniture there, so that helped pay for me to stay with the woman. I got used to the rhythm of late nights again, sleeping through most of the day, visiting the beaches, and reading hot-rod magazines and *MAD* when I wasn't playing.

I knew it was not healthy living. It's not that I was smoking weed or taking anything hard. I was just having so much fun that life became a big, fast blur. But I was drinking a lot, and it started catching up to me quickly. Once, I found myself waking up in the street in the morning, still drunk and seeing some lady taking her child to church. She pointed at me and told her kid, "See? If you don't listen to me you're going to wind up like him." I could hear my mom's voice telling me that I was definitely not on the same page as she was—that I needed to come home or I would be lost.

In my mind I wasn't just playing the blues—I was living the blues. Even then I had the same notion: the blues is not a hobby, and it's not a profession. The best way to say it is: the blues is a deep commitment to a way of life. There were a few other bands with that kind of commitment—but only a few. I saw the Butterfield Blues Band with Michael Bloomfield and Elvin Bishop in '67— they had that Chicago sound *down*. In '69, I saw Peter Green with the original Fleetwood Mac, the white British dudes who zeroed in on two things—B. B. King and Elmore James—and they played the shit out of that music. They had the sound of B. B.'s *Live at the Regal* album down almost as good as B. B. did! They lived the blues. They weren't wearing it like a suit. That's all they wanted to do; that's all they did, and they did it so well. I couldn't believe they were white. Same thing with the Fabulous Thunderbirds. They had that Louisiana sound and those Texas shuffles down.

I think the most idiotic question anyone can ask is whether white people can play the blues. If you need to know, go listen to Stevie Ray Vaughan at his peak. Playing the blues is not about what part of town you come from or what country. No one race owns it. Some people might think they do, but they don't. I can hear blues in the music of Ravi Shankar and Ali Akbar Khan. Flamenco players have got the blues. The Moors singing to Allah have got the blues. The Hebrew people in their prayers have got the blues. The blues is like chicken soup—it wasn't invented in America, and we don't own the recipe.

By the summer of 1963, I was getting older, almost sixteen. Things were changing on Avenida Revolución. Gene Ross disappeared—I didn't see him again after I got back, didn't even hear about him until he got killed. Javier Bátiz left Tijuana for the big city and the big time—for him, that meant Mexico City. During this time I think my family had been trying to reach me for a while, wanting me to come back to San Francisco. I don't remember my mom sending any letters, but maybe she did and I didn't see them. Or maybe I chose not to remember.

I did not want to go back. Years later my mom told me, "When you were in Tijuana I would get so worried. I used to tell your dad, 'We have to go get Carlos,' but he would just roll over to the other side of the bed and say, 'Nah—let him grow balls and become a man. You can't hide him with your skirt all the time.'" My dad was probably like most men at that time.

My mom persisted. Later I learned that when Tony was fired from one of the jobs he had, it gave her the perfect excuse to come down to Tijuana with him to find me—but I got word that they were coming and hid from them. They went back, but they returned a few weeks later, in late August, when I was playing at El Convoy. This time I had to face them.

Everyone remembers what happened a different way. Tony told me that he drove down with my mom and a friend. They went to El Convoy and asked the bouncer whether I was inside. "You mean El Apache? Yeah—he's passed out over there. Get him out of here; he's going to die." He meant that the nightclub lifestyle was going to be the end of me. So they carried me to the car and drove me home.

My dad remembered my being a little more awake and resistant. He told a newspaper in 1971 that he came down with my mom,

Tony, and someone else, found me at El Convoy, and they used all their powers of family persuasion to get me to go home. "We did not force him...we convinced him by crying."

The way I remember it was that my mom, Tony, and his friend Lalo suddenly were there, and I fought going back till the end. My mom knew what she had to do when she came to El Convoy. She told Tony to stand by the back door while she came in through the front. I was in the middle of a set, but as soon as I saw her standing there—*pow!* I was off like a firecracker, out the back door, where Tony was waiting. He grabbed me and lifted me off my feet while they were still moving. They basically kidnapped me—snatched my ass, put me in the car, and brought me back to San Francisco.

The one thing we all agree on is that I was silent all the way back in the car—just fuming. We also agree that all I had with me was my Melody Maker and amplifier—nothing else.

But really, what else did I need?

CHAPTER 5

This band played at the Cow Palace and opened up at the Fillmore. With Danny Haro and Gus Rodriguez, 1964.

Music and sex—those were the two things that made the most sense to me when I was in school, growing up. That's what I wanted to invest my time and spirit in. The guitar is shaped like a woman, with a neck you hold and a body you hug against yourself. You can touch your fingers up and down the strings, but you have to be delicate and know what you're doing, especially if the guitar is electric.

If I had been a saxophone player, all day long I would have wanted to hear the sound of Lester Young and Coleman Hawkins, Ben Webster and Dexter Gordon, Pharoah Sanders and Gato Barbieri. I'd need to hear a certain tone in order to dip myself in it. The saxophone has a very masculine sound.

The tone of the electric guitar is different — no two ways about it. It gets a feminine sound — unless someone's playing like Wes Montgomery. To me, Wes had a fatherly sound, gentle and wise, like Nat King Cole's voice. But when a guitar player wants to get sassy and nasty, he just has to copy the way women walk and talk by bending the notes on the electric guitar.

I believe my guitar sound is feminine — it has a melodic, female sound no matter how much bass I put into it. It's the nature of who I am — my fingerprint. I've accepted that. I think it's a powerful thing to express the wisdom of women as a woman herself would, with female overtones.

It started with my father teaching me how to get inside a note, to penetrate it so deeply that you can't help but leave your fingerprints on it. You can tell it's working if you are reaching your audience. If you don't feel it, your audience won't, either. With the violin I could do that when I was playing "Ave Maria" in church. I could tell people could feel the hug I put into a note. I mean, everybody needs a hug. I learned about legato and long notes and knowing when to use sustain and when to hit an endearing hug note. But with a guitar I felt I could go further. I mean, there are hugs and then there's someone sticking a tongue in your ear. That's what I wanted to be able to do — the guitar helped me get there.

B eing back in San Francisco was rough for a while. I made good on my promise from the year before — I locked myself in my room and refused to eat. When I finally came out, my mom had had enough. She got out another twenty-dollar bill and said, "You can go back, but this time we won't be coming to get you." I took the money and walked up to Mission Street, but then I thought about it. Then I thought about it again. I gave the money back and said, "No. I'll stay." That's the only time I felt like that. All the other times, the excitement of the music and learning was more important to me than an obligation to family. That's the honest truth.

My dad tried to make me feel better. "Son, in this country you can have a good future. There are a lot of good musicians here." I knew that. By then, all my heroes were American—B. B. King, John Lee Hooker, Lightnin' Hopkins, Muddy Waters. I was dying to hear them and to meet them. But I would have to wait—first it was back to junior high. Man, I was not ready for that—not after a year on Avenida Revolución. I was still being held back in my grade, so by then I was almost sixteen, and I felt even older than the other kids.

It was good that I had my friends—Linda, Yvonne, Danny, and Gus—to hang with and play music with. They helped me keep it together, kept me wanting to stay in America. They accepted my being back like it was nothing special. "Okay—you disappeared last year, but now you're back. No problem."

But school? My mind was always somewhere else. The one thing I remember I liked to do was draw. Linda tells me she liked to sit next to me in class and watch while I drew big, complicated cartoons—action-hero stuff. I was really getting into comic books at the time. Then, not long after I returned—just a few weeks—I remember that Kennedy was shot and the whole world was in shock. Everything came to a stop. I knew then that this country was not what it seemed like in the movies, but I didn't realize it could be so nasty and ugly. Back then I just accepted the news. But what a brutal thing to come back to in America.

We were then living in an apartment on 14th Street, in the middle of the Mission—the third place we lived in San Francisco. It was still a small place, but the apartment was bigger and better than the one on Juri Street, and the neighborhood was a step up and more mixed. Things were settling down there, but sometimes it could get tense fast, even with my brother Tony. On the one hand, I know he was extremely proud of me and would brag about me: "Oh, you have to see my brother. He's going to come up here from Tijuana and show you. The shit these guys are playing—that ain't nothing, man." On the other hand, he was the one who put me in the car and wouldn't let me stay in Tijuana. And when he would drink he could get mean and piss me off. Usually I would just take a deep breath and look at the floor, because he could really fight.

One time Tony and his buddies had been out drinking, and he came home, wanting to sleep, but my sisters and I were watching the end of some vampire movie. "Turn off the TV," he said, and then he just turned it off. Laura got up and turned it back on. "Hey, it's almost over. What's your problem?" Tony went back to the TV, but being drunk, he knocked my sister down. I couldn't stand for that. I punched him right in the eye and grabbed a chair to defend myself because I knew I would have to. The whole house stopped— my mother was just watching this go down. Tony kept looking at me, not doing anything, and I'm thinking I'm an idiot because we were sharing a bed at that time! What was I going to do, sleep on the very edge of the bed?

By the time he had a steak on his eye, we had all calmed down. But Tony wasn't happy. "I understand what you did—you were protecting your sister. But don't you ever hit me again, man."

I didn't even think of doing that, but just a few weeks later Tony came into our room with his buddies. They'd been drinking again. One of them—it was Lalo, actually—sat on the bed, right on top of my guitar—*snap!* Broke it right in two. It was the Melody Maker, but still I was mad and ready to fight again. Somehow they calmed me down.

That happened on a Friday. The next Monday when I got home from school, Tony had bought me a brand-new guitar and an amplifier. It was a beautiful white Gibson SG with a whammy bar. Gibson had only been making them since '61. Man, I grabbed that guitar—started smelling it, touching it. I couldn't believe it. That was the same kind of Gibson I played at Woodstock—an SG, but a later model and a different color.

Tony was my hero again. My eyes were tearing up. Then he said, "Hey, Carlos, I just made the down payment. You're going to have to pay for the rest of it. I'll take you to the place where I'm working so you can learn how to wash dishes and earn the money to pay it off."

That's how I began my career as a dishwasher at the Tic Tock
Drive In. I worked at the one at 3rd and King, just down the block
from our first place in San Francisco. There were five of those din-
ers across the city—they were popular and stayed open late, and
eventually a bunch of us ended up working at one or another of
them—Tony, Irma, Jorge, and I. Some of us also worked shifts at
La Cumbre, the taqueria on Valencia Street that Danny Haro's family owned. My mom was working less—she was busy being a
mom—and my dad had his regular gig at the Latin American
Club. The rest of us who were still in school and old enough had
our routines—wake up early, go make tortillas at La Cumbre, go to
school, come home, eat, then go to work at Tic Tock.

Tic Tock was owned by white guys, and the funny thing is that
mostly they treated us better than the owners of the Mexican restaurants we could have worked in, such as La Palma. And it was
definitely better financially than pressing tortillas—that's why
Tony started working there.

Not that it was perfect. I remember one day when Julio, one of
the managers, came into the kitchen. It was a Wednesday—banana
boat day—which meant that huge numbers of people were down at
the docks, right near the diner, unloading bananas for the whole
city, and the place was packed. But somehow the driver who was
supposed to deliver the doughnuts that morning did not show up.
Again.

Julio walked up to me. "Carlos! Tell your brother they didn't
bring us doughnuts again and we need them for the coffee rush.
Can he go and pick some up right away?" This is all in English. Tony
doesn't speak English that well, but he definitely understood. He
didn't blink. He kept washing dishes and answered in Spanish, telling me to tell Julio that he'd gone for the doughnuts two weeks ago
as a favor, that it's not required of him by his union, and that he
never got reimbursed for the gasoline he used last time.

"What'd he say?" So I had to translate, and by this time all the
other workers had stopped what they were doing and were watch-

ing us. "Really? Is he sure?" Then my brother said, *"Dile que se vaya a la chingada,"* and told me I had to translate it word for word.

"Yeah. He also says to go fuck yourself."

I waited for something to happen, but nothing did. Tony taught me that day that it was important not just to be a good worker but also to know your value. Know your power, and have brutal integrity if necessary. There were three of us working there then — Tony, Irma, and I. If Julio had fired one of us, all three of us would have walked. Doughnuts or no doughnuts, the Santanas did a good job for them.

There were other lessons I learned at Tic Tock. There was a bad-looking pimp who would show up late at night, dressed in a pin-striped suit and panama hat. He always had the finest women with him, drove a Cadillac, the whole thing. When he walked in all the workers would stop and stare. He had a routine — first he'd sit his ladies down, make sure they had menus, then go put some money in the jukebox.

One night he came in and did his thing, and a redneck trucker walked in with his radio blaring a Giants game — "Here's the windup, and the pitch…" Loud, loud, loud. The pimp went up to him and said politely, "Excuse me — I just put some songs on. I wonder if you can turn the radio down a little." The guy looked at him and just turned it up louder.

We're all stopped now. The whole diner is watching, thinking this is going to be a fight. The pimp — real smooth and quick — grabbed the radio, threw it hard onto the floor, then stomped on it with the heel of his shoe. It was all smashed to pieces. Then he reached into his pocket — we were expecting a gun or a knife — and pulled out a big wad of cash. He counted out one, two, three bills and put them in front of the trucker. "This covers it, man. I know you're going to let me listen to my music now." That guy's face was red. He knew better than to say anything.

Tic Tock was where I first learned about American food — hamburgers, french fries, meat loaf, cold turkey sandwiches. My favorite was their breaded cutlet and mashed potatoes—I ate that all the time, and I still love it. When we're touring these days and have a night off in Austria or Germany, everyone knows I'll be ordering Wiener schnitzel, even if it's not on the menu.

The most beautiful thing about Tic Tock was the jukebox. I put so much money in that thing just to make it bearable while washing those big pots and pans full of gravy and bleaching the floors with scalding water and Clorox. That jukebox helped me stay sane those first few years I worked there. It had Jackie Wilson, Chuck Jackson, Lou Rawls, Solomon Burke, the Drifters. Also those first Motown stars—Mary Wells, Martha and the Vandellas, Marvin Gaye. It was different from Tijuana—more sophisticated and soulful. Some of it had that gospel feel, like Solomon Burke had. The Impressions singing "Say it's all right... It's all right... It's all right, have a good time, 'cause it's all right."

Stan Getz and Cal Tjader were on that jukebox—my first real taste of jazz. There was also Latin music with Afro-Cuban rhythms—Tito Puente, Mongo Santamaría. "Watermelon Man"!

San Francisco was like that jukebox. Actually, San Francisco *was* a jukebox. The Mission was full of nightclubs, and I had friends there who had stereos. And San Francisco in general had lots of clubs and radio stations playing a variety of styles. KSOL—"Kay-Soul"—was one of the city's black stations. That's where Sly Stone started as a DJ. "Hey, you groovy cats..." He had his own thing that early. I heard a wild jazz organ on KSOL late at night—someone named Chris Colombo doing "Summertime" and just killing it. KSOL introduced me to Wes Montgomery, Bola Sete, Kenny Burrell, and Jimmy Smith. They played Vince Guaraldi a *lot*.

Tijuana was where I heard songs like "Stand by Me"—simple R & B tunes. In San Francisco I was suddenly hearing Johnny Mathis singing "Misty" and Lee Morgan playing "The Sidewinder"—a new level of hip. Basically, the city was a cornucopia of music—more than I had ever expected. I started hearing about clubs I would later try to sneak into—like the Jazz Workshop, all the way down Van Ness and over on Broadway, near the North Beach area.

Just a few doors down was El Matador, where I would hear Cal Tjader and Vince Guaraldi for the first time and later Gábor Szabó. El Matador was where I heard the amazing Brazilian guitarist Bola Sete for the first and only time. He was a phenomenon — I regret that I never got a chance to spend time with him and really hang out. I started hearing about the Cow Palace, down in Daly City on Geneva Avenue, where all the big shows were.

I remember during that first year in San Francisco I heard about a show in San Jose that featured B. B. King, Bobby Bland, *and* Ray Charles — my friends and I were like, "Oh, *shit!*" I never scrubbed plates and pots and pans as fast as I did that night. As soon as I got off work, we took off from the Tic Tock at full speed and got to the venue just in time to hear the last note and the applause that followed. "Oh . . . *shit.*"

The blues was still my thing — make no mistake. That apartment on Juri Street was where I hid in that little storage room in the dark, just my guitar and I, trying to figure out how B. B. got that tone or Otis hit that note. I was still doing that kind of thing in our new place. Jorge still tells me that he remembers I was always digging, digging, digging — working on my sound.

I also soon learned about the guitar stores around the city — seeing all the new guitars and equipment was essential to me. And of course I was still playing and hanging out with Danny and Gus. We had our little band that had no name. We had our little gigs, playing parties and dances. Listening to the new songs that were coming out and deciding which ones we liked and which ones we wanted to learn. Before I went back to Tijuana in '62, I had avoided showing them anything. I didn't want to be a teacher. But when I went back, I knew that if I wanted to play I had to swallow my pride and teach them repertoire. The good thing about it was that I could choose the songs, so I turned them away from surfer music and the Beatles. We learned James Brown and Etta James tunes together, and I taught them songs I knew from El Convoy, including "You Can Make It If You Try."

It was all fun — this was when I really began to be a teenager

CARLOS SANTANA

and do teenager things. I remember Danny had a green Corvette. We'd drive down the peninsula to one of the A&Ws along the coast, get a root beer float and some hamburgers, listen to the greatest music on the car stereo, then go home and play in his basement. I also remember that his father didn't like me for the longest time. He looked at me as if I were a bad influence on his son. I don't think I was.

I started to notice the difference between what we were listening to and playing and what most other bands were listening to and playing. We did one gig at the Stonestown YMCA on the same bill as a group of white dudes who were playing strictly Beach Boys tunes. We came in there with Bo Diddley and Freddie King tunes, and no one knew anything about that. On the way over there I remember a song came on the radio—it was the first time I heard Stevie Wonder: "Fingertips, Part 1" and "Fingertips, Part 2." Damn.

In 1963 and into '64, I was getting to know everything going on in San Francisco—I was going up and down the streets, looking at the buildings and the bridge and that beautiful bay. At home I remember Jorge was just starting to mess around on guitar, and my sisters were still putting on their records, dancing to Motown and Latin tunes that were popular then—Celia Cruz, some guy named Tito Puente. For me, San Francisco was this amazing vortex of newness.

If it sounds like I'm avoiding talking about school, that's because I was doing just that—avoiding it. It was tough because I had to switch back to English again, and when I didn't understand every third or fourth word it was very frustrating. I was not the best student and didn't like most of my courses, except for one English class in which there was a very beautiful teacher who would wear a short skirt and cross her legs. Suddenly I was more interested in her than I had been in any of the dancers in Tijuana. I'd be daydreaming, and my young body would be reacting as it's supposed to, nature doing its thing, and one time she caught me.

"Carlos, I want you to come to the board and write this down." I was like, "Um, no." She insisted, and the whole class was watching. So I got up, trying to subtly shift things around. But it wasn't working, and everybody was cracking up. What can I say? It was junior high.

My English was getting better all the time on its own. Everywhere I went—to school, the Tic Tock, band rehearsals, my friends' houses—I always spoke English. When I was talking to Linda and Yvonne, they had no problem correcting me. We'd talk all the time on the phone, and we got closer and closer. I could talk to them about anything—school, music, girls. They'd tell me about their boyfriends. They'd call me up—"Hey, Santana, how you doing?" After a while, I even opened up to them about getting molested— outside of my family, they were the only people who knew about that for many years.

I would say it took me almost three years from the time I came back from Tijuana to really get my English together and to stop thinking in Spanish. To have the right words and pronunciation. To say "Jell-O" instead of "yellow." The accent? Well, that got better over time, but it's still there, part of my identity, just like a guitar sound. It'll never go away completely.

You can see that fitting in was tough. In those first few years in San Francisco, I didn't quite know whom I was supposed to hang out with. I didn't fit with Mexicans or white people, and very early on I found out that when I was with black friends and would ask about B. B. or Freddie King, they were listening to something else—some newer style of dance music, not the blues. I learned to get rid of the notion I had when I came to America: that all black people knew each other.

Once the blues did work in my favor. I was on a city bus late one night, and though we had moved to the Mission District I still had to take a route through the rough part of town to get to the place where we rehearsed. I was carrying my black Melody Maker with me in a bag. It never had a case—I used to take it with me everywhere before Lalo sat on it. I got on the bus, and the driver looked at me and at the guitar. "Can you play that thing?"

"Yeah, I can play it," I told him. I wasn't being cocky or anything.
"What kind of music?"

"Jimmy Reed, Screamin' Jay Hawkins, John Lee Hooker." We're talking, and the bus isn't moving.

"John Lee Hooker, huh? Well, you're going to have to sit near me so I can watch you. I don't want anyone messing with you."

It was the first time someone had done something like that simply because I was a musician and because of the music I made. Without even hearing me play. That driver was one of the angels who stepped in at the right place and time—not just to watch over me but also to let me know I was on the right path. I still feel a lot of confidence when I remember that one little bus ride.

I was a musician, and that's how I identified myself—not Mexican or American. I still do. That's why I hung out mostly with musicians.

At James Lick, as at any school, there was pressure to belong to a group. They had two—the Shoes, who wore tight white pants or corduroys. They were the surfers. And there were the Barts, who were like the pachucos; they were mostly Mexican, with some blacks mixed in. People wanted to know which group I would choose—they expected me to be a Bart. I thought they both looked silly. One Latino guy said, "You don't dress like us," like I was a sellout or something. "You know why I don't dress like you? I have a job. I make my own money and buy my own clothes. I don't let my mama or any gang dress me up." At that point I was working on my own style anyway, wearing the shiny black shoes and those tight, shiny trousers the Motown guys wore—the Levi's would come later.

It was like the Jets and Sharks—whites and Latinos—in *West Side Story*. Tony took me to see the movie around a year after it came out, but never mind the gangs. Man, that was our story—about wanting to come to America and make it here. They were singing about washing machines, as I had promised my mom back in Mexico. I couldn't believe it. That's how I first came to know about Leonard Bernstein. That movie was nothing without the music. I don't know if Mr. Bernstein knew just how many people he touched with that one film. It encapsulated the whole United States at the time—and for many years thereafter.

In 1999, when I was auditioning the songs for the album that became *Supernatural*, I first heard the words to Wyclef Jean's song "Maria Maria"—"She reminds me of a *West Side Story* / growing up in Spanish Harlem / She's livin' her life just like a movie star." I had asked for a song about healing and hope, but the stuff about *West Side Story*—that was all Wyclef. And Rob Thomas on his own came up with the line "my Spanish Harlem Mona Lisa" in the song "Smooth"—and I was thinking, "We're definitely all on the same page here, brothers." Who doesn't know that movie?

After the difficulty I felt leaving Tijuana, what really kept me interested in San Francisco and not wanting to go back was my relationship with girls and music. When some of the girls at James Lick told me I reminded them of George Chakiris, who played Bernardo in *West Side Story*, I was like, "Really?" That was a handsome dude. Hmm. Okay, I was hooked.

Still, it was never a physical thing between me and Linda or Yvonne—we went to parties, and I'd watch them dance to "Harlem Shuffle," or we'd go to drive-in movies. I was more comfortable with girls than I was with guys, but I was still really shy. I had no confidence when I got to be alone with a girl because I've never been a bullshitter or a hunter. One thing I know I didn't get from my dad is the ability to hunt and charm women. That "Hey, baby" stuff was never my thing. To me, it just sounds corny, like picking up a guitar that's out of tune. That's just not my personality, even when I was with my first wife, Deborah, or Cindy or any of the other ladies. Some women I've loved may not want to own it, but they did the chasing.

I prefer to have a real conversation—that's just me.

Before junior high was over I did muster up enough confidence to get together with this one girl—Dorian was her name. She lived alone with her mom, who worked during the day. That first part of '64 I was always at her house.

I want to say that the sex was all a beautiful thing, but my memories of that time are mixed up with a gym teacher who had a crush on Dorian, and he knew I was getting with her. Every time I was in his class, he'd jump on me. "Santana, I know where you're coming from. You need to run around the school block three times and then give me fifty push-ups." It was weird—how did he know?

I think about those first times of intensity and ecstasy, and most of it happened while I was sneaking around and making sure I didn't get caught. I know some people think that can make it more exciting—like all those soul songs that say it's sweeter if you're stealing it. But I think too much of sex is wrapped up in guilt and shame. It seems to me that it should always be celebrated as a healthy thing, talked about, and studied in school—especially in junior high, when people have the most questions.

Sex should be taught as creative and spiritual expression. The whole planet is about expression—a variety of expression. We need to know about this and make our own choices. Remember Dr. Joycelyn Elders, the surgeon general who got fired for coming out in favor of masturbation as a way of preventing AIDS—how could that be anything but healthy and positive? Unfortunately we're not evolved enough yet to teach that point of view in schools. So much in this world would be better if we were taught that it's important to find a partner with whom you can talk about sex and that this needs to be an important part of your life. Instead we're left to figure these things out for ourselves—and hope we get it right.

Dorian was my girlfriend for a while—we used to go to dances together, but she'd get pissed because as soon as we got there, I'd let go of her hand and stand right in front of the band, checking out the guitarist and the rest of the guys. She would be asking me to dance, trying to get my attention, and I'd say, "No—it's okay. Go ahead and dance with your friends. I've got to see what's happening." I was at rehearsals a lot, too. She got frustrated with me. She started to feel that I was only with her for my convenience and that I only wanted to be with her when her mom wasn't home so I could do one thing.

Dorian left me for a quarterback. He'd play ball, as it were — she couldn't rely on me. A few years later I saw the same thing happen to a bass player who came into the band just after Gus — Steve De La Rosa. He had a lot of strings attached to this beautiful lady who wanted him to spend more time with her than he did with his music.

I saw it happen many times after that, too. It's a horrible thing when anyone says to you, "Choose me or the music." Please do not ask me to live according to your insecurities. That's like asking me to stop breathing. For me, there was only one possible answer — "Bye."

In September I moved on to the high school that James Lick was a feeder for — Mission High. Linda, Yvonne, Danny, and Gus were all there, too. Mission was a big change from James Lick. It was really, really mixed — blacks, Mexicans, kids from all over South and Central America, and Filipinos. Other high schools had more Chinese and Italians, but Mission was the hard-core center of San Francisco, so kids were coming from the Mission, Bayview, and Hunter's Point, and it was probably one of the most diverse schools in the city. There was a lot of tension, mostly between blacks and whites. The hippies were just coming up at that time, and it wasn't fun, because straight people would call them faggots for having long hair. Whites and blacks and Latinos would say that. If anyone was with a crowd of their own people — white, black, brown, or just straight — and someone came by alone who looked different, you knew the crowd was going to start picking on that person. That's high school.

My circle of friends got larger. It was a bigger school, and they had dances that were bigger, too. I remember that year Freddie Stone — Sly's brother — came over from Jefferson High and played for us with his band, Freddie and the Stone Souls. They put on a high-energy show, jumping over each other while playing their instruments. That was the first time I heard Greg Errico on drums.

The summer of 1964 was all about the Beatles, the Rolling

Stones, and other groups from England. I noticed the girls really liked them. They were all over the radio. I could tell some of them were coming from the same place I was—they had been listening to the blues. Groups like the Animals and the Yardbirds were trying to learn that language, too. Later I would read about how they started: pulling themselves up, hitting the road, sleeping in vans, doing what they had to do—they were comrades in arms, as far as I'm concerned, for what they went through for their music. I'm talking about Jimmy Page, Jeff Beck, Eric Clapton, Mick Taylor, John Mayall, Peter Green—all of them.

The one album that knocked me out was by the Kinks. My mom was still holding on to the money I was earning, but she'd give me a little now and then. When she did I'd get the latest Spider-Man comic and an album or two. I remember getting Little Walter's greatest hits and the Kinks' first album, and then going, "Shit! This is different—what a heavy sound." Those guys were about chords, not single notes. They were a big influence on me. Danny and others in our band liked the Yardbirds, and that was fine with me, too.

By then my band was one of the best bands at Mission at the time. Like a rhythm section for hire, the three of us would join up with other groups; then there would be different singers or guitarists or horn players in front. We were the guys to get. One time we played in the Dynamics, wearing suits and playing with two saxophone players—Andy Vargas and Richard Bean. Richard later got together with my brother Jorge and formed the Malibus, which then became Malo.

I was still working at Tic Tock while Danny was making tacos and Gus was cutting meat. We were gigging and keeping busy, playing pizzerias and birthday parties. We never did Mexican events, because most Mexicans didn't want to hear our kind of American R & B music. "You guys are too loud," they would say. They wanted to hear music from back home—mariachi, *norteño*. That was my dad's territory.

I remember one time Danny's or Gus's parents asked us to play a party where they would have asked for songs like that, and I said no. I think Danny and Gus would've been okay doing those songs—they didn't have the negative emotional attachment that I had because they didn't grow up with the things I had to see. I just told them I don't want to play baptisms and bar mitzvahs. I told them I didn't know any of those songs, even though I did know them, and that was the end of that.

The school used to hold open auditions for their Friday night dance parties, and we would win again and again. One time a student who was from Samoa saw our audition and invited us to play at his birthday party. Everything was going great until we finished our second set and asked for our money so we could leave. He looked at us and said, "You guys ate too much food, man. I'm not going to pay you." He was the one who invited us to help ourselves—we didn't know there was a limit on how much we could eat! The other guys started to argue with him, but I just pulled away. I went back to the kitchen, where our equipment was, saw his birthday cake sitting there, and carefully took it apart and laid it in my guitar case. Then I got the other guys and said, "Come on—let's just go." Later I showed them what I'd done. We ate the cake and laughed. I thought it was better to get even than get angry.

We never really had a singer. We played lots of instrumentals, and Gus sang sometimes. I would help out on songs like the Righteous Brothers' "Little Latin Lupe Lu," "I Need Your Lovin'" by Don Gardner and Dee Dee Ford, and "Do You Love Me" by the Contours. They were shuffles and boogies, mostly—more about the rhythm than about a lead vocal part.

I met Joyce Dunn at a jam in late '64—she was a *singer* singer, with a real blues energy to her voice. She was from Oceanview, just ten minutes from the Mission, so we were able to get together and work out some songs, soul tunes like "Steal Away" and "Heat Wave." It was definitely a new thing at the time—a black singer backed by Mexican Americans and a Mexican guitar player. Michael Carabello would tell me that the first time he ever saw me play was during the few weeks we played with Joyce. She was a lot of fun and later went on to work with musicians such as Boz Scaggs and record a few songs under her own name.

The first half of '65 went by fast—suddenly my first year of high school was over, and it was summer. Many biographies that I've seen say I graduated from Mission that year, but I graduated with the class of '67. With Danny and Gus and the horns, we were still playing the blues, or our version of the blues. But it seemed like the world only had room for British groups: the Beatles and the Rolling Stones, especially "Satisfaction," were *everywhere.*

Sometime that summer we heard that KDIA, which was the soul station for San Francisco back then, was sponsoring a band contest at the Cow Palace—the prize would be an opportunity to play your song on the radio and open a show for the Turtles and Sam the Sham and the Pharaohs, who both had big radio hits. Hundreds of bands showed up, but it turned out that most of them were just covering songs by the Rolling Stones and the Who, and the station wanted originality. Most got eliminated in the first round, and we got more and more excited as the day went by. We also got nervous. Because we had so much time to hang around, Danny, Gus, and I got to drinking, and we fucked it all up! We made it to number three. It felt good—until we lost.

"Wooly Bully" was Sam the Sham's hit song, and you couldn't get away from it that summer. We learned that tune and must have played it a hundred times—everyone wanted to hear it. I remember my sister Laura asked us to play for her wedding that June in Pacifica, at a place called La Paloma. We had everyone up and dancing to "Wooly Bully." I remember that because Tony's new wife was very pregnant at the time, and if you say "Wooly Bully" like you're speaking Spanish it sounds like you're saying "big stomach." Later I learned that Sam's real name is Domingo Zamudio and that he is a Mexican American from Texas.

That summer I was also listening to B. B. King's *Live at the Regal.* It was so valuable to guitarists like me, who hadn't yet had the chance to see B. B. in concert—but on this album we could

THE UNIVERSAL TONE

hear him dealing directly with his people, a *black* audience. It still makes me smile when he sings, "I got a sweet black angel / I love the way she spreads her wings," and the ladies start screaming. What could be sexier than that?

My second year at Mission started in September, and not long afterward the first album by the Butterfield Blues Band came out. To my ears, it was the best example of a musician staying true to the real electric blues—the Chicago blues—and making it work with a rock-style beat. The rock influence was not too much; it was just right. A big reason for its success was Michael Bloomfield, who played the group's lead guitar—soon he was my number two hero, just behind B. B. He was the first of the new generation of guitarists after Buddy, Albert, and Freddie.

Sometime during that fall, another singer came into the band—Al Burdett. He was from the Fillmore, on the other side of town. He sang the blues and didn't stay with us for more than a few months, but he turned me on to the most important blues album of that year—Junior Wells's *Hoodoo Man Blues*, featuring a great guitarist called Friendly Chap. Only that wasn't his real name—it was Buddy Guy, and because he was under contract to another label at the time they called him that. Everybody heard that album—the Grateful Dead, Jimi Hendrix. Buddy's way of playing guitar on "Good Morning Little Schoolgirl" became the only way to play that song.

That fall, I met Michael Carabello for the first time. He was a friend of Yvonne's and would have been at Mission High except that his baseball skills got him into San Francisco Polytechnic. He remained close with his friends in the Mission, where he lived. Carabello had gotten hooked on music when he played congas in these informal jam sessions at Aquatic Park, very close to North Beach, and had even sat in once with Vince Guaraldi. Carabello came by Yvonne's basement, which was one of the places our band would jam. Later he told me he was blown away by what he heard. I liked him—he was hanging out more than playing at the start, but we had the same enthusiasm and intensity about music. He only

had one conga when we met, but he had a nice feel when he played—
and he was listening to a lot of new sounds as well as the blues.

Most important, Carabello took me to Aquatic Park. I don't know
if they still do it, but back then, in '65 and '66, they used to let this
circle of conga players play. It would be maybe ten or twelve of them
sitting around, playing with one or two flute players, the brothers
drinking wine from leather flasks that they'd hang on their belts,
smoking weed. The sound was intense when they got going.

Carabello and I had another mutual friend, Jimmy Martinez,
who did something that totally turned my head around. Jimmy
knew what he was doing, too, because one day he came up to me,
laughing, and said, "I got an album here that's basically going to
kick your ass!"

"Yeah? Okay, bring it on." What else was I going to say?

He was right. It was Chico Hamilton's *El Chico*—the one featuring the Latin percussionists Willie Bobo and Victor Pantoja and a
guitarist named Gábor Szabó. I liked the way it looked from the first
time I saw it—Chico was dressed in a toreador cape, and some of the
songs had Spanish titles, such as "Conquistadores" and "El Moors." I
knew Chico was a jazz drummer, but the album didn't sound like
any jazz I'd heard before. It had a lot of Latin in the music as well as a
lot of other things, too—soul and lots of great grooves.

But it was Gábor's guitar that hit me hard—I heard that and
could feel my brain molecules starting to expand. His sound had a
spiritual dimension to it, and it opened the gates to other dimensions for me. You could tell he listened to a lot of Indian music,
because he put a drone part in the music. It was trance music—he
could play the simplest melody but still go deep. He was the first
guitarist who opened me up to the idea of playing past the theme,
of telling a story that isn't just a regurgitation of the head of a song
or other people's licks. Gábor took me away from B. B. King, John
Lee Hooker, and Jimmy Reed—he was also the first jazz musician
who started playing Beatles and Mamas and Papas songs and other
'60s rock and pop tunes—even before Wes Montgomery started
doing "Goin' Out of My Head."

El Chico was like a road map telling me where I had to go next. I immediately went out and got Willie Bobo's album *Spanish Grease,* and by the next year I would get Gábor Szabó's *Spellbinder*—"Gypsy Queen" was on that one—and Bobo's *Uno-Dos-Tres,* which had "Fried Neckbones and Some Home Fries." Both those songs would help shape the Santana sound. At the same time, another friend turned me on to Thelonious Monk—his live version of "Blue Monk," recorded in San Francisco, pushed me even further, made me rethink the blues and what could be done with it: "I know there's a blues in here somewhere. It must be—it *says* blues."

By the end of '65, the influence of all these new musical ideas was starting to show in the band's repertoire—and Carabello was in the band. We were still playing the blues, but we were expanding what we played, just as we were expanding what we listened to. We were playing "Jingo," by the Nigerian percussionist Babatunde Olatunji—that was a staple of those Aquatic Park jams. I was happy to be playing and making music. I did it whenever I could, wherever we could practice, and whenever we could get gigs. When I wasn't playing I was rehearsing or jamming. When I wasn't doing that I was thinking about it or dreaming about it. It really was all I wanted to do; there was nothing else. School? That was a place I went to on weekdays—and sometimes not even then.

In junior high I felt I didn't fit in because I was trying to figure out who I was. At Mission I didn't fit in because I knew who I was and the school didn't have anything for me. I could have taken music lessons, but in those days it was either classical music or marching-band stuff—nothing that had anything to do with electric guitars or blues. A lot of the classes I was taking didn't make much sense, either. In my second year at Mission High, I remember being given a test that included some historical stuff in it—and it was all about US history, which I had not had a chance to study yet. But it was supposed to be an aptitude test—not a history test.

I got angry and told the teacher I was not going to take the test. "Why not? What's wrong with it?" the teacher asked.

"Look at these questions. I just came here from Mexico. I can see already that I don't know these answers. This test is for white people. Where are the questions about Pancho Villa and Emiliano Zapata?" I wouldn't cooperate because it felt like the test was designed to make me fail—why couldn't I answer questions that were relevant to my world and my experience?

I'm not sure now how that all ended, but I do remember that I had to explain it to the principal, too. It just felt like high school and I were not meant to happen. It wasn't all bad, though. I had one teacher who inspired me to really think.

Mr. Paul Knudsen was my art teacher, and he had a funny way of doing things. He'd get the whole class into funky overalls, line us up in front of paper that was covering the walls from floor to ceiling, and tell us to dip these long metal wires—like thick guitar strings—into the paint and slap them against the paper. Or he'd give us long bamboo poles with brushes tied to the very end, and we'd have to paint from across the room. He was talented—he could look at you and draw a portrait without glancing down at the paper, and it would be great.

One day Mr. Knudsen asked another student to take over the class while he took me into another room to talk. "I took the liberty of looking at your grades since you've been here in the United States, and they're bad," he said. "But I noticed that you got good marks at James Lick in art, and you're pretty good in my class. I've also heard that you're a pretty good musician. Tomorrow we're going to the Academy of Art—I really want you to see what you're up against if you're thinking of getting into painting or drawing or sculpting."

He looked me dead in the eye. "The reason I'm telling you this is because the world is getting too crowded—there is no room for fifty percent. You must be one hundred and fifty percent in whatever you do, whether it is art, music, or anything else. Okay?" I was a little scared—he was right up in my face. When a teacher singles you out and corners you like that, you either get defensive or you open up.

No one, not even my parents or friends, had spoken to me like that before. The field trip the next day was interesting. But being in a drawing class with a naked model didn't matter. I was thinking about his words. Mr. Knudsen opened me up.

I wish I could say that my next two years at Mission got better. But I would show up in the morning and sign in, then spend more time with my friends and music than I did in the classroom. That was pretty much my routine. I wanted to be living life, not studying it. But what Mr. Knudsen told me was the most important lesson I took away from my first year of high school.

That's when I really started thinking that no matter what I did, it would have to be the best I could do. I could not be another Lightnin' Hopkins or Gábor Szabó or Michael Bloomfield. They were already in the world. They had their own sounds and integrity. I needed to get mine together. I would have to be Carlos Santana and do it so well that no one would mistake me for anyone else.

In 2010 I came back to Mission High with my wife, Cindy, to help celebrate the school's academic achievements. I think I spent more time in the school that day than I did in my last two years there. I visited various classrooms and other parts of the school, and they held a big assembly for all the students. When I spoke to them, I said, "Turn off MTV. Get into real life. Participate." I hit them with the same kind of message that Mr. Knudsen had given me.

"If you can remember only one thing today, remember this: you are significant, you are meaningful, and you matter. The best is not ahead. The best is right now. Enjoy it, don't hurt anyone, and live with supreme integrity."

Then with some of the students, we jammed on "Oye Como Va" and "Europa." We were plugged in and playing guitar in the Mission High auditorium, something I hadn't done in almost fifty years.

CHAPTER 6

The Santana Blues Band, first time at the Fillmore, 1967. (L to R) Danny
Haro, me, Gus Rodriguez, and Michael Carabello.

*You know how you'll be in a theater watching a movie so amazing that
you don't want it to end? How sometimes you have to pull your eyes
away from the screen and focus on the seats in front of you or the pop-
corn on the floor just to remind yourself that it's a movie?*

*That was what the '60s were like in San Francisco. During those
days it was a drag to have to sleep. So much was happening that I
wanted to stay awake all the time. I didn't want to miss anything. Everyone was feeling that way. For me, the '60s created a thrust of compassion and grace that everybody was feeling at the same time. The decade
propelled us out of the orbit we'd been in for generations and genera-*

tions. If you believe in gravity and you drop something a hundred times, a hundred times it's going to fall. But if you believe in grace as strongly as you believe in gravity, then a hundred out of a hundred times you're going to get a miracle. I loved the '60s because it made me believe in the law of grace.

When I talk about the '60s I'm talking about the second half, really—from '66 on. That's when San Francisco became the epicenter of multidimensional consciousness—it was the place where you could dive into all this multiplicity. It wasn't just music or clothes or politics or drugs or sex or colors—it was everything together. And everything changed—the way people were walking and talking and what they wanted to talk about. Instead of the world dragging its feet to catch up with the way people were thinking and feeling, a whole new generation was in sync. It was like that song by the Chambers Brothers—"Time Has Come Today."

That Chambers Brothers album, The Time Has Come, was released later, in '67, but to me it was a perfect snapshot of what was going on in '66. On the cover the band wore striped bell-bottoms and brightly colored shirts. They had Afros and were a multiracial band. The title song was more than eleven minutes long—it was becoming increasingly common for songs at that time to be extended past the usual three or four minutes. Songs were starting to resemble jams and grooves—the music I was getting into. "Time Has Come Today" was soulful, and it was filled with the flavors of rock—feedback, lots of echo, heavy guitar, and a hip lyric. It fit the time: "My soul has been psychedelicized!"

Never mind the hair or the drugs or the beads. That wasn't what made someone a hippie. A hippie was a rainbow warrior, a reincarnated American Indian. You know who was the original hippie? Jesus—the ultimate multidimensional, multicolor, nothing-but-love hippie. He never said, "It's my way or the highway." A hippie was not someone stuck in one perception.

I was the only one in my family you could really call a hippie. I let my hair grow long and smoked weed. Later I would leave home and live in a communal kind of situation in a house on a hill. I wanted to play *my music — not other people's songs, no matter how popular they were. Many times my parents looked at me as if I were crazy.*

You know what I miss most from the '60s? It was the idea of emphasizing individuality. The '60s were important because it was a time when you were allowed to carry your own bumper sticker. The more different you were, the more people respected you.

I miss that. Nowadays friends pull me aside before I speak, or sometimes afterward. They warn me, "People are going to think you're a hippie."

"Thank you," I say.

I was getting to know the San Francisco bands the way I got to know the scene in Tijuana — by knowing musicians and finding out where the gigs were. There were bands that came from electric blues — Chicago and Texas styles. There were electric bands that came from acoustic styles — bluegrass and folk. There were bands that were into Paul Revere and the Raiders, and wore old-style costumes or military uniforms. There were R & B bands influenced by Motown and James Brown that wore sharp suits and skinny trousers.

At the start of 1966, we didn't cross paths too much with these groups. Many came from different parts of the Bay Area. I started to hear about the Grateful Dead, who came out of Palo Alto. There was the Jefferson Airplane — they helped start a new club called the Matrix in the Fillmore area. Later that year some members left and formed Moby Grape, and they got big fast. There were groups like Quicksilver Messenger Service and Big Brother and the Holding Company. Carabello turned me on to a group called Sly & the Stoners, which had members from all over — San Francisco, Daly City, and Oakland. They later became Sly & the Family Stone, of course.

I want to say that we were all like one big family, but there were times when other musicians, especially those from the other side of town, looked at us like we were stray dogs who wanted to steal their bones. Even when we were headliners, that's the truth. We were in alliance with Sly and bands from Oakland, and we—well, we were from *the Mission*. There was a racist element to it, but we were so young I think it was just a matter of competition and insecurities. It took a while for all of us to grow up and drop our guards. I will say from the start that some bands stood out because they were really, really cool. Jerry Garcia was very gracious and embracing. The guys in Quicksilver and Janis Joplin—always supportive.

The common denominator for all these bands was a guy from New York City who had been in San Francisco about as long as I had—Bill Graham. In '66 he started producing shows that put all of us to work. We started to meet each other at Bill's place, and never mind putting us all on equal footing—he put us in the stratosphere.

If anyone ever makes a movie about Bill Graham—and someone should—it would have to be called *Bigger Than Life*, because that's exactly how he was. I saw him at the very beginning in San Francisco, just when he was starting, and I watched him become a legend around the world. He could do anything and would do everything. He was a promoter and event producer. He managed bands and ran record companies. He put together international tours and did things at the Fillmore with the same focus and intensity as he would do them in huge stadiums around the world. By the time of his death, he was the Cecil B. DeMille of rock, directing a cast of thousands. But he could also be a gaffer or a grip. "What the fuck is this?" he would scream at his people if he noticed something out of place. If no one was around, he'd move it himself or pick up the offending piece of trash. Then he'd go for the clipboard he always had with him, make a note, and move on to the next thing that needed fixing.

I have much to say about Bill because he was so important in my life and had such a huge effect on my career. If I had to bring it down to just one thing I would say this: he respected the music and the people who made it. He was the first promoter I knew who fed the bands—and he didn't feed them just sandwiches, either. It might have been before or after the show, but he would always have catering ready for all the bands. Believe me, back then some of us really needed to be fed. He created a standard that put musicians first. He made sure the toilets were clean—backstage, too.

I remember seeing him at the Fillmore at the end of a show. Everyone was gone from the place except a few stragglers. He was doing one last round, closing doors, turning off lights. First one there, last to leave.

Bill was passionate about music, and he could be profane. I have never heard someone use the word *schmuck* as many times as Bill did. I didn't even know it was a word until I met him. Nothing intimidated him. To him, confrontation was foreplay. He would stand on the street in New York City and yell at taxis for passing him by with the same energy and language that he would use to negotiate multimillion-dollar deals for the biggest acts and largest venues in the world.

Bill did not look for trouble—he looked for what was wrong or could be better. His thing was what was fair and right. I saw him argue at top volume with armed guards in Moscow who could not understand a word he was saying. In 1977 in Verona, Italy, I was surprised in a hotel lobby by a TV interviewer who wanted to know how I could be so spiritual when the concert tickets were so expensive. Bill stepped right in front of me and told me not to answer that question, then turned to the interviewer and said, "Ask the Italian promoter"—who was standing just a few feet away. Bill continued, "We had a contract saying what the ticket prices should be, but he added all these expenses and jacked up the price." That guy ran for cover like a rat when you turn on the lights.

That same night, Bill jumped off the stage in the middle of our set to stop a riot. I'm not exaggerating. You could feel the excitement all around, this huge energy. We started our set with "Jingo," and the crowd started pushing to the stage. For security, there was a line of policemen with machine guns right in front of the stage, which created a kind of DMZ that kept the audience yards away from the band—they still do that at many rock concerts.

The crowd was excited and running to get closer. It wanted to feel the music and boogie. Bill saw what was about to happen, and he hustled out right between us and got down in front of the guards, screaming at them to make room, to pull to the side, to let the crowd come down. It was like Moses parting the Red Sea. He defused the situation all by himself and stayed there for most of the show, policing the police.

His real name was Wolfgang Grajonca. It was a good thing he decided to call himself Bill Graham. He was a Jew from Eastern Europe who had escaped World War II and grown up in New York City. He spent a lot of time in Spanish Harlem, going to hear Tito Puente and other Latin groups, dancing salsa. He was a great ball-room dancer. He loved jazz, and when you look at the shows he used to do in the '60s, you can see that he brought together all those passions in one place and turned on a whole generation with his good taste—Charles Lloyd, John Handy, Bola Sete, Gábor Szabó, and of course Miles Davis.

Bill trained as a waiter up in the Catskills, and around '63 he moved to San Francisco for a straight job before he started working with the San Francisco Mime Troupe. He ran their shows and put together benefits with local bands to raise money. That's how he got started, and he learned very fast about hippie culture from Chet Helms and other people—the light shows, the posters, the kind of music that hippies wanted to hear.

Bill still dressed like a square—he never was one of us in that way. He never let his hair grow long; he never wore beads or the full hippie attire. What he did was bring a businessman's sense to consciousness-revolution culture when it was just getting started, and he did it in a way that preserved that culture's spirit and intention.

In February of that year, Bill started booking nights on a regular basis at the Fillmore Auditorium, as it was then called, on Geary Street, not far from the Mission. They weren't just concerts—not like any I had been to—and they weren't club gigs, either. Each was a really special event that showcased two or three acts on the same night. Very soon after he started, he was putting together different styles of music on the same bill—rock, blues, jazz, even Brazilian. Then he started bringing in national groups like the Butterfield Blues Band, and local groups would open for them. Then he brought in British groups like the Who and Cream and Fleetwood Mac.

All the bands would play for five nights, Wednesday through Sunday—two sets a night. Usually a matinee on Sunday. The sound system was great, and there were special light shows going on behind the bands. The posters looked like glowing paintings—bright colors and weird letters. They were on lampposts all over town. You had to stop and check them out closely to figure out what they were saying. It was mysterious and fun.

Before I got to play for him, Bill's concerts became my high school and college studies all rolled into one. I studied everything he put on at the Fillmore Auditorium and then the Carousel Ballroom—which he called the Fillmore West. You want to talk about a diploma? The Fillmore was where I really got my higher education. You can take that any way you want.

The Fillmore was like a sanctuary. At the time, things were feeling a bit desperate and very divided—Vietnam was starting to happen. I knew some people were getting drafted, and *boom*—they were gone. There was all that racial tension and rioting in black neighborhoods. At the Fillmore I could escape from all that. At the shows, there would be hippies and brothers and Mexicans. People were doing what they wanted—smoking, tripping. It was like a big, safe party.

I had no choice but to pay attention, man. How could I ignore it? I was in the middle of it. It started with the hippies in the Haight-Ashbury neighborhood around 1965 or '66. The Haight was just a dozen blocks from where I lived in the Mission, just past Buena Vista Park. Hippies' hair was long, and their style of clothes was a different kind of hip. They were wearing things and colors that suddenly made turtlenecks and tight trousers and anything that was Italian seem old. I knew about weed from Tijuana, but in San Francisco people were smoking it openly. And they were taking a new drug called LSD. It was legal then. I mean, it wasn't illegal— not yet.

In the '60s, the worst thing you could call a person was not the *n* word or some other ethnic name. The worst thing you could call a person was square. Woo—that was a horrible thing to say to somebody, and it made me think of that guy in the Dylan song who walks into a room and tries hard to understand—"Ballad of a Thin Man." The opposite of being a square was smoking pot and doing LSD.

Another big change: suddenly there was this thing called a love-in, and the movie *Guess Who's Coming to Dinner* became passé. There were these young white chicks hanging with whomever they wanted—black guys, brown guys, older dudes, and younger ones, too, like me. Later, once I left home, it was on—with hippie chicks, groupies, whatever you want to call them. It was beautiful to discover that flow—the kind of connection that happens when a girl wants to share herself with you because she loves the way you play. Oh, man. That started in junior high school, but it was as much self-deception as self-discovery. How many times do you want to make it in the back of a VW van before you say, "Come on, let's go hang out and talk"? Well, honestly, I wasn't counting, either.

You could see office guys saying, "I want some of that," loosening their ties and hanging out, smoking weed. The next thing you know they're not square anymore, and they're not going back to the office.

I think people tend to idolize certain places and times. My attitude then was that I actually didn't care to be accepted, man. I didn't want to fit into a clique—to be a hippie or a freak or this or that. I've always been anti-clique. For me, the music was it. The Fillmore was a place where the music was it, and you could be a hippie or not, and you could hear new music. The '60s were really about experimenting with music. I didn't like folk or bluegrass, but after a while I started realizing there was something even in the trippiest jams that came out of bluegrass playing.

I got together with my friends and went to as many of those shows at the Fillmore as I could afford or sneak into. In addition to Carabello, who was my age, I was hanging out with people who were a little older than I was. Sometimes I'd be a little short and ask for a dollar or two from the people in line so I could get in. One time I tried to sneak in with Carabello, but I got caught—he ran one way, and I went the other.

That's how Bill and I first met! He looked at me and shook his head, because everyone was trying to get in for free. We knew he was the guy we had to convince. Once in a while, if I got him off by himself, I'd say, "Bill, you didn't let me in on Wednesday or yesterday, but I have to see these guys at least once. I don't have money, but if I had it I'd give it to you." He'd look at me with his hand on his hip and not say anything. Then he'd jerk his head toward the door, and I knew I was in.

I don't know if Bill remembered me from the days before I did concerts for him. Only later did I see that everything he did helped me understand the value of music—that concerts cost money and that musicians and everyone else who helps make them happen should get paid. He had this thing that started at the Fillmore. He'd go up to the mike and introduce the band, always in the same way: "Ladies and gentlemen, from my heart—Santana!"

That knocked me out every time. Then Bill would come up to us after the show and say, "You owe me money."

"What? Why?"

"Every time I introduce you, you owe me five dollars."

We'd just crack up. "Okay, man. Here you go." But he was serious. He'd stand there and count it. It was a great lesson. Anyone who does something of value should get paid.

Bill wasn't the only one in town who was doing happenings like the ones at the Fillmore. Chet Helms was a promoter who was producing the same kinds of concerts. Sometimes Bill and Chet worked together; sometimes Chet did his own concerts at the Avalon Ballroom, on Sutter. Those shows were easier to get into, a lot looser. Later I learned the way Chet paid bands was also kind of loose. A few times we played at the Avalon we got a big brick of weed. Then it'd be our job to sell it and get money for food and rent! To me, Bill Graham was 50 percent Dick Clark, 50 percent hippie. Chet Helms—he was hippie, hippie, hippie.

I spent most of '66 catching what shows I could, still working at the Tic Tock, still playing gigs with Michael, Danny, and Gus, and still going to school—and when I say "going," I mean getting marked as present, then going off and doing my thing.

We still didn't have a name for the band, and I was still listening to new blues records and albums that pushed the blues further. John Mayall came out with the album *The Blues Breakers with Eric Clapton*. It was the first album that showed me that British players were checking out many of the same people I was—Otis Rush, Little Walter, and Freddie King—so I started paying attention to them, too.

The Butterfield Blues Band came out with their second album, *East-West*. It had Delta blues, like Robert Johnson, and Chicago electric blues, too, as the first album did. You could hear that the band had been listening to jazz as well—they did tunes like Cannonball Adderley's "Work Song," in which the harmonica played the same line the trumpet and saxophone played on the original. The title track was a groove that stayed mostly on one chord and had an Indian flavor with a four-beat bass pattern. I could hear the connections that were going on in the music. The song had a vibe like the Chico Hamilton and Gábor Szabó stuff I was getting into, but it was more in the electric blues pocket and was purely instrumental—the electric guitar was up-front and center stage. I could also hear how other guitarists were working it together with electric blues—I knew Bloomfield's solos on that album note for note.

I wasn't the only one listening to that album—you could tell many brains were being expanded by the same music. People were opening themselves and digging deeper into the music. *East-West* was a model for a lot of Bay Area bands. They could hear that the vocabulary of Ravi Shankar and Ali Akbar Khan was not that far from the vocabulary of Robert Johnson and Muddy Waters. The mind is a creature of labeling and encapsulating and filing things into categories. But this was music that was begging the soul to tell the mind to shut the hell up, turn up the volume, and not worry about what to call anything.

We had been exclusively a blues band at the beginning, but in '66 we started doing "Work Song" and "East-West" in our shows, adding them to the older R & B numbers we did, such as Ray Charles's "Mary Ann." We were still jamming for ourselves and a few friends more than we were playing gigs. We'd get together in friends' basements or play outside in the Presidio or in the Panhandle, near Golden Gate Park—anywhere we could make music without getting chased away by the cops or getting yelled at because of the noise.

Then we ran into Chet Helms, who told us he had heard us playing in the Presidio. "Yeah, I used to hear you guys in the park— you're good. Why don't you try out for the guy who auditions bands in the afternoons at the Avalon?" We went over there, and the guy running the auditions was a low-level folk musician with one of the jug bands in the Bay Area. He stopped us in the middle of our first tune. I think it was "Jingo."

"No, no. This won't do. You guys are in the wrong place. We don't want that kind of music here."

The guy wasn't even listening to our music—he was judging it against some idea of what he thought should be played at the Avalon. I called him out. "Hey, man—you play kazoo or washboard or whatever. You call that an instrument? You call yourself a musician? What the fuck do you know about music?" I was ready to get into it with him. My guys had to hold me back. That was the end of that audition.

It didn't matter. By the summer of '66 the band was getting better, and I was getting a reputation. At one of our outdoor jams in the Panhandle I was taking a solo. I opened my eyes and recognized Jerry Garcia and Michael Bloomfield in the audience—they were checking me out, nudging each other with their elbows, and smiling about something. Another time I ran into some guys who told me they lived in Daly City. They were looking for a guitar player and had heard about me. Would I come over and play with them? Sure, man.

But when I got to their place I said, "What kind of music do you guys play?" I should have asked before they picked me up. "The Who."

"Really? Drive me back. I thought you guys liked the blues."

Another band wanted me to join up with them, and their thing was the 13th Floor Elevators—psychedelic stuff. "No; sorry. I can't. I don't like that music, man."

I was still a teenager, doing the teenager thing. I was confident in my taste in music, and I could be cocky about my playing. The first time I ever spoke with Michael Bloomfield, I acted like a punk. It was at the Fillmore after one of the Butterfield shows, and he was standing around with a few people adoring him, and I walked right through the circle and said, "One of these days you're going to know who I am, and I'm going to cut you!"

There was silence; everybody just stepped back. Michael looked at me and smiled and without a pause said, "I want you to—I encourage you to. That's how this music keeps going." Later on I found out that Michael was a very sweet guy, and I wondered what monster came out of me back then to make me say that. Definitely some of it was the same insecurity other young musicians were feeling at the time, but I felt I had to apologize to Michael again and again, especially when he picked me to play on his live album with Al Kooper. I kept saying, "I'm still so embarrassed. I must have been fucked up." He always came back with a positive reply that was typical of his attitude: "Man, I respect you for speaking your mind. It's okay. I still want you to cut me!"

It's probably true that I was fucked up—by that time I was starting to party. At one of those outdoors gigs playing at the Presidio, I had met two guys—Stan Marcum and Ron Estrada. They were two beatnik dudes, a bit older than we were, and they always hung out at North Beach. They just really dug our music. Stan was a barber, and Ron worked as a bail bondsman, and we all got friendly. They had a house together near 18th and Castro, where I would hang out, and they would play music all the time. They introduced me to Bob Dylan's songs, showed me how to listen to the Beatles, and what LSD was. And later they became Santana's first managers.

Stan and Ron were fans, but they were also trying to help me out with my music. What did they know about management or getting the right musicians together? Well, we were in tune with each other, and that's what mattered. We would be talking, and one of them would have an idea, and they'd tell it to me—like they thought I should join another band that was going around at the time. The band's name was Mocker Manor, and they needed a guitar player. I told them I didn't know—what kind of music did they do? Did they play the blues? What does the band's name mean? They couldn't tell me.

The name came from something Ringo Starr said in the Beatles movie *A Hard Day's Night*. So we went to hear them and they were wearing mod sort of clothes and their music was going toward a Grateful Dead thing. They had a bassist who was really good, but they were playing a blues that sounded like early Rolling Stones. I gave it a try and wanted it to work. But every time we practiced a tune we'd get it down one way, then they'd go smoke a joint and forget everything we had just done. They'd look at me with that "Would you just relax?" expression. "Relax? We're wasting time. Why don't we learn the song once and just get it right?"

Stan and Ron gave me this look like, "Lighten up!" They decided to try to fix me. They all went out for lunch and left me behind with a big fat joint—like half the length of a drumstick. My assignment was to sit there, listen to some music, and light it up. I remember I put on the Yardbirds album that has "For Your Love" on it. I started smoking it, and it smelled good—not like the skunk you get today that leaves you with a headache. After a few minutes I could feel everything becoming... softer. Colors seemed brighter, and all the parts of the music were clearer. I know some people don't necessarily feel it the first time they smoke. I definitely did.

I immediately saw what I was doing—being a dictator with the band, going against the grain of the music. I realized I needed to accept and embrace a different approach from the one I thought was working. I was on the wrong side of that mind-set. Not everything needed to be thought out and over-rehearsed.

I didn't stay long with Mocker Manor, and Stan and Ron agreed with me. "You're right. This band is not going anywhere." But I did start lighting up. Getting high on weed is not like dropping acid or taking peyote or doing cocaine—or shooting heroin, which I did twice before I stopped.

People who smoke don't necessarily want to do cocaine and heroin and crack. Marijuana still carries this incorrect negative stigma that goes back to the 1930s, and parents still call it the devil's weed to scare their kids so they don't get lost.

But we hippies had a saying: "You can't find yourself till you lose yourself." You have to let go of everything that you've been taught and find a way of being happy with your own existence and bless all your imperfections. It's a way of seeing your own ego, pulling all the levers and controlling your behavior, like some Wizard of Oz behind a screen. But you can see the feet sticking out from under the curtain and say, "The jig is up. I'm no longer emotionally invested in allowing you to have power over me."

I noticed when I started smoking weed that some people use it to escape and some people use it to find themselves. I also noticed that drugs of any kind didn't necessarily make someone hip or deep. Cocaine can amplify your personality, but as Bill Cosby said, "What if you're an asshole to begin with?" Grass and peyote, those are medicines from Mother Earth. Crack and heroin and meth, those are laboratory drugs, man-made—they can imprison you, turn you into a serious habit monster.

I'm not promoting anything but the freedom to be real and have self-perception. Weed gave me an aerial view—it opened up my senses to multidimensional multiplicity. In '66, I started smoking a lot. It was easy to get and wasn't that expensive. I could smoke and function on the street and play music. But it was illegal, so I found ways of stashing it on myself and hiding it at home.

My sisters still laugh when they remember the night I came home and was scratching my head and two joints dropped out of my long hair onto the floor! I don't know if my mom didn't see them or just didn't want to see them. Maria scooped them up and gave them to a friend of hers who got high. Another time I left some weed in the hem of the white curtains at home. My mom, the clean freak, washed them, and they came out with a green stain along the bottom. She had no idea how that happened.

That was a sign I needed to eject myself from living at home. I couldn't be listening to my music and smoking weed and coming home early in the morning with the family around. Another sign was that Tony had already left home by then to start his family, and so had Laura. I was nineteen at the end of that summer, but I stayed in my mom's house for another year, still going to Mission High in the morning but then going off and doing my thing. And hanging out with Stan and Ron at their place until six in the morning. Meanwhile they were turning me on to more new music. We were listening to the Beatles and a whole lot of Bob Dylan.

Most of the time I was focused on playing with Danny and Gus, trying new things, and meeting other musicians and jamming. I didn't know what I was looking for. It's like when you go shopping for a present and you don't know what you want to get, but you know it when you find it. But I did know what I didn't like and what I did not want to play. I knew we weren't going to be part of the San Francisco sound. We called that Hippieland, and we really tried to avoid it. We were listening to some really great music then—Hendrix, the Doors, the Beatles—but there wasn't much in San Francisco that could stand up to that. Too much of it felt kind of phony almost as soon as it got popular. The whole country was going, "Yeah, baby; groovy and peace!" Sammy Davis Jr. was in a Nehru jacket and beads. Too many people were jumping on that wagon just for the ride. We had our own direction in music.

Stan, Ron, and I went to as many shows at the Fillmore Auditorium as we could that year. I was still not 100 percent sure of my English and was speaking with a thick accent. But in Stan I had someone who could speak for me when I got to the door with no money. He had no experience as a manager, but he knew how to talk to people. Nothing stopped him—he was bold, and that was a side to him I really loved. One time Charles Lloyd was playing the Fillmore, and we were there just looking up in awe at him and his band—Keith Jarrett, Jack DeJohnette, Ron McClure. Stan felt he had to say something, so just before they went on he went up to Charles and said something like, "Charles Lloyd, play it one damn time for the world, man!" He just smiled and did exactly that—played his ass off. Back then I could never have done that—those guys scared me!

One Sunday afternoon in October, Stan did his thing and spoke up for me, and after that everything started to change.

The Butterfield Blues Band was on a bill with Jefferson Airplane and Big Mama Thornton. She's the blues singer who first sang "Hound Dog" before Elvis had the hit and "Ball and Chain" before Janis did it. We had to be there. That Sunday they were doing a matinee, and Stan and I got there early and saw that Paul Butterfield was not going to be playing that night. He was totally out of it—tripping on acid, wandering around in his bare feet, watching the wall like it was a TV. He hadn't slept all night.

Onstage they were getting a jam together. Michael was directing things and playing organ because their keyboard player, Mark Naftalin, hadn't showed up. Jerry Garcia and some of the guys from Jefferson Airplane, including Jorma Kaukonen, were going to play. Stan and I could see Michael's guitar onstage and noticed that no one was playing it. Stan decided to take charge and see what he could make happen. He went up to Bill. "Hey, man, is it all right if my Mexican friend over there plays a little guitar with those guys?" Bill shrugged his shoulders. "I'm not in charge of that. Go ask Bloomfield."

Bloomfield looked at Stan and said, "Where is he?" Stan pointed to me. To this day I have no idea if Michael recognized me from that time I had challenged him. It didn't matter. His answer had the same vibe I felt that first time. "Come on, man. Grab my guitar—plug it in."

I got up onstage. They started into a blues—what else? "Good morning, little schoolgirl. / Can I come home with you?" Garcia played a solo, then they turned to me. I closed my eyes and hit it...*bam*.

We finished the tune, and I was smiling. It had felt good to be on that stage, to play with musicians who had it together and kept a good beat. Afterward people came up to me—"What's your name? You have a band?" I told them who I was, that I was part of a group, and that we didn't have a name. Then Bill came up to me. "Here's my phone number—call me. I have a couple of dates open."

That was it—we were going to play the Fillmore, and we'd be on those posters! Now we *really* needed a band name.

I did not know how important one blues solo could be—and it's not just that Bill Graham invited me to play for him. Around a week later I was washing dishes at the Tic Tock when one of the waiters came into the kitchen and said, "Hey, Carlos, someone wants to talk to you."

A young guy I'd never seen before put his head through the opening to the kitchen. "You're Santana?" He was looking at me, up to my elbows in soap. "Man, I heard you the other day with Bloomfield. That was some great playing. Listen, I live in Palo Alto. I sing and play guitar with some guys, and we need a guitar player. We're going to jam tonight. I got my car outside. I think you'll really enjoy the band."

Tom Fraser was a singer and guitarist who had been looking to put together a band and was at the Fillmore Auditorium that afternoon. I was open to anything. "Okay. Let me finish up here—I'll go." Next thing I know we're in Mountain View—the other side of Palo Alto—which is like the ghetto. Out in some old farmhouse in the fields near the shoreline. They had instruments set up, including a Hammond organ. That impressed me right away. I was already obsessed with the jazz guys playing Hammond organ—Jimmy Smith, Jack McDuff, Jimmy McGriff. That's when I first heard George Benson, playing in McGriff's band. Later he became Miles's first guitarist.

Danny, Gus, and I had found our first keyboard player earlier that year and had been working with him for around two months. He looked like that *Where's Waldo?* guy—we called him Weirdo. He played a Farfisa, and I liked it because we could get that Question Mark and the Mysterians, "96 Tears" kind of sound—and also do songs by Sam the Sham and Sir Douglas Quintet.

Out at the farmhouse I started plugging in, and the organ player came over and we started talking. His name was Gregg Rolie. I remember thinking, "I know this guy." I had seen Gregg before, before the Fillmore opened, at the Longshoreman's Hall in Fisherman's Wharf. It was bigger than a club but not as big as the Fillmore, which hadn't opened yet. Gregg played there with a band called William Penn and His Pals. They would dress like Paul Revere and the Raiders and similar groups—in uniforms with floppy sleeves and tricorn hats, like the kind we'd see on *Shindig!* on TV. I remember Danny, Gus, and I were laughing at that—it never felt like anything more than a novelty, a first-kiss kind of thing. That all came and went really quickly.

I had a joint with me, and Gregg was drinking a beer, and we started talking. We clicked even before we started playing. It turned out he was a big jazz-organ fan, too, and we were both listening to the same kind of black music.

We jammed on "Comin' Home Baby," a tune Herbie Mann had a hit with that I knew from the radio. It was one of those groove kind of things, not complicated, that came out around the time

"The Sidewinder" and other jazz tunes were starting to infiltrate mainstream radio—what we now call crossover. Gregg was listening to that music, too, and he could hang with a groove. Then we played "As the Years Go Passing By" by Albert King—a blues guitar piece, really. But Gregg knew the words to that and liked to sing it. I could tell he was a good singer, and we needed one in the band.

The noise we were making must have woken up some neighbors. Then came the cops with their sirens going, like we were breaking into a bank. They found us with our instruments, the air smelling of dope. One of them was ready to just throw the cuffs on us and haul us away. The other one started asking questions, telling his partner to relax.

"Whose house is this?"

We pointed at Tom.

"What's the name of your band?"

"We're not really a band."

"Well, you sound pretty good."

"Uh, thanks."

"Listen, you guys are playing a little loud. I know it's not that late. Can you bring it down anyway and put that other stuff away?"

"Okay."

Meeting a polite cop like that was like a blessing at the start of the partnership that became Santana. Here was another angel interceding when we needed it. He gave us a thumbs-up and looked the other way when he could have taken us all in, which the other cop was itching to do.

And he was right: we did sound good.

Playing with a good keyboard player is like having a nice, soft bed to lie down on, with a big pillow. That was Gregg. Gregg and I started talking and hanging around, and we found we had more things in common than Jimmy Smith. Later I told Danny and Gus about the guys I'd just played with, but when we met, Danny and Gus immediately didn't like them. They remembered William Penn and His Pals, too. "We don't want to hang around with them; they're squares." I couldn't argue—they did look like suburban kids from Palo Alto. Carabello said, "We're going to have to dress these guys better."

I liked Gregg and Tom, but Danny and Gus were pissed because they felt I turned my back on them. I've been accused of many things many times, but this was the first time I was made to feel I was turning my back on Mexicans. It didn't matter—all I could see was what the band needed, and these guys from Palo Alto had it.

Gregg liked us. I think that part of what endeared us to him is that we were really, really strange—Carabello and I were always kind of going at it and being crazy, but we had a camaraderie. He felt it was good for him to be immersed in the music that was playing around the Mission District. To us he was rich, but he was actually just middle-class Palo Alto. He cracked up when he found out we thought that he was rich, but where he grew up was very different from the Mission, that's for sure.

For the next few months, we were a band. Gregg was our new lead singer, and we started adding songs he liked to sing. I give him credit for bringing the band back to other-side-of-the-tracks music, like Les McCann, Eddie Harris, and Ramsey Lewis stuff. Tom was a good rhythm guitarist, and he was into the blues, but even though he was the guy who'd brought me out, something did not work with us in the end. There was a side of him that wanted to do songs by Buffalo Springfield and the Grass Roots—rock with a hillbilly thing in it. We had to tell him, "No; we don't care for that music," and so we let him go after a few months. But Tom gets the credit for being the catalyst that brought Gregg and me together for the first time.

Rock groups were starting to show the same influences I had been hearing on those Gábor Szabó and Charles Lloyd albums—Eastern flavors and groove rhythms and strange scales that sounded Indian. It all became part of that psychedelic sound in rock. The year before, the Byrds had that song "Eight Miles High," which had a middle part filled with those ideas on guitar, and the Beatles and the Stones had used sitar on songs—it was all in the air.

Then all of a sudden, that January, the Doors came out with their first album, and it had a heavier sound and lots of jazz feel, and guitarist Robby Krieger was mixing the blues with that same kind of drone that Gábor had. They were taking the basic blues—like Willie Dixon's "Back Door Man" and other songs—and turning it into an entire movie, not just a story but a big, dark novel. You could tell they were dropping acid and listening to jazz—John Coltrane and Miles Davis—and Ravi Shankar. You could hear it in tunes like "Light My Fire" and "The End." You could tell because the melodies and rhythms were not clunky anymore, like elephants or buffaloes trying to dance. Parts of the music were very delicate, like the group was working in satin and silk, and it moved smoothly, like a ballerina.

The Doors started what I call shaman music, or LSD music. Music that casts a spell and transports the listener to a place beyond time and gravity, beyond problems. The words are for real, not empty boxes. It invites the masses to move up to a multidimensional level. As Jimi Hendrix said, "I didn't mean to take up all your sweet time / I'll give it right back one of these days." He was saying, "I'll borrow your mind for right now—you'll get it back when I'm finished."

A shaman knows how to get out of the way and let the spirits use him—to be a conduit. The best music of John Coltrane? He didn't play it; it played him.

Around the same time, the new John Mayall record, *A Hard Road,* came out. Peter Green had taken over for Clapton, and his notes were like B. B.'s, but he already had his own phrasing—legato. He was just letting the notes hang. His sound grabbed me in a headlock and wouldn't let me go. And his tone! On one track called "The Supernatural"—not to be confused with my album *Supernatural*—Green's guitar sound was on the edge of feedback. That track left its mark on me. I think it was the first instrumental blues that showed me that the guitar could really be the lead voice, that sometimes a singer is not necessary. And I loved that tone.

Back then I was still learning about all this music—John Mayall, Jimi Hendrix, the Doors. I didn't know how really special all that music would become. I didn't yet have the superlatives or the language to talk about these musical orgasms. What I knew then was physical orgasm. You can't be in control when you're having an orgasm. That's what it is — letting go of control. When you have an orgasm musically, you surrender to the music. Normally, only a very few musicians on the planet can make that happen, but in the '60s it seemed like there were many. We were busy searching for that surrender, scuffling gigs at other places — like the Rock Garden, on Mission near Geneva. It was one of the first real rock clubs in the Mission. There weren't that many places we could choose to play in unless we could say we were a professional band. I never considered Santana professional until after our first album came out. Cal Tjader, Mongo Santamaría, Wes Montgomery, and Miles Davis — they were professional.

The bad news happened at the end of February. I went to school one morning, and everybody was getting tested for TB. What's that? Tuberculosis. Uh, okay — what's that? Everyone got a little shot in the arm, and if your body reacted a certain way, then you had TB, and that was serious. I thought, "No problem" — I wasn't feeling bad, and I wasn't coughing, unless I was smoking weed. Suddenly the test came back positive. Next thing I know they were treating me like a pincushion, shooting me full of penicillin and streptomycin. Then they took me off to San Francisco General, putting me in quarantine for who knows how long, in a bed surrounded by sick people, and I wasn't even feeling tired. To this day I think it happened because of the water in Tijuana and my year there on my own.

My parents didn't protest or anything. When they heard what happened, they trusted the authorities to do what was best, which meant that within days I was just so bored. I was there for more than three months! They would run test after test, shoot me with medicine, take X-rays of my lungs, then show me the spots. Then they'd tell me I was doing well, but still I had to stay. What kept me there was not the idea that I needed to get better: I stayed because the doctors convinced me that if I were outside I might infect other people, and I didn't want to do that.

I knew I had to go through with it—take the medication and let my lungs rest. I watched a lot of TV—I remember after being there a month, I was watching when the 1967 Grammy Awards show came on, with Liberace and Sammy Davis Jr.—all this corny stuff. Suddenly Wes Montgomery was playing. That was the first time I saw him play, and it made an impression. I started listening to his music—"Goin' Out of My Head," "Windy," "Sunny"—another jazz guy doing the pop songs of the '60s. He had such a different guitar sound, that deep kind of voice that made me feel like someone was touching my head, saying, "Aw, everything's going to be all right," and I believed it.

Some people came by to see me, including Stan and Ron, my dad, and my sister Irma. Carabello brought me some books to read, including a Time-Life science book called *The Mind* that I remember liking. He also brought me a reel-to-reel tape deck with headphones so I could listen to my favorite albums on tape, like Gábor Szabó's. A few weeks later I had gone through all that. I complained that I was going crazy, so Carabello said, "Well, I got a couple of joints and some LSD." Like an idiot, I took the acid later that night, right there in the hospital.

I could look around me and see older people who were lifelong smokers and had lung problems, and their skin was all yellow and their fingers were orange from all the cigarettes they smoked. It felt like everybody was dying to the left and right, and there I was, tripping in the middle of all that. A movie came on TV—*The Four Horsemen of the Apocalypse,* with Glenn Ford, about the Nazis in World War II. I got so deeply into that movie I was thinking, "Whoa: I've got to get back under the covers and close the curtains."

The next day Ron came over, and I was still hiding. "Hey, man, how you doing?" I said, "Man, I need to get the hell out of here, and you guys are going to help me out. Come back this afternoon, bring me some clothes, and I'll get rid of this freaking hospital robe they got me in. We'll get in the elevator, stop between floors, I'll change, and we'll leave." So that's what we did—I did my Clark Kent thing and got out. I heard they were looking for me for a couple of weeks, because by law I wasn't supposed to leave. They didn't find me, because I didn't go back home. I left the hospital and moved in with Stan and Ron, and that was the beginning of another long break from my family, which put even more distance between my mom and me.

Two good things came out of that stay in the hospital...well, three things. First I got healthy, and I never had a trace of TB again.

The second thing was that while I was in the hospital the people at Mission High knew where to find me—I wasn't going anywhere. They told me I could work with a tutor while I was in the hospital. If I did the work and got passing grades they'd let me graduate. So they sent this guy over in the mornings, we would talk, and he'd leave me some books to read for the next day, mostly on American history. He would come back, and I'd take some tests. A lot of the testing took the form of his asking me questions and my explaining what I got from the reading.

I liked the tutor. He knew my situation—that I had been held back because of my English and that I was nineteen and still in high school. One day he looked at me in my hospital robe and said, "Out of something bad came good, because you're not in a uniform carrying a gun. Those people would have really made it hard for you—you probably would be in Vietnam now." I hadn't even thought about that, but he was right. By all rights I was old enough to be inducted. But because I was still enrolled at Mission High, the draft couldn't get me—yet.

Staying out of the war was the third good thing that came out of getting sick. Around a year later I got the notice to report to the induction center in Oakland. I remember that place—all these young guys lining up and sitting down, filling in forms, and taking tests and sweating. You could smell the fear in there. One brother I saw had his arms crossed. His eyes were yellow from meningitis or something. He was refusing to even pick up the pen. He looked at the man and said, "Hey, man, I ain't doin' nothing. I don't have a beef with the Vietcong. You, honky, you're the one that's fucking with me in the streets. You give me a gun, I'm going to shoot your ass." I was thinking, "Whoa, he's not going into the army—maybe some other place, but not the army."

Then a guy in uniform came up to me and said, "What's your story? Why aren't you doing the test?" I gave him a letter from the doctor. By then I had been back to the hospital and submitted to a few more tests. After that the doctors decided I could just take some medicine at home. This is how ignorant the guy was: he opened the letter, read it, and went, "Tuberculosis, huh? Where did you catch it—Thirteenth and Market?" He made it out to be some kind of sexual disease and was insulting my neighborhood. I was thinking, "I'm supposed to follow you?" Shit. That's when I knew I had to keep as far away from military service as I could if the army was putting people like this in charge. I had friends at Mission High who did go over to Vietnam and never came back. I was lucky—I walked out of there, and that was that.

To this day I appreciate that the guys at Mission gave me that one last chance to graduate. I read the books and answered the tutor's questions just well enough to graduate that June. I was allowed to go to the ceremony at the Civic Center as a courtesy, but for me it really wasn't a big deal. I saw all the other families there with their kids and girls carrying flowers and stuff. I didn't have the cap or gown, and my family didn't come. No one made a fuss about it, and that was okay with me. What I remember most from that last day of school was a bunch of us students sitting in the park near Mission, smoking a joint and talking about our plans. One kid was saying, "I'm going to help my dad at the warehouse." Another guy said, "I'm going to join the marines. What are you going to do, Santana?"

I said, "I'm going to be on stage, playing with B. B. King and Buddy Guy and people like that." People just started laughing like squirrels. "Hey, man, you've been smoking too much of this."

What? I didn't say I wanted to *be* B. B. or even be a star like him. I just wanted to be next to him and be able to play with him. I didn't know how far I could get, but that was my goal. I had the feeling that the hand of destiny was touching me again, as it had the first time I heard an electric guitar playing the blues. My expectations of what I was destined to do transcended everything I experienced in my time at Mission High.

I just looked at them. "Well, you asked me."

It wasn't such a big dream. We already had a gig at the Fillmore Auditorium—the same place where all the blues legends were starting to play in the Bay Area. My band had to wait for two months to play a show for Bill Graham while I got over the TB, and then Bill booked us to open for the Who and the Loading Zone—a Friday and Saturday night in the middle of June. We had no idea how big the Who were going to get, and the Loading Zone was a local group. What mattered most to us was that we were finally going to get to play the most important venue in San Francisco. Our name wasn't even on the poster, but at least we had a name.

It was Carabello who came up with the idea. Playing the blues was the thing we were most proud of, and the word *blues* was in the names of some our favorite groups—the Butterfield Blues Band, the Bluesbreakers. He went through our last names—Haro Blues Band, Rodriguez Blues Band, Carabello Blues Band. He thought my last name had the most ring to it. Santana Blues Band became our name for the next year and a half. It wasn't that I was suddenly the leader. We were a leaderless band—not because we sat down one day and decided that, but because that's how it was.

We were already mixing other music in with the blues. We rehearsed and got our set together— "Chim Chim Cheree," "Jingo," "As the Years Go Passing By," "Work Song." Our set was short compared to what we would be doing in a few years—just thirty or forty minutes.

The first night was great. It went by very fast—and not only because I had started taking uppers at the time. I was so nervous and wired that I broke three strings that night. I didn't have any more strings with me, and we were in the middle of the set, so I looked around and grabbed the only guitar I could see—a beat-up

Strat that was Pete Townshend's! I saw Keith Moon looking at me, and he smiled when he saw my situation. "Pete won't mind—go ahead." He was very encouraging. Bill Graham was, too. He liked what he heard, and he said we should open for some more shows that were coming up.

Saturday night was terrible. We got to the Fillmore late, *really* late. Both Danny's and Gus's parents kept them late at work, and they were my ride. Man, I was so angry. But not nearly as pissed as Bill Graham was when we got to the Fillmore. He was standing at the top of the steps—the old Fillmore had a staircase that you had to haul your equipment up to get to the auditorium. His arms were folded, and he looked as big and mean as Mr. Clean, the Jolly Green Giant, and Yul Brynner in *The King and I*. He saw us trying to get our equipment up the stairs as fast as possible, and he started yelling. "Don't even bother. You will never fuckin' work for me again." He started cursing us, our ancestors, and the children we didn't have yet. He started using words I'd never heard before but would get to know because of him.

I was thinking, "Oh, shit, man. We really fucked up." We had— and just like that, we were banned from any Bill Graham concerts for a long time. He didn't even want us coming in to check out other bands, but that couldn't keep me away. I remember going home after seeing Jimi Hendrix perform at the Fillmore that summer, shaking my head and telling myself that what I just heard and saw was real. I still have never felt like I did the first time I heard him.

When Eric Clapton and Cream came to town in August and played the Fillmore, I had to sneak in to see them, too. I had to—I had no choice. I still knew how to do that through the fire escape. I wanted to see if their live show would match the sound on their records, which was so different from the Chicago blues bands that they were coming from. Bigger and more bombastic.

It did. Cream looked big in their platform shoes, and they sounded bigger. Clapton had that double stack of Marshalls behind him, Jack Bruce sounded like a freight train, and Ginger Baker looked like some kind of weird creature with his red hair, playing those double bass drums. On tunes like "Spoonful" and "Hey Lawdy Mama," it wasn't just electric blues or blues-rock anymore. They were hitting with the energy of Buddy Rich—which made sense when I found out that Ginger and Jack had experience playing jazz. Catching those first Cream shows was like someone who had only experienced black-and-white TV seeing a CinemaScope movie for the first time.

Anyway—the Santana Blues Band was on Bill's blacklist. I couldn't believe this happened. I never missed gigs. Being late was not in my DNA. My mom and dad taught me that if you make an appointment, being punctual means being there a half hour early. I'm that way now, and my band knows it. If you want to get my stomach upset, show up late to a rehearsal or a sound check or a show. I still can't stand it.

I knew how parents can be, but at a certain point when you know where you're supposed to be going, you don't let them stand in your way. You tell them, "I made a commitment. I need to be over there." For me that was the end. I was thinking, "Your priorities are not my priorities—your priority is to please your mom and your dad, and you'll end up putting that first for the rest of your life." How could making tortillas or cutting meat be more important? A gig at the Fillmore in 1967 was a major thing for any musician, and it was the biggest thing in the world to me.

CHAPTER 7

Santana in late 1968. (L to R) Gregg Rolie, David Brown, me, Doc
Livingston, and Marcus Malone.

*Before I was twenty, I could hear the difference between a weekend
musician and a full-time musician. I could tell from a person's playing
if there was enough conviction to elevate the music, to make it come
together. When I started playing with people I knew in high school, I
could tell how the music changed depending on whom I was playing
with. In our group we'd try out various tunes or keep old ones, but the
songs we played were not as important as the new players who came into
the band. I think I was lucky to have started so early in Tijuana—even
the little group that had the two fighting brothers on guitar and me on
violin helped me to hear what works and what doesn't in a group
situation.*

I think if you look at rock groups in their first few years you find two ways they got their sound. Groups like the Beatles, the Rolling Stones, and the Grateful Dead mostly came up together. Their lineups changed very little; sometimes not at all. They got better together. I think Santana developed more like a jazz band does, with different musicians coming and going until the right parts are together and the music grows into itself. We also came from R & B and Latin music: our instruments were guitar, organ, and percussion—no horns. When we started we didn't have a plan for what our sound would be like, but we knew it when we got it. I think Santana is still developing a sound that depends on the people who come into the band.

One thing we had in common with groups like the Dead and the Stones is that everyone in the band started as equals. Early on, these groups all were collectives. Then each band got tested and got successful until a leader had to step up.

I think it was a good thing Santana began that way. I think if it started out with my being the leader I might have wanted to do only whatever songs were already in my head, and maybe I wouldn't have been open to hearing the music that we were developing. I would have tried too much to control what was happening. Even with the Santana Blues Band, the idea of letting the music lead the way was there at the beginning.

The summer of 1967 was the Summer of Love in most people's minds. Flower power and psychedelic rock and hippie chicks. The Monterey Pop festival. Everybody was talking about how Jimi Hendrix burned his Strat and broke it onstage and *How could he?* Then *Are You Experienced* came out, and suddenly the sound of the electric guitar was dive-bombing, supersonic jets, roaring motorcycles, and rumbling earthquakes. Jimi made sonic sculptures out of feedback. Jimi's first album took music from the days of gunpowder to the time of laser-guided missiles. I remember someone turning me on to "Red House," and I knew immediately this was where electric blues were going—everybody was going to be following Jimi.

For me and many musicians, this was also when we started to feel that the resonance of our convictions could change the world. People like John Coltrane and John Lennon felt their music could be used to promote compassion and wisdom. It could make people better human beings. Later, Aretha Franklin, Marvin Gaye, and Bob Marley did the same thing—"Amazing Grace," "What's Going On," "One Love." Their music infused people with a different kind of message that went beyond entertainment: "We are one!" It wasn't just a cliché. It had real power to unite, just as Woodstock and *Supernatural* did. There can be unity, and music can be the glue. That's the big message, the one I've been hearing and believing since I was a teenager.

For me, the summer of 1967 was also the summer of decisions.

One day I saw the Grateful Dead stop by the Tic Tock in a limousine. Everyone in the city knew they had signed a big record deal the year before and had their first album out. I saw them from the sink where I was washing dishes and said to myself, "I shouldn't be doing this anymore." It wasn't because of the limousine. It was the idea of making a full commitment to music. I had to take the whole plunge—music had to be my 100 percent, my full-time thing. My office and my home. My eight days a week, as the Beatles said. Who you are going to be decides what you're going to do, and what you're going to do decides what you're going to be. I was telling myself, "Dude, make the eight lie down like infinity."

The decision to leave had been building up for a while. It was really motivated by seeing those Chicago blues guys playing the Fillmore in that first year. Man, I would be in such a daze for weeks after that, I don't know how many dishes I broke at work. It seemed like they were calling me—calling me to abandon, as my good friend the saxophonist Wayne Shorter would say. Abandon the need to ask permission to do this or that, to live my life. I could hear the level of the commitment they had in their music; I could hear their commitment to the way they lived their lives. I could even smell it. The other decision I had to make was to finally leave home. I could not be like those bluesmen and still be living under my mother's rules.

Then everything seemed to happen at once. We had showed up late to play the Fillmore and lost any chance at playing there again. A few days later Danny Haro's brother-in-law was driving Danny's green Corvette and crashed. He was the first person close to my age to suddenly die like that. Then I dropped LSD and had a bad trip. It wasn't my first time tripping, but it was my first bad trip. A *really* bad trip.

The problem was that I was in the wrong environment when I dropped. First I dropped with a guy who started freaking out, which made me freak out a bit. Then I left him and was hanging with Danny and Gus in the house they were living in in Daly City. They were eating pizza and laughing in the kitchen—"Ho-ho-ho, hee-hee-hee, ha-ha-ha." In my ears they sounded just like the Beatles' "I Am the Walrus." I turned on the TV, and the movie *The Pride and the Passion* was on—Cary Grant, Frank Sinatra, and Sophia Loren hauling a cannon across Europe and killing thousands of people. Not a good movie to watch on LSD. I was beginning to lose myself in a sea of darkness and doubt. It was almost like a box of firecrackers was going off in my brain, a lot of negative explosions—fear of what's going to happen to me, fear of a world that is so sick and so negative and dark. I had all these thoughts and couldn't come up with the words to describe what I was seeing. I don't remember how I did it, but somehow at five in the morning I got the mechanics together to call Stan Marcum and ask him to come and get me.

Stan was the kind of friend who would say, "I'll be right there" and mean it. He picked me up, and the first place he took me was to the woods in Fairfax, in North Bay. I was watching a beautiful golden sunrise, but what I was seeing was the world burning itself down. Suddenly I felt like I was Nero, fiddling away while a huge fire was happening all around me. I felt that the world was destroying itself and needed to be helped.

My mind was still higher than an astronaut's butt, so Stan took me to his house, and he and Ron put me in a room to try to sleep it off. But I was wide-awake. Then they put on *Sgt. Pepper's Lonely*

Hearts Club Band. The album was only a few weeks old then, and I heard "Within You Without You"—George Harrison playing sitar and singing about spiritual principles.

I needed that. Everything came together, and I finally started to come down. Stan asked me, "What happened this morning? What did you see?" I told him that I had seen the world on fire, crying for help. He asked, "What are you going to do about it?" I told him I had been thinking about that for a long time. This is what I said: "I want to help it heal."

I felt like I actually gave birth to myself that day. I went from believing the world was coming to an end to figuring out what I had to do to stop that from happening. It had been a long, long night and day—I felt that the whole experience had given me power and brought me to my purpose in life.

Stan and Ron listened to me talk. They heard the conviction. "We'll be your managers," they said. "We'll quit our jobs—no more bail bondsman, no more barber. We're going to join you, man. We're going to help you. We'll dedicate all our energy and money to you and the band." I was blown away—these two hippie dudes were ready to invest in my career. They became two more angels stepping up—coming in at just the right time. I think about it now, and it felt like they'd been waiting to hear me say what I said as much as I'd been wanting to say it.

Stan said one more thing. "You have to get rid of Danny and Gus—that's the way it is, man. They're not bad people, but they're not committed. They're weekend musicians; you're not. We can tell that. We'll drop everything for you, but you got to drop them."

I was like, "Oh, damn." I could tell that Stan and Ron had been thinking about this for a while. I knew they were right, but Danny and Gus were my oldest friends in San Francisco. Making us late at the Fillmore kind of sealed it, but if anybody was going to tell them, I would have to be the one.

Danny and Gus were upset—really upset—and they got pissed off at Stan. I told them it wasn't about their playing. It was because they just weren't ready to take the plunge. That LSD trip made me realize that our thing was done—they were my friends, I grew up with them, but it was not something that I needed to hang with. It would have been like wearing shoes that didn't fit anymore.

We stayed in touch over the years, but they never stuck with music, at least not as a profession. They're both in heaven now—they both left in the early '90s, way too early. Cancer got Gus, and diabetes got Danny—he lost a leg, and the last time I saw him I got the feeling his soul was broken because he had lost his parents and his two sisters, and he was the last one left.

I said good-bye to Danny and Gus, and I finally said good-bye to living with my mom and dad and moved in with Stan and Ron on Precita Avenue. That was the nest that nurtured the birth of the band. Their place was just ten blocks from my family's house, but my parents wouldn't know where I was for almost two years. They would look for me all over the city even though I was right next to them. But I didn't want them to do the same thing they did in Tijuana. I left without even taking my clothes.

That really was the beginning of Santana right there.

Bands living together in San Francisco was normal back then—it helped focus the energy, and it saved money. The Grateful Dead and Big Brother had their houses. So did Sly. Some were in poor, funky neighborhoods, but that was okay if it helped you to afford it. This kind of thing still goes on in Paris now among African musicians—they'll rent one apartment and cook and play music together. Same thing. You learn to trust each other.

When I moved in with Stan and Ron, I took over a small room. I borrowed clothes when I needed to and bought some stuff at Goodwill. We cooked together and closed the curtains and brought chicks in and out. People would come around, because Stan was a very social guy in a nice way, not a bullshitter. We'd smoke weed, take acid, and drink wine and discuss Miles and Jimi Hendrix and Frank Zappa. Whoever we were listening to. We listened to a whole lot of Bob Dylan. Stan and Ron had a lot of jazz in the house, too—that's when I really got to hear more of Grant Green and Kenny Burrell as well as Wes Montgomery.

The three of us—Gregg, Carabello, and I—still went to the Fillmore, sneaking in under Bill Graham's eyes. We'd stand in front of the stage, look at the bands, and say, "You better bring it, man. Let's see what you got." We heard the Young Rascals and Vanilla Fudge from New York, the Crazy World of Arthur Brown and Procol Harum from England. Certain bands didn't disappoint us. Steppenwolf was mean—they had charisma. We opened for them a lot in Fresno and Bakersfield and Lake Tahoe.

Other bands were like copies of copies. A few of them had some corny one-song hits. We'd say, "Nah—this sounds like a bad rehearsal. Let's go."

Not B. B. King. I had been so excited to see him for the first time in February of 1967. Finally, the teacher I had started with and kept coming back to was coming to the Fillmore! The first time I had heard his music was in Tijuana at Javier's house—all those LPs on the Kent and Crown labels.

B. B. was the headliner after Otis Rush and Steve Miller. Another great triple bill. I was there for the opening night. Steve was great, Otis was incredible, and then it was B. B.'s band onstage, vamping. (Later on, I learned what his close friends call him—just B.—but in my mind he will always be Mr. King.) Then B. walked onstage, and Bill Graham went up to the mike to introduce him: "Ladies and gentlemen, the chairman of the board—Mr. B. B. King!"

It was like it had all been planned to build up to this. Everything just stopped, and everyone stood up and applauded. For a long time. B. hadn't even hit a note yet, and he was getting a standing ovation. Then he started crying.

He couldn't hold it in. The light was hitting him in such a way that all I could see were big tears coming out of his eyes, shining on his black skin. He raised his hand to wipe his eyes, and I saw he was wearing a big ring on his finger that spelled out his name in diamonds. That's what I remember most—diamonds and tears, sparkling together. I said to myself, "Man, that's what I want. This is what it is to be adored if you do it right."

Gregg, Carabello and I saw B. in concert when he came back in December of '67, and I was able to study him almost in slo-mo, waiting for him to hit those long notes of his. I was thinking, "Okay, here it comes—he's going to go for it. There it is. That note just freaked out everybody in the place, man." People were in the hallelujah camp. I noticed that just before he would hit a long note, B. would scrunch up his face and body, and I knew he was going to a place inside himself, in his heart, where something moved him so deeply that it was not about the guitar or the string anymore. He got inside the note. And I thought, "How can I get to that place?"

Years later I was invited to the Apollo Theater to play in an event with, among others, Natalie Cole, Hank Jones—the great jazz pianist—Bill Cosby, and B. B. King. B. came up to me beforehand and said, "Santana, you going to play it tonight, man?" He rarely calls me Carlos.

I said, "I'm waiting for you to tell me, man."

"Come on: we want to hear the blues."

So I hit it. After I played, we walked out, and B. grabbed me. "Santana, I want to tell you, you don't have a good sound—you have a *grand* sound."

Shoot. I graduated right there. To be knighted by B. B. King himself? "Thank you, sir." That's all I could think to say. I don't remember getting back to the hotel that night.

Bluesmen are not always so gracious. Buddy Guy can be a headhunter. If you're playing with him and don't come in the right way, he's going to make sure he's looking at you while he's dissecting you. His attitude is, if you can't keep up, get the hell off the stage.

Albert King wouldn't even wait for you to start. Once at a blues festival in Michigan, Albert Collins went to meet Albert King and said, "I just wanted to meet you, shake your hand, and tell you how much I enjoy your music."

King replied, "Yeah, I know who you are. I'm going to kick your little ass when you get onstage."

I love these kinds of blues stories. To me they grab the essence of what the blues life is about—the attitude and the cockiness and the humor. Here's another one: there was a blues revue in 2001 at the Concord Pavilion in Concord, California, with an incredible lineup. I had to be there. I got there just as Buddy Guy was arriving. "Hey, man, good to see you here!" he said to me.

"What's going on, Buddy?"

He looked me up and down. "I hope you didn't make the same mistake Eric Clapton made."

"Oh, yeah? What mistake is that?"

"Coming over to see me without a guitar! But you know I always bring two." He started laughing, with all his gold teeth shining.

Then he pulled out a flask. "Santana, I know you meditate and stuff, but I got to have my little shorty dog. I need to tune my guitar—why don't you pour me some and help yourself to some, too?" So I did, and immediately he said, "Hey, whoa! You trying to get me drunk? You put more in mine than yours."

"No problem, Buddy. I'll take the bigger one, man." He's constantly testing me. I've gotten used to it.

That night he played an incredible set, connecting with people as he always does, walking out into the audience while he plays a solo, because he wants people to smell him, and he wants to smell them, too. He'll do his big buildup thing, playing a solo and building the energy to the point where you know a big sustained note is coming. There's a noise he makes with his mouth that you can hear—a grinding and churning, like it's coming from all the way down in his gut—before he hits the guitar and the note comes up and hangs forever: loud and long and deep and soulful, and he's got everyone in the crowd with him and he knows it. He grins with all those beautiful golden teeth, like he's saying, "Shit—I *willed* this goddamn amplifier and this guitar to sustain like that. I can do it as long as I want."

Then there's the song that has the lyrics, "One leg in the east / One leg in the west / I'm right down the middle / Trying to do my best"! And the women start screaming. Every time I see Buddy, he's creating a riot, you know?

He brought me out, and we jammed a little bit. He finished his set, and we were backstage, hugging and sweating, and I was just floating, man. Off to the side, we saw some people coming like it was high noon at the O.K. Corral: four big bodyguards, dressed up real sharp, two on the left, two on the right. Behind them was... who else? B. B. King himself, on the way to the stage—his band was already playing.

Buddy pushed me around a corner. "Carlos, stand here so B. won't see you. When I call you, come on out, okay?" He had a twinkle in his eye.

"Sure, whatever you say."

Buddy stepped in front of the whole procession, blocking the way. They got up real close, and B. said, "Hey, Buddy, what's up?"

Buddy looked at him without a smile. "B., how long have you known me?"

He said, "A long time. Where you goin' with this, man?"

Buddy took his time. "Well, there're things about me you don't know—like I have a son you didn't know I had." Then he called to me: "Come here, man," and he put me right in front of B., holding my shoulders. B. was still focused on Buddy, wondering what he's up to, and all of a sudden he sees me and starts laughing. "Buddy, you ain't nothin' but a dirty dog—come here, Santana!" He gave me a huge hug.

Buddy was right. I am his son, just as Buddy and I are B.'s sons.

B. grabbed our hands. "You're both walking out with me. Come on!" We went onstage together, and B. raised our hands above our heads like we were prizefighters, and the crowd went, "Yay!" Then B. turned to us with a serious look. "Okay, you guys can get out of here."

It was time for Daddy to go to work.

*   *   *

Back in San Francisco when I was living with Stan and Ron, every few weeks we'd put on classical music and clean the house with hot water and ammonia from top to bottom. It was easy for me to get used to that kind of group living because of how I grew up with my family, especially my mom. She encoded that in my DNA. And when you're a hippie, man, everybody wants to share that joint. We shared food and weed and money and chores.

In our house, most days we woke up, ate breakfast, and went to work getting gigs and finding new musicians. Intention was focused on the band: time, energy, money. Sometimes Stan would bring musicians over—we would play with them until six in the morning. We were trying out new players, but we were also just jamming and being social.

We did a few gigs at street fairs and small clubs like the Ark in Sausalito with the bass player Steve De La Rosa, who was really good and very attentive to what the drummer was doing. Drummers went in and out for a while. There was Rod Harper, who was good on certain kinds of songs but not on others. Then we found Doc Livingston, who came from somewhere in South Bay. He had certain mechanics—he could play double bass drums, but the thing I most liked about him was that when he played with mallets he could create a kind of vortex to play in. Real drummers don't need to be told when to get some mallets out. But he didn't know about just playing funky. That was too bad. I had a feeling he wasn't going to last, because he was a real lone wolf. Every time we had a meeting Doc would be off somewhere else, looking at the floor.

One night we played in a jazz bar. It was called Grant & Green because that's where it was. A bassist jammed with us on "Jingo"— he was tall with green eyes and dark skin and was really the most gorgeous-looking black man I'd ever seen.

David Brown was basically a silky person to be around—never angry, no strife. He loved Chuck Rainey's bass playing. As Jimmy Garrison was with Coltrane, David was always way behind the beat, never in the middle. I knew it was on when I heard him—I don't like bass players who play with too much precision. But I couldn't look at David's feet when we'd be playing a song because it would throw me off—he was that far back. Later, when Santana got its sound together, it all made sense—David laying back in the beat, Chepito Areas hitting it way up front—a balance of precision and conviction, you know?

He may have been behind the beat, but I've never seen anyone pick up women faster than David Brown. He was a chick whisperer. He would scratch his chin and go up to a woman real close and say something in her ear. He'd take her by the hand, and they'd walk off.

We asked David to join us that same night.

We started to look for another conga player, too. I'm not sure why we had to, but Carabello could be such a goofball sometimes, showing up late or not at all. He's the only person I know who made a U-turn driving on the Golden Gate because he forgot his Afro comb. One time we were playing the Ark, and Carabello was using the kind of conga that has the skin nailed onto it, so the only way to get the right pitch is to warm the skin. He put the conga near a stove in the kitchen to heat it up and left it while he checked out a chick. He came back, and that thing looked like a pork rind—it had a big hole in it, and it smelled horrible.

I said, "You know what, man? You're not getting paid."

"Oh, man, that's cold, man."

"No, it's not cold. You don't play—you don't get paid. You should have stayed here with the conga, man."

Anyway, we had to drop Carabello for a while. Then Stan was down listening to the *congueros* at Aquatic Park when he met this cat named Marcus Malone. He was really good—self-taught, a self-made showman. He had no knowledge of clave or anything Cuban or Puerto Rican. But that wasn't going to stop him. He had the idea for "Soul Sacrifice" and could make "Jingo" pop. I started hanging around with him more and more.

He was very, very sharp. Marcus "the Magnificent" Malone. Everything he wore was burgundy. He had a brand-new Eldorado:

the upholstery and everything was a beautiful maroon. You can see it in the early photos—Marcus rocked a different style. We were street—he was slick. He was a player, and he was a street hustler. He'd step out from rehearsals and say, "I got to call my bitches"—and we would wait.

I was with Marcus the night that Martin Luther King Jr. got shot. We had a gig that night at Foothill College in Palo Alto, and he was driving. I started crying, and he said, "Man, what's wrong with you? Why are you crying?" He was too tough, I think, to let his emotions show that way.

"Man, what's wrong with *you*?" I replied. "Didn't you hear they just shot Martin Luther King?"

He was like, "Oh"—and he just looked straight ahead.

Marcus was a tough dude, man. He had a lifestyle that was very different from ours. I don't think we could ever get him to come over to our side of thinking—to let his girls go and trust the music to make it happen for him. He'd say, "No, man. You're freaking hippies taking all that LSD and smoking pot and shit. I gotta deal with my bitches—they're taking care of me."

The band and I got tight with Marcus's mom for a little while. She had a big garage and didn't mind if we kept our instruments there and used it to rehearse. Years later I figured out that her place was very close to what is now the Saint John Coltrane Church. The one thing she asked was that we help her by painting her kitchen—so one day we all got to it and painted that kitchen. Of course I had no experience with that, but I don't think we made too much of a mess of it.

It only took a few weeks—but by July of 1967 we had the foundation of Santana. I'm still amazed at how fast it came together. That's how much talent was walking around San Francisco then. Also, it's not like we said, "Let's make this a group of people from different backgrounds—black, white, Mexican." It's just that we weren't cut off from that opportunity. Among all the bands in San Francisco, we were closest in this way to what Sly did with the Family Stone. The city had all these cultures living close together, and when Stan, Ron, and I started to look for musicians, we opened a door and it didn't matter who walked in — they fit if they had the music and the right personality.

It took a lot longer for our sound to develop. A few years later Bill Graham would say that we were like a street mutt: we had so many things mixed together we couldn't know who we were. He said that as a compliment. We continued as the Santana Blues Band — sometimes just Santana Blues — but as our music started changing we didn't know what style to call it. I already could see that the blues elevator was too crowded and that we needed to let that one go up and wait for the next one. Everybody was playing some style of blues — Paul Butterfield and John Mayall were laying it down. Cream and Jimi Hendrix were playing the blues, only louder. A year later, Led Zeppelin and Jeff Beck's band would come in with their heavier sound.

In '67 we had many new ideas and influences in the band. Everyone liked Jimi, the Doors, and Sly & the Family Stone. David was into Stax and Motown. Gregg brought his passion for the Beatles and was into Jimmy Smith and Jack McDuff. Doc Livingston also liked rock bands. Carabello was still hanging with us and still turning me on to Willie Bobo and Chico Hamilton. Marcus loved Latin music, blues, and jazz. He was the one who first turned me on to John Coltrane.

Not that I was ready for that yet. I was at Marcus's place in Potrero Hill, near the projects and near where O. J. Simpson grew up. He left me in the back room while he went to check on his women. It was like an assignment: he left me with a joint and put on *A Love Supreme*. "Here, help yourself, man."

The first thing I heard was Coltrane's volume and intensity. It fit the times. The '60s had a very loud, violent darkness that came from the war and riots and assassinations. Coltrane's loudness and emotion reminded me of Hendrix, but it sounded like his horn was putting holes in the darkness — each time he blew, more light came through. The rest was kind of mysterious — I couldn't make out the structure or the scales. I mean, I could play blues scales, but it just felt so alien to me. I remember looking at the album cover and seeing his face so calm *and* intense—it looked like his thoughts were screaming. It was one of the first times I realized the paradox of music: it can be violent and peaceful at the same time. I had to put it aside—it would take some time until I was able to understand Coltrane's music and his message of crystallizing your intentions for the good of the planet.

California was a conservative place in general, but it seemed like anyone talking about politics at that time was from the left. People were supporting things like public performances and food banks and Cesar Chavez and the Black Panthers. Either you were against the war in Vietnam and against exploitation of workers and against anything that was racist or you were old and part of the problem.

It wasn't just San Francisco. You could take LSD, turn on the news, and see people dying in Vietnam. They kept showing Buddhist monks pouring gasoline over themselves and burning to death to protest the war. How could your mind not expand? Later you saw the motel balcony where Martin Luther King Jr. was shot. Robert Kennedy lying on a kitchen floor, dying.

The '60s were in your face, and there was no remote control to turn it off. That came later. When Santana did its first national tour in '69, you could see the whole country was going in that direction—thinking and dressing differently, experimenting. Talking liberation. The thing is, this all happened in just two years. When Jimi Hendrix and Otis Redding and Ravi Shankar were playing the Monterey Pop festival in '67, I was just getting started, happy to be opening for the Who at the Fillmore Auditorium. By '69, I was playing Woodstock.

I was almost eighteen when the world started to ask questions that had not been asked before. Is there a better way than what we've been doing all these years? Why are we fighting here at home, and over there in Vietnam? Can we make this world a better place—can we infuse spiritual principles in everyday life? I had my own questions. What does that mean—tune in and drop out? What am I going to do? Where do I fit in all this?

San Francisco was the perfect time and place to experience the '60s. The combination came at just the right time—a gift. I was a guitar player who had the conviction to make music his life. I was working with songs and vibrations when the sound of the electric guitar was what people were gravitating to. That instrument became another way to take people to new places, to make beautiful paintings. The electric guitar was the new storyteller. Suddenly, with musicians like Hendrix and Clapton and Jeff Beck, it was possible to go deeper into the guitar and transcend its actual construction. Something like the Fender Strat? As Jimi said, "You'll never hear surf music again." The electric guitar was able to transcend what it was supposed to do and communicate a state of grace on a molecular level.

It wasn't just the way the instrument sounded: guitar solos were getting longer, too. The music all around us was starting to get longer. Even on the radio, songs were not just three minutes anymore— some FM stations would play a twenty-minute tune if a band put it out. Creedence Clearwater Revival was just getting started. They were already big in San Francisco and came out with a long version of "Suzie Q." It was that "East-West" influence, and from the jazz world, too—Chico Hamilton, Gábor Szabó. Hendrix had "Third Stone from the Sun"—jamming with all the psychedelic studio stuff going on and talking about "majestic silken scenes" and landing his "kinky machine." If you played guitar, you couldn't just make up something to go with a short section of a song and work it again and again. I had to open up to going on with an idea, having your own discussion. It wasn't that difficult—I could talk. I had to just learn to listen. To hear the music and know when to go higher, when to jump, when to bring it back.

I would embellish a little even when I was playing violin, though my father discouraged that. He wanted me to stay true to the melody, put the feeling into that. This was different. I was opening up to thinking about energy and sound, not just notes and scales.

After leaving home and the Tic Tock, I had more time to listen and really dissect records—listen to them again and again, maybe twenty times. I'd listen alone with my guitar or with the other guys in the house. We would sit around and smoke weed and get fuzzy and hazy. Some music sounded like it was made for that. John Lee Hooker, the Doors, Jimi Hendrix—all weed music. Definitely Lee Morgan. I used to love to smoke to *First Light* by Freddie Hubbard. If it was Bob Dylan or Miles Davis, you'd get twice as high. When I started really listening to Coltrane, I'd get high, but after a while his music sets you straight, like he had some kind of regulator tone that doesn't allow for fuzzy and hazy.

I remember talking with a lady who used to live in Mill Valley. She told me, "I heard you play, and I brought you some records." One of them was by the Gypsy guitarist Django Reinhardt. She told me he learned to play even though two of his fingers were stuck together. As soon as she left, I started listening—"Minor Swing" with both guitar and violin! Hearing Django go off on a solo gave me a whole new idea of what to do.

One night the Santana Blues Band was opening for James Cotton. Sometime in '67, we had begun playing regularly at an old movie house in the Haight that some hippies fixed up and called the Straight Theater. The place was a little raggedy, but it felt right for us. We played Albert King's "As the Years Go Passing By"—"There is nothing I can do / If you leave me here to cry..." My turn to solo came, and suddenly it was like opening a faucet. The water just flowed out. It was the most natural feeling. I wasn't repeating riffs. I wasn't repeating anything. It felt like I had turned a corner.

A writer once asked me what I think about when I'm soloing—this was in the early '90s, when all three of my children were just kids. I told him I thought about combing my daughters' hair before they went to bed, how careful I had to be so I didn't make them cry. Playing a good solo is about being sensitive and not rushing, letting the music tell you what and when and how fast. It's about learning to respect yourself by respecting the music and honoring the song.

Another time, my mom approached me and said, "*Mijo*, can I ask you something? Where do you go when you're playing your guitar and you look up? All you guys look up. What's up there?" I love my mom for having that childlike curiosity and just coming out with that question. I know she's not alone. People want to know. "What's it like in there? What's it feel like?"

It's difficult to explain—Wayne Shorter calls it the invisible realm. I call it a state of grace, a moment of timelessness. Playing a guitar and getting inside a groove and finding the notes is like the power that lovers have—they can bend time, suspend it. A moment seems like infinity, and then all of a sudden time meets you around the corner. I began to feel that when I was playing in Mexico—not a lot, but sometimes.

I don't know if my solo on "As the Years" was recorded, but the band was starting to record ourselves in concert, asking the sound guys to do that so we could listen to our performances, study them. At first it was pretty painful—it always sounded different from the way I'd remembered it onstage, and *everything* sounded rushed. I'd go home and listen to it by myself, never with anyone else. In fact I still do that—I won't listen to recordings of Santana in concert if there are people around me unless we're working on a live album or I want to show somebody something we need to fix.

We also learned to play high. Gregg usually stuck to his beer, and the rest of us would smoke weed when we played—and we tripped a lot. Without a doubt, hallucinogens had a lot to do with the Santana sound. That's the way it was with many groups then—there wouldn't be the Jimi Hendrix Experience without them or the Beatles' *Sgt. Pepper*. There would only have been electric blues and "In the Midnight Hour." Even the Beach Boys moved on from surf music because of LSD.

LSD was legal until sometime in late '68. I also took mescaline and peyote—ground ayahuasca buttons—which was a really nice trip except for when you had to go to the bathroom. It wasn't as electric as LSD, which could be a little intense because we cut it with speed.

Then we'd play.

Hallucinating is another word for seeing beyond what your brain is programmed to see. That's what those drugs did for me with music—they made me more receptive to ideas and heightened my sensitivity. Normally your brain is on a leash, with built-in filters. When I tripped and played, those filters went away, and the leash was off. I could hear things in a new way. Everything became more watery—thoughts were more fluid, and the music was more flowing. I would drop, and the music didn't sound so fragmented. It sounded like beads on a string that would go on and on.

That was the deal: it took courage to surrender and trust that when you had those hallucinations you were not in total control—and if you got afraid and tried to get that control back, you were going to have a bad trip. I always did surrender—I knew that it was going to get intense for a while but that in twelve hours or however long it took to finally pee it out, everything was going to be cool again. You learn that you can have fear or trust, but you can't have both.

We started to really hear each other, get to know one another's musical signatures. We were a collective, and everyone found a role—everyone had a chance to be lead sometimes. In rehearsals, Gregg was the stable one—he had his six-pack to drink, but he wouldn't do anything else. He was the rock in the band when all of us were doing stuff, going to extremes. The rest of us could go out with the music or go a little crazy and depend on Gregg to be the stabilizer, holding the beat together with his left hand. Somebody had to be the string on the kite.

From the end of '67 through the summer of '68, the Straight Theater gave us Friday-through-Sunday runs and put us on bills with Charlie Musselwhite and various local bands, including one called Mad River. Once we played after a Fellini movie. We started noticing people coming back to hear us, especially women—some we knew from high school and others who were new to us. They started to bring their friends, and we started to get our own crowd.

We did a few shows at the Avalon Ballroom and a few benefits at universities. We got better in front of an audience, and people started to hear about the Santana Blues Band. Then we got our first review. It was Sunday in Sausalito, and we were playing outside for spare change. Someone came up to us and said, "You're Santana, right?"

"Yes, that's us."

"You know you guys are in the Sunday pink section." That was the entertainment section of the *San Francisco Chronicle*. Ralph J. Gleason—the newspaper's top music writer, who also helped start *Rolling Stone* magazine—had named the top new bands coming out of the city. There were around twelve, including the Sons of Champlin, and we were the first he mentioned, saying that we had the X factor of excitement. I had no idea what that meant. I asked Carabello: "Hey, man, I'm still learning English. *Qué es* 'X factor'?" He laughed. "Man, fuck. I don't know, either. But who cares? We *got* it."

I like the fact that even one of the best music writers in the country didn't know what to call what we had, but he found a way to write about it. It was like the question of where Miles was going with his music by 1969—you couldn't call it jazz. Miles wasn't just jazz, and we weren't just rock. We were listening to jazz records and African and Latin music—which is really all from the same African root—learning things, getting inspired.

At the Fillmore shows, I started to hear how loose the time feel could be when I heard certain drummers—like Jack DeJohnette with Charles Lloyd or Terry Clarke with John Handy. I couldn't believe the elasticity. I started hearing words about making time more liquid, not so wooden. I heard how drums could be played very fast and light, the way some drummers could roll, and *wow*—everything hit just right. It wasn't like some bands—*clang, clang,* like a cable car. I got to hear that jazz drumming on records: John Handy had a great live album from the Monterey Jazz Festival with

"Spanish Lady" on it. I would listen to a percussion solo on *Bola Sete at the Monterey Jazz Festival* that showed me how you can add colors with cymbals and textures with percussion.

I think the most effective thing we were doing was mixing blues with African rhythms—and women really love that because it gives them another way into the music. Most men like the blues, and if you just play blues, like a shuffle, women will move a certain way. You'll get through to guys and a few women. But when you start adding a more syncopated thing—also some congas—it's a different feel, and people start opening up in another way. Now women can dance to it. They start swaying like flowers in the wind and sun after it's been cloudy for a whole month. Something happens with that mix.

There's another name for this mix—Latin music. All those African beats come through the clave rhythms that became part of the Santana DNA. That's really what you're hearing when you listen to Mongo Santamaría and Tito Puente and Santana. It's Africa.

If you said "Latin" to me at that time, I would think about what I saw on TV—Desi Arnaz and "Babalu" and guys in puffy sleeves shaking maracas—and I knew I didn't want to go there. To me, Latin music was very, very corny. The music that I did like before I really knew it was called *música tropical* or *música del Caribe* long before it was called salsa or boogaloo. I discovered Tito Puente and Eddie Palmieri the same way I discovered Babatunde Olatunji and Gábor Szabó—from just listening.

Latin music was everywhere in San Francisco—it was on the radio and jukeboxes, and later on, when I was hanging with Stan and Ron, I was getting it in the clubs. I knew that Ray Barretto had a humongous hit with "El Watusi," but I didn't know he had his own band until I started going to the Matador. That's where I heard Mongo Santamaría with his band. I had never really thought about these percussion guys having their own groups, as Chico Hamilton did. I was learning. Then I heard the percussionist Big Black— Daniel Ray—who had his own thing happening in San Francisco, more jazzy. I used to go see him at the Both/And, where Miles Davis used to play, too.

Me at eighteen months old, 1949. (© Santana Archives)

(L to R) Jorge, Maria, and Lety, 1959. (© Santana Archives)

Nina Matilde—my mom's aunt, who named me "El Cristalino." (© Santana Archives)

Josefina Barragán de Santana. (© Santana Archives)

José Santana (rear center with violin), Uncle Juan Santana (with cello), and José's band, 1945. This was the kind of Mexican orchestra dad started in; he didn't play mariachi music until we moved to Tijuana. (© Santana Archives)

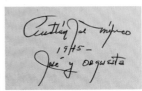

My dad's handwritten note on the back of the photo.

My dad, me, and our dog
Tony in Tijuana, 1958.
(© Santana Archives)

"Mr. 50¢ a Song"

Me at twelve years
old, on violin, in
Tijuana, Mexico,
August 30, 1959.
(© Santana
Archives)

This was one of my first gigs with my father, playing a fiftieth-
anniversary party in Tijuana, Baja California, in 1958, looking like
Cosa Nostra enforcers. (© Santana Archives)

The Strangers, Tijuana, Mexico, 1961. I'm on bass, next to the drummer.
(© Santana Archives)

My fourteen-year-old school picture, Tijuana, June 20, 1961.
(© Santana Archives)

Salon MX, Mission Street between 22nd and 23rd Streets, San Francisco, 1962.

With Danny Haro and Albert Rodriguez. (© Santana Archives)

Santana: (L to R) Gregg Rolie, me, and Marcus Malone, 1968. (© Jim Marshall Photography LLC)

Me in 1968. (© Coni Beeson)

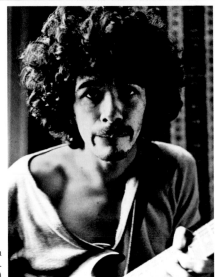

Another photo from
the same shoot.
(© Coni Beeson)

The band that started it all! (L to R) Me, Marcus Malone, Gregg Rolie, David Brown, and Doc Livingston. (© Michael Ochs Archives / Getty Images)

The Woodstock, *Santana*, *Abraxas*, and *Santana III* band: (L to R) me, Michael Shrieve, Michael Carabello, Gregg Rolie, David Brown, and José "Chepito" Areas, 1969. (© Michael Ochs Archives / Getty Images)

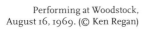
Performing at Woodstock,
August 16, 1969. (© Ken Regan)

Bill Graham takes a break while we play at Woodstock. (© Baron Wolman)

Gregg Rolie and I play to the crowd while the cameras capture the Woodstock experience. (© Jim Marshall Photography LLC)

A few moments later. (© Jim Marshall Photography LLC)

My fingers on the "electric snake." (© Photofest)

The snake talking back. (© Brandt Cotherman)

Santana at Altamont, December 6, 1969. (© Jim Marshall Photography LLC)

Santana and Clive Davis with double platinum album award, 1969.
(Courtesy Sony Music Entertainment / Clive Davis)

CBS RECORDS

A Division of Columbia Broadcasting System, Inc.
51 West 52 Street
New York, New York 10019
(212) 765-4321

Clive J. Davis, President

Dear Bill:

Historically, Miles Davis would not be of much interest to you for the Fillmore. However, I believe Miles is well on his way to really breaking out of his jazz bag. All the fantastic reviews in ROLLING STONE and Ralph Gleason's latest articles calling Miles' most recent albums the best he's heard anywhere in a decade have given him tremendous impetus. The "underground" is ready for Miles. His sales have measurably increased and I have finally softened him to play the Fillmore type emporium. I would appreciate it if you could express interest to him. In playing a role as "guest impresario" for Columbia, a bill with The Flock, Taj Mahal and Miles might be a real sleeper for you. No one of them would get that much bread as to make it hard to pay all; further, each appeals to that kind of music buff as to make it possible for all to be enjoyed. Creatively it would be a gigantic coup as each artist is felt to be a potential big artist and each has a growing fanatic following. Well, the rest is in your hands.

Santana, as you know, is unstoppable. Total sales with tape are now over 400,000 and going strong.

Warmest regards,

Clive

P.S. I saw Johnny Winter and Chicago Friday night at Fillmore. The evening was electrically exciting. Chicago was very good and Winter just keeps getting better all the time. The combination of him and his brother Edgar had the capacity house on their feet all night.

Mr. Bill Graham
Fillmore West
1545 Market Street
San Francisco, California

November 17, 1969/cb

bc: Teo Macero

Clive Davis's letter to Bill Graham about Miles Davis and Santana, 1970. (Courtesy Sony Music Entertainment /Clive Davis)

Michael Bloomfield, Coke Escovedo, and me at the Fillmore, July 4, 1971. (© Jim Marshall Photography LLC)

Me in Japan, 1973. (©
Santana Archives)

Armando Peraza
and me backstage
in Japan, 1973.
(© Santana Archives)

B. B. King and I meet for the first time, backstage at Winterland, 1973. (© Steve Caraway Images)

John McLaughlin and me at CBS Studios, 1973. (© Hugh Lelihan Browne)

John McLaughlin and me, 1973. (© Santana Archives)

Eric Clapton and me,
1975. (© Santana Archives)

Jerry Garcia and me at Bill
Graham's house in 1978.
(© Michael Zagaris)

Bob Dylan and me at the Warfield, November 13, 1980. (© Alvan Meyerowitz)

Bill Graham and me, Europe, 1984. (© Ken Regan)

Everybody was listening to Latin music—my family, too. Irma and Maria still tell me that they used to have parties at our home on 14th Street because my mom wouldn't let the girls go out. They would invite friends over, and they wore out the rug dancing to albums by Barretto and later El Gran Combo. Maria tells me that the folks who ran the grocery store downstairs would get angry because bottles would fall off their shelves from all the dancing. And poor Jorge—it was like what my sisters did with their Elvis Presley records ten years before. He says he'd go crazy hearing them play the hell out of "Bang Bang" by Joe Cuba.

Even if Santana didn't have anyone from the Caribbean in the group at the beginning, we came to Latin music naturally. It was the congas—hearing those jams in Aquatic Park and liking them, deciding that we would have some in the band and that they were going to be part of the soup. Then it was, "What music makes sense with congas"? Well, "Jingo." Then we started to hear music that could work with what we had, blues and congas, like "Afro Blue." Then it was: "We're going to write songs around the congas."

The next thing I knew I was hearing more music with congas, and I started buying Latin records with the same passion I had for the blues. By this time Gregg and Carabello and I were living together in a house on Mullen Avenue in Bernal Heights, near the Mission, and it was like we were all in a study group: "Check out the congas on this Jack McDuff record! Have you heard Ray Barretto on Wes Montgomery's 'Tequila' or on Kenny Burrell's 'Midnight Blue'? We gotta go hear him when he comes to town." Then Carabello heard Chepito playing timbales, and Chepito knew more about clave than any of us and helped us cement the full Santana sound.

We were from the streets of the Mission District, and in the beginning we were sensitive about what the "clave police" were saying. We didn't want to be intimidated by anyone thinking that we were trying something we didn't know how to do. When they first came after us, I wish I knew then what I know now—that the feel of the clave was already in blues and in rock. The electric blues guys—Otis Rush, Howlin' Wolf, Little Walter, Magic Sam—they all had songs with that Cuban feel. B. B. King had it—check out "Woke Up This Morning." Bo Diddley put tremolo on his guitar and maracas in his music and created his own electric primitive clave, and guess what? That shit went viral.

Here's another thing most people don't know about rock and clave: Chano Pozo, the Cuban conga player with Dizzy Gillespie's band, cowrote "Manteca." You can hear the influence from that song in Bobby Parker's "Watch Your Step" from '61. Parker was a blues guy from Washington, DC, who passed away in 2013, and who knows how he got to "Manteca," but it's the same pattern. When I was starting, every guitar player had to know "Watch Your Step"—including George Harrison, who played around with it for the introduction to the Beatles' "I Feel Fine." Later Duane Allman used that feel on "One Way Out." People need to know that. It all started with one Cuban song.

In 1968, Marcus really helped us show off this side of Santana—from "Jingo" to Willie Bobo's "Fried Neckbones and Some Home Fries." The chords from that one were a big part of our sound. Marcus had riffs that were his alone, and one time he came up with an idea—"Man, I wrote this song; I want you guys to help me out"—and started humming and slapping his knees. Then we each did a thing on it—I did a guitar solo that borrowed a lick that Gábor Szabó played on a Chico Hamilton track. Later we called it "Soul Sacrifice."

We were young—I didn't appreciate at the time how good Gregg was for us. He's a great soloist. I can remember watching his posture, and how he'd get into it so deeply, watching the veins appear in his throat, all that tension and conviction. He's a great arranger, too, which connects to his solo style.

Speaking of arrangers, in 1971 Santana did a *Bell Telephone Hour* show on TV. I'll never forget it: Ray Charles was on the same show, so we got to see him do "Georgia." I remember they were running through it, and suddenly Ray shouts, "Stop! Stop the band! Hey, you—viola in the third row. Tune up!" I wasn't sure if we should stay quiet or applaud.

Anyway, they wanted us to do "Soul Sacrifice" with the string section, and the whole arrangement was based on Gregg's solo. That's how lyrical a player he is. He also has a really, really powerful sense of knowing how to start a story—check out the opening of "Hope You're Feeling Better" or "Black Magic Woman." Santana likes dramatic openings, whether big or mysterious.

We started playing "Black Magic Woman" at this time, just after it came out. It was a song by Peter Green of Fleetwood Mac that was a blues-rumba of the kind that Chicago blues guys would sometimes play. It was really Otis Rush's "All Your Love (I Miss Loving)" with different words. We brought up the Latin feel in Peter Green's version, and when we played it live it made a great segue to Gábor Szabó's "Gypsy Queen."

One of the ways we stuck out from the rest of the bands in San Francisco was that we weren't really psychedelic or purely blues. We also didn't have horns, as Sly & the Family Stone did—we didn't have that funk rhythm, either. That summer Sly became a local hero. His "Dance to the Music" was everywhere, and those different voices really gave it a family vibe. Soon you could hear that Sly "sound fingerprint" all over the radio. Sly changed Motown—the producer Norman Whitfield started doing the Sly thing with the Temptations. Sly even changed Miles Davis. Miles would tell me later about watching Sly & the Family Stone just tear it up at the Newport Jazz Festival. That had to have hit Miles hard, to get him to change his music.

Let's face it—Sly Stone at his peak changed everything. The only person he did not have to change was James Brown, because James was already there. Sly had to get his funk from somebody, and he got his soul straight from the church. Sly's father was a minister and a preacher, and Sly was, too—just a more multidimensional one. He was the first guy who had female and male musicians, black and white. We were so proud that a cat from Daly City could go and change the world like that. We still are—in San Francisco, he's still our Sly, man.

It was around this time that I first met Sly. Carabello used to hang out with the Family Stone in Daly City. He brought me over.

"Hey, man, we got invited to go to Sly Stone's house. He wants us to open up for him on a couple of gigs, and he wants to produce us."

"Really? Okay. Let's go." When we got there, Sly said the wrong thing from the start—with attitude: "So you guys play that blues Willie Bobo stuff, huh?" I'm thinking, "What 'blues Willie Bobo stuff'? I'm not going to let this guy encapsulate me and define our music that way." He's a genius, man, no doubt about it, and he was already on the radio and everywhere else and he had the baddest bass player in the world—Larry Graham. But I didn't like somebody looking down at me like that.

"I'm fuckin' out of here, man."

Sly wasn't wrong; it was just how he expressed himself. Santana *was* starting to get it together with a Latin rock reputation. It was a way people could label our sound. Just don't call us blues Willie Bobo stuff.

That wasn't the end of that, though. The worst name I think I heard used to describe Santana was in *Rolling Stone*'s review of our first album—"psychedelic mariachi." Why? Just because I'm Mexican? What an ignorant, touristy thing to write.

I remember even my Caucasian friends telling me how stupid that was. I don't like to be reduced to anything other than a person who has a big heart and big eyes for a big slice of life. I'm not necessarily against music writers, but sometimes they don't think before they write. And when they *do* get it right? I remember that, too—like the jazz writer who described Albert Ayler's music as a Salvation Army band on acid. I read that and heard what he meant—and I love Albert Ayler. I thought, "Damn, that's a real badge of honor."

Here's what I think—if you're describing music that's original and not clichéd, don't use clichés to describe it. Be original and be accurate. We were open to Latin influences, and I think when we did it we did it well. Well enough to get back to playing the Fillmore.

I hadn't known that Bill Graham used to go hear Latin big bands in New York City. It was only later that he told me that he used to hang out at dance clubs in Manhattan and that he could mambo and cha-cha. It was in his blood. He knew about congas and Latin rhythms, and he liked them.

In the spring of '68 Bill was holding open auditions at the Fillmore Auditorium on Tuesday nights. Despite being unofficially blacklisted, we were welcome to play those, and we did. He didn't attend every time, but he heard us on a few occasions, and he heard how our music was changing. His ears were working. Speaking of Willie Bobo, Bill was the one who said we should do "Evil Ways" for our first album.

We didn't know it then, but around this time the Fillmore Auditorium became too small for the crowds. Bill took a plane to Sweden to meet face-to-face with the owner of the Carousel Ballroom, which was on Van Ness Avenue not far from the Mission. But the guy lived in Gothenburg! Bill flew out and met with him. They ate and drank and talked about a contract, then Bill flew back. That's how he started the Fillmore West. I don't think anyone else back then was serious enough to do something like that. If Bill believed in something or someone, he'd go after it. I admire that.

Bill would need bands to play this new, larger venue, and he knew we were getting a really good reputation with our shows. In June we played a benefit for the Matrix at the Fillmore Auditorium — the first time we had played there in a year. Stan and Bill talked, and Stan told him we had a new lineup with new songs. We wanted to play the Fillmore West, and we'd never be late.

He also told him the band had a new name — just one word, and it wasn't *blues*.

CHAPTER 8

The classic Santana lineup, 1969. (L to R) Michael Shrieve, me, Gregg Rolie, José "Chepito" Areas, David Brown, and Michael Carabello.

Santana was in New York City in 1970, and that was when we really, truly understood what clave was—when we got that word into our vocabulary. A bunch of us went to hear Ray Barretto at the Corso, a dance club on East 86th Street where all the Latin stars played, including Larry Harlow and Tito Puente. There were moments when Ray would suddenly stop the band, but the audience would already be clapping and keeping the rhythm going, hitting that clave time: ba-ba-bah—ba-bah, ba-ba-bah—ba-bah.

It was like seeing something on the wall you had never seen before but had always been there and being told, "Well, that's what keeps the wall together."

"Oh, now I see—that's the foundation for all Latin music."

Then at one point Ray grabbed the microphone and said, "Ladies and gentlemen, we have in the audience—"

I was thinking, "Uh-oh. Here it comes," because here we were, right on their turf. The clave can be like a sacrament in church to some people; to them, "Latin" can only be the music of people like Machito, Mario Bauzá, and Tito Puente. But what Ray said was:

"—some people who have taken our music to another level, to all four corners of the world, and their music represents us very well—Santana!"

You can take all the awards and accolades in places like Rolling Stone and The New York Times that we started getting—you can keep all that stuff. When Ray Barretto said something complimentary like that, there was nothing better. We had gotten props from one of the masters.

This is my thing: clave should be honored and understood and respected for what it is, but the traditional definition of clave is not all there is. When I hear Buddy Rich or Tony Williams play Afro-Cuban or Latin music, I don't think they're honoring it less than Tito Puente or Mongo Santamaría does, even though Buddy and Tony don't play strict clave—and that's their choice. But if you look at the clave as something that doesn't change, then it becomes like a ball and chain. It might be a golden one, it might be studded with diamonds, but with that attitude you're locked into one way of doing it.

Santana was never a purebred when it came to music—we were always a mutt. We were using some of the clave but not the complete conception, and we were using other ideas from Latin music. It took almost ten years for that stuff to go away about Santana not doing the clave right. When it did, it wasn't because things changed with our music. It was how people heard it that changed. We still have congas and timbales, and Santana still does not play clave in a strict sense. We play Santana.

n 1967, the world heard about San Francisco. We already knew it, but Monterey Pop had been huge—it helped Hendrix go worldwide, it got Janis Joplin and Big Brother signed to a record contract, and it put the spotlight on San Francisco. A year later it was like the whole world was visiting the city or even moving there. Bill Graham moved his concerts to the Fillmore West so more people could come. New clubs were opening up around town. Record companies were sending people to hang around and check out bands and sign them up. We didn't see them, but we knew they were there.

The summer of '68 was when everything started to roll for us. That was when we started calling ourselves just one word: Santana. You can see it on the posters from that summer. Bill was the guy who got down and lit the fuse for us. Everything that came after that happened in some way because of him: our record deal, our first time in a studio, our first trip to the East Coast. Playing Woodstock. And it all happened very, very fast, beginning with Bill bringing us back to play for him—playing the Fillmore West the first month it opened.

Bill put us on the bill with the Butterfield Blues Band—Michael Bloomfield wasn't in the band anymore. The week went great—the music felt good, but most of all it was a relief to be back in Bill Graham's embrace. He was such an important person in San Francisco to have on your side. I was gun-shy from our last experience with him, but I know he noticed that I was with a new band and that our music was more conscious, that we had our own sound going on. His ears could hear where we were coming from. Later he'd say we were the perfect child of two parents—B. B. King and Tito Puente.

Bill forgot to mention some of our other musical ancestors, but that was okay. Overnight Santana went from being the band that showed up late to the band that was on call. He was constantly calling us—"Hey, I need you guys to play tomorrow night, man. This band got busted!" Or "This freaking group canceled." We weren't headliners yet, but our name was on the poster next to national names like Steppenwolf, the Staple Singers, and Chicago—on the bottom, anyway. We got a reputation opening for every band that came through, and we put it to many of them. I think they could feel how good we were, that they should look out for us. We were capturing the headliners' fans—they were getting on our train. I think it was somebody in the Grateful Dead who said, "It's suicide if Santana opens for you. They'll steal the show."

It was great for Bill, too, because we weren't getting paid nearly as much as other bands, and we were local. No hotel rooms or transportation costs. The trade-off was that we were getting a lot of exposure. Bill actually said that out loud a few times to remind us.

At first Bill was rooting for us, not really managing us. It was more like he was a coach. He was like that with many bands—he'd do things no other promoters would even think of doing. He had that habit of carrying his clipboard and taking notes. You know that guy in the movie *The Red Shoes*—the impresario who pushed the ballerina to dance beyond limits she didn't think she could get past? Bill was like that. During a concert he would walk around backstage, onstage, all over the venue, writing things down on that clipboard. You could be working in the box office or you could be the star of the show. Bill took notes on everything and everybody. If a song went on too long, if something was set up in the wrong place—if he felt something was wrong, even if it was just okay but it could be better—out came the clipboard, and down went another note.

Then he would pull you aside at the end of the night and let you know what he wrote: "Listen, Carlos—that one song is no good: nobody's going to understand it." Or: "You could have started with this, and that one's great, but it went on too long," or, "It should have been longer." Stuff like that. That was Bill—he did that with Jimi Hendrix, and I know he took notes on Barbra Streisand and tried to do it with Bob Dylan as well. I don't think he did it to Miles.

I remember in 1985 I flew with Bill to a show he was producing with Sting in Los Angeles. Sting had a really special band—Omar Hakim from Weather Report, David Sancious on keyboards, Darryl

Jones from Miles's group on bass, and Branford Marsalis on saxo-phones. I had to hear the show for myself.

I was hanging with Sting in his dressing room after the concert when Bill came in. He was shuffling his notes. "What, Bill?" Sting saw the number of pages in his hand and rolled his eyes. "Can we do this some other time?" There was a plane waiting for us, too— Bill and I had to get back to San Francisco that night, and time was running out. But Bill stood there like a statue. "We should go over this now."

I remember Sting looked over to his manager, Miles Copeland, for help. But Miles kept smoking his cigarette and walked away like he hadn't heard anything. He didn't want to come between them. I saw that I should leave, too, so Sting and Bill could talk.

"Okay, Bill," Sting said. "But only one thing. Let's have it."

"Just one thing?" Bill looked at the clipboard. "Great—one thing. But there's parts A, B, C, D, and E…" I closed the door behind me.

Bill adopted us. He gave us space to rehearse in a warehouse where he kept all his old posters, near the original Fillmore. He gave us advice on getting an accountant and a lawyer and how to think about the band like it was a business. This was before we even saw a record contract. Bill made sure he put us in the spotlight when he could.

We were still playing all over the Bay Area and in halls like the Avalon and the Sound Factory in Sacramento. We played colleges and a few high schools. We did lots of benefits for a radio station and an arts company and a protest against the war. There was some serious political stuff going on. In one year the feeling in San Fran-cisco went from flower-power vibes to serious consciousness and revolution and "Who are they to judge us because our hair is long?" and we were right in the middle of it, and across San Francisco Bay the Black Panthers were raising their fists in power salutes and marching in their black berets.

We were living in the middle of the hippie revolution, but we were different. Our attitude was that even though we loved the principles of the hippies, we didn't wear flowers in our hair or put psychedelic flowers on our bathtubs. We were more hardass, more street. It wasn't a put-on or marketing gimmick. This was when we had those first photos made of the band—Marcus wore a jacket and a turtleneck and sometimes a sombrero, like a mariachi. That was not my idea. I wore a leather jacket, and all of us had really long hair or Afros. We looked very scruffy—except for Marcus—and very different from each other. That's who we were, and those were the people we hung around with.

It was the band 24-7, man. I had really been away from my family for a while—again. Almost another whole year and hardly any contact. My sister Maria remembers our mom asking Tony to look for me. Tony would find me and tell her, "He's fine; he's perfectly fine." Maria told me that one time my mom made her call the police to report me missing. When she told them I was eighteen, they hung up. "What do you mean they can't do anything? He's my son!" My mom was upset. She didn't really know what the rules were— but that wouldn't stop her.

I had seen my mom just once after leaving our place on Market. When I went to say good-bye she gave me a hug, and I could feel her hand going inside my pocket. She gave me a twenty-dollar bill. "Mom, I can't take this money from you."

"*Por qué no?* Why not? You need it to eat—who knows if you're eating in that place you're living?"

I said, "Because when you give me something somehow it has strings attached. I'm okay. I like the life that I'm living now. I love living where I live."

In fact, I was moving. I had met Linda Smith. She was one of the ladies who used to come hear us at the Matrix—she and her friends were listening to our music and looking for companions. We started hanging out, and the next thing I knew I was living with her and her two kids. She was white and from Oceanview. I was almost twenty-one at the time, and she was almost thirty, and she had a beautiful body and beautiful legs. She taught me many things. She also graciously took care of me. She offered me not only her body and her heart but also her support. She fed me and sometimes the whole band because we were so poor. There were some weeks when we were living off her food stamps.

Linda and I were together off and on for almost four years. I got to know her, her kids, and her family well. I wrote "Europa" for her sister when she was having a bad LSD trip—I started singing: "The Mushroom Lady is coming to town / And she's wondering will you be around." That was how it happened—the melody of "Europa" came from a lyric I made up on the spot to help calm Linda's sister.

Around this time my sister Irma was on a bus going to work and she saw SANTANA on the marquee at the Fillmore West. She told my mom, and next thing Irma knew my mom was telling the family to get ready to go out. "We're going to see Carlos play."

The rest of this story is now a family legend: my mom and dad got dressed up like it was the 1950s—Mom in her dress and nylons and heels and a nice coat, Dad in his tie and sport coat and hat. They all came to the Fillmore, and of course there were no seats— there was no place to sit but on the floor, so they all sat down. My mom saw hippies passing around what she thought was a cigarette, and she said to my dad, "*Viejo*, my God, they're so poor, they don't have any money. Let's give them a cigarette." So he opened his box of Marlboros and handed them out—they were all laughing.

I had no idea they were there until after the concert. I went out to meet them, and they were all excited. Maria says now that she liked the music, but she was thinking I was really shy because I never looked at the audience—I played to the amplifiers. Her friends who saw the band used to ask her why that was. I think it was because I was focused on the music, looking at Gregg and Doc and David—not David's foot, of course. But it was also true that I was shy—I wasn't all the way comfortable in front of an audience yet.

When I came out after the show to say hi, the first thing my mom said was, "Oh, *mijo*, the songs are too long. You have to cut

them down." I said, "Well, these are our songs—that's how long
they are." I told her I thought we could write our own songs and get
paid playing our stuff, not somebody else's songs all the time. My
mom thought I had been smoking too much weed, and she said so.
My dad didn't say much. He was happy to see me, but I'm sure he
agreed with my mom about the music. A few years later he was
interviewed by a local paper, and he told them that he was confused
because he didn't know when a song began or finished. His songs
were in the old forms—thirty-two bars or whatever.

My mom was right—our jams were long. There are some
recordings of Santana at this time that came out on a CD in 1997—
Live at the Fillmore 1968. The shortest track is almost six minutes,
and the longest is more than half an hour! We really got into that
music, and we didn't want to be interrupted. We didn't want to put
it into sound bites, like the ones you'd hear on some TV interview.
A sound bite is not memorable in the way we wanted to be.

These were not just jams: we played some jazz, including a
Chico Hamilton tune, and Willie Bobo's "Fried Neckbones"—we
never recorded that one, but sometimes even today somebody will
request it. We also played funky grooves: we were all listening to
James Brown at that time—all the bands in San Francisco were.
There was that mix of funk and Latin—what they called boogaloo.
Our brand was a psychedelic boogaloo. We definitely had enough
energy to get something across, even back then.

I like my guitar playing on these recordings because I hear
myself really getting the guitar sound right. I had been teaching
myself for a long time. The process felt like what the diamond cut-
ters who work in that one little section of New York City do—they
have a few apprentices learning how to cut the rock so it doesn't
break. Same thing with guitar—you have to learn how to bend the
note—get what you need from it—but not to the point that it goes
twang, twang, twang and loses its bite. A note has an aura, which
comes from harmonics and overtones, and *that's* where your guitar
personality comes from. Every guitar player's harmonics and overtones are different.

At the end of '68, you could *hear* my personality. A few years later Miles would tell me that he liked the way our songs sounded live more than the way they sounded on our albums—he liked the way we stretched out and the way I took my time, playing the notes in slo-mo, "endearing and with clarity." Those were his words.

One person who agreed with my parents about the length of our songs was Bill Graham. He could see we were ready for a step forward in our music and that record companies were getting interested. Bill knew they would need songs. At that time, Santana didn't know songs—we only knew jams.

Bill called us into his office. He was direct, as he always was. "You need to stop messing around with these long-ass jams and other stuff. You need to put a song in there. I'm going to play this song..." He put on a Verve record—I remember the label as it spun around. "Listen to that: that's an intro. And hear that? That's a verse."

Never mind that most of us knew all this. But the song Bill was playing for us? "Evil Ways"—written by Sonny Henry and played by Willie Bobo and his group. What a gift, right? Bill knew what he was doing. Later he told me, "I told Willie that you're going to kick ass with his song."

By thinking about our needing a song to get on the radio, Bill was preparing us for Clive Davis, who was the head of CBS—the record company we would sign with. How did Bill know? That was what he did—he knew things before they happened.

By the end of '68, Santana's name was at the top of the posters. Stan was doing business out of Bill's office, booking us, and we were all making decisions together—what gigs to do and what to do with the money. We were a collective, and we were ready for a record deal. Stan and Bill had been going around with Elektra, Atlantic, Warner Bros., CBS, and all the other labels for a while. At one point that year, Bill told us, "I want you guys to audition." We said, "What? We thought we were through with auditioning."

"You're not auditioning for me—this is for Atlantic Records.

They're coming over in the afternoon. Just set up and play for them."

I heard stories that Atlantic had not done right by some of the older R & B guys who used to be on the label. It was just a feeling, but I didn't want to be with them. At the audition I played the worst I ever played on purpose, and the Atlantic dude just walked out. The guys in the band went, "Man, what are you doing?" I said, "Man, fuck them. I don't want to be with Atlantic, man." They were pissed.

It didn't matter. We kept playing, opening for everybody: the Grateful Dead, the Youngbloods, Taj Mahal, and Ry Cooder. We kept hearing that the scouts were chasing us. One day, a guy with CBS came up to us after a show—real excited. He told us, "Man, the buzz about you guys is at a fever pitch." I remember he said he saw us four times. Then he said, "Your set list doesn't matter!" He meant it as a compliment, but we were like, "What?"

"Yeah—you could tear your set list apart, throw it on the floor, start with any song, and end with any song. I see what you guys do to the people. You take the crowd with you."

I was already fixated on Columbia, which was part of CBS. I didn't want to hear about Atlantic; I didn't want to hear about Capitol. I wanted to be where Bob Dylan and Miles Davis were. That winter in a music store I saw a poster that CBS had made for the holidays—something about Christmas caroling. The poster had cartoon faces on it: Simon and Garfunkel, Dylan, and Miles. Johnny Cash; Blood, Sweat & Tears; Johnny Mathis; Barbra Streisand. That poster convinced me more than the guy who came backstage. I wanted Santana to be on that poster.

I heard about Clive Davis at Columbia back then—he had been one of the only big record company presidents to come out to San Francisco. He went to the Monterey Pop festival, heard Big Brother, signed them, and persuaded his superiors to invest in the San Francisco sound. He started signing a lot of bands after that, which I heard pissed off some other musicians who were with Columbia because they thought these rock groups were hurting their brand. But that was not true for us. Clive Davis was unknown to me until Santana started having hits. That's when I met him and saw what he could do.

My own connection with Columbia actually started before Santana did anything with the label. That September, Michael Bloomfield and Al Kooper were booked to record a live album at the Fillmore West. It was Bill who invited me to play—"Michael's not in condition to play tonight. He's been up all night. Can you do me a favor and substitute for him?" I was like, "Are you kidding? Sure."

I think Michael was starting to show the inconsistencies that come from being a heroin user. I think he had trouble disciplining himself and keeping a schedule and getting enough sleep. That's why he only plays on one half of *The Live Adventures of Mike Bloomfield and Al Kooper*—and why I got to play on "Sonny Boy Williamson," a song by Jack Bruce, the bass player from Cream. It was the first time my name was on an album—right on the back cover. That felt great, but it was strange because I didn't get to play with Michael.

There's a photo I like of Michael and me together, onstage at the Fillmore West in 1971—a rehearsal for the closing night. We're both really into it, looking really good. Man, he looks strong. You know what I did that night, *again*? I said how sorry I was for challenging him that one time and being an asshole. He looked at me as if to tell me I'd better get over myself. "You need to stop apologizing for that. I love you and I told you, *it's cool.*"

Michael never stopped being gracious to me. I tried to stay in touch in the years after Santana got really big, but I think he was into having his own space. He was living in San Francisco, and he died there in 1981. The last time I went to his house, I thought it was unkempt and kind of crazy—I left there feeling concerned and more than a little discouraged. Whatever arrangement he made for himself was the wrong arrangement. They found him OD'd inside a car. That just tells you what kind of lifestyle he was leading—or not leading.

Michael was the first guitar player from my generation whom we all heard. Everybody else came after, including the gods, such as Clapton and Hendrix. And Michael wasn't worried by the other guitar players who came along. He welcomed everybody, as he did with me. But as beautiful as he was I don't think he had the inner strength to see his validity in that picture. I think he shunned the publicity and felt he had to pay his dues, even when he had done that already.

At the end of 1968 there were a lot of great electric guitar players in the room—a lot of chances to get discouraged and put your guitar down. But that kind of reaction is the ego talking. Whether your reaction is to stick out your chest or to run and hide— superiority or instant inferiority—either one is full of shit.

You're supposed to be you. When I saw Jimi Hendrix and Eric Clapton play, they didn't make me want to quit—they made me want to listen harder to something that they weren't listening to. I had this idea that I had to see myself in the whole picture of the time, not just in comparison to one or two others. I knew a lot of us were listening to the same blues people. So I told myself, "Maybe Hendrix doesn't know about Gábor Szabó or Bola Sete." The competition wasn't about how you played guitar, it was: "Yeah? Who you got in *your* record collection?"

I call them the Igniters: they're the musicians who make you feel that if you spend more time in your own heart you'll see that the same thing that was given to them was given to you—but you have to develop it for yourself. I'll tell you something—if Jimi Hendrix and Bob Marley were alive and they came to see my band on a good night, they'd be like, "Damn!"

Maybe some of this was me overcompensating and being a punk about it, but I thought that instead of trying to be as loud as this one or as fast as that one, I could beat him in another way, like maybe go low when he goes high or go slow if he goes fast. By then, in 1968, people who heard me play realized that I was bringing something different, not just copying Buddy Guy and B. B. King.

Santana signed with Columbia in October of 1968, and our contract took effect in December. The first person we met was David Rubinson—at that time he was Columbia's staff producer on the West Coast. He produced Mongo Santamaría and Moby Grape and Taj Mahal for CBS, so he had experience with congas. He later started two record labels with Bill Graham. He was going to be our producer, and the nearest CBS studios were in Los Angeles. That's where we got ready to go to in February of 1969.

A few days before we left, Stan said he had to tell me something. Marcus was in jail—for murder. Just like that. He had met this Mexican lady who had split from her husband, but they hadn't divorced yet. The man came home when Marcus was there, and they got into a fight. They said he ended up stabbing the Mexican guy, who later died. It might have been self-defense, but Marcus was in big trouble, and he wasn't going anywhere except lockup. We were hurt and disappointed but not really surprised. There was a side of Marcus that was about being hard and street, so his pride could put him in the wrong place at the wrong time.

I don't think Marcus's being a street guy helped him any—he eventually wound up in San Quentin. Later, when he got out, I think he began working in clothing design somewhere in North Beach.

We had to think fast—Carabello had stopped playing with the band, but he was still hanging out with us. He knew all the songs and the parts, so the decision was easy. In early February we went down to LA and moved into a big house in Hollywood that the record company rented for us for a week and a half. It was only a few blocks from the studio. I remember we all thought it looked phony and plastic compared to San Francisco. The house felt like it was the record company's, as did the studio—they just couldn't get a good sound on us. Some of the instruments sounded so thin and different from what we'd been used to. We couldn't find the energy that was in all our shows. It didn't feel like our music. Santana was different from the other groups CBS had going on—we were a street mutt. We needed a different kind of intention and independence.

A lot of it is how someone walks into a room. If a producer starts a session wearing his credentials and an attitude that the band is making an album for him, that's not going to work. We just didn't feel any authenticity with Rubinson that time. Santana recorded with him later, in '76, when we did the *Festival* album, and that was much better—I think all of us knew a lot more by that time.

It wasn't all Rubinson's fault—I think we didn't know what to expect. We didn't have to apologize for what we didn't know, and we let ourselves be led in the studio instead of taking the reins ourselves. We should have said, "No; we don't want the guitar or the drums to sound like that." Or, "That's not the right tempo or the right groove." I don't think we knew what to do with ourselves until after we did that first session. The album was going to be called *Freeway Jam,* after the tune we used to end our shows with, but this was nothing we wanted to come out, and CBS felt the same way. Now it seems impossible, but somehow we persuaded the record company to let us go back into the studio and not impose a producer on us.

We finally agreed in 2004 to let that music be released for historical purposes. Also, by that time I don't think we had any more reservations about it. But back then we thought it was like being a man from the jungle who sees himself in a mirror for the first time and just doesn't like what he sees.

We went back to San Francisco—back to the house on Mullen Avenue. Gregg had his room, I had mine when I wasn't at Linda's, and Carabello had his loft in the attic, where the floor was basically plywood over two-by-fours, and he played his music *loud.* I used to hope that everyone on our street liked Jimi Hendrix, because you could hear the speakers moving air. At four in the morning.

That was one old house — one night we locked ourselves out, so Carabello climbed in through the attic. It was dark and he was running and he went right through the floor. Gregg and I got into the house anyway, heard the crash, and found him in this cloud of dust and plaster and everything. He was okay, but man, we couldn't stop laughing.

Crazy things like that were always happening to Carabello. He was just that kind of guy — as I said, he was the goofball in the band, but he had a charisma that you could not resist. He kept the rest of us loose, especially during tense times. He would talk to anyone, and he knew *everybody*. He had his finger on the pulse. He used to hang with Sly, he was friends with Jimi, and he got to know Miles before I did. He even got tight with the women we called the Cosmic Ladies — Betty Mabry, Devon Wilson, and Colette Mimram, all the ladies who hung around Jimi and Miles. In the '70s Carabello used to stay at Miles's town house in New York City. It was easy for him to meet people and make friends and hold on to them for a long time — the two of us are friends to this day. Carabello is my oldest friend from all the Santana lineups, from back when we didn't even have a name. I never will forget that he visited me and brought me all those things when I was stuck in the hospital with TB.

Carabello used to go to the beach and play there with whoever was hanging out. While we were waiting to find out what was happening with Marcus, Carabello met a guy who played percussion and was part of a group called the Aliens. Carabello went to a club called Nite Life, just off of San Bruno, where they were playing, and called us. At first we didn't want to be bothered. "Aw, Carabello — what are you talking about?" He wouldn't let go. "There's this guy I met today at the beach, and he'll blow your mind. I think we need to add him to the band." Gregg and I came down — our place was just up the street — and man, we couldn't believe it.

The guy, José Areas, played congas on one tune, then timbales on another — then soloed on trumpet, too! He was incredible — he sounded as good as anyone on any record we had been listening to.

His rhythm was so strong and firm, like the steel beams of a huge building before they start putting the floors in. It felt like his playing could support *anything*. He was from Nicaragua and kind of small, and they called him Chepito. He looked like he just came into town—straight clothes and hair, and he didn't speak a word of English. I spoke to him in Spanish and asked him to come jam with us the next day.

Chepito fit right in. Gregg and I felt it right away. I think it took a little longer for David, but we all realized how much he added to the music—a precision, a stability without being stifling. In just a few rehearsals, Chepito knew all our music, and it felt like no matter how good the rest of us were, the wheels would fall off without Chepito. His right hand on the cowbell was like Tony Williams's hi-hat—pure and steady. He was serious, too, not gentle at all; if you suddenly had a "To be or not to be" moment with the music, he'd give you a look like, "Get it together!"

Carabello was really happy, of course, to have Chepito helping with the rhythm—he had been complaining for a while about Doc Livingston, that he couldn't get a lock together with him and get a good groove going. Doc had been part of the problem in Los Angeles—he isolated himself from the band and didn't want to talk about songs or band business or anything. He was being a lone wolf and a bit of a rebel when we needed someone to get into the huddle more than ever before. We had an album to do: we needed someone who was going to bring all his spirit and contribute.

By the time Santana went back to the studio in May for a second try, Chepito was part of the band. CBS said we didn't have to use their producer, but we had to have somebody producing, so we asked around and kept hearing about Brent Dangerfield. We had worked with him at the Straight Theater, where he had been the soundman. He had never worked in a studio before, but he had a reputation around Haight-Ashbury for being able to "get around a knob." We needed someone we could feel good with and who came from our scene.

We also needed someone to help us in the studio, to help us

arrange our jams into songs, and that was Alberto Gianquinto, a friend of David's who lived with him and played keyboards with James Cotton when he came into the city. He was an older, very stout, no-nonsense gutbucket kind of piano player who had grown up in the Mission, and he could handle blues as well as jazz and classical. Although you wouldn't know it from his name, he was a white dude—but with a black militant attitude. I remember he had a big poster of Huey P. Newton in his home, and his wife was black, from the Caribbean. He was a very assertive guy—he had to be to go up to Chicago and play with those blues bands and not get his ass whipped. We needed that in the studio.

I had gotten to know Alberto from playing around town, and I think it was Stan who came up with the idea of using him. His contribution to the Santana sound was enormous—he became our producer behind the scenes on our first three albums. We lost touch after that, and he ended up another drug casualty after having battled an addiction for many years. I heard he passed away in an accident in 1986.

We decided to use Pacific Recording Studio—a new facility in San Mateo that also had rehearsal space. The Grateful Dead had been there, and some jazz groups, too. We had definitely learned a lot from our experience in LA, like getting right into it and not wasting time, which was good because once we were in the studio we would only have a week to make the album. We went in and started rehearsing some new tunes, but nothing was coming together at first. This was when we decided to let Doc Livingston go—he kind of fired himself, really. Gregg asked him to leave, then we had a jazz drummer, Johnny Rae, with us for a few gigs—he played often with Cal Tjader and Gábor Szabó.

We weren't the only band getting it together in that building at that time—Vince Guaraldi was rehearsing there, too. At one point, he came over to our room and said, "I got to tell you, man, I was listening to your music, and I can tell the direction you guys are going—you guys are going to be big, man. Big." That was an amazing confirmation of what we felt. I used to see Guaraldi a lot because we played in a lot of the same benefits. I also saw him play at an outdoor show at Stern Grove with his trio, and Bola Sete and John Handy were on the bill, too. It was my first love-in, and everyone was smoking weed, but the music was amazing. It felt like Guaraldi stepping in and giving his approval helped turn things around.

Then it all seemed to come together. We figured out how to get the sound we wanted on each instrument. Day by day, each song sounded better. Gianquinto helped us eliminate wasted hours and figure out how to make the jams shorter—showing us how one section of a song went into the next and how to not lose the flow.

One day I saw Michael Shrieve come into Pacific looking to get some studio time for his band. He was a drummer I knew who hung with some of the guys in Jefferson Airplane, so I invited him to jam with us. We played "Fried Neckbones" together, and then he played on a tune we were putting together called "Waiting," which became the opening tune on our first album. Shrieve was really open to what we were doing and was flexible—he didn't use the same pattern every time, and we could tell him what we were looking for. We kept playing into the night. He had a looser, more jazzy feeling than most rock drummers—a kind of hummingbird energy, like bubbles bubbling. It was a little like Mitch Mitchell's playing with Jimi Hendrix, but more on top of the rhythm.

We felt a chemistry right off the bat. We asked Michael to join the band almost immediately, and he said yes. He wanted to play and jump in with us and hang out. He was from the white area of Palo Alto but was not afraid to come to the Mission. It was like Gregg all over again. Carabello and I wanted to know what kind of house his family had, what kind of cars they drove, and I got the feeling he wanted to know what kind of places we were hanging out in and what food we were eating. He started coming to the house and looking through our records, and he said, "Man, I got to turn you on to Miles and Coltrane." He did just that soon afterward, and my life would change—again.

Santana had its first stable lineup together, the one the world would get to know from our first three albums—Gregg, David, Carabello, Michael, Chepito, me, and a few people we added later. It came together like it was waiting to happen, and the music felt like that, too. You can tell we all contributed by the fact that everyone in the band shares credit on almost all the tunes. Except for the two covers we did—"Evil Ways" and "Jingo"—there's only one song, "Shades of Time," that was written by just two of us. Marcus got his credit on "Soul Sacrifice."

If I had to choose one tune from that first album that still sticks out for me, it's "Treat," which was Santana doing its version of B. B. King meets Eddie Harris. To understand that, you have to know just how big Harris's tune "Listen Here" was in San Francisco, especially up and down Potrero Hill—everybody had that album and played it all the time. You couldn't escape that groove, and that's what inspired "Treat" in a big way. I'm very proud of that one.

It was during the sessions for our first album that the ideas came together for "Incident at Neshabur," which ended up on our second album, Abraxas. We wrote it bit by bit, pulling a little from here and there and putting it together with all its tempo changes. One part in the first section was inspired by a bad groove in a TV commercial for Ajax that showed a white knight blasting people clean—"stronger than dirt!" Alberto came up with a vamp for the second part, which was basically Horace Silver's "Señor Blues." He played piano on that, going between two chords, which set me up for a solo that sounded to me like the divinity that comes after sex, when you're just lying there after giving it all you got and you both arrive at the same time and she's happy and you're happy. "Incident" had to wait to come out—it was a little too long for the first album, so we kept it safe for the next one.

We recorded the first album in five days. It took a little longer to mix it—we didn't get everything right, and we didn't feel like it captured our sound perfectly yet—but it was close and was much better than the LA session. Some genius at Columbia decided that "Jingo" should be our first single, and we had no power back then, so we went along with that. When it didn't really go anywhere I think it was Clive Davis who stepped in and chose "Evil Ways," probably with some push from Bill—it was his choice all along. That's when everything took off—we had a hit single on the radio and a bestselling album.

I picked out the cover for the album—I wanted to use the poster for the show we played at the Fillmore West with the Grateful Dead and the Staple Singers, so the artist Lee Conklin designed it again, and it really worked. When our first album came out, my favorite thing on the cover was the line "Produced by Brent Dangerfield *and Santana*." We've worked with various producers over the years, but if you look at the albums we've done after that very first effort, you'll see that we have always produced ourselves.

CHAPTER 9

Santana at the Woodstock Music & Art Fair, Bethel, New York,
August 16, 1969.

*In 2013, when President Obama welcomed me as a Kennedy Center
honoree along with Herbie Hancock, Billy Joel, Shirley MacLaine, and
Martina Arroyo, what was the first thing he said when my turn came?
Something about my being twenty-two and playing in an altered state
of mind at Woodstock—not the usual stuff people talk about at the
White House. Everyone laughed, and so did I. Obama's not alone—to
most people that's the Santana moment. People still see it in the movie
about Woodstock—Santana playing "Soul Sacrifice"—and writers
still ask about it. Yes, I was tripping, and yes, the guitar felt like a snake
in my hands. No, I still can't remember much about it, but I'll tell you
everything I do remember and what I think about it today.*

*I'll also tell you this: having the president talk about you is a true
opportunity to accept with nobility and humility the greatness of your
own life. At the same time, it's a rare moment when you can see that,
with humility, you must accept that you do not control your own life—
that you are not separate but connected to a bigger whole. At Wood-*

stock, I think Santana played a great show, but I do not think Santana was responsible for all that happened afterward. That's like a cork floating on top of a wave in the middle of the sea, bobbing up and down and telling itself it's controlling the entire ocean—that's an ego out of control.

There were a lot of things that nobody planned at Woodstock but that made it work for us. If we hadn't stayed in the town of Woodstock for the week before the festival, we probably would have gotten stuck in traffic and showed up late or not made it at all. And if some groups hadn't been late getting up there, we wouldn't have gone on early in the day and we could have gotten caught in the rain later that day and had our show messed up or even been electrocuted or forced to quit. And if any of that happened, maybe "Soul Sacrifice" would not have made it into the Woodstock movie and nobody would have seen us.

There were a lot of angels stepping in and making a way for us—the more time goes by, the more I can say that with clarity and confidence. I'll say it again: the one angel who deserves the most credit is Bill Graham. He got us the gig when nobody had heard of us. We had just finished our first album, but it hadn't been released. When Michael Lang, who was producing the festival, asked Bill for his help, Bill told him, "Okay, this is a big endeavor. I'll help you with my connections and my people. They know how to do this. But you need to do something for me—you need to let Santana play."

"Okay, but what's Santana?"

"You'll see."

Most people cannot think of Santana without thinking of Woodstock at the same time. I don't mind being linked to it—in fact I'm really, really grateful. But people need to know that Woodstock had everything stacked up against it—and that against all odds three days of peace and love and music prevailed.

Bill called a meeting for everyone in the band. It was sometime in July of 1969. He was living in Mill Valley then, the white side of the Bay Area, where the hoity-toity rich people were.

We all went over, looking at the houses—he had put together a nice outdoor buffet for us. We were all impressed. Then he sat down and told us why we were there. Usually he was always hurrying, but he took his time—he had a lot to say.

"Some groups are not doing so well right now—Hendrix is not selling; Jim Morrison's in trouble for exposing himself. I hear that Sly is doing too much coke." He gave us the full picture of what was happening in rock right then.

"I'm sending you guys to the East Coast, and when you come back everything will be different. First you'll go to Atlantic City and New York City, then Boston and Philadelphia, and finally a big festival in Texas—you'll play there with Sam and Dave, Led Zeppelin, and B. B. King. You'll go from playing small halls that hold fifteen hundred to two thousand people to festivals where there are fifteen thousand to thirty thousand people, then a huge festival in upstate New York where there will be maybe eighty or ninety thousand people. You'll do great.

"The festival in Woodstock is going to change everything for Santana. After that, people are going to recognize you everywhere, and it will totally fuck up your head. You're going to think you've always been famous. People are going to treat you like you're a god. The next thing you know you're going to need a shoehorn to walk into a room because your head's going to be so big." Bill was being direct. "Keep your feet on the ground—don't get swept up by all that."

We were like, "Oh, man, don't bring us down with that hippie shit. We're from the ghetto, we're real. We don't think like that."

Bill got serious. "Believe me: as true is true, it will happen."

Our first album was about to come out, and before we left California Columbia Records had one of their annual conventions in Los Angeles, and we went down there and played a special show for all the sales and marketing people and publicists and bigwigs like Clive Davis. I didn't get to meet Clive that time, or at least I don't remember meeting him then.

The point of the show was to get the record company people all excited about the label's bands and their new records—to get them to give us an extra push. It was there where we decided on an obvious name for the album — *Santana*. I always felt like a cat in a dog pound at those so-called industry events because of the way certain people would wear their suits and walk and "Hey, baby" you. People who'd take all the credit and the money from your music and tell you that without them you wouldn't be who you are. Clive was an exception to that rule, I later found out.

The night after we played the convention we were in New York City, playing the Fillmore East, the hall that Bill opened the year before so he could bring the San Francisco magic to the East Coast. We were back at the bottom of the bill — in fact we weren't even on the marquee, because it could only accommodate so many names and we were opening for Three Dog Night, Canned Heat, *and* Sha Na Na. That's a lot of letters. I remember Bill telling me that once he booked Rahsaan Roland Kirk there, and Rahsaan insisted that his name be on the marquee, so Bill built an extra wooden sign to hang from the bottom to accommodate him — and Rahsaan was blind!

We could feel immediately how different the crowds were from those in California — a different kind of energy, a little intimidating. New York City people don't come to you; you have to go to them. They're very astute, like sharks. They can tell if you're feeling out of place — they can smell fear. That first time we weren't anything but polite: "It's nice to be here, and we hope you like our music." Then we just played.

The other bands were looking at us like, "What is this kind of music?" and we were looking at them the same way. Three Dog Night had a smooth rock sound from Los Angeles with very radio-friendly songs. Sha Na Na was a kind of parody act of '50s doo-wop — they might as well have been a Broadway show. Canned Heat was closest to what we were doing, and you could hear they had that John Lee Hooker boogie in their music, and that was okay with me.

It was helpful to be in that kind of show so we could learn not to be afraid of competition or new audiences. Back then we were constantly monitoring ourselves to see how we fit into the music of the time—what do we like? And, just as important, what do we want to stay away from? Everybody in our band was really vigilant about not letting the band be talked into something we didn't want to be. It was fun playing with that kind of freshness—audiences still not knowing who we were, opening up for everybody, then grabbing the audience and pulling them our way. I really dug the reaction of the people to our sound back then.

Even though Bill had called it, we didn't *really* know that our first trip east was going to be our last chance to be that anonymous— that after the next few weeks we would never again be the new and unknown band coming into town. That was going to change forever, thanks to Bill, who really, really nurtured us meticulously. With that first tour he prepared us psychologically and physically for all that was going to happen.

Santana stayed in New York City for a while, playing a few shows after the Fillmore East gigs—a festival in Atlantic City, the World's Fair in Queens, and a gig in Central Park. We got to know the city on that first visit—we stayed in some hotel on 5th Avenue and walked around a lot. Bill turned us on to Ratner's, a kosher restaurant next to the Fillmore East. We took a cab up to Harlem and saw the Apollo Theater. It was August, and if you know New York City, it has its own smells in that heat, and you especially notice it if you're coming from California. It's different: the pizza joints and the sandwich shops and the garbage and the sewers—everything. It's all mixed up together.

It was amazing how fast things moved in New York. I remember walking down the street and seeing a taxicab that had been in an accident and was upside down. You could feel that energy pulsating with a kind of audacity and insanity. I would be telling myself, "You don't scare me. I've walked your streets and now I'm one of you and I smell like it." Once you claim New York you draw energy from it—it doesn't drain you and it doesn't scare you. The next time Santana came through was in November, and it was already feeling like home.

Then we played a college up in the Catskills and ended up in the town of Woodstock. Bill had rented a house for us, and that's where we stayed almost a whole week before the festival. There wasn't that much to do—so we all found people to hang out with. I remember Chepito complaining—he was sharing a room with David, who was meeting chicks and bringing them back to the house. "I'm like a mouse smelling the cheese," Chepito said. "But he's not sharing."

There were other people hanging around up there—Bob Dylan lived near there, and Jimi Hendrix had rented a house, too, but I never saw any of them. I was really shy about hanging out because those kinds of guys didn't know me then. It made me feel like a fly in the soup, and I didn't want to be a groupie for anybody—I don't want to show up unless I'm invited personally. So I said, "No, I don't think I want to go and just hang."

We saw Bill around once a day, but he was mostly on the phone, and we could tell there was a buzz going around about the festival. It was going to be big—*really* big. Some people were getting scared—people who lived around there—because many of the hippies who were coming got there early and started camping out. I remember a rumor that Governor Rockefeller was thinking of sending the National Guard in to make sure it was safe or even shutting down the festival altogether. The newspapers started talking about it like it was a disaster waiting to happen. It wasn't a disaster for us. The disaster would have been if Rockefeller had taken over and turned it into a fire drill with the police regimenting it.

Then Friday came, and we heard it was an incredible mess—people stuck in traffic on the highway, abandoning their cars, technical problems with the sound. There was no way we could go and see for ourselves. We were scheduled to play the next day and were told we'd have to be ready early to be sure we could get there on time. So we got up at five on Saturday morning, waited, and finally piled into some vans and drove to a place where there were green helicopters that looked like the kind the army used in Vietnam—they were flying people in and out. Next thing we knew we lifted off, and a few minutes later we were swooping over a field, looking down in the morning light at a carpet made of people—flesh and hair and teeth—stretched out across the hills. That's when it dawned on me how big this whole thing really was. Even with the noise of the helicopter we could feel the people when they started cheering after somebody had finished a song or had said something they liked—a huge roar came up from below.

I remember turning to Gregg and saying, as a joke, "Nice crowd!" I also remember thinking about something my dad taught me—if you're a real musician, it really doesn't matter where you are or the number of people in front of you. You could be playing Woodstock or Caesars Palace or an alley in Tijuana or at home. When you play, play from the heart, and take everybody with you.

My father's relationship with music was on a purer level than mine is. Yes, there was the money side—he did it to provide for us, but he wasn't distracted by volume. Volume is when you collect a royalty check that's so big you think somebody made a mistake. My father made a certain amount, and that's what he knew. He never heard of Carnegie Hall, so he did not factor that into the equation. Any place where he could play and where people were receptive, that was fine with him.

Woodstock was all about volume. First we were above all those people, then we landed and were in it. Right away you could smell what New York State smells like in the summer—very humid and funky, plus five hundred thousand sweaty bodies and all that pot. They dropped us off behind a big wooden stage that looked like workers had just finished building it that day—and from the look of things they still had more to do. They showed us where to put our stuff and where to wait, and I started looking around for someone I knew, and I saw Jerry Garcia having a good time and laughing. He came up to me and said, "So what do you think of this? We've been here a long time already—what time are you supposed to go on?" I had been told that we'd be going on three bands after the Dead, so that's what I told Jerry. He said, "Man, we're not going on until later tonight." That meant we were going to be there all day and into the night. So I thought, "I might as well get comfortable." It was just after noon, and the first band of the day was on.

Then Jerry held his hand out. "Do you want it?"

"Want what—what you got?" It was mescaline. That's how casual it was in those days—I took it right away. I was thinking, "I'll have time to enjoy this, come back down, drink a lot of water, get past the amoeba state, and be ready to play by tonight. No problem." Right.

Things were definitely more messed up at Woodstock than we had thought. Because of all the traffic a lot of bands were having trouble getting to the festival, so the organizers had to ask the bands that were there to play or there would be big gaps in the flow of music. Of course I didn't know this then. I remember hearing Country Joe and the Fish onstage when things were just starting to get elastic and stretch out. Then suddenly someone came up to us to tell us that if we wanted to play, we had to get on stage *now*. It wasn't Bill—I didn't even see him around. We didn't argue—we just grabbed our instruments and headed to the stage.

It was definitely the wrong time for me. I was just taking the first steps on the first stage of that psychedelic journey, when things start to melt when you look at them. I had played high and tripping before, so I had the confidence to go for it and put on the guitar and plug it in, but I remember thinking this was not going to be representative of what I can do. When a trip starts happening, all of a sudden you're traveling at warp speed, and the tiniest things become cosmically huge. The opposite happens, too, so everything is suddenly the same size. It's like that scene in Kubrick's movie 2001 when the astronaut is traveling beyond Jupiter with all the lights whizzing by—it felt like I was almost at the stage of giving birth to myself again, and we were just starting the set.

When we got onstage we saw that they had set us up really close to each other, which was great because that's what they normally did back home, and the roadie guys had come through. I think that was the best thing that happened to us that day: we could really see and feel each other and not get lost. Then someone announced us, and we could see the huge crowd in front of us — our album was just about to come out the following week, and "Jingo" wasn't being played yet on the radio, so unless people in the audience were from the Bay Area or worked for Columbia Records, there was no way they had heard about us. It's one thing to play to a crowd that big, and it's another thing to be totally unknown doing that. But I had other things to think about.

The rest of the show is a blur — *really* a blur. We started with "Waiting," the first tune from our album, and that was like our sound check. I was tripping, and I remember saying inwardly, "God — all I ask is that you keep me in time and in tune." I kept myself locked on the usual things that helped me stay tight with the band — bass, hi-hat, snare drum, and bass drum. I was telling myself, "Don't think about the guitar. Just watch it." It turned into an electric snake, twisting and turning, which meant the strings would go loose if it didn't stay straight. I kept willing the snake not to move and praying that it stayed in tune.

Later I saw myself in photos and in the Woodstock movie. All those faces I was making while I was playing reminded me that I was trying to get that snake to hold still. Then I saw the guitar I was playing — a red Gibson SG with P-80 pickups — and it all made sense. I always had trouble keeping that guitar in tune, and even though I needed a new one, the band had voted collectively not to spend the money. That's how Santana still was then — a collective. It was that way until at least the middle of 1971. Not long after the festival I got so frustrated with that guitar in a rehearsal that I ended up throwing it against a wall and breaking it, which forced the band to get me a new one.

We only played forty-five minutes at Woodstock, but it felt twice as long. Each note I played felt like it started as a blood cell moving inside a vein and pumping through my body. I had the sense of everything slowing down — I could feel the music coming up inside me and out through my fingers — I could watch myself pick a note on the guitar and feel the vibration go into the pickup, through the wiring inside the guitar, down the guitar cord to the amplifier, out the amp speaker into the microphone, through the cable into the big speakers on the side of the stage, out into the crowd, and all the way up the hill, until it bounced and we could hear the echo coming back to the stage.

Later I thought about the tunes we played at Woodstock, and I realized I had forgotten everything about the first half of our set. I did remember the last few songs, including "Jingo" and "Persuasion," and I remembered that we did "Fried Neckbones" as an encore. And of course "Soul Sacrifice," which ended up in the movie. I remember hearing the crowd yelling and clapping, then I remember going off the stage and turning back to see Gregg behind me. He had a look of victory on his face, like, "Yeah! We *did* it." Then Bill Graham caught his eye and gestured him to turn back around, like he was saying, "Not so fast—look at the crowd. Savor this moment." Gregg turned around, and his face was like a little kid's—just amazed. I turned and did the same thing. I think Bill was probably more proud of us than we were, because we were all just a little shell-shocked.

It's funny when I think about it. With everything else that was happening then, all the people and noise and getting hustled on and off, my last thought before leaving the stage was, "I'll never trip again—not for a gig this important!"

For me the best thing about being connected to Woodstock is that most of us are still around to talk about it—Gregg, Carabello, Shrieve, Chepito, and I. We're alive and vibrant. Most of all, we still stand for the same things that Woodstock represented—consciousness revolution coated with peace and love and music. The audience was filled with people who had a deep, emotional investment in making change happen. It wasn't just people wanting to smoke a joint and get laid—although many did both—and it wasn't about wanting to sell T-shirts or plastic flowers.

The original Woodstock wasn't about selling anything. It wasn't regimented or organized enough for that to happen. In fact that's the beauty of it, and that's why people are still talking about it. It came together naturally and was about using music and peace to show the system that there were a lot of freaks out there who wanted their voices heard. They wanted the freedom to be who they were, and they wanted the war to stop: "Hell, no, we won't go." We were saying that the war wasn't over there, in Vietnam. It was right here at home, between the government and the hippies at Woodstock—between the system and the people who have no voice. In '69, we had a generation with an agenda, and the groups that played Woodstock helped get that agenda out into the world and gave the people a voice.

The one problem back then was that there was no middle ground—that was not good, either. Some people were saying if you weren't supporting everything America was doing, you were not being patriotic. Meanwhile a lot of hippies were making rules of their own and talking about the servicemen who were coming back home injured or without legs—calling them baby killers. Now it seems that we are back to that same thing—people judging people and making decisions without knowing enough—and there's still no middle ground.

The true hippies thought for themselves and helped bring about a change that we needed in America. There are not enough hippies right now, in my estimation. And besides, I don't care who you are—part of the system or a hippie—you have to learn to think differently from the crowd. Think for yourself and work for a better world. Don't do anything with violence, but do make an extreme change to your own mentality. Question authority if it's not divinely enlightened. Thomas Jefferson said it his own way—rebellion to tyrants is obedience to God. In that sense, both Jesus and Jefferson were downright hippies.

That's the real lesson of Woodstock. The first Woodstock came and went, and two other Woodstocks have happened since 1969, but there's only one of them that stays in our minds, and that's because of the peace, love, and joy. I remember when I was asked to play the twenty-fifth anniversary—I was touring Australia. I asked them to tell me who else was in. "Nine Inch Nails, Cypress Hill, Aerosmith, Guns N' Roses." I said, "Man, that's not Woodstock—that sounds like nothing but white guys. In '69, we had Joan Baez, we had Richie Havens and Sly. What happened to women, and where are the black people?" I believe those are the questions that Bill Graham would be asking if he had been there in '94. I told them if it was going to be a Woodstock you can't have just one color of the rainbow, you have to have them all. They heard me—they added black and female performers, and we played Woodstock again.

In '99 they tried it one more time, but the message was gone—no more peace and love. By then, for the experience to be true to the original Woodstock, they would have had to invite music from all over the world—Native Americans, African people, Chinese people—like the Olympics but without the competition. In '99, it was about just one kind of music and soft-drink sponsorships and the TV broadcast. It was about corporate stock, not Woodstock. I didn't play at that one—no way.

In 2010, we did a concert with Steve Winwood in Bethel, New York, just a few hundred yards away from the original Woodstock site. I had just proposed to my wife, Cindy, a few days before, and I was on such a high. I had a free afternoon, so I went to walk around what used to be Max Yasgur's farm—you can still go there and see the field where five hundred thousand people gathered. It was a very emotional experience for me. They now have a museum there—and there were some people visiting who had seen Santana play that afternoon. "We were here the first time—it's great to see you again," they said. It was so gratifying to go back there and hear that.

To tell the truth, I think a lot of my memories of what happened onstage at Woodstock have been shaped by seeing myself in the movie, which didn't come out until almost a year later. The first time I saw the movie was when Santana was back in New York City in 1970. I remember I liked the way the director showed all the stuff that was happening by dividing the screen into three parts, but I hated that wide-angle lens he used that made me look like a bug.

Devon Wilson, Jimi Hendrix's girlfriend, took me to see the movie the first time. She told me that when she had seen the movie with Jimi, it had totally messed him up. "When the part with you guys came on, you should have seen his face. He couldn't stop talking about Santana."

"Really?"

"Yeah. Jimi really liked your performance, man. He loved the energy."

I had another conversation with Devon not long after Jimi's death, and she really shocked me when she told me that Jimi had once said he would have liked to have been in Santana. I still get dizzy thinking what that would have been like!

I think our music was really crisp at Woodstock, and with so many other kinds of bands playing there, I can see that we would have stuck out. Shrieve was really on that day, like a horse running free, and Chepito was playing his timbales with absolute conviction and fire, giving those hippies a taste of a kind of music they'd never heard before. We were rehearsed, like a car ready to hit the track— some of the other groups were discombobulated and still in the pit, waiting to get it together. We were hippies, but we were professional in our way. Also, some of the other groups suffered when it rained after we played— I remember talking with Jerry later, and he told me that the stage was wet when the Dead played and that their guitar cables were shocking them, so they couldn't really step on the notes. They had no insulation and no ground, so it was literally like putting your finger in an electric socket. Who can do a show like that? Jerry said that it was the worst they ever played.

If you ask me, from what I heard on the album and saw in the movie, there were three acts that had it together in terms of their music and their energy. Sly was number one—he owned that whole weekend. Then it was Jimi Hendrix, with the amazing way he presented the national anthem and the rest of his show, even though most of the crowd had left by then and it was already the middle of Monday morning when he played. Then there was a bunch of groups fighting for third place—but I think it was either the Who or Santana, and that was it.

We didn't stick around to see the rest of the festival after our show—it was time to go. The helicopters were flying people out to make room for the bands that were coming in—it was chaotic, and it wasn't like there was a backstage where you could just hang. I was still tripping and wanted to go and hibernate. The other guys were talking, but I kept quiet—I was afraid someone was going to say something about my playing out of tune. We had had enough, man. We ended up hanging out for a while in the lobby of some Howard Johnson–type hotel away from the festival, and then it was back on the road.

Woodstock was important to Santana: it was the biggest door we would ever walk through with just one step. But until I saw the movie, Woodstock had in many ways just been another gig, and for us 1969 was a summer full of big shows. After Woodstock we played pop festivals in Atlanta, New Orleans, and Dallas. We were on the road for another two weeks before we got back home, so you can imagine that by then it was all fading away in my mind.

I'll never forget two amazing things from those national tours. The first happened in Boston, where we played just after Woodstock at the Boston Tea Party. We were walking around Cambridge when suddenly we heard "Jingo" on the radio. A rush of energy went through my body when I realized that it was our song. Of course we all started talking about it, and then the excitement shifted to: "Man, it sounds like crap—we got to get a real producer." It was true—the music sounded really thin. You just couldn't feel our energy coming out of a little radio speaker. That was an important lesson—to think about how people would be hearing our music. "Jingo" was our first single, but it didn't get picked up by many stations, so Columbia went with "Evil Ways" as the second single, and that took off later.

The second thing happened when we played a few shows in October in Chicago. It was our first time in that city, and for me Chicago only meant one thing—it was the home of the electric blues! We had a day off, and we were staying at a Holiday Inn. I heard that Otis Rush was playing on the South Side in a rough part of town—it might have been at Theresa's Lounge. I couldn't persuade anybody to go with me. "No; today's a day off, man. I'm going to get a hamburger, then go to my room and relax."

So I persuaded a cab driver to take me there, and I went by myself. As soon as I got out of the cab, I was like, "Oh, damn. This *is* a danger zone." It was deep, deep ghetto—I felt people looking at me like I was a pork chop and they were a bunch of sharks. I quickly stepped into the small club, and there he was—Otis Rush, looking so cool, wearing shades and a cowboy hat, a toothpick in his mouth. I stood by the bar and couldn't move. I was just listening to his voice and looking at his fingers on that upside-down guitar. I had the feeling that this was just another night for him, that he did this every night he played, but seeing him there—playing with a real Chicago rhythm section, showing me how it's done and why it's done—was so different from seeing him anywhere else. For me, there was still nothing else that came close to the feeling that comes from the heartfelt blues—that music was just zipped into my pores. To hear Otis Rush like that, I was ready to go to Vietnam or Tehran or Pakistan. To hear that music, I'd go to hell and make a deal to stay there.

I stood out like a sore thumb in that bar with my long hair and mustache and hippie clothes. I noticed everybody looking at me. Then I saw a policeman talking to the bartender, so I walked over to him. "Excuse me," I said quietly. He looked at me up and down. "Yeah?"

"I have a hundred dollars for you—can you keep an eye on me? Let me hear Otis, and when he's finished, can you ask the bartender to call a cab and help get me to it?"

"A hundred dollars? Show it to me."

I showed him. "Okay, be cool, man. Relax and enjoy it."

I did, until the end of the very last set. Otis unplugged his guitar, said, "Thank you, ladies and gentlemen—good night!" and split. The cop looked at me. "You ready?" The bartender called me a cab, he walked me over to it, and I paid him for hanging with me. It was worth every cent. I didn't see the streets or feel the bumps driving back to the hotel. I was still hearing the music—the profound sound of Otis's voice and the way he bent the notes. Catching Otis and other blues guys like Magic Sam and Freddie King, who still played in small bars around Chicago, became part of every visit.

I think Brother Otis will always bring out the seven-year-old child in me. I'm not the only one who feels that way—Eric Clapton and Jimmy Page do, too. Even Buddy Guy will give it up for Otis. I remember one time in 1988 I got into Chicago around five o'clock and was checking in to an airport hotel. The phone was already ringing in my room when I put the key in the door—it was Buddy. "Hey, Santana! Listen, Otis and I, we're waiting on your ass here. You got a pen? Write down this address and come on over."

The address was that of the Wise Fools Pub, and I didn't waste any time. I got there early enough, when the place was only half full—Otis hadn't actually showed up yet, so Buddy and I took some solos, and we were just killing it. Then suddenly I saw that cowboy hat and toothpick come out of the shadows. It was like a scene in a movie. Otis looked around and walked through the crowd like he was in no hurry at all. This was his turf. He grabbed his guitar and stepped into the single spotlight, which hit his face in a very dramatic way. He leaned into the microphone and said: "Give them a hand, ladies and gentlemen!" Then quietly, almost to himself, he said, "Stars, stars, stars..."

It was like Otis was saying, "Oh, yeah? You think these guys were good?" He plugged in and didn't even sing—he just went straight into round after round of an instrumental blues that showed us who the star really was. He was in the middle of a solo and hit a lick that had Buddy and me screaming like shrimp on a Benihana grill. We couldn't believe what he was able to get out of each note. It was like getting a real long piece of fresh sugarcane and peeling it with your teeth to get into the middle, where the sugar is, and the sound it makes when you suck the sap out of it and the juice starts running down your chin and onto your hands. That's what it was like when Otis was hitting those notes—nothing sounds or tastes better than that!

Over the years I've gotten to know Otis and let him know how important his music is to me. He's not one for compliments, though—the first time we met at the Fillmore, I told him how incredible he sounded. His reply was, "Man, I got a long way to go." What—you? The guy who made "All Your Love (I Miss Loving)" and "I Can't Quit You Baby"? I think he's just one of those brothers who has a hard time validating his own gift, who's distant in his mind from his soul—except when he's playing. Not long ago Otis had a stroke, and he can't play anymore, and I make it a point to stay in touch, send his family a check twice a year, and let him know how much he's loved. He was never really one for words, but he'll still get on the phone and say, "Carlos, I love you, man." What can I say? He changed my life.

Back in the Bay Area in December we got asked to play another festival. It was at the Altamont Speedway—and I don't think I've ever been happier to be the first band to go on, then or now. Now that I look back on it, I think that while Woodstock was as close to spiritual as you could get, Altamont was about overindulgence and cocaine and strutting your stuff to see how badass you were. It wasn't about the Rolling Stones hiring the Hells Angels, though that was part of it. It was just a strange, rowdy kind of vibe—people pushing instead of relaxing, getting upset with each other, just the wrong kind of energy, and the people who were supposed to stop that from happening were getting the most pissed off. It smelled bad, and there was fear and anger. You could see it in people's eyes. We played and left before it all got weird—later we heard that someone in Jefferson Airplane got knocked out and that the Dead didn't want to play and that the Rolling Stones went on and a man got killed.

You can see it in the movie *Gimme Shelter*—it was all so tangible. The Stones wanted us to be in their movie, and I think we were all pretty much in agreement that we didn't want any part of that. It put everything in a bad light—the atmosphere was dark and brutal and cruel, and we didn't want to participate. We said no—more than just bad vibes, that experience had a tangibly dark, scary, cruel kind of energy that we didn't want to be connected to. We're still saying no today, because every once in a while they want to bring it out again with more footage.

If '69 was about volume and overindulgence, another part of that year was about speed—things kept happening faster than ever for Santana. How fast? By November, when we came back to New York to play the Fillmore East, we were headlining—the Butterfield Blues Band and Humble Pie were opening for us. There's a letter from that same month that I got to see years later, sent by Clive Davis at Columbia to Bill Graham, asking him to start booking Miles Davis into the Fillmores and introduce him to the rock audience. In the middle of it, he wrote about the strong sales of *Santana* and called us "unstoppable." In December, "Evil Ways" was released, and by early '70, it was a top ten radio hit. Then we got ready to go into the studio again, and after that, as Clive said, Santana really was unstoppable.

CHAPTER 10

In the week before we played Woodstock, I started hanging around a dude who was older than I was. He had some cocaine, and I said, "Nah, I don't want to do that." Then he started playing me bootleg recordings of Charlie Christian performing live at Minton's Playhouse, and man, that shit was even scarier for me! I was hearing the roots of bebop coming out of swing jazz from a guitar player who had had TB, as I had, and who had died at twenty-five. His music went straight into me. He was

*one of those guys—like Django and Tal Farlow and Wes Montgomery—
who could play intricate melodies with all these chords on every single
part of the neck and never look at it once. If you look at videos of Jimi or
me, you can see us counting frets.*

*I think Charlie Christian should be required listening if you're a
serious guitar player and not just a weekend musician. As I got to know
his melodies—and the octaves and warmth of Wes and the atomic,
bombastic sounds of Sonny Sharrock—I grew to believe that all that
music and all those musicians came to me for a reason. I think everyone
I was turned on to made me think in a new way about the instrument
and how to get at something new.*

*It took me a while, but I learned to respect Christian's way of play-
ing. It's a language that's very, very evolved. Modern jazz has another
kind of vocabulary, which came from a higher form of musical expression. It came from a special place—from Charlie Parker and Dizzy
Gillespie and John Coltrane, and it was deep in blues roots. But not the
same kind of blues I started with—string benders like B. B. and Muddy.
Django, Charlie Christian, and my former father-in-law, Saunders
King—they were not string benders.*

*I used to ask SK, "Why weren't you guys bending notes?" He'd say
almost with disdain, "Man, we never had time." I was like, "Oh!" You
can hear that when you listen to Charlie Christian hitting those notes
in those tempos. No time to bend any strings. Thank God Miles and
Coltrane moved on to modal playing; it made it easier for me—it's
closer to the blues. I know what I can and can't do and what I'm best at,
and I still don't know how to play solos around chord changes. Well,
maybe subconsciously I do. But when someone like Charlie Christian or
Charlie Parker starts doing chord changes, I can play along and hang
for the first twenty seconds, maybe thirty. I think I did okay with that
kind of feel on the end of "Hannibal."*

In 1970 we kicked off the year already riding on a rocket ship.
Santana was busy touring—back to the Fillmore East and New
York City; back home to San Francisco, where we played on a TV

CARLOS SANTANA

special produced by Ralph J. Gleason and a company called the
Family Dog; and then a fund-raiser to help the Grateful Dead after
they got busted in New Orleans. More festivals and colleges. Then
the first royalty check for *Santana* came from Columbia Records—
which was the first real money we had seen as a group. I remember
some of the other guys started buying motorcycles and expensive
cars right away.

The first thing I did was keep my promise to my mom—I
bought her a two-story, big-garage house on Hoffman Avenue in a
safe place in the upper Mission District, near Twin Peaks. Everybody was pretty much gone from the old house by then—it was my
dad, my mom, and Maria. My sister Irma lived downstairs. Mom
got her washing machine and dryer. They stayed there until 1991,
when they moved to San Rafael and then Danville. My parents were
twenty-one years in that house—longer than any other place they
had lived.

I remember when I told my mom that her Safeway bag just got
bigger and that I was buying her a house, she gave me a hug and
kept looking at me like she didn't know what to say. We had some
distance between us then—it took time for us to act like mother
and son again. I'd been out of the house for a while.

While I was away on the road, my girlfriend, Linda, found a
house for us in the North Bay area of Marin County, up on Mount
Tamalpais, with an incredible view of the bay and the Golden Gate
Bridge—hawks would be circling around there all the time, riding
the winds. We moved in there together, and compared to the center
of San Francisco, with all its street noise, it was so peaceful that I
had trouble because the quiet was so loud. It took some time to get
used to that. I wasn't meditating yet and had just started reading
the works of Paramahansa Yogananda and some other books on
Eastern philosophy. You could say that moving one step outside the
city and learning to listen to the quiet and really hear new sounds
helped open me to the spiritual path I was about to follow.

What else to do with the money that was coming in? I started
collecting a lot of music—tapes, record albums—and bought a set

of drums. I told myself I was going to dedicate one room to all my music. Later that summer in New York I would meet a man who just started to work for Columbia Records in France named Michel Delorme. He was friendly with Miles Davis and had been tight with John Coltrane, too. In fact there's a great color photo of him interviewing Coltrane in 1965 that a friend of mine turned into a T-shirt. He was instantly a hero and a friend. The second time we met was in France a few weeks later. Michel gave me a stack of reel-to-reel tapes, mostly unreleased music by Miles and Coltrane. I treated those things like they were precious metals—I took them home and carefully copied them, then returned them to Michel. He still likes to tell me how surprised he was that I kept the tapes safe and got them all back to him. He must be thinking about the three-hour interview he did with Coltrane: he lent the tape to a friend and never got it back.

Michel is one of a few special people I met over the years whom I like to call Keepers of the Flame because of what they do to keep the music thriving. They are collectors of the music and information and spirit like Michel, or Hal Miller, who has almost every jazz video ever made, or Jan Lohmann in Denmark, or Yasuhiro "Fuji" Fujioka, who has the Coltrane House in Osaka, Japan. And there's people like Michael Cuscuna, who keep reissuing the music so it doesn't disappear from the stores or the Internet. It's more than just loving the music—it's being supremely dedicated to nurturing and preserving the history any way they can.

Years later Michel gave me a compilation he called *Intergalactic Wayne Shorter*—Wayne's best live performances in France. Incredible music—one of my favorite mixes to this day. Michel and I still meet in France, and he still turns me on to new old stuff—old music that's being discovered for the first time. He also turned me on to a nice expression to use when the music's not happening, or when something's obvious—"Poof!"

Michel's tapes were the beginning of my own library of rare recordings, including vinyl albums and tapes and videotapes and DVDs—I still have them and treasure them. I always had a special room for that collection and other things, such as my guitars and amplifiers, drum kits, and percussion. Now all that music, which used to take up a whole wall, can fit onto a few iPods, so I designed some that I occasionally give to friends—one of them contains all the music ever made by Bob Marley, and it's colored red, green, and gold. Then I have one decorated with a stick figure of a trumpet player that contains every piece of music Miles ever made, including all his rare live recordings and sideman gigs—when he played on other people's records. Same with Coltrane, Marvin Gaye, and other message givers like them.

Other than the music, which I *was* ready for, I bought one thing for myself that year that maybe I wasn't quite ready for—a car. And not just any car—a special-edition, fire-engine-red Excalibur Phaeton convertible. It was beautiful. It was a 1970 model and looked like it had been made in Germany in the 1920s. It had running boards, a three-hundred-horsepower Corvette engine under the hood, and cooling tubes coming out of the engine compartment. Check it out on the Internet. This was a classic when it was new.

I never had a car before that—actually, I really didn't know how to drive. Until then I had gotten rides from my friends who drove. With the success of Santana, we all had stuff to do and less and less time to do it in. Carabello and Gregg didn't have time to come and pick me up, even for rehearsals. It was getting annoying. I thought, "I got to get me a car and learn how to drive." In that order.

So I went to a dealership in San Rafael that sold these cars—Annex Motors, I think it was. They looked at me in my hippie clothes when I walked in, and a guy in a suit and tie immediately came up to me like he was sure I had walked into the wrong place. "Yeah? What do you want?" I was staring at the car. "How much is that car?" I asked. He rolled his eyes and got ready to walk away. I told him, "No—I want to buy that car. Here..." I gave him the business card of Sid Frank, the accountant Bill Graham had connected us with. "Call him. He'll take care of everything." Later on Bill found out that Sid was ripping us off—and Bill, too—and was ready to kill him.

Sid came around with the check, I signed the papers, and the salesman pulled the car around and gave me the key. I was like, "Okay, thanks. See you all later," and I started driving away. I was fine on smaller streets, but I had to get on the 101 freeway to get back to my place—that's when I started having trouble. I was driving around twenty miles an hour in the slow lane, cars whizzing past, just hoping I wouldn't get hit. Now I think there wasn't much chance that was going to happen—you could see the Excalibur from miles away. But on that day I was squeezing the steering wheel like you squeeze juice from an orange. It was a powerful engine, but I was just crawling along—good thing it was automatic transmission, too. Right away the highway patrol saw me. Two cops pulled me over, and then another car came. Four cops were looking at the car and at me, trying to figure it all out.

I think I've just been lucky in situations like that one—there was always a good cop riding with the bad cop. One guy wanted to do a search, but the top guy came over and said, "Okay, I need to see your driver's license." Suddenly I realized I didn't even have one yet! The cop looked at me with no surprise in his eyes. "I *know* you don't have a fuckin' license because if you did you wouldn't be driving that way."

He took a closer look at me. "Hey, wait a minute: aren't you Santana?" Then it looked like it all made sense to him. He thought for a minute and said, "Okay, I'll tell you what I'm going to do." He turned to one of the other cops. "You—come over here," he said, then he looked at me. "Give him the keys."

"What?"

"We're driving you home. You're coming with me, and he's going to follow us in your car. And you see this other guy over here?"

"Yeah."

"Well, he's going to pick you up tomorrow and teach you how to drive."

Can you believe it? That's how things were. I think it was a smart move on the cops' part, because if I was going to be driving their stretch of the 101 in that kind of car with that much power, it would be better if they helped me. Thanks to them, in around four days I had my confidence together, and I had my license.

I think that story says a lot about how well known Santana was in San Francisco by 1970—we were local heroes, even to some cops. That car was also a lesson in limitations and keeping the ego in check—it attracted a lot of attention in the following two years. One time I was driving on a two-lane road when another convertible came roaring up next to me, the people all hanging out and shouting—"Santana, man, we love your shit! That's a bad car, Santana!" Only they weren't watching the oncoming traffic, and along came a big bus that almost hit them head-on. I had to pull over and stop because my heart was beating so fast. I thought, "That's not good. Those guys almost got killed because of me and this stupid car." I didn't want that on my conscience.

I toned down the Excalibur and got it painted black, which I know was like going from a 10 down to a 9.5. But it actually looked really, really good that way. I've driven many different makes since then. I'm not Jay Leno, and I don't try to collect them, but I like a good car. These days I have a Fisker Karma with blue flake paint that I like—I love when the electrical system takes over, and it just purrs. Great stereo system, too, which is important.

That year I got to feel what it was like to become a celebrity, someone people recognize, and I learned how to act graciously— even when I was trying to eat or just drive down the road. If you don't like people disturbing you, maybe you're in the wrong business. It happened so fast and so strongly that it even affected my family—my dad told me that when he was playing with a Mexican big band at La Rondalla he got more recognition and respect because of our name. My sisters told me that people would call all the Santanas in the San Francisco phone book trying to find me. They had to change their number a bunch of times, and this went on for a while. My mom told me once in the '80s that she was shopping at a department store downtown and needed some help, but the salespeople kept dismissing her. Then they saw her credit card and went, "Oh, you're Santana's mom?" and they got nice and helpful.

You know my mom by now—she said, "I don't need anything from your damn store" and walked out.

We started work on the second Santana album—which would become *Abraxas*—in Wally Heider's San Francisco studio in June of 1970. It had been a little more than a year since we recorded the first one, so we had been working on new songs and thinking about what we wanted to do differently this time or keep the same. We wanted Gianquinto to help us again—in fact, "Incident at Neshabur" was the first tune we worked on. We also knew we wanted the right producer from Columbia to work with us. I'll put it this way: Santana didn't actually like the sound of Santana until *Abraxas*.

I'm going to get into trouble, but this is the truth—Fred Catero helped many of the producers he worked with look good; their sessions would never have sounded the way they did without his help. At first he was Columbia's engineer in San Francisco and had great credentials. He worked with Sly and Janis, and on that live album by Bloomfield and Al Kooper—he engineered Mongo Santamaría at the same time we were making *Santana*. We heard that he knew how to record congas. Even more important, he knew how to record congas and electric guitars, which is why he became our producer.

I think the guitar sound was becoming clearer—it's obvious on *Abraxas*. One thing that helped my signature was my tone, and the thing that most helped my tone was a new Boogie amplifier—which, when I met the guy who invented the idea, Randy Smith, didn't have a name yet. My friend Randy gives me the credit for saying his amp really boogied the first time I heard it. I got that word from the original boogie man—John Lee Hooker.

Randy the Boogie Man, as I call him, gets the credit for making a small amplifier with enough beef to it so you could play with drive and sustain, whatever the volume was. He put turbo in it, and what a tone—damn. Some of the best things I ever played—including much of *Abraxas*—came through that first Boogie amplifier I got from Randy.

At the time, everybody was taking sounds and ideas from Jimi Hendrix and the British guys or from R & B guitar players like the ones who played for Motown. I was thinking more from the back of my brain—way in the back—like, "What's the sound of a soul praying or a ghost crying?" I think my sound was closer to what Pete Cosey would do later with Miles. Fred helped make it easy for us to paint and play without worrying whether we were getting recorded in the right way.

Fred did that when Carabello came up with "Singing Winds, Crying Beasts" in the studio. Carabello didn't play keyboards, but he could sing the melody he wanted to Gregg, who'd figure it out on organ. When I hear that tune now I still remember that I loved getting to the studio on time and finding that Gregg and Carabello were already there and they had a track ready to go—which was funny in a way, because they could fight a lot. I think they might have been there from the night before. But if that was what it took to get to the point where there was a tune that needed my guitar, that was okay with me.

Michael's a dramatic cat—you can hear it in "Singing Winds," which was a very evocative way to start an album—a little mysterious. You don't know what's going to happen after that, and then we go into "Black Magic Woman."

Gregg brought that one in, and it was an instant okay—I was already into Peter Green, and, as I said, the song was like a brother to Otis Rush's "All Your Love (I Miss Loving)." I think we took that tune and really made it our own. It's still our most requested song—and I still get women coming up to me saying, "You know, I'm the black magic woman." Of course over the years, a few more Santana songs have had the same impact. I'll get "I'm Maria, Maria" or "I'm the Spanish Harlem Mona Lisa," and if they all claim to be, who's to say they're not?

The segue into "Gypsy Queen" we thought was a perfect bridge between those two songs—we did that many times in concert and it worked so well. When I hear "Gypsy Queen" now it makes me think of how persistent Michael Shrieve was during that summer, getting me to listen and understand Miles and Coltrane. I could tell the two of them were using different scales from the ones we were using, but to me it wasn't about figuring out sharps and flats, it was about the emotion they were going for and how they went about it. In the studio we would ask ourselves, "How would Miles approach this mood?" In a way, I didn't want anyone to explain too much about their notes and scales—once I know exactly where a chord is, it's like hearing the punch line before the joke. "Damn, I wish you hadn't told me."

Abraxas was very good to a few people who had songs we covered. They all got nice royalties for a long time, and I'm happy about that—Peter Green, Gábor Szabó, Tito Puente. Tito was always funny about it in the years after the album went big. He complained that people expected to hear our version of "Oye Como Va" rather than his, and he had to deal with that. "People are always saying, 'Why don't you play it like Santana?' First I want to get mad, and then I think, I just got a new house because of that. 'Okay, *no hay problema.*'"

The first time I got into the song I didn't know Tito Puente at all—Ray Barretto, sure, but not Tito yet. I was at the house with Linda and I had just dropped some acid and was full-on into the trip, and all of a sudden I wanted to turn on the radio, which I never did normally. It was tuned to an obscure local station that was playing Latin music all night—a late-night party kind of mix. A tune came on that had a great groove, and I started breaking it down, thinking how close the feel was to "Louie Louie" and some Latin jazz tunes. The next morning I went down to the Mission to find this song, went through all the records till I found the right one, and listened to it nonstop—my own heavy rotation. It had some great solos—trumpet and flute, plus crowd noises and a kind of false ending, like one that Ray Charles would do. Just a great party atmosphere. I kept saying to myself, "We can play this song. We *got* to play this song. This will drive the hippies wild—especially the women."

There are certain songs that really get women to be women—no apologies needed, no excuses. "Oye" is one of them, and that was what I wanted, even back then—to make women crazy. I think it comes from the Tijuana thing. I think some people were more interested in playing music that could impress in the way that Jimi Hendrix or Led Zeppelin did. I couldn't care less about that.

We were getting ready to record, so we were already thinking about the number of songs we would have. I brought that song in and I started hearing, "Hey, man, that's not rock. It doesn't sound like rock." It was the first time that happened—that people in the band were uncomfortable with a song because it didn't sound like Cream or Hendrix or the Doors. Santana was about building bridges between different music styles—and apparently this was a bridge too far. To me, rock and roll was anything that felt good. So this was also the first time I really put my foot down. "No. We're recording this song because we're recording it." I think Gregg did a great job singing "Oye Como Va."

I had my own prejudices, too. Gregg was growing as a song-writer, and he had some great tunes, such as "Hope You're Feeling Better." He pushed us to record that song—we had been doing it live, but not often. To be honest, it was one of those tunes that Carabello and I thought was too rock and roll, too white. When we played it in concert, sometimes Carabello and I would pretend to hide behind our amps just to tease Gregg. We could be cruel like that—I had a lot to learn about appreciating and validating what was right in front of us. It's a great song. What I should have been doing was going up to him and saying, "Hey, Gregg—you got any more like that?"

We liked to tease each other—we used to tease Gregg about the fact that he walked like John Wayne. We'd imitate the way he talked, too, and Gregg would play along. He'd say, "Okay, pilgrim," as Duke would. "Are we going to rehearse today, or are we just going to sit here? A man's got to do what a man's got to do." Man, we'd all be laughing so hard!

I had to fight for "Samba Pa Ti." The song came to me in New York City, after our first tour in Europe that spring, when I was jet-lagged to death. I couldn't sleep; the walls were moving like I had just fallen off a merry-go-round. Then just about when I was falling asleep I heard some guy trying to get a sound out of a saxophone in an alley outside. I opened my window, and I saw the guy staggering around, not balancing so well. He couldn't seem to make up his mind what to put in his mouth, the saxophone or a bottle of booze. He took a deep breath and was just about to blow, then he stopped and hit the bottle again. I heard a voice inside me saying, "Man, that could be you, lost like that."

I grabbed a pen and paper, and a poem came to me, and as soon as I wrote it down I could hear the melody right with it. The words and music came symbiotically. The music reminded me of how my dad would sound when he'd be playing by himself, plus I could hear a King Curtis, "Soul Serenade" groove. "Samba Pa Ti" was definitely about developing romance and beauty in my playing—I wanted a naked, undressed feeling, a feeling of vulnerability.

It was fun playing it for the band for the first time. I don't think they expected something that was a little delicate. They were looking at me like, "Damn, that don't sound like rock and roll, but it's honest and real." To our credit we never dismissed any music that was honest and heartfelt.

A melody can be memorable or fleeting. "Samba Pa Ti" is not music that just passes by. If you want to see what's happening when you're on a moving train you have to look at what's off in the distance, not at what's up close. For me, it's like that with music. The best songs get the big picture and take the high road—they are long, beautiful, memorable melodies.

> Through every step in life you find
> Freedom from within,
> And if your mind should understand,
> Woman, love your man.
>
> Everybody searching
> Searching for eternal peace
> And it's there waiting for you
> All you have to do is share.

We went into the studio not knowing who would sing the lyric. I didn't have the confidence to sing it. I felt that I couldn't sing it as well as I could play it on the guitar. I think it's a lot more transparent without a vocal. Of course it depends on who sings it, but it could have been too thick, too much like...mayonnaise. I know José Feliciano recorded it with his own lyrics, but they aren't mine. When I play it now in my head, I'm still playing along to that poem—maybe I should record it again and sing the words.

That shift in the middle of the song just happened in the studio. It happened because I was listening to the grooves in King Curtis's "Soul Serenade," "Groovin'" by the Young Rascals, and Aretha's "Angel." All that music just gave birth to an idea, and we all knew to follow if one of us wanted to go someplace.

When we finished playing it the first time in the studio, we knew it was going to be big. I was going to call it "For Every Step, Freedom from Within," but Chepito was the one who came up with the name on the spot: "Eh, Carlos—*llámalo* 'Samba Pa Ti.'" I thought, "You know, I like that," and trusted my instinct.

Abraxas was a group production that was done song by song—so really Gregg, Carabello, and Chepito coproduced their own songs with Fred, and I coproduced "Samba Pa Ti" and "Oye Como Va" with Fred and "Incident" with Gianquinto. We loved that album—it was the first album we made that was as good as it could be. I love the way it looks, and I even love the name.

The title *Abraxas* came from a book by Hermann Hesse that Gregg, Stan, and Carabello were reading. A quote from the book is on the album. For the cover, we got a painting from the artist Mati Klarwein—he did the painting on *Bitches Brew*. He had done it in 1961, and we saw it in a book that Carabello had. It was perfect for us—the painting matched our music and incorporated our themes of Africa and spirituality and sexuality and Latin music. It had a beautiful naked black woman in the center, and on the left there was an angel riding a conga, which for us is now like what the Stones have with the tongue and lips—a trademark. Carabello

showed it to me, and we were sure it had to be on the new album—
Columbia Records helped make that happen.

Abraxas came together so easily that the album almost seemed
to form itself. Of all the albums I ever did, *Abraxas* was the easiest
to make. The sessions were nice and laid back and took place
between some touring in June and July, and we were able to relax
and not rush anything. We spent more time on sounds than we
had before—getting the congas and guitars and organ right
instead of settling for a compromise—and getting the room sound
right, too. Some friends came by the studio and sat in, including
Steven Saphore, who played tabla, and percussion player Rico
Reyes. Reyes and Carabello had a group called San Pacu, which
they started around '68; it was a cross between Santana and Tower
of Power. Rico was a great singer and reaffirmed the Mission District vibration around us—he was also a beautiful-looking cat, but
he became another heroin and cocaine casualty.

Another friend who hung with us was a guitarist named Neal
Schon, later of Journey and Bad English, whom Gregg and Shrieve
knew from San Mateo. They all lived in that part of the Bay Area.
Neal was already tearing it up—he was just seventeen, but he had a
reputation and was really smart. We didn't jam, but he did play one
solo on "Hope You're Feeling Better" that was not on the original
album. He had a great tone and great ideas when he played.

Clive Davis was one of the reasons *Abraxas* was so easy to make.
He was out there in CBS's office in New York and wasn't checking
on us *or* disappearing. He trusted us, and he was there if we needed
him. He understood that we made music from the heart to go
straight *to* the heart of people, and even though he was someone
who started as a lawyer, his love for music transformed him into
something beyond a tie dude. To this day, his main talent never
changed—he hears music that can hit the mainstream, and he
puts it there. That's what *he* does.

Clive will probably laugh at this, but if you played a B-flat[7] on a
piano he wouldn't know what you're talking about. He wouldn't

care—that's someone else's job. Just as Bill Graham did, he understands by hearing you—except he's not imposing, as Bill could be. Sometimes Bill's tenacity would get the best of him, and it would alienate me—like, "Dude, back up a little bit." Clive is expert in the way he uses diplomacy. "For you and your music, this is my heart; for everybody else, it's work."

"Clive, that's so sweet; thank you."

"No; I'm telling you the truth."

It's amazing to attract people who want to go to bat for you and invest in what you're doing. We were still recording *Abraxas,* and I remember one day the phone rang in the studio and Carabello answered it. "Hey, man—it's for you." Carabello had gotten tight with Miles Davis and Jimi, so it wasn't so strange when I asked him who it was and he told me it was Miles calling. But we had never met. Why'd he want to talk to me? "No, man, don't fuck around like that."

"No, really—it's him."

I took the phone, and damn, it *was* Miles, with that sandpaper whisper. "Hey, whatcha doin'?"

"Oh, hi, Miles—nice to meet you. We're recording an album."

"Yeah? How's it goin'?"

"We're learning, you know—learning and having fun."

He kind of chuckled. "Okay, just checking up on you. How long you doing that?"

"We're going to take a little time, Miles. We've been on the road for a while."

"Okay. Don't take too long."

Over the years, we got to be friends, and he'd call me up and ask how I was doing. My answer was always the same: "Learning and having fun, Miles."

The *Abraxas* sessions happened before and after our second visit to Europe—actually, our first European tour, because our first visit in April was to play a two-night Royal Albert Hall show featuring

Columbia Records acts such as Johnny Winter, Taj Mahal, and a group from San Francisco called It's a Beautiful Day, which Bill Graham was managing. Bill's role with Santana was expanding with everything that was going on—sometimes he would be the producer of the concert we were playing, sometimes the booking agent for the show, and sometimes the guy who got us recorded at the show. Sometimes he was all three.

Stan Marcum was still our manager, and I could tell that even though he had a desk in Bill's office, they didn't always agree on things. Bill was a businessman, and there was a side to him that was about the money. I learned in Tijuana that too much power can cause some people to do things that make you want to check your pocket every now and then. But I also knew that it was good to have strength on your side. And that's pretty much where I landed when it came to Bill.

Most of the guys in Santana had some distrust of Bill—they felt that when he had the chance, he would take more than what should be coming to him. I intuitively felt that what he would bring was worth a lot more than the money that he might have been making. I also know a lot of guys on the scene got pissed off at him because of deals that went bad and some other problems. But even though we didn't always see eye to eye, I always felt I could trust Bill, that he had my back.

Let me put it another way: when you consider all the other promoters and managers and agents at that time, how much they were taking and how much the artists were getting, I had no problem with Bill.

Bill was closer to me than he was to any other guy in Santana, and I got to see him in action. He was making things happen and getting things done back when the rock scene was still very new. He had used his position to get us to play Woodstock, and he had helped us work out our deal with Clive Davis at Columbia. He took the time to play a Willie Bobo tune and break it down for us. How do you put a price on all that? To me, he put more in than he took out.

Bill was like a big brother to me. He would sometimes ask me over to his house, and I'd get there just as Tower of Power or some other band was leaving. Over the years, he was a friend and adviser and helped us run parts of our business and negotiate a number of important deals. At times, people in his organization represented us and took care of paying bills. Bill wanted to handle all of Santana's business and take us under his wing, and I was tempted to accept his offer, but he never really became Santana's bona fide manager.

I had read the Ouija board—I could see what that would be like. It was like my relationship with Miles—sometimes you had a feeling that if you get too close, you're going to get burned. Bill could be very intense, and I didn't want to test our friendship. Bill accepted that, but he'd still say things like, "Well, if you're ever stuck on the ten-yard line and need someone to drive it home, I'm here for you." He always was there for me, and man, he knew how to drive it home.

CHAPTER 11

David Brown and me at Tanglewood, August 18, 1971.

I know jazz puts certain people off. I think when it comes to some jazz, people pay attention to the tools instead of the house. When you hear music, you don't want to see the tools. You don't want to know how many nails it took to build the house. Some people just haven't heard Kind of Blue *yet, or* A Love Supreme. *They haven't heard Wayne Shorter's music.*

Until I knew about Miles and Coltrane, I listened to jazz without calling it jazz —groups I heard live, or maybe a hit on the radio. I liked Chico Hamilton and Gábor Szabó and Wes Montgomery, but if anyone said the word jazz, I didn't want to listen to it. That word made me think about bands in tuxedos playing while people who were also in tuxes ate dinner. It didn't have fangs and teeth and claws. I wanted stuff that scratched you.

It was Michael Shrieve who got me to listen to Miles and Trane and corrected my twisted perception that jazz is only for old, fuddy-duddy people. He went through my record collection and saw what I didn't have, and he decided I had to hear Miles and Coltrane. So he brought over a big stack of records for me. I started to listen—"Whoa, what is this shit? This is really different from John Lee Hooker." I started playing it back and forth. Miles and Trane. Miles and Trane.

I started to get Coltrane inside of me with Africa/Brass *and the 1962 album* Coltrane, *which included "Out of This World," and of course* A Love Supreme. *With Miles,* In a Silent Way *and the* Elevator to the Gallows *sound track started it for me, then* Kind of Blue.

I would look at Shrieve and say, "Wow, this is the blues? And this is the same guy who did Bitches Brew?"

"Yeah, same guy."

I was like, "Oh, damn." I was able to feel what Miles was doing with modal jazz. You could just sit in one groove and make it happen. After a while, his music became more endearing, closer to me—I got more into it because his path really was a story, all the way back to his first records with Charlie Parker.

The album that really, really *opened it up for me was Miles's* Bitches Brew. *It had long tracks like "Pharaoh's Dance" and "Spanish Key"— on that one I could hear the connection to his* Sketches of Spain *album. Those tracks made you want to turn the lights down. One writer called it "a light show for the blind." It was very visual music. It made so much sense with everything that was happening then—like a man walking on the moon. When it came out I played it nonstop, nonstop, nonstop. I read Ralph J. Gleason's liner notes over and over—the notes in which he said that after* Bitches Brew, *the world would never be the same. Not just jazz—the world.*

During the first part of 1970, we played Europe a few times— the Royal Albert Hall in England, venues in Germany, Denmark, and Holland, and the Montreux Jazz Festival in Switzerland, where I met Claude Nobs for the first time. Claude was one of the first people I could respect the same way I did Bill Graham—he had persuaded the government and local businesses to invest in his idea to start a jazz festival, and it quickly became one of the music world's crown jewels. I could tell Claude liked us a lot, which was a good thing, because even though we had played on the same bill with jazz groups, it had always been for a rock audience. This was different, because this was really a *jazz* festival. We were the strangers there, playing for the people who came to hear Bill Evans and Tony Williams Lifetime and Herbie Mann, when he had Sonny Sharrock on guitar with him.

Claude made it work. He asked us to play outdoors next to the pool, not inside the casino, where most of the big concerts happened—that's the casino that burned down and that Deep Purple sang about in "Smoke on the Water." We did as Claude asked, and it was the first place in Europe where I felt a camaraderie that was even more pleasant than the feeling I got from hanging with hippies at the old Fillmore. At that time, people who were different from one another—who came from different generations and wore different clothes—were usually very guarded and polite around each other. In Montreux, it was loose and free—all sorts of people were hanging together, having a great time.

I played Montreux so many times over the years and did so many special shows there that it was really like another home. Seriously, if I could make three or four of me, one of them would live in Switzerland and just soak up the vibe over there. Claude and I quickly got tight, and Santana played there more than a dozen times. Every time we got there he'd open his home to us and show us his collection of recordings and videos—it was like a music museum up there, high in the snowy mountains looking out at the world. Claude was a friend and a collaborator—if I wanted to try something new, he would help make it possible—a concert with John McLaughlin; a blues night with Buddy Guy, Bobby Parker, and Clarence "Gatemouth" Brown. Or the event we did in 2006— we invited African and Brazilian musicians for three straight nights, which was like a festival within a festival. We called it Dance to the Beat of My Drums after a song by Babatunde Olatunji, who also had given the world "Jingo." If I wanted to keep playing for three hours, it was cool with Claude. I think it's important that he be validated in every way possible for all that he brought professionally and personally to musicians—we need more musical laboratories like Montreux, where musicians can come and be open, collaborate, and experiment.

I was still shy onstage then. I didn't say much into the mike, and I wasn't doing interviews. But if I wanted to meet someone I was fearless. When Santana played New York City in August—our third time there during 1970—I got to meet some of my biggest heroes, people who were resculpting the musical landscape. Nobody was bigger in my eyes than Miles Davis.

Bill was booking a summer weekend up in Tanglewood—an outdoor festival in Lenox, Massachusetts. It was all rock bands except on Sunday, when he put us on a bill with a big group of singers called the Voices of East Harlem as well as Miles Davis—jazz, gospel, R & B, and Santana. This was Bill's genius—he created that multidimensional environment consciously and honestly and brutally, and he got a new generation to hear the beauty in all this music. And that was the deal: if you want to hear Steve Miller or Neil Young or Santana, you've got to hear Miles Davis. We need more promoters like that today: if you want to hear Jay Z or Beyoncé, you have to hear Herbie Hancock or Wayne Shorter. Wouldn't that be incredible?

We went up to Tanglewood, and I remember getting there and meeting a photographer who was selling big black-and-white prints of Miles and Ray Charles performing at the Newport Jazz Festival. I bought some, and just as I'm carrying them backstage an amazing yellow Lamborghini drives in, and Miles gets out. I wasn't afraid, so I went up to him.

"Hi; my name is Carlos—would you be so kind as to sign this for me?" He looked at me and looked at the photo, grabbed a pen, and signed "To Carlos and the best band" or something like that. He knew who I was, so we started talking, and after a little while he said he had something for me. He went into his shoulder bag and pulled out a tube that looked like a big eyedropper wrapped in cowhide, and of course it was cocaine. Miles looked at me and said, "Try it."

I hadn't slept the night before, I'm with *the* Miles Davis, and I did something that I later felt I shouldn't have done. Cocaine put a distance between my heart and me, between me and the music. My body rejected cocaine as something that made my soul feel disenfranchised—it would say, "This is not for you." When I remember that Tanglewood performance, I still cringe because it felt like I couldn't get myself into the center of my heart. It wasn't the same problem I'd had at Woodstock, but I have the same kind of regret. I decided again to make it permanent: I'd never take what someone else gave me, no matter who it was.

Tanglewood had a beautiful audience with all kinds of people, many of whom, as they had at Woodstock, came up from New York. The festival was much, much smaller and was run much tighter. There were only three bands that Sunday. I loved the Voices of East Harlem. They were all about power to the people and positive message music, and they had that black church energy. There's also something about a hip choir, you know? Donald Byrd and "Cristo Redentor"; the Alice Coltrane albums, with their heavenly voices; Duke Ellington's Sacred Concerts. I think it's the prayer feeling about them that I like—the sound of voices together going straight up to God. If it has a funky, African feeling in it, I can never put it aside. The Voices had a great bass player, a young guy with a huge Afro—Doug Rauch. I called him Dougie. He became a good friend of the band and even traveled with us before he joined us. He had a nice, burly sound on bass, like an older, acoustic tone, but with a Larry Graham technique—slapping, funky. He was part of a new wave of bass players that included Chuck Rainey and Rocco Prestia with Tower of Power and Michael Henderson with Miles—they were all moving the music forward and playing music that wasn't just R & B and wasn't completely jazz. They were all supremely important to Dougie. The next year he moved out to San Francisco and ended up playing with the Loading Zone and Gábor Szabó and finally Santana.

At this time, Miles's band was getting big with the rock audience. Other jazz musicians had played for hippies, but I think the difference with Miles was that he had been listening to rock and funk groups and was bringing his music closer to rock. Without a shadow of a doubt Betty Mabry, who was his wife then, was a big reason for this. She helped transfigure her man. She got him out of those Italian suits and into leather trousers and platform shoes. She didn't want to hear any old, mildewed music at home, so she got him listening to Sly and Jimi Hendrix, James Brown, the Chambers Brothers, and the Temptations. His record collection started to be broader—as they say now, Miles expanded his portfolio. I'm pretty sure Betty turned him on to Santana.

Another thing was that, like Betty, most members of Miles's band were closer in age to the hippies than they were to Miles. You can hear that in the way Jack DeJohnette and Dave Holland played; you can hear that they had been listening to Sly and Larry Graham and Motown. Some of them were starting to use fuzz tone, and Chick was using a ring modulator. Even Miles was using wah-wah and echo.

When I heard him in Tanglewood, Miles's music was already changing from *Bitches Brew*. His group played a song called "The Mask" that made you feel like you were in an Alfred Hitchcock movie—something's about to happen, and you can't get out of the way. Miles's bands were masters of mystery and tension—they never played anything mundane or obvious. It was like what my friend Gary Rashid told me once—he agreed that Miles was a genius, but he said a big part of that genius was Miles's habit of surrounding himself with four or five Einsteins. The music always depended on who was in the band—also on what they ate and what they were thinking that day and what was going on between them.

I began to keep track of all the musicians who played with Miles—my own little list in case I got lucky enough to play with any of them somewhere down the line. At Tanglewood, Miles still had Chick Corea and Keith Jarrett *and* Jack DeJohnette with him as well as Gary Bartz, Dave Holland, and Airto Moreira. By the end of the year, the band started to change—Jack, Dave, and Chick were gone, and Michael Henderson and Ndugu Chancler were stirring the pot. Keith had stayed.

Keith's amazing, man. I have to say something about him for a minute. He's just fucking unbelievable the way he can create right on the spot. You can tell by the way he sits at the piano and improvises a whole solo show. To me, he represents a brand-new soul coming to this planet with no fingerprints, no preconceptions, no preconceived notions of what music should be. He's a giant of innocence and courage to be able to come in with a blank mind and sit down and play the way he does. I'm totally the opposite—I honor myself with melodies. I have to have some kind of melody that I can dismantle in different ways; then I try to refine it and present it the best way I can. I collect melodies like a bee collects pollen—"The Night Has a Thousand Eyes"; "Wise One"; "Afro Blue." To hear a person who discards all of them and gives you something that's 100 percent fresh—that's why I love Keith so much. What he does honors music: he goes onstage absolutely not knowing what he's going to do.

I've studied and listened to so many tapes of Miles's bands from around this time that I could tell how the sound of any given tune would be different each time they played it. The rhythm was always flexible, and the music always seemed to match the players. When Wayne Shorter was with Miles, the music sounded perfect for his horn. When Bartz came in the music sounded like it was a comfortable fit for him, too.

Miles knew what he was doing even when he didn't know beforehand what was going to happen. He was playing for a young rock crowd, and he knew he was bringing his music onto their turf, but rock bands could not come into his jazz world. He wasn't shy about it. I met him for the first time that day in Tanglewood, and we got to be very close. Later he used to tell me, "I can go where you guys are, but you can't come to where I am."

Miles was right. We didn't understand harmonically or structurally what he and his band were doing. That took years and years. They had another kind of vocabulary, which came from a higher form of musical expression. It came from a special place—from Charlie Parker and Dizzy Gillespie and John Coltrane—and at the same time it was deep in blues roots and expanded into funk and rock sounds. The sound of Miles back then was a microscope that showed everything that had happened before in jazz and a telescope that showed where the music was going. I was blessed to be around and to hear this music when it was happening. I think if you start by listening to the music he made when he played for Bill Graham at the Fillmores, you can hear how Miles helped people expand the boundaries of their consciousness—his music put stretch marks on their brains.

There's a story I love to tell about Bill and Miles because it says so much about each of them and about their relationship. I call them both supreme angels because of what they did for me and their impact on my life—and because the way they lived their lives was an example to everyone. They were both angels, but they also had feet of clay. They were divine rascals.

I first heard this story from Bill. The way Bill told it, after he got that letter from Clive Davis asking Bill to start booking Miles at the Fillmore—the one that calls Santana unstoppable—Clive left the job of persuading Miles to Bill. Bill already loved Miles, but who tells Miles what to do?

Miles couldn't get into the idea at first. A lot of it was about the money. Bill offered him a different kind of deal from what he was used to in the jazz clubs, where he would play for a whole week. So Bill made it more attractive financially for Miles. Bill also made the argument that Clive was making—that it's an investment in the future. If Miles played the Fillmore, his name would be on the marquee next to rock bands and he'd be getting through to new listeners—the hippie crowd. It might not mean so much right away, but the following year he'd double or triple his audience and then double or triple his record sales.

Bill finally persuaded Miles, got him into the schedule, and told him, "I have these dates open, and you'll open up for so-and-so and so-and-so." Bill's thinking was that even though he respected Miles he could not let him be the headliner. All those hippies coming to hear Neil Young or Steve Miller or the Grateful Dead would not stick around for Miles, and he wanted to be sure they heard Miles. He wanted Miles to go on first so he'd be sure to have a full audience, even if it looked like Miles was opening for them.

Miles did not know these bands — their music did not resonate with him, and for whatever reason he didn't see himself opening up for them. So Miles showed up late for his first show at the Fillmore East. *Really* late. Neil Young was the headliner, and Steve Miller was on the bill, too. Miles was so late that Steve Miller had to play first, and they were getting ready to ask Neil to go on. Somebody got through to Miles and got him to hustle down to the club.

I remembered how Bill would be if a band dared to show up late — he would stand with his arms folded across his chest. When Miles got there, Bill was looking at his watch and looking at Miles.

Miles played it cool — "What's up, Bill?" Miles knew he had him. Bill had made the mistake of telling him that *Sketches of Spain* was his number one album of all time, the one album he would take to a desert island. The redder Bill got, the calmer Miles was. Bill wanted to let loose some of that New York language that he had educated me with, special words like *schmuck*. But he couldn't. This wasn't some teenage rock group. This was Miles Davis.

Finally Bill let it out. "Miles — *you're late!*" Miles looked at him innocently and said, "Bill, look at me. I'm a black man. You know cab drivers don't pick up black people in New York City." What could Bill say, right? Meanwhile, Miles had his Lamborghini parked around the corner. Bill probably knew it even then.

After we met in Tanglewood I would see Miles almost every time we played New York City, sitting right in the front row, wearing something flashy, with a fine woman in the seat next to him. He would call me to hang out—he'd find out where I was, track me down, and the phone would ring. "Didn't I tell you never to come to New York without calling me first?"

"Hey, Miles—what's up?"

"Whatcha doin'?"

What was I doing? It was three in the morning. "Oh, just having fun and learning."

Miles also liked to hang out with Carabello—they would get some cocaine and get into it together. I remember a bunch of us from both groups were together at a 5th Avenue hotel—it was Keith Jarrett, Shrieve, and I in the elevator, holding it and waiting on Miles and Carabello, who were getting something from a dealer in the lobby. We were waiting and waiting, and Shrieve turned to Keith and said, "How do you do it?" He meant, how did Keith put up with all the cocaine and stuff? Keith said, "Like this." He snapped his fingers. "I just turn it off, like a button." I remember thinking, "Whoa—what button is that?" I wondered what it would take for me to turn off the cocaine conversations in Santana.

Miles and Carabello finally got on the elevator, and when we were going up Miles looked at me and out of nowhere said, "You gotta get you a fuckin' wah-wah—I got one." He wasn't taking any argument. The thing is I already used a wah-wah on some Santana songs, such as "Hope You're Feeling Better," but it wasn't something that was onstage with me. But the way Miles said it, it was like, "Come on—keep up, man."

Miles was right—Hendrix had used it, then Clapton with Cream, and Herbie Hancock had it in his group. After a while it felt like any band in the '70s had to have a wah-wah and a Clavinet or some kind of electric piano. I obeyed Miles and started using a wah-wah in all my live shows. I remember looking at Keith as Miles was giving me that advice, and he just rolled his eyes.

I got a lot of advice from Miles over the years. A few years later, after we hadn't been in New York for a bit, he called me. "What are you doing now?"

I said, "We've been on the road for a while, so we decided to take a break, record an album, and replenish."

"Well, don't stay out there too long, man. You don't want to lose the momentum. You've got it going, so don't stay off the stage too long." I said, "Okay."

Another time, Miles told me, "You can do more than just 'Black Magic Woman.'"

"Thank you, Miles. I'll give it my best shot." It wasn't a spanking, it was an invitation.

I know Miles went out of his way a lot of times to find me and teach me the ropes, tell me when to duck, stay away from this, and have you checked out that? I don't know how many other musicians Miles showed that side of himself to, but I got the feeling not many. The more I've read about Miles, and the more I've talked with other people about him, the more surprised I became that he would sometimes drop his guard and mentor me. Because Miles usually would get very intense, and he could read people, and if he saw that he could ride someone, he would mount that person psychologically. I saw him do that to a lot of people.

Miles could push it too far. There's a story that Armando Peraza told me after he joined Santana. Armando was one tough dude—he came up from Cuba in the '40s and played percussion with Charlie Parker and Buddy Rich almost immediately after he made it to New York City, and he had no problem going into the roughest part of town to collect money that somebody owed him. One time Armando was playing with George Shearing at the Apollo, and Miles was on the bill, too. Both Miles and Armando were kind of pint-size—when they met, Miles started messing with him in his usual way, and Armando got him in a corner and told him in his accent, "You doan wanna mess wid me. I break you jaw—you never fuckin' play trumpet again." I can see the words Miles was thinking in a balloon over his head—"Uh-oh. That motherfucker is crazier than me." Miles was smart—he knew when to back down.

I liked to use the term "divine rascal" to describe Miles. I later heard that around this time, Gary Bartz knocked on Miles's hotel room door and said, "Miles, I got to talk to you. I can't fucking play anymore—that Keith Jarrett is fucking up my solos, playing all the wrong shit, never backing me up. I'm going to quit, man." Miles said, "Okay, I got it. Tell Keith to come over." So guess what he tells Keith? "Hey, Bartz just told me he loves what you're doing: do it some more."

Sometimes we'd run into each other. One night I was hanging backstage at the Fillmore East checking out Rahsaan Roland Kirk playing flute on Stevie Wonder's "My Cherie Amour." *Fwap!* Someone flicked my ear from behind me—really hard. I'm thinking, "Oh, man—that fucking Carabello..." I turn around and *fwap*, in my other ear. I turn again and there's Miles running away, almost to the elevator. He saw that I saw him and came back slowly, grinning. He said, "What you doin', man?" I rubbed my ear. "I was listening to Roland Kirk."

He said, "I can't stand that n...." He used the *n* word.

"Oh?"

"He plays some corny-ass shit."

I was thinking, "Okay, that's between you two, because I like *Volunteered Slavery*."

Miles was *way* ghetto. I don't think he cared so much about what other people thought about him or about what he said, but a lot of times he used words just to fuck with people's heads. Once I asked Miles if he liked Marvin Gaye. "Yeah—if he had one tit, I'd marry him." He called Bill Graham Jewboy, and Bill would just go, "Oh, Miles." Bill wouldn't take that from anyone else—not even someone like Hendrix. Later he'd come up to me and say, "Can you believe the way Miles talks to me?" I knew underneath it there was mutual respect, but I still couldn't believe how Bill's macho thing could melt away that easily with Miles.

People could be envious of him—even scared. He made some people angry and feel hurt. Some people saw Miles as abusive toward white people. I never saw that. I thought he just abused everybody.

Backstage at the Fillmore I changed the subject. *Jack Johnson* had just come out, so I said, "Miles, man—your new album is incredible." He looked at me and smiled. "Ain't it, though?"

I met two more heroes in New York that summer of 1970, both of whom connected with Miles—Tony Williams and John McLaughlin. Tony played drums with Miles through most of the changes of the 1960s and on an album I loved, *In a Silent Way*. He was leading his own group, Tony Williams Lifetime, with John McLaughlin on guitar and Larry Young on organ. It was like all roads led to Miles— Larry and John had also played with Miles on *Bitches Brew*.

Lifetime was playing Slug's, a small, run-down club on the Lower East Side. This place was like something in a war zone; it was the club where the trumpet player Lee Morgan would get shot the following year, and they'd close it down for good. I was walking across Avenue A or B, and some guys were sizing me up, like, "What's this hippie freak up to down here?" John told me he went through the same thing—"Where are you goin', white boy?"

"I'm going to go play with Tony Williams."

"Tony Williams? Man, we'll walk you there. You can't walk alone here. They're going to take your guitar." John's story gave me the same feeling I had when the bus driver in San Francisco had me sit with him that time I was carrying my guitar. We all have our angels.

Man, the Lifetime show was loud and mind-boggling. It fried my brain. I had never heard rock and jazz ideas put together with so much intensity and with the volume turned up all the way like that. Slug's was a small, narrow place, and Lifetime filled it with a vortex of sound. Cream sort of had that energy, but not with the same ideas or sounds—it didn't surprise me so much that Cream's Jack Bruce joined Lifetime a little while later.

257

The three of them had an attitude that made them look like enforcers. You almost didn't want to look at them they were so... menacing. John was killin' brilliant in his playing, and I know that just as he scared me, I'm sure he scared even Jimi Hendrix. It was like, "Holy shit, he's got the Buddy Guy thing down *and* he can take care of the Charlie Parker thing." There are just not that many musicians who can play fast and deep the way he does. Even today I love to jam with him, then step back and just listen to him *soar*.

I met John when they took a break, and he recognized me right away. "Santana? Nice to meet you." Around a month before, I had gotten into Wayne Shorter's album *Super Nova,* which had Sonny Sharrock and John on some tracks, so that was the first thing I told him. "I also love what you do on Joe Farrell's 'Follow Your Heart' with Jack DeJohnette." I think I surprised him a little with what I was listening to, and then he told me what *he* was into: Coltrane, Wayne, Miles, and Bill Evans—in that order. That's all we needed to talk about. John wasn't into Sri Chinmoy at that point, but Mahavishnu was right around the corner.

I didn't get to talk to Tony or Larry that night, but I would get to know them later, along with many other musicians who played with Miles, including Jack DeJohnette. It was Jack who told me that he suggested John leave London and move to New York City— John, like Jimmy Page, was a session guitarist at the time, and Jack had heard him playing here and there. I always wondered, though, about Tony leaving Miles, which seemed like the perfect gig for him, and then Miles using his new band—John and Larry Young without Tony—on *Bitches Brew*.

I never asked Tony about that, but I think I can hear the reasons on a live gig at the Jazz Workshop in Boston in 1968, not long after he played with Miles on *In a Silent Way*. It sounds almost like he's having a tantrum on the drum kit—like he's a little kid throwing stuff from his high chair onto the floor. Meanwhile Miles was cool, and so were Wayne and Chick. I would have fired him. I really don't know what happened that would make someone do that, but he was certainly sending a strong signal.

Tony needed his own band—that's something I would see time and time again in other groups, and in Santana, too.

In the Bay Area in August was the first time Jimi Hendrix and I really spoke to each other as musicians, but that wasn't the first time we met. Back in '67, the week after our band was fired by Bill for being late, Carabello had somehow got us into that Fillmore show to meet Hendrix. We were trying to duck Bill, and we didn't have any money—we got in just as the sound check was starting. It didn't matter about Bill anyway, because he had his hands full with amplifiers that wouldn't cooperate. Everything was feeding back, screeching like electrified pigs. They finally got it together, and we were backstage just before the band was going on. Jimi and I hadn't said anything between us except hello, and suddenly everybody went to the bathroom—*everybody*. Somebody said, "Hey, man, you wanna come and join us?" I was young, but I knew what they were doing. "No, man. I don't want to do any coke."

"You sure? It's from Peru, really first class."

"You go ahead, man. I'm there already."

That's when I started to use my mantra about partying too much. "I'm there already, man. I don't want to get past it."

Then Jimi played—and it was incredible, both shows that night. I couldn't believe it—the way he could will his guitar to make those sounds. They didn't sound like strings and amplifiers anymore—his sound was intergalactic, with spectral frequencies that were notes yet so much more. At times it sounded like the Grand Canyon screaming.

I was like, "Holy shit." Gábor was on the bill, too, and that first night he sounded good, but I know for a fact that Gábor never wanted Hendrix to open for him again. He told me so when we were living in the same house for a while in 1971 and almost started a band together. That was the impact Hendrix had—he came and marched across the landscape like a conquistador wielding light-sabers and lasers, weapons that no one had ever seen or heard before. I saw him around seven times total, and that night was great. But no Hendrix show topped the one I heard him do at the Santa Clara County Fairgrounds in San Jose in '69. I never heard him do better.

The second time we met was sometime in April of 1970 in New York City. Devon called me from the lobby of our hotel and said, "Come on down. I want you to come with me to a party."

"What party?" I thought we were going to go somewhere else, hear some music.

"Man, just come on down—we're going to a Jimi Hendrix party. He's recording."

That sounded so strange. "He's recording and having a party? When I record I don't want anybody in the studio." Devon just laughed. "Come on, don't be such a square. We do it differently over here in New York." Devon had taken me to see the Woodstock movie the day before, and now we were going to the Record Plant. Okay, why not?

We got into a cab and got to the studio just when Jimi was arriving with a blond lady who, the last time I saw her, was with Tito Puente. Small world. Jimi opened the door for us and looked at me. "Santana, right?"

"Yeah. How you doing?"

He paid for both cabs, then looked at me. "Man, I like your choice of notes," he said with a smile.

I said the best thing I could think of at that point. "Well, thank you, man."

We walked into the studio, and it was packed with people. "Hey, how you doing?...What's happening?...How you doing, man?" As we walked from the front door down the hallway to the studio, there was a buffet of shit laid out on a table—I mean hashish, grass, cocaine. Really—it was a buffet. Jimi was ahead of me, running his hands through it, sampling stuff. He looked at me and said, "Help yourself, man."

"Thanks—I'll just smoke a joint. That's great; thank you."

Jimi and his engineer, Eddie Kramer, got started right away, talking about picking up where they had left off the night before, doing a song called "Room Full of Mirrors." I'm looking and listening, wondering how they do it in the studio—what can I learn? They played back the song, and I heard Jimi singing, "I used to live in a room full of mirrors / All I could see was me..." Then Eddie said, "Go ahead, Jimi, here comes your part." They were overdubbing a slide guitar part. Jimi started playing, and for the first eight bars he was right with it. By the twelfth bar, it had nothing to do with the song anymore. It would have been okay if he were just blowing over a groove, but this was more a structured song. I was looking around to see how other people were hearing this. Eddie was looking worried, and he had actually stopped the recording, but Jimi kept playing—more and more out.

Jimi was facing away from the window to the control room. Eddie told one of his guys to check on him, and I swear the guy had to physically pull him away from the guitar and the amplifier. He got Jimi up, and when he turned around—I'm not kidding—Jimi looked like a possessed demon. It almost looked like he was having an epileptic attack—foaming at the mouth, his eyes red like rubies.

I remember that the whole experience drained me—and that a feeling of questioning came over me: "Is this how it's got to be done? There's got to be a better way."

The last time I met Jimi was a few weeks later in California, when he played the Berkeley Community Theatre. He had made a change on the bass and was using Billy Cox, not Noel Redding. We caught the concert and went back to hang with Jimi at his hotel. Something told me that Jimi needed help, so I decided I should bring the gold medallion I wore around my neck, which my mother had given me when I was a baby—the kind that all Mexican mothers give their children for protection: Jesus is on one side, and the Virgin of Guadalupe is on the other. I was thinking I'd just grab Jimi's hand, put the medallion in it, and say, "This is for you—wear it, because I think you can use it." When we got there, Jimi opened the door and I could see that he was wearing six or seven of these medals already, so I kept mine in my pocket.

A few months after that, Santana was playing in Salt Lake City when we heard that Jimi had died. That night you could hear all the toilets on our floor of the hotel flushing—people dumping all their shit, so angry because we heard he had OD'd. Whether or not it was true, he was the first of our generation to go, and we were sure drugs had something to do with it. That's how we put it. "Fucking drugs, man."

I don't think anybody came through the '60s without taking some drugs. I also don't think anyone came through the '60s without changing—but some people changed a little too quickly. Who can tell someone who's twenty-one, twenty-two, or twenty-three to slow down? I turned twenty-three that year, and it felt like all the planets were aligning and there was a divine explosion. The Woodstock movie came out, and a few weeks later, in September, *Abraxas* did, too, and it shot up the charts faster than our first album had. It was all these streams coming together, creating a river that just kept getting bigger and wilder. I started to see rock bands, and some jazz groups, too, getting hold of congas and timbales and making them part of their sound. Celebrities were showing up everywhere we played—stars, stars, stars. Mick Jagger saw us in London. Paul McCartney was at L'Olympia in Paris, so I quoted "The Fool on the Hill" in the middle of "Incident." Raquel Welch was in the front row at the Hollywood Bowl. Miles and Tito Puente came to our shows in New York and hung out in the balcony.

Everybody wanted a piece of Santana—to be on TV, to be in various projects. At the end of 1970, we played on *The Tonight Show* for Johnny Carson and we did *The Bell Telephone Hour* with Ray Charles and the Los Angeles Philharmonic. That was the same time the Rolling Stones asked us to be in *Gimme Shelter*, the documentary about Altamont, and we had to say no.

Abraxas was on its way to selling more than three million copies that year alone. "Black Magic Woman" was a top ten hit on pop radio, and all the underground FM rock stations were playing the album *a lot*. When I heard "Samba Pa Ti" on the radio for the first

THE UNIVERSAL TONE

time, everything just froze. I was at home, looking at distant lights twinkling away, not even focusing on them, just listening. It felt good to step outside of myself and just hear the notes, which sounded like somebody else playing beautifully and with heart. At the same time I knew it was me — it was more *me* than anything I had recorded before. That opening part of "Samba" made me think, "Whoa. I can hear my mom talking, or Dad telling one of his stories." It's a story without words that can be played and understood by people no matter where they are — Greece, Poland, Turkey, China, Africa. It was actually the first time I didn't feel uncomfortable or strange hearing myself.

That year was jammed, and Bill's prediction was absolutely right — when the money got more serious, everything got more serious, and there were some ego things happening in the band. People started to change. Stan Marcum started to get the idea that he should be in the band, playing flute. He also called a band meeting around this time with Bill to basically call Bill on the carpet for taking too much money and to work out clearly who the band manager was. It was like he was drawing a line in the sand. Bill took charge of the meeting from the start. He was prepared — he had written down a long list of all the shows and tours and TV gigs he had gotten us and all the other things he did to support us that were beyond the call of duty — such as free rehearsal space and the idea for "Evil Ways." It was obvious that Stan was not in Bill's league, yet we felt we had to choose between Bill and Stan. I didn't say anything. Bill could have just said, "Woodstock."

Bill had done stuff for us that we didn't even know about, not until years later. When we were negotiating our very first contract with Columbia, Bill and his lawyer looked it over, and for some reason they inserted a line of small print on the back — something to the effect that if Columbia brought our music out again on different formats, the royalty rate would stay the same as it was on the original releases. When compact discs got big in the '80s, Santana started getting checks with lots of zeros from sales of the old albums in our catalog, and when *Supernatural* went worldwide in 1999, the same thing happened. It's a gift that still keeps giving back—thank you, Bill.

By the end of 1970, Neal Schon had been hanging around for a while, jamming with us. Both Neal and I were playing Gibson Les Pauls, but we had different signatures—so that wasn't a problem. I had a Les Paul to replace the red SG I had played at Woodstock and subsequently broken.

I liked Neal's dexterity, and he brought a lot of fire for someone so young, yet in a humble way. We had some tunes he sounded good on, and we started thinking about where to put solos so we wouldn't have two guitar solos in a row. When Gregg soloed I would comp something that would stimulate him, and Neal was able to do his own thing and find his way through it.

Neal's playing next to mine made me think of bands I liked that had two guitarists and how they worked together—the Butterfield Blues Band had Bloomfield and Elvin Bishop. Fleetwood Mac had *three* guitar players back then—Peter Green, Jeremy Spencer, and Danny Kirwan. Eric Clapton had a new band, Derek and the Dominos, with Duane Allman on some of the tunes.

In November, Clapton came to San Francisco with the Dominos, and because Bill was the promoter he arranged a special get-together for all of us at Wally Heider Studios. We were all there with Neal, and when Eric showed up the only problem was that I was tripping and too out of it to jam. I said to myself, "You better sit this one out and just learn." Eric had heard about us and was really gracious to come over and hang. We all had a good time, and I liked Eric—I was comfortable with him because I could tell we were coming from the same place.

The next thing we knew we were hearing that Clapton had asked Neal to join the Dominos, which made me think that if we wanted to keep Neal with us we only had one choice. It felt good to have another strong melodic voice in the band, and I wasn't threatened by the idea—I wasn't paranoid or too proud to have another guitarist with us. It was my decision to ask him to join us, after I spoke with the rest of the band. Neal said yes, and by December he was part of Santana.

I know a lot of people have their own perceptions about whether Santana needed another guitar player or not. I remember Miles had his own idea about it—expressed once again when we were at the CBS offices riding up the elevator one day. "Why did you do that? You don't need him." A few years after he said that, Miles had two guitars in his own band—Reggie Lucas and Pete Cosey, and then in the '80s he had John Scofield and Mike Stern together. I'm just saying, you know?

Besides, Miles had no way to know that we had some new tunes we were doing, such as Gene Ammons's "Jungle Strut," that would be on the next album and that I wanted to play with two guitar players. I asked Neal to join not because I was thinking about who played which parts or that it would free me up—it was much more about adding more flames to the band, the sound and energy we had together. The fire that Neal brought was a white, white heat.

The year 1970 ended with Columbia getting ready to release "Oye Como Va"—and by January we were preparing to go back into the studio to work on songs for the next album. We kept going ahead, playing shows, not slowing down. It was crazy energy sometimes, and we could be cocky in Santana, even before we got big.

Sometimes it was just playing tricks and pranks: one time Carabello, who was always being a goofball, poured a strawberry milk shake on top of one poor waitress's beehive hairdo. We also learned that Chepito could be crazy—he always wore long trench coats that had lots of pockets on the inside, and he'd always be filling them up with freebie stuff and other things he'd find on the road—soap and shampoo, towels, even silverware.

One time he bought a really big suitcase and filled it up with all sorts of stupid shit. We'd say, "What are you doing, man?"

"You don't get it? I'm the Robin Hood of Nicaragua. I'm bringing the poor people back some stuff that I got from the white gringos."

"Okay, but toilet paper and lightbulbs?"

Sometimes people did stupid things that really got us in trouble. Once, we arrived at LAX the same week that *Abraxas* came out, and Chepito was carrying a box of albums with him. His coat made the metal detector go off, and they asked, "Okay, what's in the box?" He said, "Explosives." *Bam!* Airport security handcuffed him and hauled him away and really put him through the wringer. We knew this was going to take a while, so we split for the hotel, and Ron stayed behind. Security finally let Chepito go when he told them he was talking about the music being explosive — "Man, it's the brand-new Santana album." He really went over the line, but he never wanted to back down from his logic. "It *is* explosive, man."

Things were coming at us fast, and it didn't help that drugs were getting easier and easier to get the bigger we got—you didn't even have to look for them; the drugs would find you. I can't deny that drugs had a lot to do with the environment that Santana came from, but my thinking was always that none of it mattered to me as long as the music kept going at the supreme level that it needed to be on. "Don't lose respect for that, man, because that's what got us here," I would say to the band.

The real problem was heroin—some members of Santana and other people around us were using, and it *was* starting to get in the way of the music. We were playing a lot, but we weren't getting together and rehearsing and thinking about songs and melodies and parts, as we had just a few months before. Some people couldn't hang with the momentum of the band. I'd wake up with cold-sweat nightmares—we'd be scheduled to play in front of fifty thousand people, and they would have been waiting for us for twenty minutes...twenty-five...*half an hour,* and we're still not ready to play because some of us are just too fucked up. I kept presenting that picture to the rest of the band. "Man, I keep having this same nightmare. First it concerned me, then it worried me, and now it's fucking pissing me off!"

They'd look at me like, "Who are you to tell us this stuff? You're doing the same kind of thing—smoking a lot of weed and messing with LSD." They had a point—I hadn't really been in a state to play at Woodstock, but at least I was together enough to pray to God to please help me. I'd tell them, "Yeah, man, but I'm not incoherent. That stuff is not getting in my way." I always felt that heroin and cocaine were more than disruptive—they were destructive. That's the best way of putting it.

I wasn't an angel about this. I tried heroin a few times—the first time because some of the people in the band's crew were shooting and they invited me to try it, and it was really incredible. I tried it a second time, and it was really, really incredible. I found myself playing all night and drinking water and thinking, "Whoa, this is easy, to play like this." It felt like worries and fears just went out the window, and you're super relaxed and just having a good time.

The rush was immediate, and it didn't make me throw up. I just went to the guitar, and the next thing I knew I'd been playing for so long that my fingers were black from the strings—and they didn't hurt. Playing after shooting up was very seductive and deceiving— while you were doing it, it felt like you attained a facility to articulate on a level beyond what you had previously known. You could play up and down the neck of the guitar without doing anything wrong—you thought. But the next day you'd listen to the tape you made and realize that you were deluding yourself. Heroin will do this to you.

It was important for me to know, really know, that I never needed heroin to get into that kind of trance with my guitar. On any given day I can be playing and look down an hour later and see drool hanging from my lip down to my shirt—I'm that euphorically into it. I look at myself when that happens and go, "That's great—that's a badge of honor." But I do try not to do that onstage.

The third time I was getting ready to shoot up, I was in a bathroom with a cat who couldn't find my vein. By the grace of God, just as he found a place to inject me, the door to the medicine cabinet opened by itself, and the mirror swung right into my face. Suddenly all I could see was myself up close, and I looked like the Wolfman in one of those movies on late-night TV. I was like, "Holy shit"—it really freaked me out.

I said, "Hold on, hold on."

"No, it's okay—I found it."

"No. Please take the rubber band off. Don't put that in me. You can have mine." He looked at me. "Really—I don't want it."

Something in the way the mirror opened up and the way my face looked in it told me once and for all that heroin wasn't for me and that I would never touch it again. Thank God I wasn't hooked yet and didn't need to take it. I'm pretty good at listening to signals, and this one felt like more than an omen. I really got the message: heroin and cocaine are not for you.

So I knew how heroin felt and why people would do it—but by the end of 1970 I couldn't stand watching what was happening to some of the people in the band and what it was doing to our music. There were more fights and arguments than making music—the joy of it felt like it was leaving. Being onstage in Santana was like being in a football team, but when you start throwing the ball and the same guys keep dropping it, then it begins to wear on everyone, and you can feel it coming apart. But every time I said something about it, people would deny it, and if I said anything about the drugs, they would react like I had a huge thermometer in my hand and I was going to put it in somebody's butt. People would look at me and say, "There is nothing wrong with us; what's wrong with you?" It was frustrating—it felt like there was no way to get through that.

On New Year's Eve we played a festival in Hawaii and had a few days off. The morning after the concert I woke up around five thirty in the house we stayed in, right on the beach. It was still dark, but I couldn't sleep, so I went and woke up Carabello. I said, "Michael, I need your help, man. I need you to wake up and take a walk with me." He saw I was serious. We started walking down the beach, and he listened to me.

"You and I started this thing, man. But something has to change, because we're not making any progress—we're getting worse with our attitude to the music. We're getting really arrogant and really belligerent. It's becoming a drag now to even deal with going to the studio, and if I'm feeling that then I know it's got to be like that for the others. This merry-go-round is not going anywhere, and we're not creating music that I feel has the same power as what we were doing at the start.

"Look, I'm in this and with all of you—I'm part of it, but I want to change. I want us to go back to the way we started, rehearsing new songs and trying out different things. I want to bring that joy back. But if things don't change, I might have to leave the band.

"I need your help, man. I think we need to have a meeting and bring this up and talk about it and really, really deal with it."

Carabello and I still talk about this conversation today. He brought it up recently, reminding me that I woke him up and took him walking. "You really tried to talk to us about changing our course before we hit a brick wall or went over a cliff. You were right."

That morning on the beach, Carabello looked at me and said, "Okay, man. Let's take care of this." But it was a long time before we did.

CHAPTER 12

Me in my Jesus T-shirt, Ghana, March 6, 1971.

I want to talk about Africa. I've only been there a few times, but each time I've gone the first thing my whole body is thirsty for is the rhythms — to hear the music and see the dancers. It's about connections between us and where we came from. To this day, African music is my number one hunger. I can never get enough of the rhythms, the melodies, the second melodies, the colors, the way the music can suddenly change my mood from light and joyful to somber. If people ask me, I tell them that we play 99.9 percent African music. That's what Santana does.

Ralph J. Gleason reviewed our album Santana III *in* Rolling Stone *—everything he said was right on. He said that the rhythms we use should be put under a microscope so people can tell how each one leads back to Africa. In my mind, I can see a map that shows how we can trace all the rhythms we have over here in America back through Cuba and other parts of the Caribbean and Latin America, all the way to different parts of Africa. What was the rumba before it was a rumba? The danzón? The bossa nova? The bolero?*

Maybe music doesn't always fit into maps so well, but I'd like to see someone try. Some places need to be bigger on the map than they actually are because they're more important than people know—Cuba; Cape Verde. It's crazy—Cape Verde gave birth to music in Mexico and all over South America, especially Brazil. When you hear a certain kind of romance in music—the bolero, the danzón, the slow cha-cha— it all came from that one little island. You would have to bring the focus in on Colombia, too, with those bad cumbias that Charles Mingus loved to play. Then you have Texas, Mississippi, and Memphis shuffles, and all those street rhythms from New Orleans. It would be fascinating to see where the arrows point.

I wish there was a school here that just taught one thing—how to have some humility and recognize that Africa is important and necessary to the world—and not just because of its music, either. When it comes to African music, I got nothing but time to learn. I think I've surprised a few African bands because I was able to hang with the music—there's too much groove not to!

One more thing about Africa: one of the greatest compliments I ever received was not on an awards show but from Mory Kanté. He's a great singer and guitar player from Mali. I love, love, love his music. He was part of the "Dance to the Beat of My Drums" concert we did with Claude Nobs in Montreux. I was there in my tuning room, and an African gentleman came in and said he was Mory's representative and that Mory apologized because he did not speak English, but he had a message to tell me. He told me the message in their language, then he translated: "Mory wants to tell you that your belly is full, but you're hungry to feed the people."

"Okay, thanks!"
Then the man bowed and walked out.
Wow. It sounded like a great compliment. I'll take it.

I f music is from many places it's also from one place, and Santana could not have happened without San Francisco. If you needed to meet a good bass player, somebody always knew somebody else, or maybe you'd hear about a new piano player or drummer or group you had to check out. My own brother Jorge was coming up with his band, the Malibus, and getting a reputation on guitar—then they changed their name to Malo and got together their own mix of rock and Latin rhythms and Spanish lyrics. A few years later some musicians from Malo would come to Santana as well as certain players from Tower of Power, the great horn band from Oakland. Even today I look at bands close to home for people who might come into Santana.

That's how things flowed in San Francisco. Santana was never exclusive—like many bands, we played and jammed and did sessions with each other and found new ideas and people to go on the road with. Just as Neal eased into the band, we were open to thinking about playing and recording with other musicians. We were open to having other people sing lead besides Gregg, too—as we did on "Oye Como Va."

You get all that on our third album. We started the sessions for *Santana III* at the beginning of 1971. Rico Reyes came back to sing on another song in Spanish, "Guajira," and Mario Ochoa played piano on it. We had the Tower of Power horns on "Everybody's Everything," which became the first single from the album later that year. We opened the door and invited Luis Gasca to play on "Para Los Rumberos," another Tito Puente song we wanted to cover. We made it our "Dance to the Music"—we sang the names of Carabello, Chepito, and me before playing our parts. Greg Errico from Sly's band and Linda Tillery from the Loading Zone played percussion on some songs, and we had Coke Escovedo playing percussion all over the album.

Coke came in and added so much to the sessions from the start that we had to give him credit for the inspiration he brought to that album. Coke's roots are Mexican, and he had played with Cal Tjader before he played with us. He's one of the famous Escovedo brothers — the whole family makes music. His brother Pete also plays percussion and is Sheila E.'s father. The brothers had a Latin jazz group together that played around the city, and in '72 they formed Azteca, the Latin rock-jazz group that many musicians got started in. Coke helped write "No One to Depend On," the second single from *Santana III*, and he started touring with us.

The challenge of the third album was finding new tunes and new ideas to fit with our sound. We put the pressure on ourselves because, for a little bit longer, we were still at a point where we could be a unit. We would be rehearsing, and suddenly someone would say, "Hey, I have an idea" and play it, or someone would want to start playing a Latin tune or a B. B. King riff he had been hearing, and we'd work out our own interpretation of it right on the spot. The tune "Batuka" came from a musical arrangement that Zubin Mehta sent to us to play with the Los Angeles Philharmonic on *The Bell Telephone Hour* on TV. The piece was written by Leonard Bernstein as "Batukada," and it's a long score, and we were looking at it like monkeys trying to figure out schematics for a computer! "What the fuck is this?" But we liked the name, so we shortened it to "Batuka" and said, "Let's just make up our own shit, man." That's how that tune came about — it was just based on the name of the score Mehta gave us.

That's also how we were able to come up with "Toussaint L'Ouverture" in the studio. It was one of the last things we did with Albert Gianquinto. "Everybody's Everything" was based on a 1966 song called "Karate" by the R & B vocal group the Emperors — it had a great hook that I couldn't get out of my head. I had heard it once on the radio, then a few years later I was in Tower Records, where I always did some research, buying 45s of old hits from the '50s and '60s. I found it still on sale, and the staff played it for me, and I was thinking, "Damn—this is like black hillbilly, hoedown kind of music," and I loved it.

The song was about a new kind of dance, but that wasn't what Santana was about, so I made the thing happen with the lawyers, who called the two guys who wrote the song—Milton Brown and Tyrone Moss—and got the okay for us to come up with our own words. Neal played the solo, and we kept the "Yeah, I'd do it" from the original.

I looked through my Rolodex of music that I loved and brought in "Jungle Strut" by Gene Ammons. I played it for the band, and they said, "Yeah, that sounds like Santana. We can do that." We wrote "Everything's Coming Our Way" together—it was my way of sneaking some Curtis Mayfield into our music. David was getting into Latin and Afro-Caribbean music more and more—he worked out some ideas with Chepito and Rico Reyes and came up with "Guajira."

We normally did one song a day in the studio, but because of our touring in '71 the sessions for *Santana III* stretched over more time than any other Santana album—we started in January and were still recording in July. We would record in San Francisco, hit the road for a while, and on the way back home go into a New York studio with Eddie Kramer. We were crossing those time zones—both in the United States and overseas. The road could be rough if you let it get that way. Chepito could burn like a two-ended candle—but then he had an aneurysm and got so frail he couldn't play for a while. We asked Willie Bobo to come in and take over timbales, and he did.

In March we got on a plane in New Jersey that took us farther from home than we ever thought we'd go. We received a phone call about going to Ghana to help celebrate the country's anniversary—they wanted Santana to play in a festival with Ike & Tina Turner, the Staple Singers, the Voices of East Harlem, Les McCann, Eddie Harris, Wilson Pickett, and Roberta Flack. We had a choice: we could go to Ghana or stay home and see Aretha Franklin and Ray Charles at the Fillmore West—they were recording a live album. That was tough. But we said, "Let's go to Africa."

Next thing I knew I was on a flight sandwiched between Roberta Flack and Mavis Staples, and they were singing "Young, Gifted, and Black"—I got it in stereo. I said, "Whoa. This is going to be fun." Next to us was Wilson Pickett's horn section.

The whole plane started partying as soon as we took off. There was no one but musicians on board—everyone started smoking weed and doing coke. Willie Bobo turned out to be like a running comedy act, an instigator of practical jokes and funny stories. He knew how to poke you to see if you had the wisdom to laugh at yourself, although a lot of people may not have been ready for it. You'd either get pissed off or you'd laugh. It seemed that half the material he could have created for Bill Cosby. Willie had that kind of presentation. He and I got really close at that time.

It was the longest flight I'd ever been on—more than twelve hours. When we landed the whole airport looked like a tsunami of Africans—they were all there to greet us, all colors, sizes, and shapes. Some were so black they were almost iridescent blue. It was beautiful—they came right up to the plane. We walked down the stairs, and the crowd started parting like the Red Sea in front of Moses, and suddenly there was a line of local people representing Ghana's twelve nations coming to meet us. Each nation had its own dancing style and costumes, some decorated with big buffalo horns and seashells. Each group greeted us one at a time, then the mayor of Accra and his party got their turn.

The whole scene was incredible to see and hear first thing after landing. Then we saw a witch doctor kind of guy—he was wearing animal skins and shaking a big gourd that was as big and round as a basketball. He made it rattle like a Buddy Rich roll. It was obvious by the way he took center stage that he commanded a lot of respect. Even the mayor's people got out of his way, and the people who were filming the trip and concert loved him. We were like, "Who is this guy?"

Willie decided he would show off—he had an amulet that he wore, and he started saying that his voodoo was more powerful, that he had his own thing going on. Back then I figured we all had our own way of dealing with the invisible realm. I just wasn't flaunting mine. But that holy man fascinated us and scared us at the same time. I could tell right away that he was a sorcerer and had a way of dealing with the invisible realm—he could reach the spirits. And that wouldn't be the last time we saw him.

We got through customs and went straight to the hotel to get ready for a big dinner that the president was hosting. Before we started eating everyone was asked to rise, and a group of men and women sang Ghana's national anthem, which was in a kind of call-and-response form. Suddenly I recognized it—it sounded very close to "Afro Blue." I couldn't believe it. If this wasn't where Mongo Santamaría got the song, then they were close cousins, man. Both were coming from the same place.

We were there for almost a week, and there was a lot of looking and learning going on. The next day Carabello ate or drank something and came down with dysentery, which kept him in the hotel, close to the bathroom. Shrieve and I went into town to the market to just look around, and our taxi got stuck in traffic—bumper to bumper, all the windows down. I had brought a cassette player along and was listening to some Aretha Franklin on my headphones. A woman who was walking by stopped right next to the car and was staring at me like I had just stepped out of a flying saucer. I took the headphones off and showed her how to put them on her head. She did, and her eyes got real wide, and she smiled a huge smile. It was connection with penetration—it was like family there.

Workers were still constructing the stage when we got there, so we had to wait for them to finish. At night we were on our own and would all hang out in the only place we could—in the lobby lounge of the Holiday Inn. We ate there, drank there. We laughed when Willie Bobo was holding forth, making everybody hoot. One night he started picking on Wilson Pickett—"Hey, Wilson Pickle. Wilson Pickle." Pickett could be a tough dude. He was serious, like Albert King—he didn't take any mess. But Willie kept at it. "Man, let me show you what you're going to be doing in your show." He got down on one knee and put his coat on like it was a cape. "Just like James Brown, but it ain't gonna work, because here in Africa, James Brown is number one. Sorry to tell you."

I couldn't believe it—I got myself over to the other side of the lobby as fast as I could, away from the intensity. I think we were all getting itchy to get out more, and at the same time I remember wishing some of us had been more understanding and respectful of the people and their culture. I remember Pickett would say that Africans needed to use more deodorant, and Willie was ragging on the holy man we met at the airport—he was really a charlatan, a guy who had people convinced he had some kind of power. I also remember hoping that the witch doctor didn't pick up on any of this—just in case.

The next night in the lobby bar I heard an African guy in a suit and tie talking about how we were there just to steal their shit and exploit their music. He said it just loudly enough for me to hear him. I walked up to him and said, "Excuse me." Then I handed him my guitar and said, "Here, man, play me something."

He said, "What? I don't play the guitar; I'm a lawyer."

"Then it's not your fuckin' music—it's only yours when you play it." I could be cocky, too, and I liked to make my point. He grabbed his drink and gave me my guitar back.

I went back down the next day—it was the same place, the same people, like they hadn't moved from the night before. Later that afternoon, someone came up to me in the lobby—"Mr. Santana? Mr. Pickett wants to see you in his room."

"Uh, Okay."

I went upstairs, knocked on the door. A young lady opened it. I heard a voice from inside go, "Who is it?"

"I think it's Carlos Santana."

"Yeah? Let him in."

I went inside, and Pickett and Ike Turner were doing coke. "Come on in, man."

"How you guys doing? What's going on?"

Pickett looked me up and down. "So you're the magnificent one, huh? You're the Santana? You're that guy?" I knew from back in my Tijuana days where this was going—I didn't want any of that. "I heard that you wanted to talk to me, so I'm here, but before we do that I just want to let you know that I have all your albums. I play all your songs and love them. 'In the Midnight Hour,' 'Land of 1000 Dances,' 'Mustang Sally,' 'Funky Broadway,' 'Ninety-Nine and a Half (Won't Do)'..." I kept going down the list, and it was true— I learned all of them. "I love you, man."

Wilson looked at Ike. Ike, to his credit, just shook his head, like, "It's cool. Carlos is okay." I politely got out of the room.

It wasn't the first or last time that happened—meeting a musician I love who was mistrusting or not happy with praise. But I have to say it very rarely happens—I think over the years I can count on one hand the number of those kinds of meetings.

I met Eddie Harris in Ghana on that same trip and asked if we could play together on one of his songs. "Hey, Eddie—you want to jam? Let's do 'Listen Here' or 'Cold Duck Time.'" He shook his head. "No, Santana, you're not going to beat me with my own shit. That ain't going to happen." I wasn't looking at it like that and tried to explain. "Man, I just love your music."

It happened another time just a few weeks after we got back from Africa, when we shared the bill at the Fillmore East with Rahsaan Roland Kirk. The night Miles was there and flicked my ear, I knocked on the door to Rahsaan's dressing room, something I rarely did. It opened, and I remember it was almost pitch-black in there. Rahsaan and some of the guys in his band were in the room. "Mr. Kirk, my name is Carlos Santana, and I'm just here to thank you from the center of my heart for bringing so much joy in your music, man. I've listened to *Volunteered Slavery* and *The Inflated Tear*..." As I had with Wilson Pickett, I started naming the songs I loved, then I waited. All of a sudden they all started laughing like hyenas, just laughing and laughing. I quietly found the doorknob, opened it, and walked out. I told myself, "Okay. I'll never do that again."

Another thing I won't do is mess with any black magic. We ran into that holy man again walking near our hotel in Ghana, and a chicken crossed his path. He stopped and looked at it in a weird way, and *pow!* The chicken suddenly fell over dead, even though it had just been looking fine and healthy. Everyone backed up and gave the guy room. We got back to the hotel, and at the restaurant all the guys in Pickett's band wanted to tell him the story. "Pickett, man, you're not going to believe what this voodoo guy did. Man, it was freaky!" Pickett kept saying, "No, no. I don't want to know. Don't tell me, don't tell me." But they wouldn't stop—they were like kids coming back home and needing to tell their parents about something that happened at school. They told Pickett about the chicken, and he just shook his head. "I told you not to tell me this shit, man. Now I'm going to have nightmares." Meanwhile Willie Bobo was cracking up.

The last day before the concert in Ghana, the organizers found something for us to do. They invited us to the Cape Coast Castle, which was a place where Africans were held before they were put on the slave ships that would take them to various parts of America. It was basically an old brick fort painted white, right next to the ocean, with cannons in front. We had a tour guide explain what had happened there. He showed us the "gate of no return," which the slaves went through as they walked on African ground for the last time. He took us down into a horrible, hellish basement where the slaves were stuck waiting for the ships. All of us got really quiet—you could still feel the intensity from all the souls that had been crammed in there.

The wind picked up on cue and started making a whistling, lonely sound as it blew through the cracks and crevices in that old fort. All of us got chicken skin—it was like the sound of souls howling in pain and horror. *Woooohaaauuuiiiiiii!* Tina Turner heard it, and her knees got weak and she started crying and people had to carry her back to the bus. The wind kept blowing harder, and the whole thing got more and more creepy. Thinking about it now still gives me chills.

Willie didn't come with us to the castle because he wasn't feeling right. When we got back to the hotel he was really sick—sweating with a fever and vomiting. It was the same thing that Carabello had during most of the trip, but worse. He had a serious fever, and it wouldn't go down. We all took turns staying with him and putting cold towels on him throughout the night. Around midnight, a local doctor in a suit and tie came by while I was watching him and started looking at him.

The doctor said it was dysentery, and I couldn't help thinking about that holy man and all the things Willie had been saying and wondering—well, we all felt that way, suspicious and not sure what to believe. Just then somebody knocked on the door, the doctor got up to answer it, and sure enough, there he was—the holy man, stopping by to look at Willie. The doctor let him in, but I got up and blocked his way. Our eyes were locked on each other, and we had an inner conversation—I spoke to him inwardly.

"Man, I know you got the power, and I know you did this to him." Then I pointed to my T-shirt, which had a picture of Jesus on it. I kept talking to the holy man in my mind. "I respect and honor the beliefs that people have all over the world, as I do yours—but can you get through Jesus? You may be able to go through me, but you also got to go through him, because I am not only with him but I also belong to him."

You have to understand that I respect and honor Jesus Christ—he was a remarkable historic figure who stood up to authority and believed in common people and the power of his message—and he was killed for it, pure and simple. The thing about Jesus that gets lost, I believe, is that he was a man—that he was born and that he had to grow up to become who he was. He was a man, and he must have been a very attractive one at that, because he had charisma and people loved him. Women loved him. It's strange that the Bible says nothing about when he left home as a teenager and came back later. Where was he between the ages of thirteen and thirty? I believe the man went around the world—to Greece and to India. He got around, and he did things. He had to so he could learn to feel what it's like to live, how it is to eat well and be loved but also to be hungry and scorned. To feel the sensation of what it is to be a man and also hold divine mysticism.

There's a scene in Franco Zeffirelli's TV miniseries *Jesus of Nazareth* that's one of my favorites: Jesus walks into a temple just when the rabbi is about to open the holy scriptures and read from them, but Jesus politely asks the rabbi to move over. He does, then Jesus grasps the open scrolls and closes them, saying, "Today before your eyes the prophecy is fulfilled" and "The kingdom of heaven is upon you."

The people in the temple all get twisted and think it's blasphemy, but they don't understand his message: we can stop suffering—the divinity is already here, in each one of us, which ultimately is not what the church wants us to hear because they want the control and the message to come through them. From his aerial view of the situation, whether he speaks through Jesus or Muhammad or Buddha or Krishna—or whether he communicates directly to each of us—God can reach any part of anyone and say what we need to hear. No one should have a monopoly on that connection; no one can say with certainty, "You have to go through me to get to him." That sounds like a pimp to me.

I have a problem when that message gets twisted so that certain people are in a position to control and manipulate others, which is what religion has done for centuries, without coming to the aid of people who need help—when religion lets people suffer because of its dogma and traditions.

There's something else I like about that scene: Jesus was one of those guys whose duty it was to stand in the middle of a crowd and say, "Hey! The world is *not* flat," and that takes a lot of courage. It's how I feel about someone like Ornette Coleman, who came to New York from out of town with a different kind of music when everybody else was doing a more established kind of jazz, whatever that was. I have a lot of respect for people who not only have the clarity to see but are also not afraid to step up and speak out.

If Jesus were around today in the flesh there wouldn't be a Christmas. That's about business, and religion is an organized institution like the Bank of America, and it has a lot more money than the Bank of America. There's a saying that I love: "You got to give up the cross, man. Get down from there—we need the wood!"

Jesus was never about rules and requirements. He had a Christ consciousness, and he was not interested in dividing the world into believers and nonbelievers and saints and sinners and making everyone feel guilty about being born into sin and telling them they need to suffer because of that.

It wasn't a "my God versus your god" thing when I stood up to that shaman in Ghana. I was just facing my fear and calling on the power of love, which is the most supreme force of all—love and forgiveness, allowance and willingness. With just those few things, miracles can happen and human consciousness can be advanced and fear can be eradicated.

The holy man glared at me. I could see he understood what I was thinking. He looked at my eyes, then at my T-shirt, then he turned to the doctor, and they nodded at each other. It almost seemed to me like they had a thing going—one of them would get people sick and the other collected when he brought the medicine. Then that holy man walked out. Nothing happened to me—I didn't catch dysentery.

Check out *Soul to Soul*, the movie of the concert—Willie was able to play the next day, but you can see he was very listless. You can also see the crew getting fascinated with that holy man, turning the cameras on him whenever they could. Who knows? Maybe he worked some voodoo on them, too.

I remember Ike and Tina went on first—they had the theme song for the concert, "Soul to Soul." Wilson Pickett was the top headliner, and I think we played pretty well. What was peculiar was that the crowd didn't know when to clap. We would finish playing a tune, then...nothing. You could still feel that they were thinking it was really cool, that they really liked us, but I think the long songs and the various sections confused them, as they did with my father. They were learning through all the music, though, because they applauded when we finished the set and were clapping and dancing by the time Pickett played.

The Voices of East Harlem, with Dougie Rauch still on bass, played that night, too, and they impressed me more than the first time I heard them, in Tanglewood. They had a great song called "Right On Be Free" that sometimes I will play with Santana even now, more than forty years later. I like music with a message like that, music that I call brutally positive—such as Curtis Mayfield's songs or Marvin Gaye's "What's Going On" or the Four Tops' "A Simple Game"—because people need a constant jolt of "Kumbaya" that's not goody-goody. There's a lot of African music like that, too—I love Fela Kuti and his son Seun, who does a song that goes: "Don't bring that shit to me...don't bring bullshit to Africa." I love songs that say, "I'm going to take all those words and tell you straight about what's goin' on and whoop your fears with it."

After I got back from Africa, that trip stayed with me for a long, long time. I brought albums home with me and started to collect more wherever I could find them. I said, "Thank God for Tower Records" when they made a separate section for African music. I wanted to have one room in my home just for African music because I wanted to learn how to play it. It was rough trying to find the records at first, then starting in the '80s, when I would be in Paris you could see me making a beeline for the African section in those big music stores on the Champs-Élysées. I'd get a basket and just start grabbing.

Chepito recovered from his aneurysm, and he and Coke Escovedo joined us after we got back from Africa. We toured from the Bay Area to New York and then went to Europe, where we played the Montreux Jazz Festival again in April. We returned to the United

States and toured, sometimes with Rico Reyes or Victor Pantoja, who played congas on the first Chico Hamilton record I ever heard. And in July, we finally finished recording for our third album— *Santana III*.

We were doing a lot *as* a band, but things were not getting better *inside* the band. I think the first real cracks in Santana, the cracks that started forming the winter before, had started to show in terms of our musical tastes. At first the differences in what we were listening to helped us develop as a band: we shared it all, and it held us together. But by the time we were in the middle of recording our third album, our differences had us wanting to grow in our own separate directions. Gregg and Neal wanted to do the Journey thing—more of their kind of rock sound. David Brown was getting deep into Latin dance music, and Chepito was already there, listening to Tito Puente and Ray Barretto. I was pregnant with John Coltrane and Miles—Shrieve was, too. I was also getting into Weather Report, which had musicians who played with Miles on *Bitches Brew*—Joe Zawinul and Wayne Shorter were the nucleus of that new group.

You could really sense those differences after our shows, when we'd be hanging in the hotel. Shrieve and I would get together to listen to our favorite music in his room or mine, turning each other on to different records that had just come out. It could be jazz or soul or whatever. Girls would come by, looking to get high and party, and they'd get bored when the two of us would be going, "Check out this groove!" or "You gotta hear this solo." They'd move on to Chepito's room or David's.

I'm not judging one thing against another—there's time for everything. But it wasn't just music—by 1971 differences were also showing up in the priorities of some people in the band. The rock-and-roll lifestyle was taking over; it wasn't just the women or the cars or the cocaine and other excesses, it was also the attitude. We used to say that we were from the streets and we were real—we'd look at other bands that were making it and judge how they acted. "We're never going to be assholes like that," we'd say. But I saw how some people in the band were acting, and I was thinking to myself, "It's easy to see why a lot of bands fail—they OD on themselves."

I thought Santana was becoming a walking contradiction. The soul wanted one thing, but the body was too busy doing something else, and we were trying to be something we weren't anymore. Everything that Bill Graham said would happen was coming true—our heads were getting so big it was starting to feel like there wasn't enough room for everyone. I think we were all equally guilty of this.

For me the worst thing still was that we weren't practicing or working on new music, and I was hungry for that. I'd have to work at getting us together to play. I'd say, "There's dust on those platinum albums, man. Our music is starting to get rusty. We need to get together, and it shouldn't be like I'm saying we have to go to the dentist and deal with an abscess. We should get together—I'll rejoice with your songs, and you'll rejoice with mine, as we did on the first two albums."

Being a collective made us possible in many ways—it's what we *were*. But there was basically no discipline, and nobody but Shrieve wanted to hear that we might be making incorrect choices. We were very, very young—even our manager was young. He was supposed to be looking out for us, but he was participating in many of those excesses. He was using and helping to supply the band, and he still wanted to be in the band.

Some people in the band were angry at me because I was not happy most of the time. It's true: I probably wasn't a pleasant guy to be around, because I was complaining about this and that. I was feeling myself in conflict with so much money and so much excess, and the spiritual side of me was being crushed.

I was starting to lean more deeply in a spiritual direction at this time. It started with a few books. The only thing I had read when I was a kid was comic books—*Amazing Stories;* Stan Lee's Iron Man and Spider-Man. At the start of Santana I was already moving over to books about Eastern philosophy. In the Bay Area it was in the air—everybody was reading *The Urantia Book* and Paramahansa

Yogananda's *Autobiography of a Yogi* and Swami Muktananda's memoir. I read all of them, too.

There were yogis who came through San Francisco, and they would speak to whoever came to hear them—followers and friends who were curious. Sometimes I heard that John Handy or Charles Lloyd might show up, which was one more reason to go. I got to know the names of various gurus, including Krishnamurti and a young, pudgy guy called Maharaj Ji. There was also Swami Satchidananda, whom Alice Coltrane was into. They'd sell books after they spoke, and I would pick them up.

Everyone had heard about the Beatles and Maharishi Mahesh Yogi, the guru they followed for a while, and some people saw him as a trickster. I began to understand that these gurus were not charlatans but very wise men who could help people see their own luminosity—the divine light each person has inside, which enables us to lessen fear and guilt and ego. I learned new words for these ideas—words like *awakening*. That was really the job these teachers were doing: awakening people to a higher consciousness.

The next thing I knew my molecular chemistry began to change just by being curious and considering the metaphysical questions these gurus would talk about. It was a new language I was learning. I started asking questions like, "How can I evolve and not make the mistakes that everybody around me is making? How can I develop a bona fide, tangible spiritual discipline—with or without a guru? How can I connect this to my rock-and-roll lifestyle and the music I'm making?"

I was starting to get an inner urge to read more books and listen to music that resonated on the same frequency. I started to put aside Jimi's music and even Miles's for a while. I looked for the resonance I was getting from these gurus and found it when I was listening to Mahalia Jackson or to Martin Luther King's speeches—just his words and his tone and intention. John McLaughlin came out then with his new group, the Mahavishnu Orchestra—I played that first album over and over and felt their intention.

I also played lots and lots of Coltrane. He stayed on my turntable for a long time. I was learning, trying to comprehend the language of ascension. "The Father and the Son and the Holy Ghost" was *the* door for me. That was not easy, because the first ten times you listen to it you can't even find 1—the downbeat. It's all 1, and the only close resemblance to a melody in there is "Frère Jacques."

I could play guitar and hang with the modal music Coltrane was doing later, around the time of *A Love Supreme,* but Shrieve helped me get a feel for Coltrane's earlier stuff—and that of Miles and other jazz guys—because the idea of thirty-two-bar songs and AABA parts was all new to me. He would say, "Here's the bridge" and "This is a tag." "See how they modulated to another key?" or "Hear how the first sixteen bars are played two-beat and then the bridge is in 4/4 to get a swing feel?" Shrieve started in a high school jazz band, so he had some training and could be a guide.

As intense as Coltrane's music is, that was becoming my peace of mind. I'd play Coltrane or Mahavishnu, and I could be by myself. Cocaine and partying and all that fast living do not go well with *A Love Supreme* and *The Inner Mounting Flame*—that music was like daylight to vampires. Sometimes I'd play Coltrane for my inner peace, but to be honest sometimes I'd do it to get people who were hanging out too long at my place to leave. It would work every time—*whoosh!*

I know Coltrane was about peace and nonviolence, as Martin Luther King was—you could hear that in his music. But the intensity that I saw turning some people off was coming from the supreme intention there—the kind of intention I connected with in the Black Panthers across the bay in Oakland. We had gotten to know about them through David and Gianquinto, who was the first white Black Panther I knew. We had learned about the programs they established to help their community, like providing lunch for schoolkids. The government didn't see it that way—they were coming down hard on the Panthers. By the time we played for them they were on the run—Huey P. Newton and Bobby Seale were in jail, awaiting trial, and Eldridge Cleaver was in exile in Africa.

Some San Francisco groups, such as the Grateful Dead, did benefits to raise money for the Black Panthers so they could fight their legal battles. I remember we did two concerts for them, and I got to see how scary things were up close. We showed up in a limousine at the Berkeley Community Theatre, got out, and the first thing that happened was that security guys in black berets and black jackets asked us to stop and assume the position—"We need to frisk you."

I said, "Uh, okay, but you know we're playing for you."

"We know that, and we thank you, man, but up against the wall. We still have to do this."

Later on I understood that they had many infiltrators and people in their own organization spying on them. They didn't trust anyone. They had to protect themselves. They were living as if every second could be their last. I could feel that, and that impressed me. I remember talking with one of the Panthers. He pushed his face close to mine, saying, "I got one question for you, man. Are you fucking ready to die right now?" He was talking about what it meant to be in the Panthers back then. "Are you ready to die right now for what you believe in? Because otherwise get the fuck out of here; if you join the Panthers you got to be ready to die right now." I kept my mouth shut. It was scary. I was like, "Damn. This is not the Boy Scouts." It was brutal then, and that was their level of commitment.

I know seeing that kind of supreme intention had an effect on me—it felt like it was time to make decisions. Not long after that it was clear to everyone that David was not doing well—his heroin use was showing, and his playing and the music were starting to suffer. Sometimes he'd take too much and would be nodding out and not capable of presenting the music the way it was meant to be. He couldn't hang on the bandstand, as jazz musicians say. He was too buzzed to be open to any discussion or accept any offer of help.

Drugs had taken Jimi the year before, then Jim Morrison died that summer in Paris. In 1971 many people were getting scared—some of us were feeling that everything we had been building was falling apart. At the end of that summer, it felt like some of Santana was on the same route. Just a few months later, they'd find Janis with a needle in her, and she'd be gone, too.

I felt I had to put a stop to anything that had to do with cocaine or heroin in the band. I didn't have any problem with marijuana and LSD, but the harder stuff had to go. It was also a matter of who was hanging around with us: dope dealers, pimps—some real San Quentin material. I had the radar for that from Tijuana, and it had gone on long enough—these people were just bad news. It was getting dangerous, and it was making us look bad.

This was when I really started to feel that it meant something that my name was also the band's name—that started to be my explanation of why I cared so much about so many things. Why I couldn't chill about people showing up late, or showing up in no condition to play.

"I told you why," I would say. "This is about the music, not me. But this thing happens to have my name, and since it does I have a responsibility."

"We just called it that because we didn't know what else to call it. But it's not your band," some people said.

I would think, "Well, not yet."

I made the decision to fire David. It wasn't like I fired him directly, but really I did it by saying I wouldn't play with him anymore. This was the biggest step I had made toward taking charge. I think everyone understood that it had to be that way. But we weren't getting rid of him—it was more like we were giving David a chance to get straight, because he came back to Santana just a few years later.

We had dates to play, so we replaced David with Tom Rutley, an acoustic bass player Shrieve had worked with in a big band in college. I liked Tom—he was a big, huggy-bear kind of guy, and he had a low, low voice that I could barely understand and a great upright bass tone. He recorded some tracks with us on *Caravanse-rai*. He was only with us for a short time before Dougie Rauch took over, but Tom helped us at just the right time—when Shrieve and I were trying to navigate jazz music and imagine we could actually play with people like Joe Farrell and Wayne Shorter.

David might have been gone, and we had a bass player, but many things were still wrong—the drugs and lowlifes and hang-arounders were still getting in the way of the music. It had gotten to the point where people would wake up in the morning still drunk and fucked up from the night before, still totally buzzed on cocaine. Then they'd do more cocaine to wake up, so then they'd be tired and wired, and I was the one who kept putting my foot down. "They" were mainly Stan and Carabello.

Sometime in September, before another tour across the coun-try, I opened my mouth, and there was an argument, and by the end of it I said, "I'm not going unless we get rid of Stan Marcum and Carabello, because they're supplying the band with the heavy stuff and we sound like shit. We're not practicing, and it's embar-rassing. Either those guys are out or I'm out." I had to do what I had to do.

Stan and Carabello were in the room and I said this in front of them. They laughed and said I couldn't do that. "We leave on Mon-day, man. If you don't show up, then you're not in the band." And that's exactly what happened. It felt horrible. It felt really, really hor-rible to be part of a band that had just left on tour without me. But that was it—there was no official separation announcement, no press release, and no legal agreement. Everyone left, and I stayed behind, licking my wounds.

My consolation for the next few weeks was going to various jazz clubs around San Francisco and hanging out, playing with guys like George Cables at Basin Street West. I had gotten tight with George when we both played on Luis Gasca's album *For Those Who Chant* that summer. He was playing in Joe Henderson's group, with Eddie Marshall on drums, and they told me to come down and sit in with them.

I was also hanging with Dougie Rauch, who had moved to San Francisco and was playing at the Matador with Gábor Szabó and Tom Coster on piano and the drummer Spider Webb. This was when Gábor and I got tight—we'd get together and play, then we'd talk and listen to music. I was just breaking up with Linda after almost four years together. He would come over to the house, and he'd feel uncomfortable because of the arguments and the vibe. After I got back with Santana a few weeks later, Linda left, Gábor moved in, and we started hanging out with a group of chicks that included Mimi Sanchez, who was a hostess at the Matador and was an incredibly beautiful, very strong woman.

Mimi is the lady on the cover of *Caramba!,* the album by the great jazz trumpeter Lee Morgan, and she's the same Mimi who later married Carabello. I want to mention her—and Linda and Deborah and other women who have been in my life. There are people who are strong, independent forces in the lives of many musicians—there have to be. They help unfold us in a way that makes sense with all the craziness that can go on. They help us to not be afraid of ourselves and to learn to deal with brutal confrontations that seem so important but that really didn't mean anything. For many of us, these people are our teachers. They nurture us and keep things together when we're out on the road.

Mimi and my first wife, Deborah, were friends. In the '80s Carabello and I were also friends again, and when Mimi came down with terminal cancer, Deborah threw a party for her and her family. I remember I didn't recognize her because of her illness. Mimi had one request—that I play "Samba Pa Ti" for her. Such an outpouring of love came to her that day from her family and from Deborah's divine giving—she washed Mimi's feet. There was a reason Deborah and I had thirty-four years together.

Gábor and I stayed close, even after I got back with Santana. I remember so many things about him—he never talked about his time with Chico Hamilton or listened to Chico's music. I'm not sure why. But I could tell he was thinking about a different sound when we got together—something he was working on with Bobby

Womack that he later called "Breezin,'" which George Benson made famous.

One time Gábor invited me to come and sit in with him in the studio — he'd brought in another amplifier for me. "Oh, man, thank you," I said. We ended up just hanging out, then Gábor wanted to go for a walk. We stepped outside on Broadway in San Francisco, a funky area of town. At one point he stopped, turned, and said, "Carlos, I heard that Santana is starting to have some problems. If you ever want to start a band together, you and I, let me know."

I was like, "Really? That would be a great honor, Gábor, but what the hell do you need me for?"

One thing I think people have to know about Gábor is that even before Wes Montgomery was putting a jazz thing on rock and pop tunes, Gábor was really the first jazz guitarist to say it was okay to blatantly borrow songs by the Beatles and the Mamas and the Papas and other radio stars and record them in a jazz style, with his own thing. Later other jazz people did that, and no one could help noticing: "Hey, this idea is selling a lot!"

I was honored that Gábor wanted to build a group with me, and I did think about it, but I think he saw me as a freelance musician when really I was still part of a band. I was part of Santana, and I felt connected to Gregg and Shrieve and Carabello, even with the drugs. Later on I developed the kind of perspective that made it easier for me to do collaborations and play with other bands and still be completely in Santana.

Three weeks after Santana left for the road (minus this Santana), the phone rang. It was Neal. The band was going through the East Coast and was at the Felt Forum in New York. "Hey, man, I don't want to say this, because it's probably bad for your ego, but the audiences are screaming and booing — they want to hear you. They know you're Santana. Come on — why don't you get on the next plane?" I wasn't changing my mind. "No. Not unless you put Carabello and Stan on the next plane home. Then I'll be there."

I heard later that when the band made up its mind to get me back and send Carabello and Stan home, the two of them went around to everyone's room, letting people know how upset and hurt they were. I got on a plane and flew to New York to meet the band at their hotel. It was really awkward, because when I got there, Stan and Carabello were right there in the lobby, looking daggers at me. Carabello said, "Okay, man, you got your fuckin' way. This is what you wanted, right?" I didn't take the bait—I just looked at him and said, "What I wanted is the band to be thriving."

The feeling right away was that this was going to be a new chapter for Santana. It wasn't just that we had to find a new *conguero;* we also needed to do that while we were thousands of miles from the musicians we knew best. So one night in New York City we decided to put it out into the world, and we asked if there was a conga player in the audience. That's how we found Mingo Lewis. He was a street musician with a lot of energy. We put out the request from the stage—I was probably the one who did it—and the next thing we knew this cat showed up and sounded good with us. He knew almost all the parts for our songs, so we asked him to join the band right there and then.

During those first few shows there was definitely a division, or the feeling of a divide, in the band. Half the members wanted to beat me up, as did some of the crew; they were pissed off because they felt I was killing a good thing. My thing was, "It's already dead and will be more dead if we don't cut off the diseased leg." I also think I might have done some people a favor by helping to prolong their lives.

The energy in the new lineup was immediately different onstage, too, where it felt like Gregg, Neal, and I were fencing each other and Michael was the guy in the middle, which actually was a good thing. When Dougie came in on bass, and with Mingo on the congas, it was a whole new kind of rhythm—more flexible and looser. That really was when I started to feel that maybe Santana could go in a different direction, one that would be evident on our fourth album, *Caravanserai.*

After we finished the US tour we flew for the first time to Peru to do our last concert of 1971—but something happened that stopped us from playing. And thank God we didn't play, because we probably would have sounded horrible. Just think about it and repeat these words: *rock band; Peru; 1971*.

The twin brothers who booked us there were heavily involved with cocaine, so they met us at the plane in New York and brought a flour jar that was filled to the top. The party started in the air, and when we landed the whole Lima airport was filled with people— you would have thought the Beatles were coming on the plane after ours. We looked like...well, you know the story about Ulysses and the sailors who are turned into swine and grunt and act like pigs? That was Santana coming off that plane. By the time we landed the jar was almost half empty. I was ready to have another cold-sweat nightmare about going onstage and finding everybody in the band frozen like popsicles.

There was another part of the picture we didn't know before we got there. Some people were not happy we were there—communist students who thought we represented American imperialism. Not everyone who hears the word *America* thinks of *Howdy Doody* and Fred Astaire. There was a protest, and someone started a fire in the place where we were going to play.

Later I heard that Fidel Castro wouldn't let people listen to our music for the same reason. I also already heard that Buddy Rich used to throw people off his bus for listening to Santana. I'm okay knowing that we are not going to be everybody's golden cup of tea.

When we got to Lima, we hung out with the mayor while our luggage went to the hotel. We got the key to the city, took some pho- tos, and then we went to visit a few churches at my request—I was in Latin America again, and I wanted to see the churches. We were at the first one for just fifteen minutes when suddenly the place was surrounded by cops. They escorted us to a municipal building, where we waited and tried to figure out what was happening. The cops kept saying that everything was being done for our protection, but they revealed nothing else.

We were supposed to play the next night, and some guys were getting angry. Gregg was like, "Hey, man, fuck this." I told him not to pull the John Wayne act. "I'm telling you, lawyers are not going to help you here, man. Be cool." I could see that our situation was no different from being in a Tijuana jail. Then the cops told us there'd been some more problems with students; we were in danger, and we had to leave. They asked a plane that was flying from Brazil to Los Angeles to land and pick us up so that we could get back safely. We went straight to the airport. Our tour manager was Steve Kahn, who worked for Bill Graham—we called him Killer Kahn. He went back later to get all our equipment and luggage, which we had left at the hotel. He had to put on a wig to hide his hippie hair and shave his mustache so that he wouldn't be recognized as an American.

So we get inside the plane that will get us out of Peru, and there's only one place for me to sit—next to a weird-looking chick with raggedy blond hair who's wearing a big muumuu. We took off, and she asked, "What happened?" I told her the whole story, then she looked around and said, "I wouldn't worry about that. Look what I have." She lifted up her dress, and it was like that guy in *Midnight Express* was sitting right next to me. She was a mule, and she had so much cocaine strapped to her that she looked pregnant. "Why don't we go to the bathroom and do some coke?" Just what I needed. "No thanks," I said. "I need to sit somewhere else, man." As soon as we landed at the LA airport, the FBI and other people in uniform wanted to interrogate us about what happened. "Sure thing, man; let's go." I wanted to put as much distance as I could between me and that pregnant chick—and fast.

The story we got was that the government actually was trying to help us. I hear that people in Lima still talk about the time Santana came there but never played.

I was talking with Miles one time about changing the players in his bands and always going forward with his music. "It's a blessing and a curse, man. I *have* to change," he said. I liked the idea of a band being like that—loose and natural, open to the gift of new ideas.

I wanted Santana to be that way. But at the end of 1971, Santana was falling apart. Two of my oldest friends were gone from the band, and the mood in the band wasn't pleasant—things were getting intense.

We could have used some time off the road to turn down the heat. When you're busy playing and creating new music and recording—repeat, repeat, repeat—you don't know how long to keep it going. You don't know how long the phone will keep ringing with offers to do shows and make records. We never asked, "How much time can we afford to take off? A few weeks? A year or two?" But maybe we should have.

Santana III came out in October and was another number one album for us. I say "us" because on the first three albums everybody played his part and nobody told anyone else what to do. But when we started recording *Caravanserai* in 1972, I began to tell people what to do and what *not* to do. *Santana III* was the last album featuring most of the original Santana members, including Gregg. I could tell that there was a hurtful rub when I was in the room with certain people, and I'm sure it was the same for them, but what happened had to happen. When something is over, it's over.

It would be around eight months before Santana got a new lineup and really got its groove together and went back on the road. It was the only time Santana did that—leave the scene for so long and come back with new personnel and a new sound.

We had gone from rooting for each other to tolerating each other to being two bands in one, in conflict musically and philosophically. On one side you had Gregg and Neal, wanting to do more rock tunes, and on the other side you had Shrieve and me. Chepito was always on his own path—dealing with his distractions and never really involving himself with what the band was doing or where it was going. He had songs that he wrote, and his sound will always be an important part of the band, but through all the changes that would happen in Santana, he always seemed to be in the dugout—never really in the game.

Shrieve and I were like gardeners, trying to let the music relax a little bit and grow on its own. We were listening to and thinking about jazz and rhythms and how many musicians we could meet and jam with. I think our way was more true to the idea of the original band, which gave everyone the freedom to say, "That was beautiful. Let's try that again a couple more times, maybe in a different direction." The big change was that by the time we were recording *Caravanserai*, I was the one saying that.

CHAPTER 13

It took me around a year to go from being part of the band to being at the point where I was feeling that the name of the band wasn't just a cool-sounding name: it was my name, and I had a responsibility to it. I think it's good that I got to that point in my perception, because I wasn't wired or equipped to deal with maintaining a Who or Rolling Stones or Led Zeppelin kind of band—all for one, but no clear leader. I am

Santana—if I'm not in the band and it has the name Santana, then it's a Santana tribute.

I'm very lucky to have worked with all the musicians who played in Santana. They all brought different rhythms and beats, different ways to articulate chord changes, and different energies. I have learned from each one, and my mind is very clear about what and who—I can name you all the keyboard and conga players, all the drummers, all the bass players. They've all been important.

If you see a musician up there playing in Santana, he's not there just because he knows the songs. It's because of trust. I trust each one of them to be genuine and to have a deep respect for three things that they will never drop: the tempo, the feel, and the groove. We talk about that all the time. The tempo and feel have to be right for each song, and the groove—man, the groove is king.

One reason Santana survived all those lineup changes over the years is because every new keyboardist or bassist or singer wasn't there just to sound like the records from thirty-five years before. Each Santana band has had its own identity. Every new musician has to show his own heart and bring new commitment into the mix and make it work with everyone else. Some guys ask me what they should do or rehearse. I tell them if you want to do research before playing in Santana, don't research Santana. I wouldn't even be talking to them if they didn't know our music already.

I tell them to go and check out Marvin Gaye—get a video of him from 1974, and see that you have no choice but to believe every word he sings. Or Michael Jackson in '83. Or Miles in '69. Jimi in '67. Howlin' Wolf in the '50s. You believe every note they play. I tell them, don't justify the music and talk about chord changes without talking about how to make it come alive every time—like Frankenstein, up from the dead. I can see why Wayne Shorter likes those old movies—"It's alive!" That's what we need to hear in Santana.

One time we had a discussion on the bus. One band member said, "You know, we really don't like it when you tell us what to do and what not to do."

    I said, "Okay, then surprise me. Don't bring the same thing to every song. Don't play me something you learned. They don't teach audacity or sass or motherfuckingness at Berklee or any other school of music." It's not that they have to get to that every time. But I can tell if someone's just slipping by, and it's my role to say something, just as it's my job to let a musician know, "Hey, that was some great shit you played tonight. Thank you."

A lot of projects came out of guys hanging out, playing, and talking about ideas to work on together. The concert in Hawaii with Buddy Miles came out of Buddy and Greg Errico getting together with people like Neal and Coke Escovedo. Buddy and Greg had a mutual affection, so it was natural they'd do something together. And when I visited Buddy at his house in Nevada, he told me about a New Year's gig at the crater on Diamond Head that he was going to do with Greg and other musicians.

Buddy Miles had been Jimi Hendrix's last drummer and had been with Wilson Pickett and the Electric Flag before that. Then in 1970 he had a big hit with "Them Changes," and at the time of the concert he had just signed with Columbia. From my point of view, things weren't happening with Santana anymore, and who knew what the future held? Doing this concert was like imagining what Santana on steroids could be. It felt like it was the last part of the parade, and it was fun—an all-star band that was mostly Bay Area people, like Neal, Gregg, Coke, Luis Gasca, saxophonist Hadley Caliman, and Victor Pantoja. Carabello was there, too, and he played—but I had started to hang out with Coke more after we split, and Coke and I really bonded there.

Buddy and the others brought some tunes, but mainly we jammed on some loose ideas. We played them first and named the tracks later. The whole concert was recorded by Columbia, then Buddy and I went into a studio to mix the music. I got my first lesson in collaborating musically and finding the right way to say something that has to be said—away from Santana, in a studio filled with musicians, friends, girlfriends, and Buddy, who had a lot more experience than I did.

After a while Buddy got into the mixing room with the engineer and put the rest of us out. Hours and hours later, he played it for us. I listened to what were going to be the first two sides of a double album, and when it was fading out, I just said, "Buddy, you ain't enough." He said, "What?" with a hard look on his face. I said, "Man, I have to hear voices and horns and guitars. It can't be just you. You're too far up in the mix, and where's everyone else? You ain't enough. We need to mix it again."

Everybody was looking at me, then back at Buddy, like, "Damn, he just sounded you, man." Buddy started looking at me like, "How could you say that in front of everybody?" It had to be mixed again, there was no question about it. "Come on, Buddy, let's do it once more, and this time make sure we can hear everyone enough."

I liked the music — I was honored that he trusted me to bring something different out of him, and he definitely brought something different out of me. That's the way I still hear that music. Buddy just sang his ass off on "Evil Ways" and "Faith Interlude" — he's a phenomenon.

Buddy and I got tighter after that album, which was good, because we had to get behind it and tour that music when it came out. We found a way to speak with each other and to respect the music first. Buddy would say, "You talk to me in a way that most people don't." Most people were afraid of making him angry and saying the wrong thing. I told him, "Buddy, I'm never trying to put you down. I love your drumming and your singing. Sometimes I'm just saying you're getting in the way of a lot of things with the mask you put on. I just want to get to Buddy Miles — the soul, the heart, the gift that God gave you."

Buddy had a voice that could sing in any key, and he also played great guitar. The problems occurred when he wasn't playing. He'd need to be the focus and have things serving him. It was Buddy, Buddy, Buddy, or he would get into trouble really, really quick. I still love Buddy in spite of Buddy Miles. We got together again in 1987, after I saw him with my friend Gary Rashid at the Boom Boom Room—it felt so good I invited him into the band. I have a good habit of using a bad memory, so I forget stupid shit that happened and I will give a person a second chance. We had fun for a few shows, until the same things started happening again.

Buddy was a pocket drummer—meaning he played in the pocket, which is great if you're going to play "In the Midnight Hour" or "Knock on Wood" or other R & B grooves like that. If you're going to play "Manic Depression," that style doesn't neces-sarily work. Buddy, and even the famous Stax drummer Al Jackson Jr., as great as he was playing with Otis Redding—they're some-times too tight. With cosmic drummers like Roy Haynes and Jack DeJohnette and Tony Williams and Elvin Jones and Mitch Mitchell, there's a chemistry of bubbles and sparkles that is an entirely dif-ferent kind of pocket. The extreme is Rashied Ali, Coltrane's last drummer—that was a pocketless pocket.

John Coltrane and Pharoah Sanders and Antônio Carlos Jobim and Alice Coltrane, with their looser rhythms and spiritual, prais-ing melodies, were inspiring a change in the kind of music Shrieve and I wanted to do. If you listen to the music from the sessions we started doing in early 1972, you can hear that we sound like we were working with divining rods, looking for water—you can hear things changing in our music from February to March to April and May.

We were looking for our new identity beyond Santana. You could say we were looking for Weather Report and for Miles Davis—I mean, Don Alias and Lenny White, who played on *Bitches Brew*, are also on some Santana recordings. I think what we were all doing was looking for our identity in the same places—rock and jazz—with a spirit of exploration and the courage to try something new, even if it didn't make sense or we weren't supposed to do it. *Caravanserai* was the album we weren't supposed to do.

For the next five months we were Santana mostly when we were in the studio—the band only did a few live shows under that name, and it wasn't clear what the future of Santana was going to be. We went ahead with sessions from March to June of '72 in CBS's new recording studio in San Francisco—where we had done *Santana III* with Glen Kolotkin. The studio had originally been Coast Recorders, the place where John and Alice Coltrane had done one of their last sessions on the road in 1966, and it made sense that we'd be making the same kind of cosmic music in the studio they had used.

What was strange was that instead of the usual tensions we went through while making the other albums, these sessions were really smooth. We weren't fighting—that part was over. Instead there was a kind of sadness. David Brown, Stan, and Carabello were gone, and Gregg and Neal agreed to do the music that became *Caravanserai* but were thinking about the music that would become Journey. For me, it was the sadness of feeling the original Santana coming to an end. I think about those months, and I remember I found myself crying a lot—asking myself what was wrong. My body was shedding tears at the dismantling of my relationship with everyone, mourning the fact that we didn't have each other's backs, like we used to. To this day I listen to "Song of the Wind" and break down inside hearing Gregg's playing on that one—no solo, just a simple, supportive organ part that is not flashy or anything but supremely important to the song.

Transitions can be painful, but this period was made more organically smooth by Michael Shrieve. Musically he and I felt that we needed to walk a tightrope with *Caravanserai*—we knew it would mean trying new kinds of music, really stretching. It was Shrieve who said, "Let's check out Jobim," and we decided to record "Stone Flower" and write lyrics for it. Players on the album included Gregg, Neal, and Chepito as well as a few new members, such as Mingo and Tom Rutley on bass, who left after these recordings to go back to the jazz world, where he came from. We had Dougie Rauch on some tunes. You can really hear what he brought to "All the Love of the Universe" and "Look Up (to See What's Coming Down)"—when we heard those tracks, we realized how much we needed Dougie.

Gregg was getting ready to say good-bye, too, but I had heard Tom Coster in Gábor's band at the same time Dougie was playing with them. Tom—or TC, we called him—was a jazz guy, no two ways about it. He could play everything. I knew if he took over for Gregg he would bring something different to the organ feel in the band and would bring other keyboard sounds, too. He plays that high-energy electric piano solo on "La Fuente del Ritmo." TC would help create some great songs for Santana when we needed them, such as "Europa" and "Dance Sister Dance."

With Coster and the others I started to find my own way of talking about what I was hearing in the music. I was learning that especially with new people in the band I needed to be as respectful as possible but also as clear as possible about what I wanted, like: "The chord I'm thinking feels like this—you have to picture a sunset, when the clouds are painted red...no, that chord is the middle of the day. Try this other chord. Okay, that's like four in the afternoon. Can we get to six o'clock, right before the sun goes down?"

To me, music has always been visual. I can see when there is color or mood, or water or fire or a tear rolling down from an eye, or a smile. That's the business of a musician: to make the chord or the rhythm or whatever "sound-match" a certain memory or emotion and connect to something real.

I told Glen Kolotkin at the beginning of the sessions that I wanted the album to start with the sound of nature, and he said, "I got just the thing—in my backyard I have a cricket chorus, and you won't believe how loud they get." So that's how the album starts, and then you hear Hadley Caliman playing the saxophone part—the fog whooshing in after the crickets. That's also Hadley with that wild flute solo on "Every Step of the Way." There were other local people we brought in—Rico Reyes sang on one tune, and a local guitarist, Doug Rodrigues, played with me on "Waves Within." Wendy Haas played keyboards on this album, as she would on some other Santana albums. I decided my solo on that tune should cut through the music like a hot knife through butter—some of what I played came from listening to Freddie

Hubbard's "First Light" and Miles's "Concierto de Aranjuez." Neal and I were quoting a lot and using ideas and feelings that we got from other music. "Astral Traveling," from Pharoah Sanders's album *Thembi*, helped give birth to the opening song on *Caravanserai*.

The making of *Caravanserai* was when Santana really got into people working separately in the studio — Shrieve and Dougie and Chepito would get their tracks together and come to me and say, "Okay, we need you to come in and play your solo." I'd hear it for the first time right then, and I'd wet my finger and point it up in the air like an antenna on the Empire State Building and let the melodies and inspiration come to me — I was thinking "Nature Boy"; "Love on a Two-Way Street." Gábor Szabó licks. They're all on that album. People would tell me later, "Whoa — that was a great solo on 'Stone Flower.' " I'd say, "Thank you, man," and be thinking, "I hope nobody busts me for it!"

For two reasons my favorite song on *Caravanserai* is still "Every Step of the Way" — first because it sounds like what we really loved back then: Herbie Hancock's *Crossings*. The song also reminds me of Shrieve because he wrote it and because of how we played together. Shrieve was there to complete the journey that became *Caravanserai*. He was in my corner, and I was in his — we helped each other complete it. When it came time to figure out the order of songs for the album, he and I kept making cassettes of different sequences. Then separately, we would drive around San Francisco and listen to them. We would give them to each other and discuss them until we knew exactly how the tunes should run. More than any Santana album, *Caravanserai* was meant to be a full album experience, with one track connected to the next — a body of work like *What's Going On* or *A Love Supreme*.

I remember telling Shrieve, "I found the word *caravanserai* when I was reading something by Paramahansa Yogananda."

"Wow, sounds great . . . what does it mean?"

"The caravan is the eternal cycle of reincarnation, every soul going into and out of life, from death to life and back again, until you arrive at a place where you can rest and achieve an inner peace. That place is the caravanserai. How you live now determines how you will live again, if you can get there. Reincarnation is in your hands."

It made a lot of sense to me — the cycle that happens to all of us: mineral, vegetable, animal, man, divinity. It's in our hands. I remember thinking that I was glad I had become acquainted with Eastern philosophy, because up until then I thought that you just die and that's it — you go to hell just for living. That's why we put the quote from Paramahansa Yogananda's *Metaphysical Meditations* on the album cover:

> The body melts into the universe.
> The universe melts into the soundless voice.
> The sound melts into the all-shining light.
> And the light enters the bosom of infinite joy.

For me, Armando Peraza was the most important person to come into Santana that year — maybe any year. He played in two tunes on *Caravanserai* — he added bongos on "Fuente" and later joined Santana on congas. He was one of the top four *congueros* to come over from Cuba in the 1940s, along with Patato Valdez, Francisco Aguabella, and Mongo Santamaría. Since the '60s, he'd been living in San Francisco.

Armando was older and wiser than all of us — he was almost fifty then. He had been in the game for years. He was older than Miles Davis, which was another reason he didn't take any mess from him. Armando was compact and tough. You could hear it in his congas — Armando was like a cheetah and a laser. He penetrated, and he was really fast. Meanwhile, alongside Armando, Mongo had a beautiful, burly, fatherly sound. It was a great combination.

Armando was an amazing spirit and force in the band. For me, he became a mentor and a tutor and a divine angel. He told me things when I needed to hear them, and he told great stories. He had stories about all the people he'd played with and the crazy things he'd done. He'd challenge people with his credentials—his badge of honor was that his first gig after arriving in New York City was playing with Charlie Parker and Buddy Rich. "Afterward they both wanted me to come play in their bands," he'd say. Then he'd say, "What've you got?"

Another thing Armando liked to do: after a gig he'd look at his hands. He had tiny little hands and a big, big sound. Armando would say, "And I don't use a goddamn sticket, man." In his vocabulary, it wasn't a drum stick. "I don't need no goddamn sticket." He had his own way of speaking—instead of saying, "Don't gimme that shit," it was "Don't gimme that shick." If he was into the way somebody played, it would be "I like that guy's shick."

I was called Carlo. McLaughlin was Maharishi, not Mahavishnu. Lionel Richie was Flannel Richie. There was Argentina Turner, Roberta Flop, and that Weather Report guy, Joe Sabano. "Hey, Carlo, you know I was with Sabano when he wrote 'Mercy, Mercy, Mercy'?"

"Really, Armando?"

"Yeah, I helped him out."

There was one story Armando told all of us a few times about being in Tijuana, where he did a little bit of everything—he was a dancer, a baseball player, and a bouncer. One night he bet a bartender that he could jump into a bullring and deal with the bull. You want to talk about full circle? Years later a beautiful, elegant woman saw him with me on the street in Daly City, California, yelled out his name, and came over. She said she was the wife of one of the Nicholas Brothers, then she said, "How come you don't remember me? I was with you in Tijuana when you bet that bartender that you could face the bull!"

Armando turned to me. "You see, Carlo? Sometimes people accuse me of being senile, but I just have a great memory." I still don't know what that means.

I first read about Armando on the liner notes to one of the early Leon Thomas albums, which describes him playing in New York

City. The first time I heard Armando play was in a park in San Francisco in 1968—he and a guy named Dennis were going at it. Nobody was buying or doing anything—there was just a big crowd focused on the two of them. They finished, and people were freaking out, jumping up to give them a standing ovation. Armando came straight over to me, sweating and not caring. "Carlos Santana?" He knew who I was.

"Yeah?"

"Someday I want to be in your band, man."

I didn't know what to say. "Oh, man, that would be an honor."

"But I can't do that right now because I'm playing with Cal Tjader at the Matador. Come see me."

Another time, in New York City, Carabello told me that Armando was sitting in with Mongo at the Village Gate. We took a cab straight to the club, and all these drummers were there—on my right was Roy Haynes, and Tony Williams was on my left. Mongo was playing his songs—including several cha-cha-chas and "Watermelon Man." Armando was up there, too—putting more and more "something" into the music. Then all of a sudden it was just Armando and Mongo—what everybody came for. The look they gave each other was, "You're my friend, but I got something I need to show you."

I've seen Armando go up against Francisco Aguabella and Billy Cobham. He'd do his thing, then pull back a little and put his hands out like a toreador working a cape—"Eso—there you go! What've you got?" Every time musicians like that get together, the walls start to sweat. I swear to you, they actually do rearrange the molecular structure of the joint.

Armando was still one of the most important people to come into my life—he was another angel who showed up at just the right time. He carried so much music inside him and could be such a character. By being the way he was, he instilled confidence in me. He helped me believe in what I was doing and where the band was going. I needed that in 1972, because when we finished *Caravanse-*

rai all the people around us were shaking their heads, saying we had gone too far.

By that time Santana was almost six months past the first breakup, when Stan and Carabello were let go. Carabello was around, playing with other folks in the Bay Area, and starting his own band. David was trying to get himself together. But Stan was hooked, and eventually he became another drug casualty.

One good thing was that it hadn't been a messy divorce—at least not financially. We never fought over royalties or anything like that—we don't even now. But it was messy in the sense that people were very disappointed in each other, laying blame and guilt on each other like I don't know what.

Santana was moving forward, and I was the one talking for the band inside and outside the studio. When we were finished with *Caravanserai,* Clive Davis asked for a meeting at CBS's studio. It was just Clive, Shrieve, and I.

Clive was definitely not happy. He had heard the music, and he was not smiling. It was one of the most important meetings we ever had about Santana, as important as the one we had with Bill Graham before Woodstock. By that point, with the band falling apart, Bill and Clive were handling a lot of the energy around us, trying to help us keep it together. But when it came to the music, Shrieve and I were the ones to go to.

There's a funny thing that Clive does sometimes, usually when he's in his own office. He'll look away from you and talk to you indirectly, through one of his people: "Uh, Harry—tell Carlos that we should release the album on this date." Meanwhile I'm in the same room; I just heard him say it. It didn't matter. "Uh, Carlos? Clive thinks that we should release..."

I remember we were sitting across from each other, and there was a candle on the table between us. Clive was looking right at me. It probably seemed strange to Clive, but I kept looking at that candle when we spoke—not to ignore him, but I knew something was coming. I knew he was going to try to persuade me to take the band in a different direction. But we were too deep into this thing with *Caravanserai* to turn it around.

Clive said, "I'm sorry; I have to ask. Why would you want to do this?" I have to say that he came into the conversation patiently. He was not pushy, just very gracious. I said, "Why would I want to do what?" He said, "Clearly there's not one single within a thousand miles of this album. There's nothing here to take to radio and get a hit with. It feels like you're turning your backs on yourselves. The jazz stuff is great, but there's already a Miles Davis; there's already a Weather Report. Why don't you just be Santana?"

I said, "It's going to go like this, man. This is a body of work—the whole thing is a single." I kept looking at the flame of the candle because I didn't want to look in his eyes and be swayed into saying, "Okay, let's go back to the studio and create another *Abraxas* kind of thing."

I bored my eyes into the candle. I knew Clive was doing his job, and I knew Bill felt the same way. They were both right—there was no single on *Caravanserai* to take to radio.

I remember Quincy Jones once telling me about Ray Charles standing up for his music—the two of them had come up together in Seattle. When Ray got ready to do songs with strings and voices—a produced, pop kind of thing—some people who liked his R & B sound said, "I can't get with that. I don't like this 'I Can't Stop Loving You' or 'Crying Time.' What are you doing?" Ray's answer was, "Well, man, you're not going to be ignorant your whole life, are you?"

I wasn't going to put it that way. I had too much respect for Clive, so I said, "Clive, thank you for coming here and saying what you needed to tell us. You need to do what you need to do, and we need to do what we need to do. But we can't be doing another 'Black Magic Woman' over and over and over. We can't go back—with all the changes in the last few months, we literally cannot go back. We have to learn to change and to grow." Clive didn't really argue, he just thought for a moment. "Well, I do need to tell you there're no singles in here."

Clive was disappointed, but he didn't try to put the screws to us: "Do it this way or else." It wasn't that kind of thing. Clive has always been very artist-friendly. He'll give it to you straight, but he's not a person who's going to make you feel like a stupid child who doesn't know what he's doing. Bill Graham was kind of like that, only he would be straight without pulling any punches. When he heard what the title was going to be, he said, "*Caravanserai?* More like career suicide."

"Career suicide"? Okay, it sounded a little like *Caravanserai*. Ha-ha. But no, I didn't think we were doing that.

With all I know now I believe I still would make the same decision today. But I could not argue with Clive—I knew he was right in his thinking and that he was looking out for our best interests as well as Columbia's. In hindsight what I wish I had said was, "Clive, let us do this one, and the next one we'll work on together, okay?" But I didn't know how to do that then—how to be diplomatic. Now I know. It's all in the wording—all in the timing, presentation, and tone. Today I want to be able to invite people to invest emotionally with me and not consider it my music or theirs—it's *our* music.

Columbia put out *Caravanserai* two months after *Carlos Santana & Buddy Miles! Live!* There were no hits on the radio and no gold records coming from either album, but they got great reviews. In *Rolling Stone*, Ralph Gleason really liked *Caravanserai* and reviewed it along with Miles's *On the Corner,* but the general reaction was "What the hell is this?" It still sold well because a lot of people were curious about it, and we got so many compliments from musicians for that album. But without a radio single, sales went down compared to our first three albums. It didn't matter. We couldn't go back. We had to go forward, and *Caravanserai* is what we felt was right at that time.

A few months later, in '73, there was an argument over money at CBS, and they let Clive go. Clive, in his way, had adopted us, as Bill had. Like Bill, he had a system and the right people working for him so that he could say with supreme conviction, "If we work together and you come with me, I'll get on the phone, and your music is going to get on the radio. You are going to get not only gold but platinum records." Clive and his people always know how to get music into the mainstream. Santana was still able to continue, but with Clive gone, there was never the same feeling at CBS.

Gregg left San Francisco by that summer—he got to the point where he was really over the whole rock scene. He started a restaurant with his dad in Seattle, where he's from. I knew I was going to miss him. But he was just too caught up in what he wanted to do away from Santana at that point, just as I was focused on where I thought Santana should go. If there had been any chance for reconciliation and getting back together, it was gone by that point. I had been doing a lot of jamming with other bands around the Bay Area starting that spring and summer—playing in concerts with folks like Elvin Bishop and Buddy Miles; Malo, my brother's band; and Azteca. In July I was invited to be a featured guest with Tower of Power at the Marin County Civic Center—they were on a double bill with the Loading Zone. I showed up in my Excalibur with two blond chicks who were friends of Neal's. I got out my guitar, and we went backstage.

This is the night when Deborah and I first really noticed each other. When I saw her, I remembered she had been with Sly—she looked like she was Sly's girlfriend. This time Deborah was by herself, looking very attractive in her eyes and her skin and holding herself with elegance. It was in the way she walked—like a queen—which was something I would come to know over time. I didn't know yet that she was from a musical family or that her dad was a famous blues guitarist. I didn't even know her name.

I was very single at that time, not really looking. In those days, women found their own way—guys didn't always have to take the first step and do the walking and talking. I know what Deborah says in her book about my chasing her. But in my book, it went down like this: I went to get a drink from a water fountain, and when I straightened up she was right behind me. She really looked beautiful and had long eyelashes. We spoke for a little bit. Then I soloed on "You Got to Funkifize." I went home, and the next day the phone rang. It was Lynn Medeiros, Jerry Martini's old lady — Jerry is the saxophonist who helped put together Sly & the Family Stone. Lynn said that she and Deborah were working on a cookbook — favorite recipes by the ladies of rock musicians. Would my lady like to participate?

Man, I saw right through that. Come on. But it was nice and charming and kind of funny the way they did that. I said, "Okay, no. No lady over here. Thanks. Sure, I'd like to talk with Deborah. Put her on the phone." That's how it started.

Our first date was a week or two later, and it didn't take long at all. She loved music, and she understood musicians, and she wasn't someone who would get between a musician and his music. She was young and beautiful and was very close with her family, which attracted me. She talked about her mother and grandmother a lot. She had a strong foundation and confidence. Looking back on it now, I think that's what attracts me most about women. Whether they are with you or not, they're okay — they may want you, but they don't need you. I don't like women who are needy or whiny. If there's any of that "Oh, without you I'm just nothing" stuff, then I know I got the wrong one. Got to go!

Deborah also had an inner beauty as well, a divine kind of spark. I found out almost immediately after we started dating that she was aspiring to a higher consciousness, as I was. She was reading about Swami Satchidananda and I was reading Paramahansa Yogananda and we were both disenchanted with the trappings of the rock-and-roll lifestyle and disappointed with people who were close to us. For some reason we always got to talking about that when we were crossing the Golden Gate Bridge — the hurt and disappointment that came from people going their own way and getting lost.

Whatever happened between her and Sly is in her book, and that and what was happening with me and my band had left us both needing support and consolation. I think a lot of what brought us together so quickly was that we were both like birds with broken wings: we needed mending. We were consoling each other.

There was still a hole in me from what happened with Santana, and Deborah came and stood next to me at the right time. Dougie Rauch used to say that everybody has a hole to fill. Some people try to fill it with sex or drugs or money or food, but everybody has a space inside that they need to fill—that's the closest I ever heard Dougie get to having some kind of philosophy.

Did I know Deborah was the one at that time? I knew how I felt at that moment, and that was all I was thinking about. I was open to the possibility without even thinking about it. I think the important thing, looking back on it, is that people should know that you don't attract whom you want or whom you need. You always attract who you *are*. So if you do whatever inner work needs to be done and deal with who you are, then your heart will be open and you can be flexible and vulnerable again and invite in your queen and take your existence to another level. I don't believe it was a coincidence.

Deborah was sexy and exciting, and she made me comfortable. There was a side of her that was very generous and nurturing. Very soon after we started dating I had the feeling that one reason we met was that I needed help cleaning my inner closet. Then she started asking me to come over to Oakland to meet her mom and dad.

Deborah was the younger daughter of the Bay Area bluesman Saunders King—he was black, his wife, Jo, was white, and they were serious, churchgoing people. SK had been known around San Francisco during World War II, playing blues and ballads for black servicemen with his big band, or "orchestra," as they called it back then. He had a smooth way of singing songs—"S.K. Blues" was his big hit in '42.

SK had history. He was one of the first electric blues guitarists on the West Coast, the same generation as T-Bone Walker—he had heard Charlie Christian playing guitar with Benny Goodman, and that was it. SK got his own instrument, put a band together, and was playing in shows with Billie Holiday when she was at the top.

From what he told me later, I got the idea that he sometimes got her West Coast band together for her. SK had known Charlie Parker and worked with him. SK was also a veteran of the old TOBA circuit—the black-owned Theater Owners Booking Association, the *real* chitlin' circuit—and he had toured through some rough places and stood up to some serious racist shit.

To understand just how respected SK was, you have to know that B. B. King called him his personal god. SK's response to hearing that was, "B. B.? I knew that boy before he knew how to hold the guitar."

SK didn't have a problem with his daughters getting with guys who had some sort of public profile. He had practice with that: Deborah had been with Sly for a while, and SK's older daughter, Kitsaun, was dating Kareem Abdul-Jabbar at the time. Years later, Kareem and I would tell each other SK stories—he told me that he got some advice from SK when he was getting beat up while he was with the Milwaukee Bucks, which I guess was the only thing they could do to stop him. SK told him to defend himself, to not wait for the referee. Just once, just one good hit. He did, and that was all it took—opposing players started to leave him alone.

Later, when I started to call him Dad, SK would tell me stories. One of his favorites was about playing on a session with Louis Armstrong—a radio broadcast, I think. Everyone was looking over the sheet music before they went on the air, except for Louis. When they asked him what he was going to do if he didn't know the music, he said that to him playing music was like walking through an orchard full of fruit trees and that each note was like a fruit hanging off a branch and that he was going to pick only the ripest ones.

Another time SK was looking upset, and I asked him what happened. "Man, I got this phone call last night, and this cat starts talking to me. I could tell he was a musician, but he was calling me the *n* word. I can't stand it when someone calls me outside my name." That's how they talked about it in SK's generation.

SK said, "I didn't even know who it was! I hung up and I got so angry and suddenly I said, 'I know who that was.' It was Dizzy Gillespie, but I didn't care. I got back on the phone and called him. 'Man, don't you ever call my house and call me outside my name again, you hear me? My name is Saunders King, you got that? Now I know why they call you Dizzy.'"

Kareem and I used to talk about how long it took to get past the probation stage with SK. He wouldn't even turn his head to look at you; and with a toothpick in his mouth, he looked like Otis Rush. You can talk about Checkpoint Charlie and airport security and all that stuff, but it only scratches the surface of how it felt each time Deborah took me to her parents' home. It took a while to get SK to actually open up.

It was Deborah I was getting close to, not her parents. But the more time I spent with her, the more I spent with all of them. I was getting another family. I remember Armando looking at me not long after I met Deborah, then just shaking his head, like he was thinking, "It's too late to save this guy now."

Caravanserai was released in October of '72, and, as we had for our other albums, we got ready to go on the road, playing concerts to help introduce our new music. Santana was then Shrieve, Dougie on bass, Armando, Mingo and Chepito on percussion, and two guys on keyboards—TC and Richard Kermode, who had a bad, straight-ahead *montuno*, a consistent Latin feel in his playing and was steady like a horse. In my mind, TC was the Keith Jarrett of Santana, and Kermode became the Chick Corea. Kermode had been in Jorge's band, Malo, and I remember my mom telling me that I should be more careful about taking musicians from my brother's band. I didn't think I *took* him—my thinking was that Santana was another opportunity for musicians, and if they wanted to they could try playing with us, see if it worked, then decide what they wanted to do. That was a really nice combination—TC and Kermode.

The *Caravanserai* tour started in North America in October. It was Santana, Bobby Womack, and Freddie King — rock, blues, and soul groups all together. I was in heaven, man, playing next to those legends. We played a number of chitlin' circuit venues that didn't usually have rock bands, so there were a lot of black folks in the audience who normally wouldn't come to a Santana concert, and of course there were a lot of white rock fans catching Bobby and Freddie, whom they normally wouldn't go and hear.

The one problem was that when we started playing the longer pieces from *Caravanserai,* our fans started screaming. "Hey, Santana — play 'Oye Como Va'!" They weren't shy about it, either — I'd be into a long, slow solo, and suddenly somebody would yell at the top of his lungs: "Play fuckin' 'Evil Ways'!" Oh, man. I remember turning around and looking at Shrieve, and then we'd go into "Stone Flower." The people got loud on that tour. Other bands were picking up on that — I remember Freddie King saying, "Hey, Santana, that's some weird-ass shit you're playing now. Why don't you play some 'Black Magic Woman'? I like it better when you just play some blues."

Changing musical direction is never easy, but that first tour after *Caravanserai* felt like it caused the most tension — both inside the band and between us and our fans. It even caused tension within my own family — my mom couldn't understand why I would play original music, and my dad was still trying to figure out the structures to Santana songs. Both of them thought I was crazy to change Santana around. Meanwhile, we were on the road, and I was thinking about Deborah a lot and about my growing spirituality. I was meditating, and I had been introduced to a new spiritual guide by Larry Coryell.

Coryell and I were already going down the same path musically — he was a guitarist mixing jazz and rock intentions before I ever thought about doing it. He had even cut tracks with Jimmy Garrison and Elvin Jones, Coltrane's bassist and drummer, the year after John moved on. Earlier in '72, before I met Deborah, Coryell came through San Francisco and stayed with me. We meditated together, and I noticed a photograph he carried with him — it was in a little frame, and it was scary. It showed a man in the middle of meditating so deeply that the photo was humming! His eyes were half closed, and it looked like he had a small smile on his face. I asked Larry who it was. "This is a transcendental picture of Sri Chinmoy in a high state."

A *very* high state — I could feel the intensity from the man just through the picture. I would come to know that photograph and that face very well — I'd soon be meditating on the photo, just as Larry did, and would continue to do so for almost ten years. That face became the note I would use to get myself in tune with a Christ consciousness, a Buddha consciousness.

Sri Chinmoy was a guru who had moved to New York City from India and had started an ashram and meditation center in Queens. Larry was one of his first disciples, but that didn't matter; if Larry had asked me to come meet him then, I think I'd have run the other way. But nine months later, after getting together with Deborah and finishing *Caravanserai*, I was ready. It started with John McLaughlin — he found me in a state of openness and helped plant the seed.

Here's how it happened: just before the *Caravanserai* tour began, John called me about doing an album with him. I guess because of the Buddy Miles album, some people saw I was open to collaboration, and John knew that we both had a special place for the music of Coltrane. John's album that year, *The Inner Mounting Flame*, connected with me in the same place — so it made sense. Later I learned that Mahavishnu was the name that Sri gave to John.

But John had been a guitarist in Tony Williams's group — the guy who played with Miles on *In a Silent Way* and then on *Jack Johnson*. People ask me if it was intimidating to play with John back then — it's *always* intimidating to play with John. He was busy restructuring the way a guitar sounded in jazz — in *music*. What could I do next to him?

It's funny — I had no problem sticking up for Santana's music; I could do that on my own. But when John asked me to record with him, I spoke to a lot of people, including Shrieve and Deborah, before saying yes. I remember Armando had good advice: "Don't worry, goddammy." (He'd say "goddammy" instead of "goddamn it.") "You let him do his shick, let him play. When it's your turn, you already got something he don't have."

That made sense to me — I'm there to complement what John does, not compete with him or be compared to him. Before I said yes, though, I was telling myself to get ready to wait — wait to see what he would play and how he would play it, then do the opposite. If he plays up and down the neck, quickly and staccato, answer him slowly, with longer notes, and it's going to be a beautiful contrast.

It was like Miles had taught me — I'd always be learning, no matter what, because that was just who I am.

Those lessons never went away — I still carry all of them. I feel them today if I have to play with someone I know is great or even if I have to just meet someone like a president or Nelson Mandela. Fear and intimidation are like anger and hatred — all part of the ego game.

Saying yes to record with Mahavishnu — by that time I was calling him Mahavishnu, and he was calling me Little Brother — came down to this important lesson: my mind works for me; I don't work for it. Whatever it is that I tell my mind we're going to do, we're going to do. I told myself, "Yeah, it's going to be a little shaky the first couple of times in the studio with John, but I'll find a way." I still have that attitude, no matter whom I'm going to play with or where I'll be playing.

We sealed the deal when John flew out to San Francisco to sit in with the new Santana at Winterland at the start of October, which was really the first time the new, full lineup performed. John sat in for the last half hour, and Deborah was backstage for the first time at a Santana concert. I felt so high from everything that was happening — the music coming together and falling in love. I felt light and open to whatever was coming next — like a weight was lifting.

The *Caravanserai* tour across the United States and Canada

didn't last long—it ended with a few shows around New York City at the end of October. Deborah met me there, and then McLaughlin and I went into the studio with our respective rhythm sections. We used Larry Young and Jan Hammer on organs, John's wife, Eve, on piano, and Don Alias and Billy Cobham on percussion, balancing it out with Shrieve, Armando, Mingo, and Dougie on bass. The music included a few originals by John—he can come up with some long, gorgeous, celestial melodies, and I know that's just one reason why Miles loved him. He did two for this album—"Meditation" and "The Life Divine." There was also a beautiful, meditative spiritual called "Let Us Go into the House of the Lord," which became a favorite song of mine to play at the end of concerts, because when people heard it they really understood: "Okay, it's time to go home."

John and I also did two of our favorite Coltrane pieces—the opening part of *A Love Supreme* and "Naima." Coltrane was the reason the recording came together, so we had to celebrate his music and acknowledge him, even if we were rock musicians doing some of his holiest songs only a few years after he died. I was too naive to think anything about that—even after the music came out, I didn't read any reviews about whether or not we had committed sacrilege. I know there's a jazz police, just as there's a clave police. Gábor Szabó had a name for them. "Eh, they aren't musicians," he'd say. "They're just a bunch of jazzbos. Real musicians don't think like that." That's how I felt. It wasn't like we were putting a mustache on the *Mona Lisa*—it never felt wrong to play that music.

John and I would get together again in early '73 to finish the music for the album. In the end we called it *Love Devotion Surrender,* which was the spiritual path of Sri Chinmoy. Coryell had been the first to tell me about Sri, then John started speaking about him with even more intensity, with a consistency of serenity in his persona. That last week of October, John and Eve took Deborah and me to meet their guru for the first time.

The meeting was at the Church Center for the United Nations, across the street from the main UN buildings. There were a lot of people around as well as Indian food and some live music. Later, some people read poetry—not that different from the meetings I was going to in San Francisco. I brought along a couple of flowers as a sign of respect—I had heard other spiritual leaders speak, but I didn't know what to expect. Sri was a short, balding man wearing red robes and a big white smile—an incredible, sweet smile.

John introduced us, and Sri said, "Oh, Mahavishnu has told me about you. Good boy. I am so happy that you're here." I learned later that he greeted all his disciples that way—"good boy"; "good girl." He looked at me intently and accepted the flowers. Then he said, "I can see your soul wants to be here so bad."

Sri started speaking to everyone who was there—telling stories and speaking about his philosophy. I found out right away that *desire* was the word he used to describe uncontrolled forces of the ego, forces that separate and divide people. *Aspiration* was the effort of the spirit to get away from the yoke of those forces, reaching for a higher conscious and bringing people together. "Aspiration is the inner cry," he would say. "It cries for endless bliss, boundless peace and light. Aspiration harmonizes; desire monopolizes."

I closed my eyes, and the next thing I knew it felt like he was getting closer and closer, brighter and brighter, until he was right in front of me, even though he was still yards away at the front of the room. I kept my eyes shut, and in addition to Sri's voice I remember hearing another voice inside me telling me that this is a man of the elements, that inside him he carried sun, water, and earth. The inner voice said, "You are a seed. A seed needs sun, water and soil. Together you will be able to grow and give divine fruit to humanity."

I'm not making this up—that's actually what I heard. Sri stopped speaking, and I had a feeling that I was inside a waterfall, but instead of water there was light, and instead of falling down, the light was all going up. I was thinking to myself, "Did this really happen?" By the time I opened my eyes, I knew Sri's teaching was meant to be my path. Sri could see that, too. There was no contract to sign or handshake or anything like that. There was no official welcome—just Sri standing in front of me, smiling and saying, "I take you; I accept you. If you want, I take you as my disciple. But you got to cut your hair and shave your beard."

I knew that Sri advocated no drugs, no drinking, and no sex until marriage. John had told me about all that. Sri was about discipline—that was the "surrender" part—and he was not into any hippie sort of lifestyle. I was happy he asked me, but I wasn't sure. Cut my hair? I couldn't even think of anyone asking me to do that except for someone like Sri. In 1972, your long hair was not just a mark of honor—it was your identity and your strength and your connection to a way of life that said, "I'm done with the old way of doing things." What Sri was asking felt like some Samson and Delilah sort of thing.

When we got back to the hotel, Deborah asked me what I was going to do—if I was really going to join. She told me how she was feeling, that she was ready. I said, "I don't know. I don't want to sound weird, but I got to have some sort of sign." I had hardly said that when suddenly a bird came swooping into the room—we had left the window open. It flapped around, then flew back out again. Deborah and I looked at each other with our eyes open wide. I was thinking, "Holy shit. Did that just happen?" After a few seconds, Deborah said, "Okay. I guess you're going to cut your hair."

We found a barber in the Village. I remember the look on the lady's face when I walked in, like maybe I had walked into the wrong place. The next time I saw Sri, I was looking all clean. I was wearing a white shirt, and for the first time in maybe six or seven years my hair wasn't touching my collar. All that was left on my face was a neat mustache.

Deborah and I were welcomed by Sri into his ashram. I felt like I had gotten over a big hump, like I had gotten rid of a cancer of anger and fear and come back from a very, very deep meditation. I immediately could taste and smell better. I felt healthy; my own saliva tasted sweet, with no bad odor, and I noticed that I didn't smell funky even when I had finished a long concert and hadn't yet taken a shower. Something had changed in my molecular structure—molecules obey your thoughts, you know.

Then almost immediately we had to leave New York and join Santana in London for the start of a European tour. When the band saw me they were shocked. I could see in their faces that they thought someone had kidnapped Carlos and sent his twin brother instead. I explained to them that Deborah and I had accepted Sri Chinmoy as our spiritual guide, our guru, and that he had accepted us. I think most of them understood, though my short hair was a big change. The one who really got it was Shrieve, because we both loved Coltrane and because we were both on this planet searching for the same thing: spiritual, mental, and physical stability. Not long afterward, he cut his hair, too, and became a disciple of Swami Satchidananda.

The European leg of the *Caravanserai* tour was a triumph after that—we played at Wembley Arena in London, and I remember that any doubt or frustration and anger I had about people not liking our new music went away after the reviews of our album and our show came out in *Melody Maker*. They were both written by Richard Williams, who was one of the best rock journalists in England then. He said *Caravanserai* was the "Hot Rhythm Album of 1972" and called the progress we were making "logical, organic, intelligent." He said that each tune blended into the next. The review also compared some of the orchestral arrangements to the sound that Gil Evans got—and any comparison to Miles's music made me smile.

The praise Williams gave our live show at Wembley Stadium pushed it up even higher—he said, and I'm quoting exactly, "It seemed like the Gods had descended from Olympus and were walking the earth once more." He said this was the best version of the band yet, and he could tell how I was comfortable being the leader of the group, interacting with everyone onstage. He compared us to Miles's band again—he gave special attention to Tom Coster and Richard Kermode, calling them a "couple of Keith

Jarretts," and to the balance between funky and sophisticated in the music.

To this day it's my favorite Santana review. It wasn't just the applause Williams gave us—there was power in what he said and in how he said it. He really understood the work we had put into *Caravanserai* and the chance we took going in a new direction. Who would've thought it would come from a British magazine and not one back home?

I was on a cloud—the band was working so well. We played various places in Europe, then Montreux again, and the blessings continued. Claude Nobs welcomed Deborah and me into his home. He cooked for us—cheese fondue, even cherries flambé. He gave us an amazing bedroom where he had hooked up his phone with some technology so that it would call up music that he had recorded at his festivals when you hit certain buttons. The music would play through the sound system in the room. Aretha Franklin's "I Say a Little Prayer" was keyed to the numbers 1–7–9. I'd push the numbers, and the song would play. This was 1972, remember. How Claude got that technology together back then I still don't know.

When we came back from Europe, we did a few more shows across the States that Bill Graham set up. He had asked me who I'd like to have open for Santana on that run, and it took me less than a second to say Weather Report. They agreed to be on the bill, and during every show I'd be backstage listening to them play—Wayne, Joe, Eric Grávátt on drums, and Miroslav Vitous, who was playing acoustic bass through a wah-wah!

I was loving the music, but I got such an uncomfortable feeling when people would scream "Santana" while they were playing. I wanted to go onstage, grab the mike, and say, "Hey, shut the fuck up! This is Weather Report—this is *Wayne Shorter.* You're embarrassing me!" I had to take a deep breath. I was thinking that maybe we could open for them and get the Santana thing out of the way and then let them go on, but I remembered Bill saying that it wouldn't be fair because people would leave as soon as we were done. "They just don't know the value of this music like you do."

Wayne is a harmonic genius and was one of the reasons Miles's band sounded the way it did in the '60s and why jazz sounded the way it did in the '70s. He and Joe Zawinul brought electric rock and jazz together in Weather Report with elegance and supreme commitment and courage at a time when people would be complaining about it from both sides. Neither the jazz police nor the rock crowd knew what to think about it.

Later on I got to know Wayne and found that in person he is sweet and warm. He's now one of the closest friends I have, and I'm very proud to say that. But it would be a few more years before we got tight. I need to express how much I feel for the man. I'll put it this way: if there could be seven of me, one of them would stay with Wayne and just take care of him from the moment he gets out of bed through the time he gets on the plane or in the car to go to the show or the studio to the time he gets back home again. Just making sure he's always okay, doing what he does. There are few things more important to me than being able to be of service to Wayne Shorter. That's how much I respect and revere him.

Wayne's temperament is like a mix between a kid with a new box of crayons—who's just discovered orange for the first time— and an old Jedi Knight who has the wisdom of the ages. He might be giggling, thinking about a scene in an old movie he likes—and he remembers them all—then he'll turn around and say the most profound things.

Once I was with him, the drummer in his band was really mad about the kind of road stuff that can happen anywhere, anytime. Wayne let him go on, listening, giving him respect. The guy finally stopped to take a breath, and Wayne said, "So what did you *learn?*"

What a perfect way to put it and make him think and end the complaining at the same time. Wayne has a way of framing things that gets you to totally change your perspective, such as the way he thinks about music. One time I saw him sitting at a piano, thinking, sweating, hanging over the keys like a praying mantis, getting ready to hit a chord. All of a sudden he brought his hands down, then jumped back and said, "Did you hear it?" Someone else there said, "Well, that's an inversion of a B-flat augmented seventh with..." Wayne didn't even let him finish. "No, it isn't!" The other guy said, "But, man, it is—see, you have..."

"No. It. Isn't! It's a texture—a texture in sound."

I had never seen Wayne get that way—what he was saying was, "Don't always try to put music in a box with a pin sticking through it, like some dried-up butterfly in a collection. Let it live and be alive at least for a little while before you analyze it and nail it down. Keep the imagination open and flowing." Wayne is in the business of creating music that sometimes doesn't make sense but that always gives people chills.

Bill was right back in '72. Most people couldn't hear what Wayne and Weather Report were doing. Back then Wayne didn't really know how I felt, either, so when I went up to him at the end of that run of opening for us, he was a little cool to me. I could tell that opening for Santana was not his favorite experience.

By the time we got back to San Francisco at the end of that tour, Deborah and I were looking at each other in a way that I had never, ever before experienced. We were in love, and it was time to introduce her to my family, which I did before the year was over. Then I went to Oakland—where her mother, Jo, welcomed me like I was coming home. She was totally accepting of me.

Next I spoke to SK—this was about the third time I got together with him, and this time he dropped his guard to the point where he came up to me and said, "Let me ask you something."

"Yes, sir?"

He looked at me very seriously. "Do you believe in the Universal Tone?"

I said, "Yes, I do, sir. Universal Tone means that there's one note that can connect alpha and omega, that can connect heaven and flesh. There's one note that you can play at any time, in any place, that can make you communicate to all hearts at the same time."

The first time I heard about the Universal Tone was not from

SK but probably from the hippies, because of their connection to Charles Lloyd and Coltrane, the Beatles, the Doors, and the whole San Francisco scene. I didn't know much then about the sacred sound, but I knew about *om* from my spiritual reading and of course from the John Coltrane album of the same name. I knew about the idea that there is a Universal Tone and that many religious paths, even those of Native Americans, use it to connect with Father Sky and Mother Earth. I understood that the Universal Tone is about a collective conscious. It's not about one person but rather about everyone—it's a way of using sound to connect with the divine in all of us.

I was surprised to hear SK ask that question, and I think he had seen many musicians who were out of balance, who were disconnected from the Universal Tone—some from my generation and I'm sure some from his generation, too. It was the first time SK had asked me a question like that, and I knew that it meant that he was starting to look at me a different way.

CHAPTER 14

I'd love to share something with you: I really get high on gratitude. Gratitude is one of the highest things that a human being can aspire to, because when you're grateful you go beyond the halo and the horns. Halo and horns are just words for energy with the guilt. Angels and demons—they give you a standing ovation when you do your best to be grateful. I invite you this second, this moment to embrace unconditional love. Unconditional love is a love that is greater than your issues, greater than your luggage and baggage and illusions. Love makes you and me necessary as opposed to unnecessary. Love does away with distance and

separation. Love turns all the flags of the world into a river of colors. Love is the light that is inside all of us, everyone. I salute the light that you are and that is inside your heart. I salute you.

Anyone who's seen a Santana show in recent years knows I like to inject a dose of reality into the concert. Four or five songs along, maybe after we've played "Black Magic Woman" and "Oye Como Va" and just before "Maria Maria," the singers will take a break, and I'll start talking to the crowd. I'll welcome them to the show, then tell them about the light that they each have inside them, that they *are* light—*luminous* is the word I like to use. I ask them to please consider accepting the nobility and greatness of their lives. I say, "Please consider acknowledging that you're not separate from your own light, which is what so much of culture and religion wants you to believe—that you're not worthy, that you're a wretched sinner, that you came into this world a sinner before you even opened your eyes for the first time. That you need to atone and that you're alone."

Sometimes at that point someone will scream, or a few people will yell that they want to rock and yell out what song they want to hear, and I'll say, "Hey, man, just listen for a moment. I'm grateful you paid for a ticket, and I know the songs you want to hear, but here's something maybe you need to hear even more. How about a higher level of consciousness for a minute?"

I feel that now, in this part of the book, I want to stop, like I do in concert, and say a few things that connect the dots. I want to explain again why I'm doing this book, to talk about the Universal Tone, and remind everyone that it is not just a saying—we really are all one. I hang all my beliefs on that one note.

I'm many things—a father, a husband, a guitar player, a bandleader, and a believer. I'm also a preacher and a teacher— that's a big part of who I am now, and it comes from the work I have done on myself, starting years ago with the teachers I decided to follow. One of the most important lessons I learned was to listen to what they were saying and take the time to stop and listen to myself.

There's a very noble concept that Eastern Buddhists have: you are the gardener of your own mind. It's the idea that you have to take responsibility for your thoughts, to catch and stop yourself from thinking thoughts that are inappropriate or hurtful.

We should write it in big block letters: THE EGO IS NOT YOUR FRIEND. The ego likes doubt, and it will criticize and guilt-trip you to death. It will condemn and judge and draw you into a pit and then laugh at you. That's why meditation can be very hard. It's easy to *do* nothing, but it is very, very difficult to *think* nothing. You can never really do that, anyway—the thing is to step back from all those thoughts, like getting out of a rushing river, then just sit there and let the river keep going. Meditation is the first step to controlling all that talk, talk, talk that keeps going on inside you so you can finally decide whom you're going to trust—your light or your ego. Can you tell the difference?

For a long time I have thought about the exchange between Eastern philosophy and the Western mind in the 1960s and the relationship between the two. There were many gurus and spiritual teachers coming around during that time, and each had a different priority and path you could follow, even if the basic message was the same. There was no guidebook or website you could read to know which one was best for you. You had to listen to each of them with your heart and common sense and look at who was hanging around with them and decide if their ways of talking and their requirements and disciplines made sense for you. If they were real gurus, their messages were about love and connection.

It was an exciting time, and the ideas that these gurus were bringing to us were shedding light on a map that was always there—we just couldn't see it. Suddenly there were all these paths we could take that we didn't know existed. Even today I think Eastern philosophy is like a wise old uncle trying to help the Western mind, which can be enmeshed in adolescence, acting like a spoiled teenager, wanting to party, smelling like unwashed socks and beer. Those gurus came on the scene, teaching us how to be spiritual. They helped me face that part of my life with maturity at a time when I needed it.

There's a big difference between religion and spirituality. I know now that you can only believe in both if you are willing to take personal responsibility. If you see yourself not as a drop of water but as a part of an entire ocean, a part of everyone and everything. If you can master that idea, and if you can master the ego— which many religions count on your not being able to do—then you know your responsibility is not just to yourself but to everything. Loving yourself is loving others, and hurting others is only hurting yourself. If you believe this, then it doesn't make sense that there can be only one religion and that you're going to see God but everyone else is wrong and going to hell.

I don't buy the idea that only one kind of person gets to walk the red carpet, you know? You can keep the kind of heaven that's selective. I want the heaven that's for everybody. That's where Sri Chinmoy helped me the most. He would say that there is only one goal but there are many paths, and that each religion is right in its own way. In the West we have a way of thinking that comes down to this: the devil made me do it, but Jesus has got my back. Another way of saying it is: the devil made me do it, but Jesus will still carry me across the river of life.

Damn. What sort of responsibility is that? Even if you didn't do anything the devil told you to, just how many people does Jesus have to carry? How about climbing down and doing some of the walking?

Even before 1972 and making *Caravanserai* and getting together with Deborah and meeting Sri, I had made a conscious decision to step away from the churning of conflicts and ego games in my life. It was a once-in-a-while thing, but it was a dedicated thing— regardless of the consequences, no matter what people said, if they came along with me or not, and even if I was on my own.

The reason for gurus is that you can't do it by yourself all the time—definitely not at the beginning. You need someone else to hold up the light so you can see where you're going on your new road. A true guru is someone who brings light and is a dispeller of darkness. Jesus was a guru. Sometimes it's nothing that gurus say or do but how they change things by their presence. Miles, onstage in the 1970s with all his musicians, without saying anything or even blowing into the trumpet, would shift the whole focus of the music just by looking this way or that or by walking up to someone who would then stop playing shit. That's how a guru works.

John McLaughlin used to tell me that Miles would say to him, "Don't forget—*I* was your first guru." Miles could be funny, but he wasn't wrong.

I think that's why gurus and Eastern teachers sought out musicians—because people pay attention to them. Those gurus were smart—they knew what they were doing. They weren't going to take out ads or do radio commercials. They were talking, and a lot of people were listening, and a lot of those people were musicians whom other people were listening to. I'm not sure why so many musicians were going that way, but I know for everyone there comes a time when you have to make a move for your own betterment. Even the oldest turtle with the hardest shell has to stick its neck out once in a while—and I think it was easier to do that then than it is now. The Beatles stuck their necks out with the Maharishi. Before them John Coltrane was reading Krishnamurti and talking about him with people, educating himself on spiritual principles.

People might still wonder about that—which musicians went with which gurus and for how long. But that's a distraction—the point is not who studied with whom, it's the why. For me it was about needing to evolve and elevate and share that with other human beings—to send letters home from the front line while I was waging the battle over the ego. I was with Sri Chinmoy for almost ten years, but my spiritual path never stopped.

I think you can guess by now that the ego battle is never totally won. It takes diligence, patience, and willingness, and from the start it's got to be a gentle transformation. If you want to make progress in winning the battle over the ego, you can't just chop off the head or jump into the deep end. It's got to be gentle, and it has to start in a safe place. Even after you learn to meditate and to focus every day on love, devotion, and surrender, every day is also a chance to fall back into old habits. Even now I must remember to let my ego go and stop investing in the illusion of separation and unworthiness. It's a day-to-day thing.

Sri used to say that at every moment we have to decide if we want the division-desiring mind or the union-aspiring heart. I used to think about it this way: when Santana was flying around the world in the '70s and '80s, we'd be up above the clouds. I'd look out the window at a big, soft blanket where everything was sunny and quiet and looking perfect. But I knew in an hour or so we had to go back through the clouds and deal with whatever was happening underneath, just waiting for us.

Being human is not easy for anyone. Everyone has to deal with his or her own humanness. If we all could just tell ourselves, over and over, that the spark of the divine in us will triumph over our feet of clay—done. There'd be no need for gurus or guides. If only it were that easy.

It took years to say that with confidence about myself and to be able to speak about my convictions in public and onstage. But there's no magic bullet that will work for everyone, no perfect master you can go to who can fix everything for you. I learned many things from Sri Chinmoy. Then it was time for me to learn on my own and from others. These days, there are two wonderful thought adjusters—Jerry Jampolsky and Diane Cirincione—who help me stay on the path with their gentle wisdom. I also read from the book *A Course in Miracles* every day and discuss its message with Jerry and Diane and try to apply its spiritual principles.

In the end I think we all have our own experiences and our own emergencies. We need to consider our choices and listen to the messages that various people have for us and choose a path for ourselves. I think that everybody is meant to find his or her own way home.

I believe I am a spiritual kind of person who's well-rounded and balanced. I like to laugh and don't carry this stuff around like it's a heavy message that needs to be weighed and delivered with special handling. To be enlightened means to be light in all senses of the word.

There's a story I've heard about two monks who made a vow to never touch a woman. They're walking along and come to a river where a beautiful girl asks for their help getting to the other side. One of them lets her get on his shoulders and carries her across. A little while later the monk who helped the girl sees that the other is angry and upset. He asks what's wrong. "What about our vows? How could you carry her?" the other monk says. The first monk looks at him. "Hey, I put her down a long time ago—you're the one still carrying her."

I'm still going to share during my shows—that's just who I am, and I think people need to hear what I have learned. And if you listen—*really* listen—you can hear the message, the Universal Tone that I speak about, in all the music that I play.

It's not just my music, either—the Universal Tone lives in any number of songs that speak with the same message of love and connection, that take away the filters and reveal the best of who we are and who we can be. Sam Cooke—"A Change Is Gonna Come." Marvin Gaye—"What's Going On." John Lennon—"Imagine." Bob Marley—"One Love." John Coltrane—"A Love Supreme." Even "Row, Row, Row Your Boat" and its line "Merrily, merrily, merrily, merrily / Life is but a dream." These are songs that time cannot wither or diminish.

Thank you for being here. We love touching you with our music, and when you leave this place and you wake up tomorrow and you have to deal with you, I invite you to look in the mirror and say, "This is going to be the best day of my life." Say it with clarity and soulfulness and sincerity. When you can say that, then you truly are divine, and I salute you because I can see Christ in you. I see Buddha, Krishna, Allah, Rama, Shango. I see holiness in you. If you remember anything from tonight, let it be this. Say to yourself, "Hey, that Mexican said it is my choice. It is my choice alone. I can create heaven on earth." God bless you and be kind to one another. "A Love Supreme," "One Love," "Imagine": thank you. Good night.

CHAPTER 15

Santana, 1973: (L to R, top) Tom Coster, Richard Kermode,
Armando Peraza; (middle) Leon Thomas, Michael Shrieve,
Chepito Areas; (bottom) me, Dougie Rauch.

*My time with Sri Chinmoy lasted from 1972 until 1981, and I believe
both Deborah and I felt we got what we needed, that we benefited from
his style of spiritual discipline—and that's exactly what it was, a discipline. In an interview I did back in the late '70s I said that I was "a
seeker with Sri Chinmoy...even music is secondary to me, as much as I
love it." I think many people were surprised to read that then, and it's
still true. I was a seeker—now I feel I'm a guider.*

I should be clear: it's not about music or spirituality. For me, music is part of being spiritual, an extension of my aspirations in this lifetime. If I wake up only to be a musician, or only to go to work, or only to do this or that other thing, then I would be missing the big picture. But if I wake up and my first thought is that I am here to be a better person, then the musician in me is just going to come out naturally.

Music is the amalgamation of sound and intention and emotion and wisdom. To this day my chant is the same—"I am that I am. I am the light"—and that's what I chant if I feel myself scattered, pulling away from my core, if I feel the Universal Tone separating into different notes. I need all that I am to hit that one note and be in tune. Five things go inside that one note: soul, heart, mind, body, and cojones.

I knew I had made the right decision to be a disciple of Sri Chinmoy when that feeling I had when I closed my eyes and heard him talking and chanting did not go away. The joy, the light, the lightness. When I went back to San Francisco and would visit the meditation center that Sri had started there, it stayed with me. When I would wake up to meditate at four in the morning, I felt the same way.

Love, devotion, and surrender—that's the name of the path of Sri Chinmoy. Most people think of it as the album I did with John McLaughlin. Some even think that I joined Sri so I could play with John. That's funny. First, it's not easy to tell yourself to play guitar next to someone like John; and second, it's much, much harder to be next to Sri! It was not like joining a garden club and meeting every Wednesday night.

The love part of Sri's path is the thing that all gurus and spiritual leaders agree on—love is the unifying force of the universe; it's what holds us together and brings us life. Love is the breath that flows through us all and connects us. Devotion is the commitment to living with spiritual priorities, which was the direction I was already going in when I started to move away from drugs and toward the idea of inner work; it was where I was going when I met

Deborah, who was moving in the same direction. Devotion is not just inner dedication but also listening and learning a new vocabulary so I could talk about the incubation I was going through.

The surrender thing—that part was 100 percent Sri. Surrender was discipline—Sri's discipline. It wasn't just about short hair and guys wearing white shirts and pants and looking neat and women wearing saris. It wasn't just abstinence from drugs and smoking. Surrender was about a pretty strict diet and schedule—agreeing to stop eating meat, agreeing to wake up at five in the morning and meditate for an hour or two hours straight, even when the brain and the body both want to do other things—anything but that. Sri was also one of the first gurus I know of who had exercise as part of his path. Sri was healthy, and he looked it, too.

One of the most important lessons I learned from Sri was his fearlessness—he believed so firmly in what he was doing that even before the whole guru thing was popular, he was doing it right in the middle of New York City. He wanted his disciples to be healthy, so he got us into jogging. Later he got into tennis and he put together teams and played with professionals. He wanted his disciples to be vegetarian, but there weren't many places that served that kind of food back then—so he inspired people to start restaurants. John McLaughlin and his wife, Eve—Mahavishnu and Mahalakshmi—helped invest in and run a place called Annam Brahma in Queens, which was close to Sri's ashram. Later, Deborah and her sister, Kitsaun, and I put together one of San Francisco's first vegetarian restaurants—Dipti Nivas. I think eventually there were more than thirty of them around the world that Sri had helped bring into being.

Sri's fearlessness in inspiring all this to happen in a world that mostly didn't understand what he was about was one of the qualities I most respected. He didn't just take his disciples and move to some jungle overseas, like Jim Jones did in Guyana. Jonestown was all about self-deception and darkness. Sri was self-discovery and light—right in the middle of Jamaica Hills, Queens.

If anyone asked me where Deborah and I lived in the years from

1973 to '81, I would have said Queens first and San Francisco second. The reality was that between all the touring and recording and running the restaurant, which we opened in September of '73, we would come out and stay in Queens usually three or four times a year. Each time it would be for around two weeks of meditation and exercise, like a pilgrimage. It was usually spread out through the year, and we were there for some special occasions, such as Sri's birthday and Christmas, when we had to be there, and I'd make sure Santana's schedule did not interfere with those dates.

When we were in Queens Deborah and I could relax and settle into the routine that Sri made for us: on most days around 4:00 a.m. we would wake up, take a shower, then go over to Sri's house, because we were two of the few privileged ones—the first circle of disciples—who would meditate on the porch with him, which was a great honor. Then we would walk or take a nap, and later we'd have breakfast together. Deborah would work in the kitchen or some other enterprise such as the store, selling books and Indian saris, and I would help her or spend time speaking with Sri.

Later in the day Sri would talk to the disciples, play a little music on a toy organ, and get everyone to sing with him. Sometimes he'd sing songs he had written himself; sometimes he'd make them up right there and teach the words and melody to everyone. Then we'd stop and close our eyes and he would speak about music and its special power to make us aspire faster, to achieve a universal feeling of oneness, and to connect the outside—the music that man makes—with the music that everyone has inside but doesn't always hear. One type of music helps reach the other—from one note to the Universal Tone.

The relationship I had with Sri was different from the relationship Deborah had with him, because I was not with him as much as she was. She would spend a lot more time with him while I was out on the road. I would come back and be overflowing with questions, wanting to know about how things functioned on the way to finding the light, and whether this or that was proper, and what she thought about various things. All the time I was with Sri I never called him Guru or Master or anything like that, but I showed him respect. He was a guide more than anything else, and it felt like I was part of a fellowship. It was a fellowship that I needed to return to so that I could be with souls who were aspiring toward the same path—just as certain people who want to climb Mount Everest or explore Africa will need to hang together and speak and support each other. Like attracts like.

It took a major commitment of time and energy from Deborah and me, and because of Sri and who he was, we were prepared to do it—a commitment of energy to excellence. For a number of years through the 1970s, our work with Sri was more rewarding than all the things the world was offering—the money, the praise, the other rewards that came from being in Santana.

I knew that I needed to surrender and do the things Sri required if I wanted to get past the ego games, get outside of myself, and have a different view of my persona. It was a commitment like being in the Marine Corps. Once you put on the uniform, you wear the uniform. This was spiritual boot camp—24-7—not just going to church on Sunday. I kept my conviction and my consciousness high, and I could feel much of myself changing. Everything started to change.

I think about it now, and these changes all made sense. It was as if they had been planned. One life change led to another and another and then one more—turning away from drugs and the crazy rock-and-roll lifestyle; thinking about spiritual questions and changing my diet; the band coming apart; finally accepting that I could not fix the break between Gregg and me; going in a different direction with the music; meeting Deborah; meeting Sri. I can't see any of that happening if I'd still been smoking cigarettes or weed or eating junk food. It felt like it was all supposed to happen— later I understood inwardly that it was the invisible realm working its way through me.

It was my own inner journey, but to the fans of Santana and people around the band I was still the same Mexican guy onstage with a guitar every night hitting those notes. They didn't know what was going on until I showed up dressed all in white, with my long hair cut short. Even people close to me, including other members of Santana, didn't see these changes coming. When Deborah and I got to London at the end of 1972 for the European shows, everyone thought I'd gone off the deep end. Everyone except Shrieve, of course, who joined Swami Satchidananda.

When I got back to San Francisco, everybody including my mother thought I had lost my mind or just given it away. My family and friends from the Mission were the most certain of it. "You've been brainwashed. Those people will eat your brain—there is nothing happening but Jesus Christ, and that's it. Anything else is the devil." My dad was the one who was cool about it. He honored me by not saying anything, respecting my decision, and allowing me to work it out and find out what it was all about.

To the older guys who had left the band—and of course to Bill Graham and Clive Davis—this was just one more piece of evidence that I didn't know what I was doing, that I was willing to commit career suicide. Most of them didn't say anything, but I could feel it—and their suspicions didn't go away until 1975, when we went back to the older Santana kind of music. Until then, every now and then people would point to other Latin rock groups, such as Malo and Azteca, and say, "Man, they're playing Santana better than Santana is, know what I mean?" I knew *exactly* what they meant, but still I'd look at them and say, "No: what do you mean?"

The one guy who kept at it was Bill. He came by the house a couple of times, and I'd say, "What's up, Bill?" and we'd talk. One time he was being very polite. "Can I come in?"

"Sure."

"You know I love you like a brother, like my son," he said, and he started crying.

I said, "Bill, what's going on, man?" He shook his head. "The decisions that you're making are breaking my heart because I can see how hard you've worked so far, and it feels like you're just throwing it away."

Bill had been taking things hard not only because of my decision to go with Sri Chinmoy and to change the sound of Santana but also because there was a big problem with how Sid Frank had managed—*mismanaged*—the accounts. Money had disappeared and taxes hadn't been paid, so the IRS was getting involved, too. Almost all the money we thought we had put away had leaked out. That year, partly because we were told we'd better keep busy to make the money back, Santana played more shows than ever—we were constantly touring.

Yes, our music had changed, but people still wanted to come out and see Santana—they were buying tickets. I said, "Bill, now I'm going to cry. But if I do what everybody tells me to do, man, it won't be me. I know you want to encourage me to make better decisions, but I'm not going to kill my career, and I'm not going to let anyone kill who I am, either. I have to go through this with Sri Chinmoy, and I'm working on this thing with Deborah." I told him, "Bill, it's just that simple."

By that time Deborah and I were living together. I remember the day I knew we had crossed that line and I could tell that we were a couple. She called me over to her, and she had the keys to the Excalibur in her hand. She was making a face, holding the keys up with just two fingers, like she was holding a dead rat. "What?" I said. I had no idea what she was doing. She said, "Now that you're with me, you're not going to need this." I said, "What do you mean?" Then I got it.

I was thinking, "Who does she think she is? That's audacity, man." But I liked how she did that—she had my respect, and I could feel right away what my answer was. I said, "I'll tell you what—you don't like it, you get rid of it." I think Deborah sold it in half an hour.

That's when I knew that we were in it for the long haul. In April, Sri was talking to us, and he said that he could see we were good together, that we were helping each other with our spiritual progress. He said, "You two should get married." We looked at each other with questioning in our eyes, because back then young people were not so formal and were pulling away from those kinds of old, traditional ways. I was twenty-five and Deborah was twenty-two and we were in love, but we hadn't even been together a year by then. I think we could have lived together forever at that point, but Sri convinced us that he saw something more. "I think your souls need to be tied together—this will help you both with your aspirations even more."

When Deborah and I got back to our place, she asked me, "What do you think?" I answered, wanting to first get her reaction: "What do *you* think?" We went back and forth like that, neither one of us wanting to take the first step. It wasn't a very romantic proposal, I admit, but then again I hadn't really been trained in that department. We did love each other and wanted to be together, and we wanted to be on our spiritual path together, and Sri had told us how that should happen, so we decided to go ahead.

Deborah quickly told her parents, and not long after we got back to San Francisco, on April 20, 1973, we got together at city hall to sign the forms. Then we held a small ceremony and reception in Oakland, at SK's brother's house—he was a preacher, and he married us, too. I remember wearing funky white platform shoes, which made me a lot taller than Deborah, and I remember I wore a tie. I think I had shaved only half of my face. I also remember that everyone asked if my parents were coming.

In fact, I didn't invite anybody when I got married—no one. No family and no friends. Deborah's mom asked, "Where are your parents and your sisters and brothers?"

"They're not coming."

The rest of the guests looked at me with their mouths open. "They're not coming?"

"No."

"Why aren't they coming?"

"Because I didn't invite them."

In the '60s, when things were going smoothly, as they were supposed to, almost with no special plan, we'd say it was a groove. That's what our wedding was like and what my priority was—very quick and simple, no hassles. Deborah and I were in love, and we were living together, and that's what seemed important then—we knew we would also be having a divine ceremony back in Queens with Sri.

The hassle that I wanted to avoid was my mom—we were probably farther apart then than we had ever been, and we had not seen each other for a while. I was still holding on to all the hurt that came from that list of things she had done beginning in Mexico, such as spending the money I had saved for a new guitar. The tension in my muscles when I thought about that was still there—it would take years before that started to release. That's how I was feeling about the idea of a ceremony, anyway. When Jo asked me why my mom wasn't at the wedding, I didn't know what else to say. I told her, "My mom is very domineering, and she would want to change everything."

I did call my mom afterward, with Deborah next to me, and told her that we had gotten married. I could tell she was hurt. There was silence, and after I hung up I didn't know what to say to Deborah. When we had our second wedding in Queens with Sri Chinmoy, another very simple and unpretentious ceremony, Deborah persuaded me to invite my family. I remember flying to New York with my father, mother, and my sister Laura on the plane. The whole way over, my mom was letting me have it—making it really difficult—and she didn't care who heard. All I could do was sit there and take it—this time I couldn't walk away; she had me. I remember looking at Laura, and she was just shaking her head, trying to look away.

I'd never seen my mom so hurt; I'd never seen her react that way. The whole trip she would bug out and start crying and then get angry again. Laura would try to step in and be the shock absorber, and I would say that this is what I didn't want to have happen at the wedding in San Francisco. I knew that I wouldn't have done anything intentionally to hurt my mom, but still I had done just that by ignoring her and keeping her out of my life. I was already getting closer to Deborah's family than I was to mine—I remember we spent our first Thanksgiving after getting married in Oakland, cutting the turkey and watching O. J. Simpson break another football record in Buffalo. To me it felt natural. Her family never made me feel anything but invited—"Come on, you want some more sweet potato pie? How about more of this?" Just like that.

I was still young and growing up and evolving, and I still had a habit of going away if I saw a verbal conflict coming, especially with a woman. I could feel a door close, and I would be gone. It was automatic. That was one of the things I had to take care of with the inner work I did. I'll say it here: all the prayers and the spiritual coaching, all the inner and outer adjusting—I now see that it was really for my mom, which is why I'm dedicating the book first and foremost to her, with my thanks for being so strong and patient.

It would take a few more years for my mom and me to really get together again, and for almost the last thirty years of her life we were the best of the best. Before that, it was rough for a while. It was a crazy time, and I was so discombobulated with thoughts and emotions. I'll put it this way: I wasn't all the way present.

Even at our first wedding, when it was just Deborah, her family, and I in Oakland, I told her family that I couldn't stay for the reception because I had a rehearsal with the band. Once again, they looked at me like they just couldn't believe it. "Thanks for a great wedding day, everyone, but I got to go and get ready for this next tour." Deborah knew about it, but I don't think I was scoring many points in my favor that day. I went out to the car, and because it wasn't the Excalibur anymore I forgot what to do and had locked the keys inside.

I remember standing there with Deborah while SK worked a coat hanger into the window to open it for me, all the while looking at his little girl so hard I could hear what he was thinking. "Are you sure you want to marry this Mexican cat?" Over the years, whenever Deborah and I got into it, she'd say, "I should have known right then that it wasn't going to work." But we stuck it out.

In April of '73 we started working on the next Santana album, the follow-up to *Caravanserai*, staying with the same jazz flavor and spiritual vibe. By that time we were running on our own steam.

(L to R, top row) Tony, Irma, Maria, my dad and mom; (bottom row) Jorge, Lety, me, and Laura, 1982. (© Deborah Santana)

(Clockwise) Alphonso Johnson, Alex Ligertwood, David Sancious, Raul Rekow, Chester C. Thompson, Chester D. Thompson, Orestes Vilató, Greg Walker, me, and Armando Peraza, 1984. (© Jim Marshall Photography LLC)

Salvador and me at a video shoot in San Francisco, 1985. (© Ken Friedman)

"I see your brain. I see what you are thinking." Sentient Salvador, 1987. (© Santana Archives)

"Are you ready for me?" Stellabella, 1987. (© Santana Archives)

Stella and Salvador, 1988. (© Santana Archives)

"Ready for the world."
Angelica, 1992.
(© Daniel Valdez)

Angelica Faith, 1996.
(© Santana Archives)

(L to R, top row) Me, Irma, my mom and dad, Tony, Laura; (bottom row) Lety, Jorge, and Maria, 1988. (© Deborah Santana)

(L to R) Alphonso Johnson, Michael Shrieve, Chester Thompson, José "Chepito" Areas, Armando Peraza, me, and Gregg Rolie, backstage in 1988. (© Ken Friedman)

Performing at San Quentin Prison on December 10, 1988.
(© MarkBrady.com)

With my mother in San Rafael in 1988. (© Santana Archives)

Sitting in with Stevie Ray Vaughan and Double Trouble at the Oakland Coliseum, December 1989. (© Jay Blakesberg)

José and Josefina's fiftieth anniversary, 1990. (© Santana Archives)

José and his sons: (L to R) José, me, Jorge, and Tony, 1990. (© Santana Archives)

(L to R) Salvador, Angelica, Deborah, me, Stella, and Champ the dog, 1991. (© Linda J. Russell)

Bill Graham and me conversing onstage in 1991.
(© Santana Archives)

Clive Davis and me at
the Grammys,
February 23, 2000.
(© Rick Diamond)

"Supernatural Evening with Santana": (L to R) Everlast (aka Erik Schrody), Sincere (aka David McRae), Wayne Shorter, Money Harm (aka Marvin Moore-Hough), me, Rob Thomas, Sarah McLachlan, Dave Matthews, and Carter Beauford, 2000. (© Neal Preston)

(L to R) Deborah, me, Stella, and Angelica, 2000. (© Mark Seliger)

Josefina, Dolores Huerta, and José José at the Latin Grammys in 2000.
(© Santana Archives)

Gary Rashid and me in 2003. (© Santana Archives)

Hal Miller and Kitsaun King backstage, 2003. (© Santana Archives)

Getting down with the Universal Tone. Sitting in with Buddy Guy at the San Francisco Blues Festival, September 26, 2004. (© Gabriel Bronsztein)

(L to R) Chad Wilson, Gary Rashid, Chester Thompson, Tony "TK" Kilbert, and me in Hawaii, 2007. (© Hal Miller)

Embracing the future: Cindy and me on our wedding day in Maui, December 19, 2010. (© Jimmy Bruch)

Sealed with a kiss. (© Jimmy Bruch)

Onstage in 2011. (© Gary Miller)

Martin Sandoval and me at Santuario de Luz, 2012. (© Santana Archives)

Me, Cindy, and
Claude Nobs, 2011.
(© Michael Vrionis)

Dolores Huerta, me, Angelica, Cindy, and Juana Chavez, December 2012. (© Santana Archives)

President Barack Obama and First Lady Michelle Obama greet Kennedy Center Honoree Carlos Santana and family in the Blue Room during the Kennedy Center Honors reception, December 8, 2013. (© Official White House Photo by Lawrence Jackson)

Santana Band, 2014: (L to R) Pepe Jiménez, Tony Lindsay, Benny Rietveld, Karl Perazzo, Tommy Anthony, me, Jeff Cressman, Paoli Mejias Ramos, Bill Ortiz, David K. Mathews, and Andy Vargas. (© Libby Fabro)

(L to R) Hal Miller, me, and Ashley Kahn in Woodstock, New York, June 15, 2014. (© Benny Rietveld)

Who was around to tell us anything anymore? Maybe Bill, but CBS had fired Clive Davis around the time we started the new album, which was called *Welcome,* and we didn't have a tight connection with anyone else at the record company—not the way we had with Clive. The people who came after him did what they had to do, but I never really did work with any other record person who understood and could speak to musicians the way he did, except for Chris Blackwell at Island Records.

There was also no one left in the band to complain about changing our style or going in a different direction—Shrieve, Chepito, and I were the only guys left from the original lineup. Still, that didn't help me with the transition—the change in the band and the changeover to the next part of my life were still spinning around in my mind. I actually played John Coltrane's music over and over and over and over, for focus. I still do.

This time the title track, "Welcome," was actually a Coltrane tune. Shrieve and I talked about who should be on the album. We liked the idea of two keyboards and also two percussionists, which we had on *Caravanserai,* so we kept Richard Kermode and Tom Coster, and there was Chepito, who was the Tony Williams of the timbales, and Armando, who—well, he was the Armando Peraza of the congas! Dougie, of course, stayed with us on bass, with his nice, funky consistency, and we invited some special friends, too—some of the same people from the Bay Area who played on *Caravanserai*—plus John McLaughlin, the saxophonist Joe Farrell on flute, Jules Broussard on soprano saxophone, and others.

For some reason I didn't pay as much attention to the guitar player as I think I should have on that album. On *Welcome,* I focused on the moods of the keyboard players and congas and timbales and stuff like that. The one tune I really thought about for my guitar was "Flame-Sky," which has McLaughlin on it. The title comes from something Sri said when I played him the song.

"You're such good boys, you and John"—he said that endearingly about us. "If you could only see how you affect the audience—both of you inflame their hearts to aspire again to be one with God.

Most people forget, and they invest in a nightmare of separation and distance from their Creator and they play roles they make up, but the only role that is real is the undeniable relationship with the Creator and being in your own light. When people hear this song, a flame will shoot out of their hearts straight up to the sky, which will tell the angels, 'This one is ready. This one is aspiring and not desiring.' "

Another thing I remember about that tune: when John and I did our tour together later that year for around two weeks, we played "Flame-Sky" to open our shows and always closed with "Let Us Go into the House of the Lord." What a great band—John brought Larry Young and Billy Cobham, and I brought Dougie and Armando. I remember that Armando took on Cobham in one rehearsal after Billy said that he'd never met a conga player who could keep up with him—congas versus drum kit. I thought it ended in a draw, but Armando was still unimpressed. He held up his hands and said, "I don't need no stickets."

The first three gigs were really fast and loud, and I could see people yawning and covering their ears and walking out. In Toronto I told John we needed to have a meeting with everybody. "Okay, Little Brother. What's going on?"

"I think we need to do some sound checks and really rehearse some of the intros, the endings, and the grooves, because all our songs are sounding the same. We need to break down the songs, bring down the volume, and put a groove in some parts. Slow down a few and add some variety. I'm not used to people yawning and walking out of our concerts."

We had our meeting, and I might have been a bit immature in the way I called out the group for being unprofessional, which hurt some feelings. Eventually I heard that John had said that not even Miles talked to him like that. But I was surprised that nobody else had brought it up. I was feeling that if you're going to pack a place with thousands of people, as we were doing, you owe it to them not to play like it's a Tuesday night at some little bar. Something good came from my speaking out, because we started playing different moods, creating valleys and meadows and mountains. It was very successful. And yes, I was working on knowing how to talk to the band. I'm still learning.

The big question for the *Welcome* album was vocals—who was going to sing after Gregg left Santana? We looked at our record collection again, and we thought about Flora Purim and invited her to join us. She came from Return to Forever and sang "Yours Is the Light." I really liked Pharoah Sanders's album *Karma,* on which the song "The Creator Has a Master Plan" was sung by Leon Thomas, who sometimes liked to yodel. Leon was doing his own albums at that point: he put words to Gábor's "Gypsy Queen," and he was being produced by John Coltrane's producer, Bob Thiele. Asking him to record and tour with us was Shrieve's idea: "What if we get Leon Thomas to sing 'Black Magic Woman'? Can you imagine that with him?" I said, "Okay, let's do it!" and Leon agreed. I love Leon's singing on *Welcome*—on "When I Look into Your Eyes" and on "Light of Life," with strings arranged by Greg Adams.

My friend Gary Rashid—Rashiki—had just started working with us then. His very first job was to go to the airport and meet Leon, and he was asking, "How will I know what he looks like?" Leon arrived wearing a kind of safari outfit with a big hat and a cane. No problem. Leon became an important part of Santana, recording and then touring with us from spring of '73 through the end of '74. But at the start I don't think he really trusted us to treat him right. He saw that I was eating a specially prepared vegetarian meal every night, so he told our tour manager he wanted something special. "Okay, what would you like?" the manager said.

"Liver and onions"—which I think was like asking for a high-priced menu choice like steak. So our tour manager made sure that at every meal—in the hotel and backstage—a plate of liver and onions was waiting for Leon, and you can guess what happened. By the third day he was done with that. "Don't you guys get to eat anything but liver?"

The first tune on *Welcome* is "Going Home," which was inspired by Antonín Dvořák's *New World Symphony* and was arranged by Alice Coltrane. I asked Richard Kermode to play her arrangement on the mellotron and Tom Coster to play the Yamaha organ the way she played her Wurlitzer. I'll be honest: Shrieve and I had Tom in a headlock, telling him he had to listen to Alice Coltrane, to Larry Young, to Miles playing the Yamaha, and God bless Tom, because he never threw up his hands and said, "Fuck it" and walked away. Instead his attitude was, "Okay, I'll try it." Once he got the tone down, it was all easier after that.

"Going Home" came out of meeting Alice Coltrane that year, which for me was maybe the biggest realization of my spiritual dream—going from being a dishwasher to meeting the widow of John Coltrane and then getting to make music with her.

We met for the first time in the spring of '73, when Alice invited me to come stay with her in Los Angeles so that I could meet her and her friend Swami Satchidananda. By that time she had adopted the Hindu name Turiya. I liked Satchidananda, and maybe he was another guru I could have followed, but I can be intense, and I think that Sri's own power and intensity were good for me. If there's such a thing as discipline in romance, then that's Sri Chinmoy, because he is a lover of the supreme, and I tend to gravitate to lovers. When they hug you it's really close. They're not going to let go.

Deborah and I were making a life that had two homes, one in Marin County and the other in Queens, at the place we rented on Parsons Boulevard near Sri's ashram. We were going back and forth, and we had enough trust already in our marriage that she could go to New York and meditate while I stayed and recorded in San Francisco. So when Turiya invited me to spend time with her, which she did after she got to know about me from *Love Devotion Surrender*, Deborah knew that it was an opportunity for me to develop an important musical and spiritual relationship—one that needed to be developed. So Deborah went to see Sri in Queens while I went down to Los Angeles.

We're all interconnected anyway, but I felt more open than I had at any other time about playing music and learning. I tried to take *all* the lessons I could find from the teachers I could find. You could say that during this period, all the meditating and discussing and listening I was doing were like peeling an artichoke, pulling away the outer layers to get to the core of who I really was, who I'll always be, without playing the hide-and-seek games that people play with themselves.

I spent close to a week with Turiya. She opened her house to me, and I was very grateful that she did. I remember listening to her speak about music and her spiritual path and of course about John—but she never called him John. It was either Ohnedaruth, his spiritual name, or a few times she called him the Father. She used to tell me that he never stopped playing, even when he was home, long after a gig. When he had the day off, he'd still be at it— she told me that he could spend an hour just looking at the saxophone in front of him and then another hour fingering it up and down, all over the horn. Finally he'd put it in his mouth and start playing—hallelujah! So first he visualized the music, then he got to the mechanics. I think Coltrane wouldn't stop thinking about and playing the horn because he didn't want the stove to get cold— if it does, you have to start all over again.

I also spent time hanging around Turiya's children. I watched them jump in the pool during the day, and every night after the kids went to sleep she and I would talk for a little bit. She'd go to her room, and I'd relax on the sofa. Then around three thirty in the morning, we'd both get up, and she would play the harp and the piano. I would listen, then we'd both meditate some more.

One morning, almost at the end of the week, we started meditating. When you meditate at three in the morning, the first half hour is like being on a plane flying through turbulence. Your eyes are red, you know it's dark all around you, you're trying to stay awake, and you're shaking. Then all of a sudden things get really smooth. That morning I could see a beautiful flame in the candle that was burning—it was like a flame inside the flame. So in my mind's eye I went into it, as I had done many times before. But this time I began to feel the presence of somebody in the room besides

Turiya. It was John Coltrane. Then he materialized in my vision. He was looking right at me—and he was holding two ice-cream cones, each of which had three scoops!

I looked at John, and he smiled and said, "Would you like to try some?" Then it was as if Turiya had entered the vision from the corner of my left eye, and she said, "Go ahead and try one." So inwardly I took one of the cones and licked it, and it was sweet and creamy—just delicious. "Good, huh?" John said.

"Yes, thank you. It's very good."

"Well, that's a B-flat diminished seventh chord."

"What? Really?"

Then I heard Turiya say, "Try another one," only it seemed like she was saying this out loud in the room next to me, like she knew what was happening in my meditation.

Man, that *freaked* me out. How did she know? I have no doubt when people read this they're going to say something like, "Oh, sure—this cat just took too much LSD, and the hallucinations were still coming." But I stopped doing drugs from '72 to '81. Maybe once, a year later, I'd get curious again and try a hit of mescaline, but at that point in '73 I was really straight—totally clean.

You have to understand that to this day, when I listen to John Coltrane's music, it reassures me that God never lets go of my hand. No matter how dark things get, God's still in me, no matter what. For me his music is the fastest way of getting away from the darkness of the ego—darkness, guilt, shame, judgment, condemnation, fear, temptation, *everything*.

It's not just *A Love Supreme* and *Meditations* and his more spiritual albums. If I hear "Naima" or "Central Park West" or "Equinox" or "The Night Has a Thousand Eyes"—or any of the older ballads he recorded—I find that every note is laced with spiritual overtones. There's always a prayer in there that anyone can hear.

Even when Coltrane is playing a song, it's much more than that—and I like songs. I like "Wild Thing." I like "Louie Louie" and anything by the Beatles or Frank Sinatra. But Coltrane wasn't just about songs—at least I don't think he was. His music is about light, and his sound was a language of light. It's like the solvent that they put into dirty, murky water: stir, and instantly the water goes back to being clean. John Coltrane's sound is a solvent that clears the muddiness of distance and self-separation. That's why we all love Trane—Wayne Shorter, John McLaughlin, Stevie Wonder, and so many others—because his sound reminds us that everything is redeemable. That's what Coltrane was telling people: crystallize your intentions, your motives, and your purpose for the highest good of the planet.

I never was able to meet Coltrane, but I feel him through so many other people—Alice Coltrane, of course; Albert Ayler; John Gilmore—especially through their spiritual practice and their intergalactic music. Today you can still hear Coltrane in Wayne Shorter and Herbie Hancock and in the music of Charles Lloyd, Pharoah Sanders, Sonny Fortune, and many others.

I know some people scratch their heads when I tell them that John Coltrane's music has the power to rearrange molecular structures. I found myself once at an Olympics ceremony—I was talking about the healing power of Trane's music, and Wynton Marsalis was next to me. He shook his head and made a face. I just cracked up. Maybe Wynton's changed his perspective, but at that time I could tell he didn't want to hear what I was saying. You know, it's such a blessing to be able to play from your soul and to reach many people. It's also a blessing to be able to listen and hear the healing power that comes from other people's music. That is what I mean when I talk about the Universal Tone.

CHAPTER 16

Deborah and me, Day on the Green at the
Oakland Coliseum, July 4, 1977.

*Around 2004 I had a very, very meticulously detailed dream. Check
this out: I was in a building in Milan at night. John McLaughlin was
there, too, and we could see outside through a window to a park with
really bright lights in the middle. They were like interrogation lights, so
it was dark everywhere except where the lights were shining, and some
guys were playing soccer there, but they couldn't go too far because they*

had to stay in the light. So John and I were watching this soccer-in-the-lights game, and suddenly I saw Todd Barkan—the guy who ran the Keystone Korner jazz club in San Francisco—walking across the park, and with him is somebody who's carrying some saxophones and pushing a bicycle. It was John Coltrane!

John and I watched the two men come up to the building we're in, and we were getting more and more excited. Coltrane left the bicycle outside, came up with his horns and some sheet music, and Todd introduced us. "Hey, Carlos, John's got a song that he's working on, and I think he wants you to play with him."

"What? Really?"

Coltrane looked at me. "Hi; how you doing?"

"Uh, hi, John." I was so nervous, just thinking, "Oh, my God, I'm with John Coltrane, and he wants me to play something with him!" I looked at the music as Coltrane was taking his horns out, and it was a black church song, something like "Let Us Go into the House of the Lord." I was thinking, "Oh, yeah. No problem. I can handle this," and I started working on my part.

But when I looked up Coltrane was suddenly gone. I asked Todd, "Hey, what happened to John?"

"Oh, man, somebody just stole his bicycle, so he went looking for it, but I think the thief got away." So I decided to help him and left the building, and suddenly I was on the parkway between Nassau Coliseum and Jones Beach. I saw Coltrane's bicycle, but it had been stripped—the wheels and the seat were gone. I picked it up anyway and brought it back with me and found John. Then, with a jolt, I woke up.

Man, that dream left a powerful impression on me. It was still early in the morning, but I had to tell somebody, so I called Alice: "Turiya, I'm sorry to call at this time." She said, "That's okay—I've already done my meditation. How are you?" I told her about the dream, and she said to her it made perfect sense. She broke it down this way: she felt that the kids playing in the park were the kids who listen to music today, bouncing in and out of the dark, looking for music that will bring them into the light, music like John Coltrane's. The stolen bicycle with no wheels represented how difficult it was for that music to find a way to get to people. There was no vehicle anymore to help carry Coltrane's music to those who need to hear it. His music gets so little airplay and so little press, but it's important to bring people into the light of his music—to make Coltrane a household name.

I've been trying to put the wheels back on that bike since 1972—recording "A Love Supreme" and "Naima" with John McLaughlin, recording "Welcome" and "Peace on Earth," pointing people to John's music and to Alice Coltrane's sound, which, I believe, is sadly overlooked—but her music is really timeless, too.

I have lots of other ideas. I went on a quest to get the Grammy people to name their annual lifetime achievement awards after him: the John Coltrane Lifetime Achievement Award. I'd like to put together an entire album of Coltrane performing "Naima": three or four disks that include some of the best performances he did of that beautiful song, live and in the studio. I support Ravi Coltrane, John and Alice's son, and his wife, Kathleen, in all they're doing to preserve the Coltrane home in Dix Hills, on Long Island, where Coltrane wrote A Love Supreme and where he started his family with Alice.

There's another thing about that dream of John Coltrane and the bicycle, and people are free to say that I'm tripping. They wouldn't be wrong, either—in some ways I think I was born tripping! But many times it's hard to tell the difference between dreams and imagination. Anyway, the same morning that Alice Coltrane interpreted the dream, I got a phone call from my friend Michel Delorme in France. I told him about the dream, gave him all the details, and he kind of shrugged it off in his typical way: "Poof! Of course, Carlos. I am on the road with McLaughlin. We were in Milan just last night, talking about you and John Coltrane."

The year 1973 was one of spiritual discipline, and it was also a year of extreme endurance and madness. It felt like Santana was on the road more than we were at home—some nights we did two sets. By my estimation I think we did more than two hundred shows. Why did we work so hard? A big part of it was the feeling that while people were paying, we should be playing. We didn't have enough confidence to believe that the audience would still be there if we took time off and then went back to New York or London or Montreux. We also didn't know better—if our manager was telling us that we needed to be making a certain amount of money, and if we were hurting because of the IRS, who among us had the experience to stand up to that? We were young, we were eager, and we believed in our new music. It was our decision. Nobody was putting a gun to our heads.

What helped me was that I was meditating and my diet was healthy and I wasn't partying, and Shrieve was the same way. This was when we started to have incense onstage and when I put a photo of Sri Chinmoy in deep meditation on my amplifier. I don't think I could have made it through that year without the spiritual strength to support what we were doing on the road. We had traveled a lot before, but you can ask anyone who was in Santana that year—there were times it was like going to war. For me, it felt like Shrieve and I were comrades on the battlefield. It was hard, but we were in love with the music, and nobody ever complained.

When I look back on those times, I realize that I wasn't always the easiest guy to be around. I was like an ex-smoker hanging with a bunch of smokers and telling them that they needed to change. I think that like most people who are not ripe with maturity or spirit, I tended to get all huffy and puffy and holier-than-thou. Maybe I did come across as having a sense of superiority and some kind of rigidness about the spirituality thing. I'll put it this way: there was room for me to grow, and it took me some time to realize it.

I think a few of us who were following Sri Chinmoy back then felt that we had some sort of key to heaven and that everybody else was a dumbass. I wish Sri in his teachings had also said, "Look, if you're going to be on a spiritual path you need to be gentle with people who are not going the same way." I didn't know it, but I had much growing to do—I was still very, very green at conducting myself with gentleness toward people. By contrast, I could tell from listening to the interviews John Coltrane did that he was very considerate of other people's spiritual unfolding, or their lack thereof, whenever he spoke. That was what I needed to aspire to—not just his music. There was a lot of learning going on in 1973.

The other thing that made it easier for me that year was that I think the band was one of the most amazing versions of Santana ever. Actually, I'll put it this way: in hindsight, that 1973 band—with Leon Thomas, Armando and Chepito, TC and Kermode, Dougie, Shrieve, and me—was musically the best and most challenging band I've ever been in. And the thing is, when we were playing at our best we were really just trying to find ourselves.

That lineup was the closest I think Santana ever came to being a jazz band. At sound check we would try out new things, and it was fun. I remember we would take inspiration from little musical segments written by a keyboardist named Todd Cochran, who wrote for Freddie Hubbard and others and recorded his own music, too. He had a song called "Free Angela" that we started doing, which I thought sounded like it could have been on Herbie's album *Crossings*. To this day we have sound checks and try out new stuff all the time, even if we're in the same place for two or three nights and have already tested out the system. "You still want to do a sound check?"

"Yes, of course. Let's try something new..."

I think the best way to explain that year is to start with Japan—that was our first time in that country and that part of the world. Like Switzerland, it became a country Santana came back to again and again, and it was where we found another enlightened music lover, like Claude Nobs in Montreux, who had become a big music promoter there—Mr. Udo. Some people call him the Bill Graham of Japan, because he was the man who really started bringing big rock acts there. I agree with that, but he also earned his moniker because he respects the music and treats the musicians well. He never stopped believing in Santana and what we were doing—ever. He's always been dignified, a snappy dresser, and always has some great stories—when he laughs he doesn't hold back. He's another keeper of the flame, one of the angels who arrived at just the right time to guide and support us. Mr. Udo is the only promoter I have ever worked with in Japan.

When we came through in '73, Japan was still very traditional — you could see there were as many people in kimonos as there were in suits. McDonald's wasn't there yet, and neither was Kentucky Fried Chicken. Mr. Udo made sure we ate well, though, and he was always the perfect host, taking us out to dinner — he still does that, and I still make sure we leave time for it when Santana goes to Japan. On our last visit there he presented Cindy with the most beautiful, mind-blowing kimono decorated with all this embroidery, which made her just melt — it was fun watching my wife turn into a six-year-old!

Japan has always been the best place to get the newest electronics, especially stereos. The Japanese had Beta-format videos when those first came out and compact discs and DATs when no one else had them. That first time we were in Tokyo, we discovered Akihabara, the district where all the electronics stores were set up, and that's when I found out that Armando, with all his supreme confidence, was also a supreme bargainer.

He was amazing to shop with and watch. Armando had a routine in which he would go into a store and pick up a tape player or something, put it back down like it smelled bad, go away, and come back to it as if he felt sorry for it. Then he'd say to the salesman, "Remember me? My name Armando Peraza. Here with Santana. This...*thing*...special price for me? How much?" The salesman would be smart enough to know what to say. "It's three hundred and ninety-five dollars. But for you, three hundred and fifty dollars. And maybe a good deal on some headphones." Armando would say, "Hmm. That's not too bad. Write that down for me."

Often I could tell that this was the first time anyone had asked the salesman to do that. So the man would write down his offer, and immediately Armando would go across the street to another store, where he'd been just ten minutes before. "Hey, remember me? Armando Peraza from Santana? Look at this — same thing you have here. He wants three hundred and fifty dollars. What can you do for me?" So he would get the price down to three hundred and twenty dollars. "That's the best you do? Because everyone in Santana is looking for this thing, too—I bring them all here to you. Just write the price down for me—I show them." You can guess what would happen next. Armando would go back to the other store and walk away with something like a 40 percent discount. Then the two salesmen would phone each other to talk about that crazy Cuban!

Armando wasn't that way just with electronics—he loved nice coats, and he was a shoe addict, too. It was fun to watch Armando at work—I learned a lot.

In Tokyo, Mr. Udo had us play a whole week at the Budokan, a beautiful arena that had been built for judo competitions. The Beatles had been there in 1966, and it became another jewel in the rock touring world, one of those places every group had to play—and record, if they were lucky. Our shows were taped for TV broadcast and packed every night. I thought maybe it was time for the first live Santana album to come out—and so did Mr. Udo. So we also recorded our concerts in Osaka in another beautiful theater called Koseinenkin Hall. It was such an amazing experience: the love and respect from the audiences, the support from Mr. Udo, the level on which we were playing. When we left Japan to play Australia and New Zealand, I knew we had recorded some of the best music we had ever performed.

We did the tour of the Far East and Australia on a plane we rented—an old propeller plane that Chepito nicknamed the Flying Turtle because all our trips seemed to take forever—I remember that going from Hong Kong to Perth felt like a twenty-four-hour flight. But at the time it didn't matter, because we were so high on the adventure of it. We'd finish playing a great show and be buzzing, then we'd get on the plane and I'd close my eyes and wake up in a new country I'd never seen before—Indonesia, Malaysia, Australia. I was also really high because the press was complimentary, even though they might have been disappointed at not having

heard the original Santana band and the kind of concerts we were doing back then.

The last concert of the tour was in New Zealand—Christchurch—and I remember the band being so together, as if we had made it to the summit of a mountain. It really felt like the best concert of the tour, the best that band had ever sounded. We didn't record all our shows back then, but I knew that fans were able to either record Santana in concert or find people who did. I knew that there were bootlegs floating around, although it wasn't as extreme as the Grateful Dead's situation with the Deadheads and all the taping and trading that went on. For some reason, though, I wasn't able to find a recording of our Christchurch show until 2013, when we got a copy through one of our dedicated Santana followers. We call them the gatekeepers because they know more about the band and its history than just about anyone. The recording needed to be fixed in the studio, because the tape had deteriorated and was wobbly. But once it was repaired, the playing sounded crisp, and it validated everything I remembered feeling about the show. There was a sense of adventure in our playing; we were stretching out and trying new things, even on the last date of the tour, and there was no more turbulence—no problems with the structure of songs or the segues. It felt like the show just played itself—it was that good. It still blows my mind.

From there we went back to the United States and toured for another five weeks. It was during this period that Deborah and I got our spiritual names from Sri, which he had promised us the year before. Devadip, which means "lamp of God" and "eye of God," was my new name; Deborah's new name was Urmila—"Light of the Supreme." At this same time, Deborah and Kitsaun were getting ready to open Dipti Nivas, the vegetarian restaurant that Sri asked us to start in San Francisco because he would not accept any donations. He preferred that his followers do the kinds of things that expanded his message of love. "Do not try to change the world," he would say. "The world is already changed. Try to love the world."

A new vegetarian restaurant aspired to that spiritual goal and was the kind of contribution he wanted.

The restaurant opened in the Castro, which was becoming known as the center of San Francisco's gay community, and as the neighborhood grew it helped all the businesses there. At first I wasn't sure if we were ready to run a restaurant, but I got to see Deborah in charge, and because Kitsaun was also a disciple by then, I knew the two of them would be okay. I remember Deborah once going up to a tall drag queen and saying, "Excuse me, sir. There's no smoking allowed." He looked like he had spent half the day getting himself together. He looked down at her and put out the cigarette. Deborah was no-nonsense when it came to that.

Soon anyone who was vegetarian or was thinking about giving up meat or was just curious came by. The frittatas and casseroles and fresh juices were delicious, and the place got great reviews. Deborah and Kitsaun started doing meditation classes there, and bands such as Herbie Hancock's came in to eat when they were in town. The name for what we were doing was what Sri first called it—a love offering. People could taste our intention and feel what we had to offer on a spiritual level. Dipti Nivas stayed popular for a long time.

The next leg on our tour was Santana's first real run in Central and South America—ten countries, including Mexico. It was my first time playing there since I left in 1963. In fact the first show was in Guadalajara, in my home state of Jalisco, so you can imagine the attention I was getting. I'll be honest: I don't think I was ready for it. I was still getting myself together spiritually, still figuring out my identity. And musically I was much more American than anything else, still loving the blues and the jazz of Miles and Coltrane. In my mind, even before I met the press in Mexico I was already thinking that they'd be wanting to claim me. You know what the first questions were when we started doing interviews? "Why don't you play Mexican music? Don't you like music from your home country? Why don't you speak Spanish?"

Asking me those kinds of questions was like waving a red flag in front of a bull. The reporters would do the press conference in a very confrontational way. My mind was spinning with all kinds of possible answers, like: "I'm not Mexican, I'm a Yaqui Indian, like my father." Or "You know, what you think is Mexican music is really European—two-beats and waltz rhythms. Even the word *mariachi* comes from the French word for 'wedding.'" But interviewers were looking for a lesson in music history about as much as I was looking for an interrogation.

Things between those Mexican writers and me did not get off on the right foot. There was a bit of a war between us that went on for years: even my mom heard about it back in San Francisco. Friends would send her the newspapers, and she'd call me. "Can't you tone it down a little bit? You might be telling them the truth, but you're pissing them off like crazy." She read everything. "Why are you so angry?" she'd say. My whole family has been like that— Tony, Jorge, now Maria—checking up on me, asking me to watch my words. That's a family tradition now; even if I sometimes have to respectfully disagree with them, I love them even more because they care so much.

Things did get better with the Mexican press over the years, and it never stopped me from going there and playing the same kind of shows I do everywhere else in the world. It took time—when I went back after *Supernatural* hit I think that was the first time I really felt comfortable being Mexican and being in Mexico, even with all the questions I would get. One thing's for sure: there never was a time I did not feel the love of the people when I played there. Mexican audiences always made me feel right at home—even that first time, in '73.

One highlight of that tour made me extra proud of being a Mexican. When we got to Nicaragua, Chepito's home, we agreed to play a benefit for the survivors of the huge earthquake that had hit there just before Christmas the year before. Actually, this was the second benefit we did—the first one was in California the previous January, with the Rolling Stones and Cheech and Chong. This time we played in a soccer stadium right in Managua, where the earthquake had hit. Who was the emcee for the show? I couldn't believe it—Mario Moreno, or, as every Mexican knows him, Cantinflas!

Everyone in Central and South America knew the movies of Cantinflas and loved him. He was like all the Marx Brothers rolled into one—making fun of rich society people; getting away from the cops; getting over without changing who he was. The fans crowded the airport when he arrived. When he got onstage at the stadium, the placed was packed. He went up to the mike and said, "*Hermanos, hermanas!* I got a phone call while I was in Barcelona that I was needed here to be master of ceremonies tonight, and I said right away, 'Of course! For my brothers and sisters in Nicaragua, of course.'" The stadium was filled to the top, and everyone was cheering. Then Cantinflas got serious. "I have just one thing to ask." The whole place got quiet.

"Whoever took my wallet, can you give it back?"

Man, I've never heard such a huge explosion of laughter. It wasn't just the sound; you could feel it. In a single moment fifty thousand people who had been messed up by the earthquake and by months of waiting for help all let go of their tension and their worries and were laughing together. It really was spiritual. With one small line, just a few words, Cantinflas connected with every person in that place. That was a huge lesson to me—the power of laughter.

It also reminded me that in church when I was growing up I saw a painting of people on Judgment Day—those who were damned and going to hell and the other, lucky ones who were going to heaven. I was still a kid: this was supposed to inspire me? I would think, "Keep that to yourself," and I'd take what little money I had and go to the movies to see Dean Martin and Jerry Lewis acting goofy. I'd laugh my ass off. I've always loved comedies and comedians—especially those who know how to make fun of themselves without being racist or vulgar.

Laughter can be a very spiritual thing—if you ask me, I think getting in a good, gut-busting round of laughter is worth more than a month of meditating. It can take you away from yourself, help you let go of a lot of layers of fear and anger. If you get someone laughing, *really* laughing, you're dealing with Christ consciousness and Buddha consciousness and divine illumination. To me, Rodney Dangerfield and Bill Cosby and Richard Pryor and George Lopez are all holy men in the way that each of them looks at life and finds a way of making fun of it. It still makes me laugh to think of how Mel Brooks dropped Count Basie and his big band in the middle of the desert in *Blazing Saddles* and had the black sheriff ride by on his horse with the Gucci saddle—that's comic *and* spiritual genius. There's so much going on in that one moment. Laughter is lightness, and if you don't have a sense of humor things can get dark really quick.

One of the other lessons to come out of that tour of South America in '73 was that because I spoke Spanish, I got a lot of practice doing interviews and talking to the audience from the stage. More and more I was stepping in front of the band in public, even though Shrieve and I were still making the decisions together about the music.

Bill Graham produced that first Nicaraguan earthquake relief concert back in January of '73, and I think that had to be another reason he and I were so compatible. I always believed that music could help people who needed help, and I still do, and in fact that's how Bill got his start—producing concerts to raise money for the San Francisco Mime Troupe, then to help some people who had been arrested, and the one thing that never changed about him was that he never stopped doing benefits and fund-raisers and putting together concerts for good causes, no matter how big he got. Being around hippies and that San Francisco thing, he couldn't have ended up any other way—doing what he could to help people and to protest what was wrong.

Remember the S.N.A.C.K. concert Bill put together in 1975 with Bob Dylan and Neil Young and other bands that raised money for after-school programs? Or when he helped raise two million dollars after the '89 California earthquake with all those rock bands and even Bob Hope? Whenever he called me for stuff like that, I would always say yes—put Santana's name on the list. In fact, put us on the list first, because I know he could then use our name to get other big names.

Just before Bill died, in '91, we were talking about an American Indian benefit at the Shoreline Amphitheatre in Mountain View to mark the anniversary of 1492—"500 Years of Surviving Columbus," we were going to call it. The last phone message he left me was about that project: "Stay well, my friend. I'll see you tomorrow."

By the end of '73, we were all tired of being on the road, and Ray Etzler was our new manager. Bill was still overseeing the business side of Santana, and though we really managed ourselves, we hired Ray to take care of stuff that needed taking care of, like dealing with Columbia Records, which seemed to be less and less in our corner.

Welcome came out that November, and we had wanted our next album to be our concert from Japan. We had heard the tapes of our concerts in Osaka, and they were great—they caught the band at its best, and we were really proud of it. We had a great plan for bringing that music out, for making it an entire Santana concert experience: three LPs, with a booklet and images from Japan, including one of the Buddah, all done by talented Japanese artists. The album included a tune we put together during those concerts and named after Mr. Udo.

It was beautiful and ambitious and the music was fresh, but it was nothing that Columbia could handle. With the album cover and packaging and the three disks, it was just too expensive for them. They didn't believe it would sell enough. Even after the Japanese finally released *Lotus* in the summer of 1974 and it became the bestselling import at the time, Columbia wouldn't budge, and even Bill couldn't make them. That's how different things were after Clive was forced to leave. I was learning just how bureaucratic things could be in the United States and how differently record

companies were run in Europe and Japan. You know what Columbia did around the time *Lotus* came out? They put together a single-
disk greatest hits album, as if we were some over-the-hill group,
and released it around the same time. That was a low point.

We'd pushed so hard to be as good as we were on that album, to
deliver hundreds of shows that year, that if you look at the Santana
schedule for the first half of 1974, you can tell I was recovering—
everyone in the band was. There were a few Santana shows, but
most of my energy and intention was focused on meditating and
being with Deborah in Queens. I did a few spiritual concerts with
Deborah and John and Eve McLaughlin, and sometimes with Alice
Coltrane and her group, and sometimes when Sri was there he
would start the night and read his poetry.

Hanging around Turiya inspired me to write some spiritual
melodies, and when she heard them she surprised me by coming
up with some arrangements to go along with them—symphonic
oceans of sound, tides flowing in and out. Those first tunes became
"Angel of Air/Angel of Water" on the *Illuminations* album, which
was the first album to have my spiritual name on the cover. All the
planets aligned to make that one happen: Turiya was in between
record companies at the time, and Columbia agreed to it but wasn't
expecting any radio hits, so the attitude was that they'd figure out
what to do with it when it was finished. Basically, Columbia told us,
"Go and have fun." The album was like *Abraxas*—no hassles at
all—but the music really took me farther away from that classic
Santana sound than almost any other recording—farther away but
closer to where my heart was.

We did the sessions at Capitol Studios in Los Angeles, where
Frank Sinatra used to record, because Turiya knew it and there was
space for a full string section. Everything was done live, and it was
amazing to be in the same room with Jack DeJohnette and Dave
Holland—both of whom had played with Miles—and Armando
and Jules Broussard and Tom Coster. There was a great vibe:
Armando would tell a story, and we'd crack up, then Turiya would
say something that made us all laugh even harder. Everyone thinks

of Alice Coltrane as being a serious, deeply spiritual person who was somehow close to the divine and was not allowed to joke around. But she loved to laugh and have fun.

I remember riding with her once in a limousine, and she said, "Carlos, I have to tell you something, but please don't laugh."

"Okay, Turiya, I won't."

"I want to play you my favorite song now." She was giggling like a little girl. She put on the track, and it was Ben E. King's "Supernatural Thing." I was like, "This is your number one right now? It's cool—that's a great tune." It was great to see that part of her—enjoying music in a pure way, without needing it to be one style or another.

I love the string arrangements on *Illuminations* and what Turiya played on harp and organ, especially on "Angel of Sunlight," which, like many of Turiya's songs, opened with tabla and tamboura; two disciples of Sri Chinmoy played them. I played my solo, and the engineers got an amazing tone on my guitar that I think was partly because of the room but also because the Boogie amplifier I brought with me had a second volume knob, which let me play softly but still with a lot of intensity. There's a joke that goes, "How do you get a guitar player to turn it down? Put a chart in front of him." Well, in that session I was tiptoeing, walking on eggshells because of everyone there, so I wasn't going to blast my guitar, but the Boogie helped me turn it down and still be loud in my own way.

My favorite moment on the whole album came right after I finished that solo. Suddenly Turiya blasted off like a spaceship, playing that Wurlitzer, bending the notes with her knees—she had some gizmo that stuck out of the side of the organ—and Jack and Dave and I all looked at each other like we were hanging on for dear life! It was one of the most intense things I ever heard her play.

It was my idea to get DeJohnette and Holland for the album; Turiya had wanted a young drummer in Los Angeles, Ndugu Chancler. She introduced me to him, and he told me he had played with Herbie, Eddie Harris, and many others. He had a sound that I immediately liked, very much like Tony Williams. In fact, Ndugu had also played with Miles for a little bit. He didn't play on *Illuminations,* but I got to hear him play, and I kept his name in my head because I definitely wanted to get together with him at some point. I still do that with musicians I hear and like. I'll file the name away in my mental Rolodex, and sometimes it will be years later when I think about them and give them a call.

At the start of summer Shrieve and I started working on the sessions that became *Borboletta,* which I think of as the third part of a trilogy, along with *Caravanserai* and *Welcome.* I call them the sound tracks—those three albums were like a set. They all had the same loose, jazzy feel and spiritual mood. The sessions were in May and June, and TC became very important to us in the studio—he would get a production credit with me and Shrieve—and we kept some of the same band as we had on *Welcome,* with a few changes. Flora Purim and her husband, Airto Moreira, were very important to that album. Leon Patillo—who sang and played keyboards—joined the band, too, and brought a gospel kind of vibe, which was different from what Leon Thomas had brought. We asked Stanley Clarke, who played bass with Return to Forever, to help us out on some tracks, and he did. Dougie left to go work on other projects, such as playing with David Bowie. David Brown came back into the band and played on some of those tracks, too.

They were fun sessions—I was getting used to seeing new faces for each album, and I enjoyed seeing how we reacted when they played with someone new for the first time. There was always going to be someone who would be checking out the other guy, testing him. We were playing "Promise of a Fisherman" when I looked over at Armando and Airto, and they really seemed to be going at it musically, really pushing each other. Airto looked at me as if to say, "What's with this guy?" Later he asked me, "Is he always that competitive? He has those congas, and all I had was a triangle, but still it felt like he wanted to kick my ass." I got used to those kinds of surprises.

Another surprise? We were almost done with the new album and getting ready for our first tour in six months when Shrieve got very sick and had to go into the hospital with kidney stones. I called Ndugu—he played on one track for *Borboletta* because it looked like Shrieve needed more time to recover—and I asked him to come on the road with us.

I could tell immediately that Ndugu was the right choice—he was especially good with a funky backbeat and could still handle the jazzy numbers. A lot of drummers can only do one or the other, and their backbeat can get really stiff and stifling. Ndugu had no rigor mortis—he was open and not suffocating. He was also blessed with knowing how to tell which kind of groove was best and was able to bring the kind of feel that was coming from Marvin Gaye and Stevie Wonder, which helped move Santana toward a '70s kind of funk. Michael Shrieve was more meshed with Elvin Jones and Jack DeJohnette, and he had his own sense of funk, but it wasn't as tied into the '70s as Ndugu's was. It was just two different ways of playing.

I wasn't thinking of disengaging Michael Shrieve from the band when he got sick, but that was what happened. I knew we weren't going to cancel the tour, and I was getting very curious to know how our sound could change and develop in a new direction. So there were those reasons for pushing ahead, and I know they didn't all sit right with him. We never formally decided that he was going to leave the band, and we never made his departure official or public. When I think about it now, it wasn't handled ideally or in as gentlemanly a way as it could have been, what with Michael being in the hospital. But the decision to go ahead with the tour was what made us realize that we needed to go our separate ways.

I cannot speak for Michael, but I think the separation gave him a kind of freedom to take time away from touring and explore some different music ideas, because that's what he did. He's a super-talented drummer who made music in other bands and for film—to this day he still contributes songs to Santana. He moved to New

York City and lived there in the '70s and '80s, and I visited him there almost every time I came through. He was always gracious and welcoming—I think we had been through too many of the same things together in music and on our spiritual paths for the sediment of anger and resentment to muddy the water between us.

Shrieve leaving Santana was the band's final step in its evolution from being a collective to being a group with two leaders to finally being a group in which I alone was in charge. Shrieve was the last connection to the old band, the last person whom I would confer with and sometimes defer to. Chepito was still in Santana, but he still had his own agenda; he was more like a hired sideman in the band, and I think that touring so much in '73 had kind of distanced him from me and strained the relationship between us, the way it strained us all.

If you want the date that I took on the full-on duties of leading Santana and it really became my band, it would be sometime in late June of '74. Since then I've tried to do my best to be true to the original spirit of the band and to the music. And since then it's been a blessing and a duty. There has been freedom from having to be responsible to another person, but at the same time there is the everyday responsibility of making decisions and plans, and I am still trying my best to navigate Santana with honesty to a place where it's all milk and honey.

I was almost twenty-eight then, and when I look back I don't remember it being difficult—switching to that role of being the leader. I didn't feel too young or too naive or lacking in experience. We'd already been through the big move that put me and Michael at the helm. I'd say it felt natural: the way I looked at it was that Santana was really me even before there was a Santana band. What was difficult was resisting other people's interpretations of what they thought Santana was or what it should be, both from outside and within the band. The people closest to me who encouraged me to be myself and to trust myself were Bill Graham, Deborah, and especially Armando. He was the only one inside Santana who was always in my corner with a supreme confidence that was conta-gious. He'd say, "There's only one Santana in this band—that's you, Carlo. You tell them this is your shick now."

In the middle of the 1970s it felt great to be young and leading one of the most important rock bands on the road. The music and the hits from our first three albums and the Woodstock movie were like a wave of energy that did not stop carrying us through those years. The blessing was that we could be as busy as we wanted to be, even without any new radio hits—though we did have a few more hits in us that would come later in the '70s.

The other blessing was that we had an inner balance and focus that, for much of the time, kept most of us away from the tempta-tions and excesses of the era. We were starting to have a language with which to deal with the spiritual world and the so-called realities around us. There was a bridge between the seen and unseen realms that was important if we wanted to keep going with our music and stay relevant and connect with the past and continue into the future.

When I think of those years in the '70s, I think of the many musicians and legends I was able to meet because of where San-tana was in the music world. Some were heroes, some were friends, and some were not—and there was always something to learn from all of them.

I remember feeling uncomfortable that Muddy Waters was opening for us. We should have been opening for him, always. His blues music was so important to so many people, and he was the one blues legend I was too intimidated to introduce myself to, even in 1974 and '75. I loved seeing how he put together his shows— who played first; who came on next. For example, I was wondering why Muddy needed three guitar players in his band. But then in the middle of the show he'd point to one of them, who'd play a solo in B. B. King style. Then Muddy would point to the next guy, who would play a solo in Freddie King style. Finally the last guy, who sounded a little like Albert King, would play. Then Muddy would step up with his slide guitar and just kill it—show everyone who was in charge—and bring the house down.

By the end of the show the audience had their mouths open, wondering how it was possible that this older guy had so much energy and soul. Then Muddy would show them one more time in the encore. He'd say, "Thank you so much. It's so wonderful to play for y'all. Right now I want to introduce you to a very special person—please give my granddaughter a nice hand!" He would bring out a lady who was in her twenties. Big applause. "Okay, now I want you to give a hand to my daughter." Of course, everyone was expecting a woman in her fifties, but out came this little six-year-old girl. Everybody would suddenly get it, and with perfect timing Muddy would go, "Now you see I *still* got my mojo working...one, two, three, hit it!" And he'd go into his last number.

You can't make this stuff up. I have so much love for the mentality and spirit of that dude.

Here's another special moment from '75: the same day I got to meet Bob Dylan for the first time, I got to jam with the Rolling Stones! I was staying at the Plaza Hotel, across from Central Park, and so was Bob. I knew his music from the '60s, of course, but in the years since then I had really begun to treasure his genius. I remember once sitting down with "Desolation Row," listening to the words and breaking it down for myself: "Einstein, disguised as Robin Hood / With his memories in a trunk / Passed this way an hour ago / With his friend, a jealous monk." I mean, this guy is like Charlie Parker or John Coltrane the way his imagination flows—absolutely astonishing.

We were introduced, and we were hanging out in a suite, just getting to know each other, when I got a call that the people from CBS Japan were there. I remembered that I had a meeting with them. They were there to show me the *Lotus* album, and I asked Bob if he wanted to see it. So the record people came up and started to take the album apart, spreading the artwork out on the floor, unfolding the pages in the book, and it was just an incredible package. I saw Bob's eyes getting big.

The phone rang again, and this time it was the Rolling Stones' people—the band was in town playing Madison Square Garden. Did I want to come and jam with them? "Well, I'm here with Bob Dylan."

"Well, please bring him, too!"

So a little while later we got into a taxi—Bob, my Mesa/Boogie amp with the snakeskin cover, and I. Nobody sent a limo or anything, which was no problem until we arrived at the Garden, told backstage security who we were, and it was obvious they didn't believe us. I guess they were probably thinking, "Bob Dylan and Carlos Santana together? Showing up in a taxi? Nah." We called the Rolling Stones' people, and they came down to get us.

The concert was incredible—I think it was the last night of the band's run there, and the place was electric. There was an opening act with steel drums, and Billy Preston was hanging out and playing with the Stones, so I got to meet him. They did their show, and near the encore they came up to me and asked me to come on and play on "Sympathy for the Devil." Mick sang his part, then turned to me, and I put my finger on the string and... *wham!*

Suddenly I noticed heads turning and eyes looking at me. I don't know if the band had miked my amp too hot or something, but somehow I don't think they were ready for the sound of that Boogie amp—the drive and the intensity. I was thinking, "Yeah, *that's* how it's supposed to sound."

I'm not taking any credit for what happened after that night, but I will say that if anyone remembers the Stones' next tour, in '77, it was all Mesa/Boogie amps onstage. And the year after that Dylan played Japan, and they made a nice-looking double album from the concert.

That same summer I finally got to jam with Eric Clapton. When we play together I don't hear Eric Clapton or Santana. With Eric, it's a conversation about whom we love most. "Oh, you got some Otis Rush? How about some Muddy Waters?" When we play it isn't about crossing swords and dueling, which is how some people think of jamming. It isn't Fernando Lamas versus Errol Flynn. It's "You got Robert Johnson, and I got Bola Sete."

I think the best guitarists have the biggest boxes of heroes—some British cats tend to limit themselves to one kind of style, but not Clapton and Jeff Beck and Jimmy Page. They listen to Moroccan and African music—recently Jeff Beck has been checking out Romanian choirs. George Harrison listened to Indian sitar. I think Stevie Ray Vaughan could be fearless when it came to listening: he didn't just check out T-Bone Walker, he also checked out Kenny Burrell and Grant Green and Wes Montgomery. It wouldn't be fair to call Stevie a blues guitarist. You can hear it on "Riviera Paradise": his vocabulary went far, far beyond Albert King. All these guys I mentioned are open to many influences, but they'll always be rooted in a certain thing. Each musician to me is like an airport—there are a number of different planes coming in and landing and leaving. It's never just one airline.

It's always changing—right now I want to hear some Manitas de Plata, because he's blues and flamenco together. I want some of Kenny Burrell's *Guitar Forms* with Gil Evans arranging and Elvin Jones on drums—I could live with that on a desert island forever. As much as I love John Lee Hooker, sometimes I have to say, "Hold that thought: I'll be right back. I got to hang out with some elegance and 'Las Vegas Tango.'"

I noticed later that all the heavy metal guys—at least those who play very fast, like Eddie Van Halen and Joe Satriani—remind me of Frank Zappa's kind of fearlessness, which leans toward a Paganini vibe as opposed to a B. B. King or Eric Clapton vibe. A blues connection might not be there anymore, but that's not good or bad; there's a nice contrast to all of it. It's just a matter of apples and oranges and pears and bananas. Santana's not going to be everybody's favorite music every time.

"You're not made out of gold"—that was my mom talking.

"Oh, yeah? What's that mean?"

"Not everyone's going to like you. You can't be everyone's golden boy."

She was right. That was another lesson I learned in the '70s. At the end of '76 we played a double bill in Cologne, Germany, with

Frank Zappa—two shows, one that he opened and we closed, and the other that we opened and he closed. I wasn't thinking that this would be another situation like the ones we had with Rahsaan Roland Kirk and Wilson Pickett, but when I went to Frank's room to say thanks for the music, I could tell that he was someone who wasn't going to let me into his awareness. I don't remember what he said, but I got a feeling that I wasn't supposed to be there.

I quickly offered my respect and gratitude for his music and left. I was sincere—I liked his music, especially "Help, I'm a Rock" on *Freak Out!* and that raw and dirty blues, "Directly from My Heart to You," on *Weasels Ripped My Flesh*. Whatever it was Frank didn't like, it came out a few years later when he made "Variations on the Carlos Santana Secret Chord Progression," and in one listen I knew it was not a compliment. But in a weird way it was like a compliment because he went out of his way and spent time and energy to make a point about my music. You know how I found out about it? I was still buying Frank's albums even after we met back in '77. I loved the title *Shut Up 'n Play Yer Guitar,* so I got the album, and there it was.

My answer to anyone who's so invested in that kind of criticizing or hating or toxic feelings has never changed over the years. My phone would ring, and it would be Miles or Otis Rush. Today the phone still rings, and it's Wayne Shorter or Buddy Guy. Do I care what you think about me?

By '75, there had been many calls from Miles, especially when I was in New York City. One time back in '71, Miles called me at my hotel in New York and got me to come down to a weird gig at the Bitter End. "Write down this address. I want you to come over and bring your guitar."

"Okay, Miles," I said. I went down there but left the guitar behind. When I got there Miles was screaming at the owner of the club—screaming with that hoarse voice of his. In the middle of all that cussing he suddenly turned to me and got all nice, like, "Hey,

Carlos, how you doin'? Thanks for coming by." Then he turned back to the owner and resumed the yelling and foul language.

Richard Pryor had just started his set—he was the opener, and he was cracking everybody up. Then Miles said, "Where's your guitar?" I just shrugged my shoulders. "Oh, I see." I didn't say anything, but this was the band with Jack and Keith and Michael Henderson on bass. The way those guys were scrambling things, I couldn't even find 1. They started playing, but Miles was still pissed at the owner, and it was like he went on strike. He stood his trumpet on the floor and then just lay down—right there in front of the stage—while the band was working on colors, not really songs.

Whatever needed to happen must have gotten worked out, because eventually Miles got up, put the trumpet to his mouth, and everything fell together. Suddenly there was a theme and a focus and a feeling of structure. It was amazing—he changed the music without even playing a note.

I think Wayne and Herbie would agree that a lot of what made them the way they are today was because of being with Miles. I think it was like that with anyone who played with Miles—even to this day Keith Jarrett, Chick Corea, Jack DeJohnette, Dave Holland, Gary Bartz, and many others are all making music that is the best in jazz, making music that makes other stuff sound like easy listening. I remember Branford Marsalis talking about this after he played on Miles's *Decoy* album. He said that with Miles he was able to play stuff he had never thought about playing, but as soon as he got back on the road with his own band he was playing the same old way as before. He credited Miles for bringing new things out of him.

I know how Branford felt, because Miles's consciousness permeates many musicians, not just those who played with him. It permeated me even before I heard him live, just from listening to his albums and reading the liner notes and playing along with John McLaughlin on *In a Silent Way*. You know, Miles never really came out and asked me, but I sometimes got the feeling he was checking to see if maybe I would be in his band. He'd ask, "So you like living in Frisco?" It was the closest he came to inviting me, but then my stomach would tighten up and I'd say to myself, "No, don't do it. It will break up a friendship." With Miles I knew enough not to get too close. Also it was an honor to think that it was even possible, but I never thought I'd be able to hang with the music he was making then.

The other thing about Miles was that you couldn't rely on knowing what he had done in the past. That can be intimidating. He was moving forward with his music and not looking back. I only remember one time that he changed his mind, just for a moment. Miles was at the Keystone Korner in '75, and his band started with some deep funk stuff. Miles was playing organ; his trumpet wasn't even out of its beautiful leather case. The music sounded like a freaking cat in the alley, with a subwoofer that only gophers could hear, way down there. I was thinking, "Oh shit, that's the opening song?" All of a sudden a big lady in front yelled out, "Miles! Miles! Play your trumpet!"

The whole place was looking at her, and her date was trying to hush her up, but she wasn't having any of that. "What? I paid for your goddamn ticket, and I paid for mine, too. Miles, play your goddamn trumpet! We don't want to hear this shit."

It was on Miles what to do next. He looked at her, then opened the case, took out the trumpet, and brought down the band. Then he got down on one knee right in front of her and gave her a little taste of *Sketches of Spain*. Only a woman could have gotten away with that, and I loved the way Miles handled it.

At that time I was starting to see a few things about Sri that weren't endearing him to me. He was still treating me with favoritism, but sometimes he'd say things that didn't feel right. I didn't feel that a holy man should complain about his disciples and be ragging on their imperfections. My feeling was that as disciples we were supposed to be the ones who were human, who needed inner work, and he was supposed to be the one showing us how to be compassionate.

My pulling away from Sri was gradual but efficient and tangible, because for me, everything that used to be honey was turning to vinegar. By '77 it felt like it was time for me to go. Larry Coryell and John McLaughlin had both left by then, but Deborah wanted to stay. I was starting a long tour with Santana at the beginning of that year, and that's when I told her I was leaving him. "You can stay with Sri if you want, but I'm gone."

The Santana tour in the first half of '77 went on for months and months. I was disconnected and cut off from my life in many ways. Deborah and I were on the same frequency when I left, and I felt our spiritual paths should be together whether Sri was guiding us or not.

But when that long tour came to an end in April I could tell it was time to come home and be with Deborah, or we were done. We got together, and she got very, very serious, and I knew what I had to do to not lose her. I asked Bill to come by our house in Marin. He had booked Santana to do some dates at Radio City Music Hall—after a sold-out US tour, this was going to be the crowning jewel of those four months. I recognized and respected that. I knew what I was risking, but I told Bill, "I can't make those gigs, man. I need to spend time and reconcile things with Deborah and heal the situation. It has to be now, right away."

The first thing Bill said was, "Carlos, you must be out of your mind. Those tickets are already on sale!" I said, "Well, I probably am out of my mind, but I feel that right now this is what's supremely important to me, and there's nothing that can change my mind." I put it in words I knew he'd understand. "The Santana machine is not more important than my relationship with Deborah." Bill looked at me, and in his face I could see him slowly go through a full mix of emotions—anger, hurt, frustration, and finally defeat and deep sadness. Then he said, "Carlos, I hope that someday in life I will know love like this."

CHAPTER 17

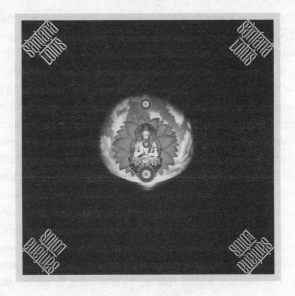

Do you ever get tired of smelling bread when it's just been baked and it comes out of the oven early in the morning, even if it's the same old recipe? Water doesn't get tired of being water; the sun doesn't get tired of being the sun. It's the ego that gets bored. That's when I have to tell my ego, "I'm in charge here, not you." If the ego gets to be in charge, everything will be old, or it will have a date stamp on it. So I have to tell myself, "No. I'm not afraid to play 'Black Magic Woman' or 'Oye Como Va' and make it new again."

Great music has no expiration date. In the '70s I was starting to feel that some of the music on the radio was becoming very disposable—

and that feeling never went away. I call songs that come and go sound bites—they're like meaningless quotes on the nightly news. How can you get meaning or timelessness or elegance from a sound bite? To me, a sound bite is the opposite of a "memorable forever." "Light My Fire" by the Doors—that's not a sound bite. "No Woman No Cry" and "Exodus" by Bob Marley—those are memorable forevers.

In the '70s we had the Bee Gees and Tony Orlando. Disco and punk. People were glorifying the Ramones and the Sex Pistols, and I was telling myself, "Okay, let me look at the energy." I felt it—it was valid. At the same time, Jaco Pastorius and Tony Williams—that was punk to me. My point is that no matter how intense it might be, I don't know any punk music that's more intense than Tony Williams Lifetime.

What was really happening for me back then? Marvin Gaye and Al Green. I think there will always be a time and a place when I'll listen to Led Zeppelin or AC/DC and love it. But when I really need to replenish myself—when I feel I've been under water too long, and I need to come up for air—it's always going to be Coltrane or Miles.

At the end of the '70s I would not allow myself to think that some other music was "happening" and my music was old hat. But when I read interviews I did for *Creem* or *Rolling Stone*, my values seem like they were from another generation. In a sense they were: the '60s was, "Let's change the world." You hear it in the music—let's help people, and let's be gentle. Let's be *this* kind of people—kind people. It was a consciousness of healing.

Bob Marley was the heart and conscience and soul of the '70s. No question about it. I think he is the most important artist of the '70s. When everything was going disco or dis*cord*, he was the glue that made music meaningful. His was music with a purpose, to spread the Rastafarian mission of oneness—I and I—which was no different from the philosophy of claiming your own light, which Sri was talking about. "One Love," "A Love Supreme"—I don't get tired of saying those two back to back. Bob Marley had purpose, and his music had beauty and movement and sex and truth.

I started listening to Jimmy Cliff and *The Harder They Come* back in '73, and then I got interested in music from Trinidad and Brazil. Do that and you'll start to hear all the sounds that came from Africa, you know? But I'd come back to thinking, "What is this music from Jamaica? Okay, reggae. First they called it calypso; now it's roots reggae."

Third World, Burning Spear, the Abyssinians: Bob Marley had a whole other spin on it. The first album I had of his—*Catch a Fire*—looked like a big lighter that you could use to light your spliff. I was saying, "Wow, this music is really different, man. Really, really different—where's the 1? How's that beat work?" He had two brothers in the band—Carlton and "Family Man" Barrett—on drums and bass. He took them from Lee Perry, who had been Marley's producer, and I don't think Perry ever forgave him. I don't think I would have.

I never met Bob Marley—we never crossed paths. But once I left Sri, I lit up again and listened to him more and more. He was the saving grace of the '70s—each album he put out just got better.

What was amazing, though, is that there were not a lot of black people who were into Bob Marley. Especially strict black church people—they couldn't get with his philosophy or his hair or his ganja. Some people were trying to change that when they made a decision to have Marley open for the Commodores, and he played Madison Square Garden. Same thing happened with Jimi Hendrix— he never had much of a black audience, and I think it troubled him.

All that reggae music introduced me to the island kind of life. It helped me see that someday I could slow down and relax and live in a place like Maui. You cross a road, and the ocean is your bathtub. The sky is your roof; the food is fresher than fresh. This is better than the Ritz-Carlton. That made me realize that this is what reggae is about and where it's supposed to take you: no problem, man, no worries. Far away from "What is wrong with me? Why can't I learn to relax?" Listening to Bob Marley takes you on a natural, mystic flow. These guys were never in a hurry. It still sounds good.

I'll tell you the best bands that came out of that scene. One was the Police. They were straight-ahead punk, and because of Sting, they wrote intelligent songs with that punk energy. Another group was the Clash—they wrote smart songs with a message and a purpose, and they loved Latin music. I met them backstage in '82, when we both opened for the Who in Philadelphia. They were playing *cumbias* on a boom box they had, and Joe Strummer was humming the lines and the whole band was into that music. Then they were playing black music—early hip-hop stuff. I was pleasantly surprised. Their music had a symmetry of Africanness in it.

Sometimes the music in the '70s and into the '80s was surprising, like rock getting together with hip-hop. There was Afrika Bambaataa with Johnny Rotten and James Brown, and a few years later Run-D.M.C. teamed up with Aerosmith and then came black rock and white hip-hop—Living Colour and the Beastie Boys. That was in the '80s, but that kind of unexpected mixing had been there before—for example, in what Miles did at the Fillmore. That's how things change in music—one kind of music comes up next to another, and suddenly, *shift!* That's what's important to me.

Columbia Records supported us reluctantly. With Clive Davis long gone, no one was putting pressure on me to produce radio hits, but I knew they wanted another *Abraxas* from Santana. They didn't say it, but I could feel it. I was ready to return—I'd gone so far out and up ahead with Santana, and with Alice Coltrane and John McLaughlin, that I figured we should try to take Santana back in a song direction, to be more radio-friendly. It was like taking a walk back down a familiar path. *Amigos*—with the songs "Europa" and "Dance Sister Dance"—came out of that.

Greg Walker is a very, very soulful singer, and we needed someone new in 1975, when Leon Patillo left. Ndugu brought Greg to a rehearsal at SIR in San Francisco, and that was it. He came into Santana right on time—just when we started *Amigos*. The first song he sang with us was for the album. Leon's voice had a clean gospel sound, but Greg's voice was coming from Luther Vandross. Greg has that same facility and presentation of soul.

The one thing I remember saying to Greg was not to *sell* a song. Don't make it like, "Hey, buy this tire." Offer me your heart. I still say that to singers in Santana, because they're the front part of the show. Treat the song like you're making a love offering; don't look or sound obvious.

Greg had some fearlessness in him—many musicians who join the band and get onstage for the first time will say, "Damn, we didn't know it was going to be like this. It's like a 747 taking off, and I'm holding on the best I can." Then they have to decide if they want to be hanging off the tail or up in the cockpit. Greg was up front from the beginning, no problem. He helped define Santana for a time, because he was right there, front and center, on four albums—*Amigos, Festival, Moonflower,* and *Inner Secrets.*

We reconnected with Dave Rubinson because of Bill Graham, and this time around we all had more experience and worked better together. He wrote "Dance Sister Dance" with Ndugu and TC—to me, it sounded like their version of what they imagined Spanish Harlem to be like. When I first heard it I was like, "Okay…" But I really like the ending, with its synthesizer chords. We could work with synthesizers and other technology from the start because Weather Report made it okay, and I loved Jan Hammer and George Duke and Herbie, of course.

I wasn't afraid or ashamed of that technology—I tried an ARP Avatar for a while, playing my guitar directly through the synthesizer. But I always felt that as soon as I played the guitar, all the other stuff was just stuff. I mean, if you play Albert King next to just about anything on the synthesizer, what can I tell you? It's like putting up a whale next to a goldfish.

I think the best Santana tribute is a song Sonny Sharrock made just before he died. He told me about it one night in San Francisco at Slim's. I went to see him, and he said, "I wrote a song about you, man. It's called 'Santana.'" I kept looking for it, and I finally found it. I remember I said, "Brother Sonny must have been listening to the ending of 'Dance Sister Dance.'"

Columbia told us that *Amigos* was a hit, so everyone was happy and loved Santana again. We made another album with Rubinson— *Festival*—for which Paul Jackson came into the band on bass and Gaylord Birch on drums. Ndugu left and recommended Gaylord.

Usually when someone leaves Santana it's because it's time for us to grow in different directions. Sometimes a player will know it himself, and sometimes it will be my job to say that it's time to go and grow and be prosperous and maybe see you again—thank you for everything. That happens the majority of the time. Very seldom will people leave because they want to. But Ndugu had other things to do, and he was the one who decided to leave.

Ndugu is a perfect feel musician. He played beautifully on "Europa." He could play with us, then with Marvin Gaye or George Benson or Michael Jackson. And before us he played with Miles! You can hear what I mean on the beginning of "Billie Jean"—that beat is swinging. In 1988 we got Ndugu to come back as part of the Santana-Shorter Band.

Santana was still a rock band, but it was creating its own identity—it was changing, creating new music, coming up with new hats for us to wear. About "Dance Sister Dance": I'm not trying to be facetious or funny, but I'm always surprised when any Santana song becomes a hit. Even when we released "Black Magic Woman" and "Oye Como Va," there was a voice inside me saying that maybe it was a mistake; maybe it's just not rock and roll enough to be popular.

Then another voice answers, "Excuse me: why would you put any limitations on yourself? You don't want to be a prisoner of yourself. You don't want to be putting out your hand, saying, 'Hi, I'm Carlos Santana, the Latin rock guy.'"

By 1977 *Lotus* was selling enough copies as an import to make Columbia want a live album—that was part of the inspiration for

Moonflower. The album was half live tracks and half studio songs. Bill Graham is credited on the album for his "direction," and he was the one who wanted us to cover a song by the Zombies. He kept insisting, asking us to choose either "Time of the Season" or "She's Not There." Bill was more directly involved this time around—sometimes he was even in the studio.

That was a challenge, because Bill could be strong in his opinions anywhere he was, even though he wasn't really a producer. One time we were recording a song, and somehow he got the notion that he needed to step in, like a producer would. Tom was playing a solo, and Bill started going, "Stop, stop"—he stopped the take! TC goes, "What's going on?" Bill starts explaining that he needs to do the solo again and think about when he enters, and he's saying, "I'm picturing a helicopter above a beach and it's got a rope hanging down and holding on to the rope is a naked woman and there's a horse running along the beach without a saddle and she needs to land just right on the horse, okay? Your solo should be like that, so you need to try it again."

Everybody was quiet. I said, "Bill, why don't you just tell him he started too soon?" He said, "I just did, schmuck."

The other thing Bill loved to do at recording sessions was tell stories. When he did, we knew we were going to be there for a while—at least until someone would say, "Hey, who's going to pay for this studio time?" It was worth it. We decided to do "She's Not There," and it was another hit. Over the years, Bill picked two songs for Santana, and both were hits.

I like the artwork for the two albums we did with Bill—man, I've been blessed that few people try to stop me once I make up my mind about an album cover. The cover of *Moonflower* is a photo taken from the top of a mountain that I loved, with the gold of sunset spread across the clouds. I found that in a photo book on the Himalayas. The photo on the cover of *Inner Secrets* was taken by Norman Seeff, the photographer who did the cover of Fleetwood Mac's *Rumours*. In the photo, I was dancing while the band was clapping. I forget what song we were dancing to—maybe one from

THE UNIVERSAL TONE

the album—but I remember that Norman made me feel more comfortable than I had felt in any other photo session.

You can see it in the covers and in the music: things were changing again inside Santana. We did *Amigos,* and a year later Gaylord Birch left and we got Graham Lear on drums—another Ndugu recommendation. He had heard Graham with Gino Vannelli, and said, "This cat is bad!" He was right—like Steve Gadd, Graham had precision and soulfulness. He stayed with us for almost seven years, into the '80s, and I learned a lot from him. Chepito liked him, too, and used to call him Refugee because he was from Canada—that coming from a Nicaraguan. Onstage I would announce him as "Graham Lear the Great." If you want to hear how good a feel Graham could bring to a track, check out "Aqua Marine" on *Marathon* from '79 or any other instrumental from around that time. Soulful precision!

Around the time *Inner Secrets* was about to come out in '78, Greg Walker was getting ready to leave Santana, and we brought in Alex Ligertwood, someone else who was in my Rolodex. I first heard him when he was singing in David Sancious's band, Tone, and they opened for us at the Beacon Theatre in 1975. David is a bad dude. He plays guitar and keyboards and came from Bruce Springsteen's band and wore Zorro hats like the ones Lenny White used to wear—a real rock fusion guy. I noticed that David's singer had a great R & B voice, even though you could hardly understand him when he'd speak to you—he has such a thick Scottish accent. I called Alex, and he did a few gigs with us with Greg singing, too, and I found I liked the idea of two singers. They could cover for each other—one higher and clearer, the other lower and more bluesy, more across the tracks.

Over the years I've tried that again and again. That's how we do it today, with two singers—Tony Lindsay, Andy Vargas, and sometimes Tommy Anthony, who plays guitar but can also go high and clear with his voice. It's like basketball—some guys bring the

385

toughness, and other guys are like cheetahs. Still others are like anchors to a song. We need the versatility, but I need you to not drop the ball. I perceive the musicians in my band as players, and our goal is to reach the heart, any way we can.

By the end of '78 Greg left us, and Alex fit right in. He became the voice of Santana on many of our albums and on most of our tours in the '80s and into the '90s. He can make you feel God in his singing—as he did when he sang "Somewhere in Heaven" on the *Milagro* album in '92. You believe him.

One thing that hadn't changed: I was still Devadip. When I did my own albums at the end of the '70s I used that name because those were albums between albums: there was Santana the band, then there was Devadip Carlos Santana the person. *Oneness* and *The Swing of Delight* are two of my most personal albums. I did *Oneness* in 1979, and I was influenced by Weather Report and synthesizer sounds and their great album *Mysterious Traveller.*

I did *The Swing of Delight* a year later, and Dave Rubinson helped me persuade Columbia to do that one, too, so I could get Herbie Hancock, Wayne Shorter, Ron Carter, *and* Tony Williams to play. That was Miles's band from the 1960s.

I looked around the studio and was scared to death, thinking, "What the hell am I doing?" That will make a guitar player turn down—turn it down and go deep, deep inside himself for the inner stuff. In the middle of the recording Wayne had a moment of doubt, which was very unusual for him. He stopped the song. Everybody stepped back from the mikes, and Tony put his sticks down. Wayne just shook his head and said, "That wasn't me. I never play desperate or frantic. Let's start again."

I was feeling very blessed that we achieved everything I set out to do with that album at a high level. *DownBeat* magazine gave it a great review. I guess they could feel the intention. That album came from my wanting to honor Sri for what he had done for us— Deborah and me. He made the painting on the cover, with its pattern of gold and cherries.

I really started to get friendly with Wayne and Herbie during the making of that album. That was when I got to know them, to sit and talk with them. Wayne was much easier and more relaxed than he had been eight years earlier, when we first got together. He opened up and started to tell me stories about Miles and insights about the music that would take ten minutes to explain. Or he would show me something from a big, thick book of drawings he had. Once he showed me a picture of a woman from Venus. I asked Wayne why she had four feet. He said, "She doesn't have four feet, she's just moving really fast." Okay, thanks for clearing that up. One thing I can say about my relationship with Wayne is that I often have to slow down to catch up with his velocity. He's the one who's always moving fast.

Wayne never takes anything too seriously—least of all himself. Here's something else he told me once: "I'm going to go on the road as a comedy act, just me and a soprano saxophone. And I'm going to be the straight man."

From the first time I got to hang with Wayne and Herbie, I could tell they were about spiritual principles and observations and cracking each other up. They were about being themselves, untainted by any particular way of behaving, like children with integrity and pristineness.

Herbie is a supreme genius and sweet as ice cream and pie, as Elvin Jones would say. I first met him when he opened for us at the Boarding House in '72, and after that we would see each other around and he'd tell me about his chanting and that he liked to eat at Dipti Nivas, which by the end of the '70s was the number one vegetarian restaurant in San Francisco. In '70, he was recording in San Francisco with Ndugu, and Chepito told me that Herbie wanted me to come over and sit in. I was honored but didn't have time to play, because we were leaving the next day for Brazil.

Herbie is from Chicago, and that's in his sound, by way of the blues. Once I was telling him to listen to some Otis Spann, and he said that he wasn't familiar with him. I realized, "Oh, right. There are always two sides of town—at least two. There's the blues sentiment of Otis Spann and Sunnyland Slim and Jimmy Johnson, who backed up Chuck Berry—that's one side, and there's Wynton Kelly and Red Garland and John Lewis on the other. Still, Herbie can give you all of them at the same time.

Nobody's more modern or fearless than Herbie is with electric pianos and synthesizers—real artists are not afraid of technology. Starting when he was with Miles, he found a way to utilize those instruments so they didn't sound offensive or weird. Years later, when he and I were welcomed together at the Kennedy Center Honors, Snoop Dogg thanked Herbie for giving birth to hip-hop. I'm not sure how many people understand how huge that is and how true. Just listen to his album *Sunlight*, which came out even before "Rockit"—everybody uses those ideas now.

Today if I put on *Oneness* and listen to those tracks I remember that by then Deborah and I had gotten back on track and I was hanging with SK a lot more. Some of the music came from that, including "Silver Dreams Golden Smiles." SK played guitar and sang on that one, and Clare Fischer did the string arrangements.

In 1981 Deborah agreed that we should both leave Sri—it was time to dust off our feet and get moving. We left our place in Queens late one night, leaving behind all our things, just like that. Later I heard that Sri was going to take my name back and told some disciples not to associate with us anymore because Deborah and I were going to drown in a sea of ignorance, which I didn't like hearing because I didn't want to back down from what made me go to him in the first place. I didn't stop believing in the principles and the divinity and light within—but that was a dark thing to say.

The Sri I knew would say things like, "When the power of love replaces the love of power, man will have a new name: God." I'm not sure how it happened, but many people think Jimi Hendrix said that. He didn't; that was Sri.

Sri helped me be more than just Santana the guitar player. He helped me get to a deeper awareness of my own light, a deeper awareness of my own connection with divinity and humanity and the invisible realm. It's God, no matter what you call it, and he is beyond all praise. He doesn't need a billboard—he doesn't need us to worship and adore him. We need to honor and worship and work on ourselves, to crystallize our existence by discipline. That's the most important thing I got from Sri, and I'm still guided by that principle.

CHAPTER 18

Miles Davis and me at the Savoy, New York City, May 5, 1981.

In the '80s Santana could tour just as much as we wanted. We navigated across the country, playing the same venues in the same cities, from Detroit to Chicago to Cleveland to the usual places in the New York area—Nassau Coliseum, Jones Beach. You could hear us on classic rock and oldies radio stations. I'm proud that those songs kept good guitar playing out there for many years, even when there were few guitar solos on popular songs. You could hear oldies on the elevator or at Starbucks with a solo by Eric Clapton or Jimmy Page, and sometimes the solo itself was more memorable than the song.

One of the best compliments I got after *Supernatural* was from Prince. He said, "Carlos, because of you I can play a guitar solo on one *of my songs and it'll be on the radio." I had never thought of that. I replied, "Yeah, it wasn't cool to have guitar solos on songs for a while."*

In the '80s, radio wasn't making or breaking Santana. I think our reputation was always more about our shows, because people need to be given chills. When you get chills you immediately become present in the now. And because of that our audiences can feel that the intention and purpose of the band is a whole lot more than entertainment. It's to remind everyone on a molecular level of their own significance, to convey the idea that each of us has the power to bring forward abundance from the universe right now. Santana is a live experience, bringing the moment more than the memory. That will never change.

In 1981 it was time for a new start and a new home—a family home. Deborah and I left the East Coast and moved from Marin County to Santa Cruz. It was the first house we bought together since we had met, and right after that her parents and my parents came to visit. We started to spend more time with our friends, and Carabello and I reunited because he had married Mimi Sanchez, who was still one of Deborah's best friends. They started coming to the house a lot. We were both older and smarter by then.

Watching Carabello grow to become a proud man who is positive and honorable has been gratifying to see, because I want people to understand that we need to believe in each other. It makes us stronger than we are by ourselves, and it can make us change. There's always someone in every neighborhood who in the end redeems himself. In my neighborhood it was Carabello—we have so much history between us, which goes back to my Mission High days, and I'm very pleased about that.

Just as I did, Carabello remained friends with Miles—he stayed at Miles's town house when he visited New York City. In '81 Miles was coming back after he had stopped playing in '76. Nobody had heard from him for around five years. All the stories said that he was in a dark place with the curtains closed. I sent him cards and flowers once in a while, and I heard through Herbie and Dave

Rubinson about him because they used to visit him. I know he thought of me, and I thought of him.

Santana played Buffalo that year, and as we were getting ready to come to New York City to play the Savoy we were listening to some Miles. I remember Rashiki asking if I thought Miles would ever put the trumpet to his lips and play again. We still didn't know. I said, "Nothing is really impossible—maybe when he gets bored."

Sure enough, a few days later, when we got to New York, I heard Carabello was coming to our show at the Savoy and bringing Miles. I couldn't believe it. We finished doing the sound check, and there they were backstage. Miles had on a suit that made him look a little raggedy, like he was living a funky life.

It didn't matter. Man, it was beautiful to see him. Bill Graham was producing that tour and got as excited as a kid. "Miles, it's so great to see you! Thanks for coming out. How are you doing? How do you feel?"

Miles seemed to think Bill was checking up on him. "What?" he said.

"How do you feel, man?"

Miles said, "Put your hand up like this." Bill put his hand up, and Miles punched it real hard—a Sugar Ray Robinson jab, up close and hard. "I feels fine, Jewboy." Same old Miles.

I went to my room to meditate, as I do before I go onstage, and Miles followed me. I told him what I had to do, and I closed my eyes and started getting quiet and going inside. I wanted to do that for at least ten or fifteen minutes. Miles was very respectful—he didn't talk, but I could feel his eyes, like two lasers, focusing on the medallion I was wearing. I could hear him breathe, and I opened my eyes. He was looking at the medallion like he was going to pierce it with his gaze, so I said, "Miles, do you want it?" He said, "Only if you put it on me." I took it off, put it on him, and he said, "I pray, too, you know."

"You pray, Miles?"

"Of course. When I want to score some cocaine I'll say, 'God, please make that motherfucker be home.'"

I was like, "Oh, dang!"

There's a thing I used to do whenever we played and Miles was near—I still do it when we're in New York City. I'll play a little bit of "Will o' the Wisp" from *Sketches of Spain*. We played it in the concert at the Savoy, and after the show Miles mentioned it for the first time. "Yeah, I like the way you play that. A lot of people don't know how to do it right." I said, "Miles, we got a limousine. Would you like us to take you home?" So five of us got into the limo—Miles, Carabello, saxophone player Bill Evans, Rashiki, and I. When Carabello got in the front he slid the seat back, which hit Miles on his foot, which was already hurting for some reason. Miles got real brutal, and he immediately went off on Carabello.

We started driving around, then suddenly Miles turned to me and said, "Carlos, this Puerto Rican bitch tried to get some cortisone in me to help me with this thing I have with my foot. She was saying, 'Cortisone this, cortisone that.'" I thought about it and laughed. "Miles, she's saying *corazón*—that means 'sweetheart.' She loves you."

God loves characters, and God loves Miles. That whole night was incredible, crazy. It felt like we had fallen into someone else's weird version of Wonderland—like we had slipped down a rabbit hole into some other dark, scary world. Miles was telling us where to go. He was in charge, and everywhere we went you could see that people knew him well. Whether they were happy to see him was another thing. He'd try to get away with a lot of stuff—testing people, doing his street act.

Miles took us to one of those nightclubs that looked like it had come out of *Escape from New York*. It had steel shutters everywhere. We got out of the limo, and I was wondering why we were there, because it looked like an abandoned factory. Then a big security guard carrying a baseball bat came up to us. He said to me, "You guys are all right. I know who you are." Then he pointed to Miles and said, "Why do you have to bring him here?" Miles walked right past him into the dingy building, and I just followed.

Miles went straight to the piano, which was beat up and out of tune. He said to me, "Come here—I want to show you something."

I said, "Okay," and went over to him. Miles looked at the keyboard and stretched those long fingers of his. Man, you could do a whole movie just on Miles's hands. He was doing the same thing Wayne does at the piano—look, wait, then pounce. It's funny—my wife eats that way: Cindy with food, Wayne and Miles with chords. That night, when Miles hit the chord, the whole club just disappeared— suddenly I was in Spain, in a castle in an old adventure movie. Miles said, "Do you hear it?"

I said, "Of course—that's incredible. Thank you." He got ready to show me something else, but some guy got up and put a quarter in the jukebox, and the song "Muscles" by Diana Ross came on, totally changing the mood. Miles looked over at the guy, who knew what he had done, because he was looking back. Miles stared at him some more and then said, "Man, you know who I am?" He said, "You're Miles Davis. Big deal." Just like that. That was all Miles needed to hear. He smiled and went up to the bar. "Give me a fucking rum and Coke. And whatever he wants."

Miles started to get bored with the place, so we all got back in the limo, and Miles said, "Carlos, are you hungry?"

"Yeah, I could eat something."

"I know a great place where they have black bean soup." So he told the driver where to go, and we got to talking. Suddenly Miles looked up and saw that we'd driven too far. This was through his sunglasses and the tinted windows and all that. He opened the partition behind the driver and shouted, "Hey! You passed it—it's two blocks back. Back up the car!" The driver said, "I can't go back: it's a one-way street." *Slap!* Miles reached through the little window and whacked him on the back of his head! "I'm telling you—go back!"

So we backed up the narrow New York street and went into the restaurant, another funky place. We found a table, and Miles said, "I'll be right back; I got to go pee." On the way to the men's room he saw a woman and stopped and started talking to her and then whispered in her ear. When he was gone, she turned to me and said, "You're a nice man. Why are you hanging around this filthy-mouthed guy?"

While Miles was in the bathroom, the soup arrived, and a big, burly waiter with huge arms came over and said, "Hey, Santana, want some bread with that soup?"

"No thanks—I'm cool. Just the soup." But when Miles came back he didn't see a bread basket, so he told the guy to come over. "Hey, motherfucker, where's the bread?" The waiter looked at Miles and put his big arm on the table right next to Miles's face and said, "Man, what did you just call me?"

This is the part that was like *Alien vs. Predator*. Miles had some really long fingernails, so he put his beautiful black hand around the guy's arm really slowly, looked up at him, and in a really creepy way said, "I'll scratch you." The guy shook his head and kind of slithered away. Rashiki and I were looking at each other like, "Man, this is some scary shit."

A whole night with Miles in New York—it was really challenging sometimes to be with that dude. That night ended when the sun was starting to come up and Miles took us with him to score some coke. We drove to a neighborhood where I didn't want to get out of the limo, so I told him that I had to get back to the hotel because we had an early flight later that morning. Rashiki and I stayed in the limo—I took some money out of my wallet and gave it to Carabello and said, "Here's some cab money for you and Bill Evans." I waved good-bye to Miles, but he was already walking away into the dawn, getting smaller and smaller.

I remember thinking he seemed like a kid walking through Toys"R"Us who knows he can pick out anything he wants. Everybody in New York knew him. He had carte blanche—he was Miles Davis.

I saw Miles again later that year in New York City when he played Avery Fisher Hall. He came right up to me and gave me a hug, which was the first of only two times he did that. I really cherished those moments—I didn't see him hug many people. At Avery Fisher it was the strangest hug—he locked his hands behind my head and put his nose to mine, so we're looking straight into each other's eyes, then he picked himself up from the ground while holding on to my neck. So he was hanging from me, and he looked at me and said, "Carlos, it means so much that you're here."

The second time Miles hugged me was at his sixtieth birthday party in 1986, on a yacht that was docked at a marina in Malibu. I felt so moved afterward that when he went to greet somebody else I went off the boat just to take a moment. I was looking at the ripples in the water when his nephew, Vince Wilburn, came over, and I said, "Man, it really affects me when he greets me like that." He said, "I saw that. Right after you left he said, 'That's a bad mother-fucker right there.'"

It's something to be validated by a giant like that—a giant who was a divine rascal, too. I remember he was an hour and a half late to his own party that day, and while we were waiting I was talking with Tony Williams, who was smoking a cigar next to the boat, and he told me, "This isn't the first time he's done that."

Zebop was the album I made when I started playing a Paul Reed Smith guitar—which would become my main guitar. Paul is still my main guitar maker to this day. He and Randy the Boogie Man have given birth to creations that have done so much for guitarists and pushed the boundaries of excellence, each in his own way—Paul with his guitars and Randy with those Boogie amplifiers.

Paul Reed Smith—I like his heart and the people he hires. His workshop is like the set of a science fiction movie. More science than fiction. From the carving to the measuring to the fine-tuning to the varnishing, he knows the science of it and how to get the balance right so the guitar has—here's the word: consistency. No matter the weather or the place or the circumstances, a PRS guitar will not fail you, because it behaves itself. One other thing: whenever Paul ships them, the guitars always come out of the case in tune. It's a personal touch.

The funny thing is that when I first fell in love with two of those

PRS guitars, they were the prototypes. I had models 1 and 3, but meanwhile Paul had moved on and redesigned his guitars and was manufacturing them. It wasn't just the shape—the new model of what I had been playing sounded different to me, a little more nasal. I asked Paul to go back to the old style, but he said it was cost-prohibitive at that point to redo the guitar. My argument was that I know what happens when somebody sees Tony Williams playing a Gretsch or Jimi Hendrix with a Stratocaster or Wes Montgomery with a wide-body guitar. I just knew if kids could see me with that guitar they'd want the same thing—and I knew there would be enough of those kids to make it work on the business side. I had a feeling about product endorsements—my name could sell things besides albums and concert tickets.

Around 1989 some of my guitars got stolen, including those original PRSs—we had someone in our organization who trusted somebody he shouldn't have to store some equipment he shouldn't have stored. We did a big APB campaign to get them back, and by the grace of God we found them in hock somewhere because they were so unique. The happy ending of that story is that we found the guitars, and Paul decided to use the original mold to make some new guitars in the old style, and now we've had a long relationship and PRS has my endorsement.

I have learned about the value of product endorsements and have also learned to trust my first instincts about some things. Here's another example: like Paul Reed Smith, I will always have affection for Alexander Dumble and his amplifiers and of course for Randy the Boogie Man and his Boogie amps. In 2013, Adam Fells, who works in our office, sent me a video that the people at Sony Music had found of Santana in Budokan in '73. I watched it and heard the guitar sound and looked closely at the amplifier and it hit me—"That's my old friend. I miss that sound!" It was Randy's original snakeskin Boogie amp that I had long ago moved on from and hadn't thought about in years. "Adam, you guys got to find me one of those snakeskin Boogies!" He told me, "We still have them—we haven't seen them in a while, but they're in the warehouse." Adam found them, then Randy fixed them up and worked on the contacts, and I plugged in—and there was that voice. That's what I'm playing now, along with a Dumble, and I'm getting the best from both.

The point is that after this Randy went back to that old model and design, too. He made more than seven hundred snakeskin Boogie amplifiers. Then he and I signed them, and now everybody wants them. They're selling like crazy in Japan. So please don't tell me about something being cost-prohibitive.

By 1981, it felt like the spirit of the '60s had left America and gone overseas—that was the year Santana played the Live under the Sky festival in Japan, an event that put rock and jazz together. Santana played, Herbie Hancock's V.S.O.P. band played, and then we played together, along with Herbie and Tony Williams. The old Fillmore Auditorium spirit was alive again—there, anyway.

At that point, when everything in America got so big and was sounding the same to me, I felt free enough with Bill Graham to express myself and call him on what was happening in the music business. If he could walk around with a clipboard taking notes on my show and critiquing me—well, it goes both ways. At least we had that kind of relationship. So I asked him, "What happened to you, man?"

"What do you mean, what happened to me?"

"You used to put Miles Davis and Buddy Rich and Charles Lloyd on the bill with rock acts. You used to stretch everyone's consciousness and show us all that there was great music out there that was not just what we heard on the radio. But now you've stopped."

He looked down. "Good point." He had stopped doing concerts in ballrooms and theaters and had started packaging stars such as Peter Frampton.

"I'm sorry," I said to him, "but why are there no more jazz musicians on the bill?" It was still possible to make that Fillmore spirit happen again—that was my message to Bill. Yes, I know—the business had changed. But it was Bill who had built the business and set the example, and he still had the power.

I'm proud of all the albums Santana recorded in the 1980s and '90s. Each of those records captured a moment in time; they're like snapshots of where I was and what I was listening to at the time. They each had an identifiable spirit. With each Santana album I had learned to be present with openness—to listen a lot and be open to not only the musicians and the music itself but also to the producers, because Santana is like the Raiders or the Seahawks—a team. Maybe I'm in charge, but Santana is a collective vision and includes many spirits and hearts and aspirations. We're going to have to carry that music out of the studio, take it on the road, and play it night after night—maybe not all of it, but you never know until you see how the songs feel and how they are received after the album comes out.

When I did my own albums, my only responsibility was to myself—it was just my vision. In '82, I made *Havana Moon* on my own as Carlos Santana, with Jerry Wexler producing. The album started from the idea that Chuck Berry wrote the title song, which is part of the architecture of rock and roll, by pulling from T-Bone Walker and Nat King Cole, especially Nat's "Calypso Blues," which had Nat, accompanied only by a conga player, singing as if he had been born in Jamaica. My dad got to play and sing on *Havana Moon*, and we recorded my mom's favorite song, "Vereda Tropical." I also got to collaborate with the fabulous organist and arranger Booker T. Jones as well as one of my favorite vocalists, Willie Nelson.

The songwriter Greg Brown wrote a song that Willie was going to sing called "They All Went to Mexico," and when I heard the lyric "I guess he went to Mexico," I thought, "Whoa: this is like something that Roy Rogers or Gene Autry used to sing; it's like Wayne Shorter's quotations from 'South of the Border' in his solos." Then it dawned on me that most of my friends saw something about Mexico that was different from what I saw. But I was still a little too close to it all. I grew up in Tijuana, so a lot about Mexico was not necessarily all that groovy for me. But others see something good in the country, and I was trying to see that and see myself in a different light, too. I also started thinking that Willie is from Texas, and that used to be Mexico, so really Mexico is part of his roots, too. Then I thought, "It all connects — we are all part of it. Let's do this song."

I have Willie Nelson to thank for helping push me with that tune. Two years later, after Deborah and I were blessed with Salvador, I went to visit Mexico on my own, and the real reconnection began.

As a result of *Havana Moon* I also discovered Jimmie Vaughan, whose playing I just loved. Jimmie and his band, the Fabulous Thunderbirds, could play shuffles like nobody else, and Jimmie had that Lightnin' Hopkins and Kenny Burrell thing down to perfection. We bonded right away, and he kept telling me, "Wait until you hear my brother."

When I met Stevie Ray Vaughan for the first time in 1983, he had a little bit of an edge to him. He tried to challenge me: "Here's my guitar; show me something." Show you something? I looked him straight in the eye and told him to put the guns back in the holster. "I love your brother, I love you, and I love what you guys love. Let's start with that." He stopped right away and apologized: "Sorry, sir." I told him he didn't have to call me sir, but don't come at me like that.

As I had with Jimmie, I had a profound connection with Stevie from the start — both of us had an incredible, deep devotion to the music we call the blues. When I say "deep," I mean from the center of the heart. Stevie Ray knew that, and you could hear it in his music, the same way you could hear it in the music of Eric Clapton, Jeff Beck, Jimmy Page, and Peter Green before him. Now there are people like Gary Clark Jr. and Derek Trucks and Susan Tedeschi and Doyle Bramhall II and Warren Haynes, along with many others, who keep the flame burning.

The thing that was so different about Stevie Ray is that he wasn't playing just the flavor of the blues, as many others were at that time. Maybe you can do that with some kinds of music, such as "lite rock" or "soft rock" or "smooth jazz," but not with the blues.

For it to ring true, you got to be all the way in it. Believe me, Stevie Ray was all the way in it. Man, I miss him.

In the fall of '82 Deborah and I went to Hawaii, and our parents came along, too. One day in front of everyone, my mom told Deborah, "I had a dream that you were pregnant." I remember my dad jumped on her for saying that, for saying that out loud in front of everyone and putting her on the spot. My mom said, "What? I can't tell someone about a dream I had?" Mexican moms take their dreams seriously — I guess that's where I get that.

It turned out that Deborah was already two months pregnant — she asked me how my mother could tell. "She was pregnant eleven times — she knows." The following May, when I was home from a long tour of Europe, Salvador was born. Just like that you become a parent.

I believe Salvador was a culmination of many, many years of praying by both of our moms. He also came from divine design. Deborah and I would meditate and ask for a special soul to be selected, and then we each took a shower, and we got together. Salvador was conceived with divine intentionality. So were all our children.

Years later I told Sal how he came to be — a few times — and the older he got the more he understood. The first time was when he was just five or six years old and going to public school. Deborah and I knew we could afford to send him to private school, but we wanted him to have a full experience of cultures and people and not be separated by privilege. Sal was very smart — he understood what we were trying to do, and he was okay with that. When he didn't understand something, he would ask questions.

I came home one day, and Deborah told me, "Your son wants to talk to you," which was code for "This isn't going to be a piece of cake." He had heard some rough words at school — one in particular — and he could tell it was wrong for some reason and didn't want to talk about it with his mom. I asked Salvador what word it was. "It sounded like 'duck,' but it started with an *f*."

I was proud of Sal for figuring out a way to say the word without saying it. I explained to him that it was a bad word for something that could be very good, and that something was part of why he was here. I said, "Your mother and I—we prayed for you, we lit a candle, we meditated, we asked for your soul, and then we got in bed and we made love and that's how you got here. You were made in love. That's the opposite of that word." I remember Sal looked at me with his head to one side. "Oh, okay. Thanks, Dad."

Then he thought for a second. "But what's it mean?"

"You'll really have to find that out for yourself when you're old enough, son."

Three times it happened—and it was almost always the same thing. Deborah got to the hospital first, and I would get there and see my parents and in-laws waiting. Then the nurse would come with the baby wrapped in a blanket, and we'd all crowd around to get a peek. The first thing we'd see would be the eyes, sparkling just like diamonds. All our children—Salvador in '83, Stella in '85, and Angelica in '89—were born with their eyes open. They were so pristine—we'd all look at Deborah and go, "Good job, Mom." Then each time I would need to go to the car and suck up some fresh air because the experience was so intense. I'd be alone, sitting there quietly, and slowly I'd start to hear a song.

Every child brings a song with him or her. It's up to the parent to hear it and get a tape recorder or a pen or something and get it down. "Blues for Salvador," "Bella" for Stella, and "Angelica Faith"— each one of our kids has a special song, whether it was written for them when they were born or it came later. You look at the child and you just hear the melody. Probably some of my best melodies fell into the couch and got lost while I was sitting there making up a song to sing to the babies—to stop their crying and get them to sleep again.

At three in the morning, when the baby can't stop crying and his mother is already spent and out like a light—just gone—it's your turn. So I learned how to hold the babies, strong and secure, tummy-down, and they'd relax. It would get them out of the crying mode. We had a clown doll that you could knock down but it always sprang back up. I hit it by accident one time, and the baby stopped crying, looking to see what happened. We turned it into a game, and it worked almost all the time, at least to break the crying rhythm. There are things any parent can do to be creative with silly stuff lying around at home.

Even before Sal was born, Deborah and I agreed that once he arrived I would never go on the road for more than four weeks — five weeks at the most. Five weeks and home, no exceptions. This was family time. Maybe I could do some recording, but only in San Francisco, and we kept to that. This way I did not miss birthdays or graduations. We have a lot of family videos that I am in — I'm very proud of that.

Sal was only a few months old when we took him to Japan in the summer of '83, and he was pretty happy his first time over there. He was a big boy, a butterball, for his first few years. He looked like a sumo wrestler. Mr. Udo was helpful, but for Deborah and me it was a wake-up call because of all the crazy hours and the fact that we got sick for a few days. Then we thought about all the germs we could catch by traveling on a plane. Rookie parent stuff. We said, "Let's not do this anymore." But when our next two children were born, we still took them with us as much as possible until they started school. I wanted them to see their dad at work, to know what he did when I couldn't be at home with them — I wanted them to see the world.

I was amazed, but I shouldn't have been surprised. As soon as the kids came, so did the family. My mom came around, and my sisters and brothers would help out, and Deborah of course had the support of her mother and father and sister, whom the kids loved. They would yell "Auntie Kitsaun" every time they saw her. Not long after Stella was born, we decided to move back to Marin County to be nearer to family and friends. We also had to think about schools. All this pulled me closer to my parents and got me thinking about the fact that my son was part of their legacy.

In 1985 Salvador was almost three, and Deborah and I visited Mexico incognito—my hair was still pretty short, so no one recognized me. I have to say that one of life's greatest luxuries is to be anonymous in a crowd. Most people should take that to heart. We had decided to go with my mother to visit her relatives in Cihuatlán, so because we were in Jalisco anyway we made a snap decision to visit my hometown of Autlán. We had a driver, but for some reason it took most of the day to get there—four hours there and six hours back.

We met a lot of people who remembered my mom. I was still a kid when I left. Sal was still just a baby but was starting to grow, and he had big feet then. He still does—size 15, bigger than Michael Jordan's. I know that because when he was a teenager Sal got to spend some time at Michael's summer basketball camp. It's crazy sometimes the details I remember.

The whole town was passing Sal around as if he was the first baby they'd ever seen, to the point where Deborah and I were getting paranoid. "Hey, where's our baby?"

Autlán was so much smaller than I remembered, which of course is normal because *I* was much smaller the last time I had been there. It felt like what it was—a small town, or a big village. I started kissing my mom on her forehead, kissing her hands. It was in that moment that I began to see clearly what she had done for us. I was thanking her for taking us out of that town and to a place that had bigger opportunities and better possibilities. This is not a put-down or a negative comment about Autlán. I've gotten to know the town again, and I'm proud to call it my original home. This is about the immensity of my mother's conviction in taking us to a place so far away and changing the destiny of our whole family—all because of just one decision in her mind.

CHAPTER 19

Angelica, Salvador, and Stella, 1990.

I call it domestic rhythm, and it's something that many musicians have trouble with. But I think any parent who has to do a lot of traveling has to deal with it. I open the door to that subject all the time when I'm with other musicians: "Hey, man, how's the domestic rhythm?" They look at me—some will get it, and some will go, "Domestic rhythm? What do you mean?"

"You know, man. How long have you been on the road?"

"Oh, that."

Even with my kids grown, and now with Cindy as my partner, I still do my best to keep the domestic rhythm balanced with other rhythms in my life, like the music and the shows and the traveling and the recording. It's easy enough on the music side when you think about it — once you have the music down, all you really have to do is show up and do your best with the band. But I learned early on in my family that when it was time to come home, I had to do a lot more than show up. I had to be willing to become a mopper or a duster or a rug cleaner or a hair brusher or a sandwich maker. I had to be willing to put the same energy and care and intention into my life with Deborah and the kids that I put into a great guitar solo.

I remember how my father would do it when he came back after having been gone for months. There'd be all this craziness going on around him, kids walking in and out of the place, and he'd find a place on the hard floor and just stretch out. It was like some sort of Mexican yoga — he would extend his arms and legs, then he'd shake his fingers. I tried that once after a long tour because it felt like the walls kept spinning and wouldn't stop. It eventually worked — the walls stopped moving, and I had arrived, ready to get up and help out and say, "Okay, how can I help?" or "What can I do?" or just go ahead and take out the garbage.

I think a lot of people, not just musicians, are not secure enough in their inner peace to handle the madness of domestic rhythm — children screaming; parents and family dropping by. Relatives mean well, but sometimes their visits can add to the pressure. But that's the rhythm you're supposed to enjoy the most — being part of it and letting it happen.

The first few years with the kids were fun, and with the family coming around to visit — my parents and sisters and brothers and in-laws — it was a new experience for me. I hadn't thought about family that way. Each of the kids' steps along the way was a new thing — learning to walk, to eat grown-up food, to talk — and it was amazing to see their personalities develop.

We took them on the road when we could — I remember one time when Sal was already in second grade and Stella had just started school and Jelli was really small we all went to Europe together. We went to Switzerland, where Claude Nobs was an amazing host; then to London, where the kids loved riding in the city's big taxis; then to Rome. Then there's the other side of touring— the sadness when the kids knew they couldn't go with Daddy and I'd be getting ready to leave, waiting on the car to pick me up. Every time this happened they would all run and get their crayons and paper and start drawing pictures and get really focused so that they wouldn't have to hang with a feeling of separation. I'll never forget the sound of their scribbling with so much force and concentration. That was their way of saying, "It hurts us to see you go, so we're not going to wait with you and look at you. Good-bye!"

Damn. Of course it reminded me of the fact that my dad was gone all the time when I was a kid, and I remember how it felt in my stomach. "Where is he? When will I see him again? Did I do something wrong to make him go away?" I know kids have a habit of blaming themselves when parents can't be present. I didn't want that for my kids, so I would speak to them and explain what Daddy had to do. No tour more than four weeks—and even in the middle of the tour I would get on the plane and fly back home for birthdays and graduations and special occasions. I decided to do all I could do to see them as much as possible. When the car would come to take me to the airport, I would go over to each of them and remind them how much I loved them.

We went through that moment a bunch of times. Around the mid '80s Santana was touring a lot with other big acts. We'd be opening for the Rolling Stones, and I was always grateful for those opportunities. Bill Graham put together many of those tours, and they were all great and memorable experiences—including the one in 1984, when Santana was opening for Bob Dylan. I loved that Santana band of the mid-'80s. It was a powerful, fun band, and when that band hit, it was like, "Oh, damn." I learned so much from all of them.

On bass we had Alphonso Johnson, who came to us in '83 and had just the right kind of mix and experience for Santana at the time. He had played with Billy Cobham and Phil Collins and was a consummate gentleman and pure class. I first heard him when I went to see Weather Report in '75 at the Berkeley Community Theatre. The band was fluid and powerful, but the cat on bass absolutely freaked me out. What is it about bass players from Philadelphia? Stanley Clarke, Victor Bailey, Jimmy Garrison, Reggie Workman, and Jaco Pastorius were all born there.

Alphonso is intelligent and warm, and I could hear that in his playing. He was with us for a few years—he had many great moments with Santana, but you can start with "Once It's Gotcha" on *Freedom*.

We also had David Sancious in that band. I admire him like crazy. He's just as I described Alphonso—a gentleman with great spirit and no baggage. Besides being a wonderful keyboard player, he's a hell of a guitar player. He wasn't afraid to plug into a Marshall and play from his heart. He reminds me of Coltrane in the way he looks. He could play Trane in a movie—he's got that quiet loudness.

We had two Chester Thompsons. One was the amazing Chester C. Thompson on drums, who had played in Weather Report with Alphonso and later in Genesis. The other Chester Thompson played organ, piano, and synthesizers, and just as Ndugu was vitally important to the sound of the band in the late '70s, this guy was the cat who helped to define where Santana went after the mid-'80s and for the following twenty-five years. If you want to know who he is, check out his organ solo on "Victory Is Won," the song I wrote for Archbishop Desmond Tutu. When Chester and I first played the song, it was for Tutu himself when he visited my house in 2001.

I met Chester—everybody calls him CT—around 1977 or '78, when I was doing a lot of sessions in San Francisco, trying out different things, not necessarily for albums. I remember it was very easy to connect and play with him, but he was in Tower of Power at the time so I didn't think any more of it. It wasn't until around 1984, after Tom Coster had left Santana, that I thought of CT again.

I figured I had nothing to lose, so I asked him if he'd be interested in joining Santana, and he said yes.

CT came into Santana with some of everything I love: some McCoy Tyner, some Herbie Hancock, a lot of church, and a whole lot of soul. I knew he was going to fit in right away, because that's what the music calls for—if you're going to cook bouillabaisse you have to know what ingredients you need to put in the pot. With CT it was all about camaraderie. We could talk until six in the morning after a show, just talking about the music we love. I don't think I was closer to any keyboard player in Santana other than Gregg Rolie.

I had needed someone in the band who had different ideas from mine. I had been wanting someone to bounce things to me; I didn't want to have to be constantly feeding others. After just a few shows I could tell that CT would be comfortable with bouncing ideas, and he had a lot to bounce. I also knew that every time he took on a solo he just tore it up. You can hear it on tunes like "Wings of Grace" and "Hong Kong Blues." Onstage, he'd get a certain look, almost like he was possessed, and I'd say to myself, "Man, I want *that* in my band." Then he'd just take over, and while our albums stayed with the song format, onstage he liked to stretch out, and so did I. Even with his intensity, he made it really easy to go on tour because he is very stable—I never saw him throw a tantrum or do anything desperate or frantic. CT was cool and soulful, and I appreciated that.

It was also very easy for CT and me to write together—we came up with songs like "Goodness and Mercy" and "Wings of Grace" on the spot. "Brotherhood"—from the album *Beyond Appearances* in '85—was written by CT, me, and Sancious. For some reason, Miles really focused on that one, with its funky line and preacher's message. "Really, Miles?" He put his face close to mine and said, "Yeah, and you ain't even black."

In '87 we recorded the album *Freedom,* and that title really ties into things that were happening at the time, such as Buddy Miles getting out of jail and getting his life together in the Bay Area. He sang his ass off on some of the tracks, including "Mandela," which Armando wrote; of course the whole world was looking at South

Africa then and asking themselves, "What can we do to accelerate change in the apartheid system and get Nelson Mandela out of prison?"

It was like the '60s for a brief time, a period when we felt that music could make things evolve. That was really when the Santana shows got to be more socially aware again and I would remind people in the audience that they were giants who could create miracles and blessings. We wore T-shirts with our heroes on them and announced that no woman or man is free until we're all free, as Martin Luther King said. I asked the sound crew to put together special songs — message songs — to play on the PA before and after our shows to deepen the meaning for the audiences.

Freedom is also special because Graham Lear had come back, and, briefly, so did Tom Coster — so we had TC and CT together. For the *Freedom* tour in '87 we kept the band personnel down to Alphonso, CT, Graham, Armando, and Alex, with Orestes Vilató and Raul Rekow on percussion. We traveled to many places in Europe we'd been before and some places we hadn't been, like East Berlin, with Buddy Miles as a special guest, and Moscow, where we did a historic Soviet-American concert with the Doobie Brothers, Bonnie Raitt, and James Taylor. I remember Steve Wozniak paid for it, and because it took place on July 4 it was called the Interdependence Concert — Give Peace a Chance.

I also remember Deborah knew someone living in Moscow whom she had gone to school with and had been a '60s revolutionary. She wanted to take a cab by herself in the middle of the night to visit her friend, so she did. That's part of Deborah — very fearless. There's a video of me talking with some Russians through a fence, and some of them were young enough to have grown up with "Black Magic Woman" and *Abraxas*. They told me that our music had made a big impact on people's consciousness, that it got people through hard times.

In Moscow the music started off with a Russian marching band playing "When the Saints Go Marching In," then some Russian bands played, then Bonnie Raitt, James Taylor, and the Doobie

Brothers went on, so the program was building in intensity. By the time we went on the crowd was flying, and we rode that energy, man. We tore it up so bad that when we played the last note and were walking offstage we started hearing a rumble with screaming on top—"Santana! Santana!! Santana!!!" I remember Bonnie kept looking at me afterward, not saying anything, just shaking her head.

One of the best compliments I ever got came from Bonnie after some other concert featuring us both.

"Hey, Carlos!"

"Hi, Bon!"

"I got a new name for you—Fearless! You're not afraid to play with Buddy Guy or Ry Cooder or Ray Charles or anybody."

I said, "Thanks, Bon!"

Why should I be afraid? This isn't the Olympics, and it's not boxing. That's still how I feel—playing music should be a win-win situation.

In East Berlin I realized we had a different energy from any band that the Russians had seen before. Music does break barriers. Their country was just starting to really open up back then—I think they had to catch up faster than they were expecting, too.

Santana played Jerusalem for the first time on that tour—the city where Jesus preached and ran into trouble. I remembered all the stories from the Bible that I heard in Autlán about that city, and there really was something special about it. I remember waking up in the morning and seeing the sun coming out, just as it's done for thousands of years, and it's so beautiful. Then you see the twilight, and you can't help but wonder why people fight so much there. I went walking around, and I realized that on the one hand Jerusalem is a very, very sacred and historic place, but on the other hand it's like so many other cities in other parts of the world—vendors and marketplaces and people hustling each other, just trying to get by. Parts of that city are about as pristine and spiritual as the backseat of a New York City taxicab. I was thinking it really doesn't matter where you are when it comes to the invisible realm—it's what you bring to that place in your heart that can make it divine and holy.

* * *

All those dates in the Soviet Union and Israel? That was Bill Graham—he put those together. He was putting together a lot of international tours. Just the year before he put together the Amnesty International tour that was supposed to be like the old Fillmore days—rock, jazz, African, Latin. All flavors, multidimensional. And big headline names, including Peter Gabriel and Sting. I played at one of those concerts—at the Meadowlands in New Jersey—but not with my band. That was okay—it was the only time I played with Miles.

Being who I was and who I still am, I got into a conversation with Bill before the tour about whom he was booking. "Why don't you work on putting Miles Davis on at Amnesty International?"

He was like, "What?"

"Do the same thing you did at Woodstock—tell them that if they want your help they have to put Miles in there."

Long silence.

Later, I was on tour in Australia when the phone rang in my hotel room—it was four in the morning, New York time. "Hi, Bill. How you doing?"

"Miles is going to play."

"Holy shit, Bill. You did it!"

"But I need you here, and I can't afford for you to play with the whole band because I already used up my favors with Miles. Can you come by yourself?"

That was my reward for pushing for Miles. Of course I was coming. I flew from Australia to Honolulu, then from Honolulu to San Francisco. I picked up Deborah, flew to New Jersey, and went to the Meadowlands. When I got there, Bill said, "You're playing with Rubén Blades and Fela Kuti and with the Neville Brothers." No problem. "And Miles."

Wait. "Bill, I'm playing with Miles?"

"Yes, and Rubén in half an hour. Miles wants to see you in the trailer." This was epic. Did Miles ask for me to play with him? Why didn't he mention this before?

I had a major case of jet lag. My eyeballs were red, and my brain was just not functioning. When I went into his trailer, Miles was in a state I'd never seen him in before. He was looking at me a little sideways. He looked at my shoes and at my shirt, grabbed my pants, and said, "You're even trying to dress like me and shit." I was like, "What?" And he went off on me, telling me I'm just following him. I could see that maybe he was thinking I arranged this gig just so I could play with him. Before he got too far I said, "Look, man. I don't need to play with you. I asked Bill Graham to bring you here because I felt that this thing would not be complete without you. Whatever he said to you, that wasn't part of my condition." And I walked out.

Wow—okay, so that was how it felt to get on Miles's bad side. I thought he'd give me the benefit of the doubt on that one. I was on his side. He should know that.

Just a few years before he had called me. "What are you doing?" he asked.

"Listening to a CD, Miles—*Thriller*."

"What's that?" I told him about a new format—compact discs— and about the new album by Michael Jackson that everyone was crazy about and that Quincy had produced. "I can't stop playing a song called 'Human Nature.'" Next thing I knew Miles did it on *You're under Arrest* and was playing it in concert every night.

I had to go get ready to play—even if Miles was pissed and it was going to be awkward. I was waiting next to the stage, and just before my turn to play it came into my head to check the tuning of the guitar. It had been tuned by the guitar tech, but it had been sitting out there by itself with a lot of people onstage, and who knows what had happened, but it was totally out of tune. On the video of that set, when it's time for me to come in, you can see me standing with the audience behind me. I'm facing away from them, toward the camera, because I still have the guitar up near my face so I can work on the strings. Just when I got it tuned, it was time for me to play. I turned around and was on my tippy-toes, the energy was so intense! Then I hit the note and just killed it. Later, Deborah came up to me and said, "That's what I want to hear! Why don't you do that all the time?" She used to say that now and then.

We played "Burn," and I thought I played well for being so jet-lagged—I was really zonked out of my head. When we were walking off the stage, Miles was a totally different guy. "Hey! How was that for you?"

"It was great, Miles; it was really an honor to play with you."

Man, I thought Miles was going to chew me out again. That day, before we played, had been the only time he ever snapped at me. Later on I realized he had just gotten nervous before doing such a big show.

"Oh, yeah. It was weird for me. I couldn't hear shit."

I said, "Well, you know, if that happens to me, I move around like a boxer until I find the sweet spot somewhere between the bass player and drummer, and I make my own mix."

Grandma Jo and Deborah and Emelda, who was married to Deborah's cousin Junior, started taking the kids at a young age to a church in Oakland, and when you go to a black, no-nonsense church like that you go a certain way and you sit a certain way. You learn a code of behavior. Sal's got that church in him—so do his sisters, but about Sal the British might say, "He's *proper*." I remember all three kids always acted that way when we went out—they'd say thank you in restaurants, too. When you're a parent, you start to watch what other families do in public, and I'd sometimes see kids out of control—extreme, like the kid in *The Exorcist*—and I'd be glad not to be embarrassed that way when we'd go out of the house.

I think Deborah is a great mother and I'm a great father and that a lot of our success was about communicating honestly and clearly with all three kids so they understood what was expected of them. In everything we did with them, we maintained a consistent system of ethics, moral compass, and integrity. We never spanked our kids, but there were words and looks that got across the message that they needed to be quiet and be respectful. When they got older I would tell them that if we didn't see eye to eye on something, they could raise their hands and we'd go for a hike and break it down. "You have that option to walk and talk it out," we'd tell them.

Of course, the older they got, the more they'd test the limits. I remember having to say to one of them, "You know, I've spent a lot of time meditating and reading spiritual books to learn to be peaceful and compassionate, but all that stuff is going to go out the window the next time you disrespect your mother in front of me!"

Deborah had what she called a pow-pow stick that she kept on top of the refrigerator. It was there, and the kids knew that if they ever went too far she was ready to get it. I really can't remember it ever being used, though she did pull it down a few times. Deborah and I were a good team, because the kids would come up to me and say, "Mom said this was okay."

Parents are going to make mistakes, like everyone else. But we learned and got better at being parents, and they learned that the usual play-one-against-the-other stuff wouldn't work with us. "Really? Let's go and ask Mom to tell me herself." They tested us, we set the limits, and although there was a lot of room in between, some things were not for bargaining.

Nobody said being a dad wasn't going to be challenging, but I can tell you that it was and that it's been fun, too. I've learned from my children, and one of the most important things I learned was how to laugh with them and sometimes how to laugh at myself, too. I remember Stella wanted a little Chihuahua dog—please, please, please—so she got one. Of course it was not only her dog, it was the family's dog, but who's going to feed and train it? One night I came home from a concert, and Stella was on the sofa watching TV with her friend. Jelli was there, too. I settled down and started to get comfortable, but all of a sudden there was something warm and weird between my toes, and the smell hit me. Everyone was looking at me. "Stella, it's dog poo!" She was just looking at me. "And it's *your* dog!"

Nothing. So now it's really stinking and I'm up and cleaning it and cleaning my toes and wiping the carpet and I can't believe it and suddenly it comes out of me. "Man, I am *not* supposed to be cleaning dog poo! *I'm a rock star!*"

Of course I wasn't being 100 percent serious, but at the same time it was just the kind of thing you would hear from a rock star, so it was funny both because of what I meant and also because of what I didn't mean. There was a moment of stunned silence, then suddenly Jelli started busting up, rolling on the couch with tears in her eyes. Then Stella and her friend and I started laughing, too, and soon we were all laughing hard at what I said and the way it came out.

I want for my children the same things I want for everyone I love in my life—health, happiness, and peace of mind. At the same time those are the three things I cannot give them. I can show my kids what those things look like and maybe how to achieve them, but I also say that they have to get them, sustain them, and, most of all, appreciate them for themselves.

The music continued, the children grew, and the spiritual discipline was there, too—that never left. One thing Deborah decided when we left Sri Chinmoy was that we would not fall short in our spiritual race—we were runners, and we would not slow the pace of aspiration. Aspiration is the flame—the desire for divinity. Deborah and I decided to not lose our love of God or abandon our principles and practices—meditating in the morning, eating healthful food, and reading spiritual books.

On the road in every hotel room I would stay in I would light incense and burn a candle and close my eyes and go inside. Backstage in every dressing room before we went onstage, I would do the same. If anyone in the band wanted to join me, they were welcome to. Most of the time the spiritual discipline was self-discipline. There was no more guru, but I still did a lot of reading and got a lot of guidance from books.

I had found *The Urantia Book* before I met Sri Chinmoy and was still reading it after I left him. I would always be looking for books that brought me a tangible sensation of being. I keep moving up by selecting books that help me broaden my view of myself. I found I would be thinking of something in the airport, and I'd pull out a bunch of books I had stuck in my bag and one title would stand out. "Oh, this is exactly what I need." I'd get on the plane, and in some chapter in the middle I'd read something that was exactly what I needed to visit and identify with right then. "Let me take this message and live with it for a week."

I still find those kinds of books today. This is my strategy: set forward your intentionality like an arrow, and the bull's-eye appears. You attract who you are. That's how I found *A Course in Miracles* and *The Book of Knowledge: The Keys of Enoch* by J. J. and Desiree Hurtak.

For Deborah, the spiritual path meant going back to church. After a while she left the church in Oakland and discovered Unity in Marin, a church with a progressive, universal attitude. It wasn't about doing things only one way, but I still couldn't see myself going to church unless there were congas there, and because there weren't, I didn't go too often. Sometimes I did go with Deborah and the kids, but usually when she'd be at church I would be with her dad talking about things like spiritual traction.

SK was the one who said that: we are all here to dig in and make some spiritual traction, not to slip and slide and shuck and jive and make excuses. When he said that, I was like, "Right on." I love the idea of explaining spiritual discipline in a street kind of language so people don't have to say, "What the hell is he talking about?" I like the idea of spreading a spiritual virus that instead of making people sick makes them totally alive. The virus can spread from one person to another until they and their neighbors see a decrease in violence in their community.

The spiritual path was presented to our children very naturally, normally, and organically. They understood that we read spiritual books, which were there for them to read, too, if they wanted. But there's nothing like living a spiritual path so your children can see the light in you. When you wear it every day, that does more than anything else to encourage them to live it, too. They saw us meditating and went with Deborah to Unity in Marin. When they started to get older and I would present something to them—a principle or some way of looking at something spiritually—they'd resist, as kids tend to do with everything their parents present them with. But they'd retain it. Maybe a week or month later I'd hear one of them on the phone with a friend quoting almost exactly what I said: "I don't want to invest emotionally in something negative." "I don't want to wear that like a badge of honor—that's not who I am."

I still speak to them on that level—I'm constantly asking Jelli, Stella, and Salvador not to be afraid to let people know about their intentions and be clear about what they mean to say. It's their daily spiritual reality check. Stella was in the studio for the first time not long ago, making some music, and I texted her, "Ask God to help your music connect with all hearts on this glorious planet and remind them of their own divinity." And to this day, anyone who's been to a Salvador Santana concert will hear him say, "It's a blessing to be in your presence, and it's a blessing to play for you." I love that. By the end of every tour, the groups opening for him all start expressing their gratitude to the audience, acknowledging their presence and thanking them for being there.

In 1987, when Sal was just four, I was jamming in the studio with CT when one of those magic moments happened. But the engineers were still messing with calibrating something, and we wanted to record what we were doing right then. "Hit RECORD right now! Get this on tape, man—I don't care how you do it!" So we got it on a two-track reel-to-reel—one track for CT, one for me. Just as I played the last note and it faded, the tape ran out—*flub, flub, flub.* Years later I found out that one of Stevie Ray Vaughan's blues was recorded exactly the same way—suddenly, on the spot, on a two-track reel-to-reel. And just as he played the last lick, the same thing happened—the tape ran out. The really weird thing? It was the same engineer both times—Jim Gaines.

I have to say a word about Jim and the other engineers Santana has been blessed to have in the studio and sometimes on the road. Fred Catero, Glen Kolotkin, Dave Rubinson, Jim Reitzel—they've all been instrumental in our success through the years, and I feel they all need to be honored. Jim Gaines worked with so many great artists, from Tower of Power to Steve Miller to Stevie Ray Vaughan, before he came to us. He brought a really earthy quality to the sound and did what he did without any ego—he was a pleasure to work with. He was with Santana just as things were going from analog to digital, so he helped with that transition and was as great with the computer as he was with the knobs. Recording technology was up to thirty-six tracks at that time, before Pro Tools came around, but he was really patient and knew what to say and when to say it in a very gentle way that would help make the music a lot more flowing.

After that jam with CT in '87, Jim gave me a cassette of it, and I left it in the car. The next day Deborah went shopping in that car, and when she came back she asked me, "Why don't you play like that?" There was that question again, the one she asked after the Amnesty International concert—sometimes she'd say that and I'd have to think, "What does she mean?" Before I said anything she was already asking me the name of the song on the cassette.

"What song?"

"You know, that song you played with CT. I heard it and couldn't drive. I had to pull over."

I decided to call it "Blues for Salvador," not only for Sal but also because San Salvador was going through some hard times then, with an earthquake and a civil war. That song inspired my last solo album as Carlos Santana. I love it because it has Tony Williams on it, and more of Buddy Miles's singing, and that band—CT, Alphonso, Graham, Raul, Armando, and the rest. I dedicated the album to Deborah, and the song "Bella," for Stella, is on there, too.

"Blues for Salvador" won a Grammy as the year's best rock instrumental performance—the first Santana Grammy, but not the last.

CHAPTER 20

Wayne Shorter, John Lee Hooker, and me, backstage
at the Fillmore, June 15, 1988.

Maybe it looks like I'll record with anybody, especially after Supernatural —
*"Carlos the Collaborator." And maybe I still have a lot of spiritual books to
read, because I'm supposed to see the same thing in everybody, but in
music I don't, and I won't. There are some songs that even if you put them
into me intravenously my body's not going to let them go in. It's like,
"Thanks for asking me to play on this tune — I mean, thank you for inviting me, but I don't hear myself in that." I've said no to certain musicians
because quite frankly I don't like their music. I'm actually surprised they
would even invite me. It's never been about money at this point: it's
mainly about whether I'll like a song ten years from now.*

In the '80s I recorded on albums by McCoy Tyner and Stanley
Clarke and my old friend Gregg Rolie and Jim Capaldi from Traffic. In
'85 Clive Davis asked me to play with Aretha Franklin, which was

perfect because I was working with Narada Michael Walden at the time, and so was she. She is the queen of soul. I could not say no to her. Or to Gladys, Dionne, or Patti, but I did once say no to another R & B singer because her version of "Oye Como Va" was a little too LA slick for me. I know she was disappointed, because I had told her that I would do it.

It would be a privilege to do something with Willie Nelson again or Merle Haggard. Anybody in the Coltrane family of musicians I would say yes to, and I would say yes to almost everybody in the Miles family. I said no to a West Coast rapper because the song he sent sounded corny and plastic. I can still hear myself with Lou Rawls.

These days collaborations don't happen in the studio—they're just files e-mailed between engineers. I've adjusted to that. I'm lucky because I was born with a highly active imagination. I can close my eyes and you can grab a Sam Cooke song and I can play on it as if he were next to me and I can say, "It's an honor to work with you, Mr. Sam Cooke." Imagination gets past time and distance and separation, which is what any collaboration has to do, too. Imagination is like, "I'm right here, and you're right here, and let's get it on."

Prince is a bad dude, a giant dude. It would be an honor to do something with him from scratch. I have the songs that would work for us. He's a hell of a guitar player, a hell of a rhythm guitar player, and he's sat in with Santana a few times. I've heard him play piano, and sometimes he goes into a Herbie place. He's a genius genius. The only thing is, we'd have to find common ground—swamp–African–John Lee Hooker stuff—so it doesn't get slick-a-roni. I like it down and dirty and barefootin', and I think that's what he loves about the music, too. We got to go to the jungle, man.

The best-paying jazz gigs today are usually the festivals, and many of them take place in the summer. The winter before the summer of '88 I asked Wayne Shorter if I could start a rumor. "A rumor about what?"

"That you and I are in a band going on the road."

He smiled with a twinkle in his eye, as he often does, and said right away, "Yes, you may."

Wayne and I brought together a group that we thought was perfect for both of us: there were two keyboardists — Patrice Rushen, who brought an element of Herbie Hancock, and CT, who brought elements of Joe Zawinul, the church, and some McCoy. Plus we had Alphonso, Ndugu, Chepito, and Armando. We split the set list between some songs Santana usually played and Wayne's originals. I asked him if he would mind doing "Sanctuary" in a boogie way. I think I got a couple of dirty looks from somebody in the band, but Wayne smiled and said, "Yeah, let's do it" — and he took that song back to his early days in Newark.

We did twenty-nine concerts together, and we should have called it the Let's Do It tour — it was fun and different every night. I think Wayne could feel that there was a camaraderie in the group. I'm glad Claude Nobs helped us record our performance in Montreux. We did a concert at the Royal Festival Hall in London. Backstage before we went on, Wayne, Armando, Ndugu, and I were hanging with Greg Phillinganes and a few guys from the Michael Jackson tour, which was in London at the same time. John Lee Hooker, the original Crawling King Snake, was also in London, and he came by. I called it Hanging with Some Heavy Hitters. I couldn't have been happier than I was that night.

Playing with Wayne taught me how he goes into a melody. It's like a blind man checking out a room for the first time, or like a dancer trying out a stage so he can memorize it. He purposely plays almost as if he doesn't know how to play, with a lot of innocence. But his playing is not naive: it has an innocence and purity, without desperation. It's like he's having fun discovering even though he already has everything that he's looking for.

Playing with Wayne gave me courage — courage to go deep and high. It made me play with more vulnerability instead of just bringing the hard licks that I'd practiced and prepared, which can be like a shield that you carve carefully before you come out of your room. Wayne taught me to present myself as open and vulnerable, inviting the other player to present his or her wisdom. It's an invitation to learn together.

Wayne does that when we talk—he'll ask a question not because he doesn't know the answer but because he wants you to hear the answer yourself. Then all of a sudden things start to fix themselves. You don't have to try so hard—sometimes you don't have to try at all, and if you try harder you end up making it worse. That's what I really learned from Wayne—and Herbie, too. Okay, you can be upset. But like Wayne told that member of his band one time, "What did you *learn?*"

There were some strange things, too, that happened on that tour. Every night it seemed Chepito was going through a new crisis. Thank God Wayne's wife, Ana Maria, was there, because she would dismantle it. He seemed close to the edge all the time, saying stuff like, "Chepito is very upset today" and "Poor Chepito. He's going to die next Tuesday." It was always going to happen on a Tuesday. Armando would look him at him and say, "Why wait? Do it now, goddammy." You could hear the tears suddenly stop. "Okay. What time is rehearsal tomorrow?"

Miles was part of the big jazz tour that we were on, and when he peeked in on our show in Rochester and was getting ready to leave before we had played, Chepito almost lost it. He went running up to Miles. "Wait—you haven't heard Wayne and Carlos and me. Where you going?" Miles looked at him and just said, "Chepito, you're still a bad motherfucker," and walked away. "Did you hear what Miles called me? I am a *bad motherfucker!*" Then the tears started again, because he was happy.

Chepito always reminded me of Harpo Marx with a voice. Clown, troublemaker, and super talented—all in one. Earlier that year there had been a memorial concert for Jaco Pastorius, who had been killed in '87. He had come to our concert in Miami the night he died, but afterward he hadn't been able to get in some other club, and that led to a fight with a bouncer. Jaco went into a coma that he never came out of. Backstage at the tribute concert in Oakland was everyone who had a connection to Jaco or Weather Report or Miles: Wayne, Joe, Herbie, Hiram Bullock, Peter Erskine, Armando,

Chepito. I had a bootleg tape of Coltrane we were listening to, and Marcus Miller came in. He said, "Hey! How's everyone? What's going on? What are you listening to?" We waited a second, and I said, "It's good stuff—you should check it out."

"Yeah, okay. Sounds good!"

I'm not sure if Marcus could make out who it was—the recording wasn't the best quality—but Chepito picked up on this and couldn't resist. He went, "So who are you?" Marcus looked at him and said, "I'm Marcus Miller—I play with Miles."

"Yeah, I know Miles, but I never heard of you. What do you play?"

"I play bass."

"Hmm. Okay, never heard of you."

Marcus was hooked, and he tried explaining some of his other credentials, but Chepito just kept saying, "Never heard of you, man. Sorry." Of course Chepito was just pulling his chain. By the third time he said that, Wayne and Ana Maria and Herbie were cracking up, and Marcus finally realized: "Oh! Okay—very funny." That was definitely one of Chepito's finest moments.

One night on that '88 tour I said, "Hey, Wayne, you look so happy, man. What happened?"

"Miles just gave me back the rights to my song."

I suspect that it was "Sanctuary," because that was one of Wayne's tunes on *Bitches Brew*, and it ended up with Miles's name on it. I was happy for Wayne, but this happened almost twenty years after that song got recorded. Some things you have to watch out for in your life as a musician. Sometimes you have to stand up and say, "Look, man, this song is my song." And you have to do it yourself. Even if you're standing up to someone like Miles. That was the kind of advice I got from Bill Graham and Armando—you don't have to be crass or vulgar or get upset, but speak up. The worst thing anyone can say is no.

The other thing that happened on that '88 tour was that I got to see firsthand how certain jazz musicians were treated on the road compared to the way a Santana tour was run. I expected that things would be different in terms of the quality of hotels and the backstage thing—I'm not talking about that. Although I did get upset once when we were picked up in what looked like a laundry truck instead of a car.

I'm talking about a lot of stuff the concert producers were not paying me and Wayne for, like putting our likenesses on big posters and T-shirts and broadcasting the concert on the radio and recording it. None of that was ever okayed by us; we were getting paid only for the gig. Even then it was standard practice in the industry that if your show was to be recorded for radio or TV you were to receive another payment besides the fee for the concert. Same with merchandise.

So I found myself speaking up a lot on that tour, and I know to some people I must have looked like a prima donna—I remember some of the other jazzmen on that tour looking at me that way. But I just didn't want to cooperate with an old-fashioned plantation mentality that seemed to be standard for jazz festivals and clubs. "Turn off those cameras, man, and don't turn 'em back on until you guys ask permission and negotiate with us properly."

Experiencing all that on the '88 tour made me realize that it was imperative for me to be more hands-on with my own business. I have Wayne to thank in a way, because that tour forced me to be even more of a leader with Santana. I realized that some people around me weren't even asking me questions, like whether I wanted to be on the radio and how much I thought I should be paid for it.

"Oh, it's for later release on CD, but it's to raise money for a charity."

"Okay, what charity?"

The fact that these questions weren't coming my way really started to bug me, and suddenly it all became a priority, and I became more involved with the band's business decisions.

In a way I was waking up to the responsibility of caring how Santana was presented, so that the feeling and the message and even the spelling was all correct and accurate on album covers and posters and advertising and tickets. A lot of times other people just don't have the same consciousness as you do or are too busy or just don't have good taste. I remember thinking about how abysmal some of Miles's and Coltrane's album covers were. I started to demand to see everything—artwork, photos. "Okay, these three are the best—we'll choose from these. These over here I don't ever want to see again. Got it?"

The first example of this was *Viva Santana!*, which came out in '88 and was a compilation that showed how far Santana had come in twenty years. It wasn't just a "best of"—it told the Santana story through thirty songs and included a booklet with new original artwork that also used images from the covers of older albums. There were a lot of details and work that went into it, and everything came through me—this album I actually produced from top to bottom. We also did a documentary in which I talked about the band and myself and which included footage of Santana performing. It came out on VHS, then later on DVD, and now I think you can find most of it on YouTube. It really was the first attempt to show and explain Santana's complete history, from "Black Magic Woman" to "Blues for Salvador," in one package and in all the new technology and formats of the time.

At the same time we wanted to do a twentieth-anniversary reunion tour. It made sense—*Viva Santana!* was all about our history, so why not? Things were good between Gregg and Shrieve and me; Chepito and Armando were still in the band; and we had Alphonso to play bass, because Dougie was gone. David was not well at all, and we already had Armando and Chepito, so Carabello, who had his own band, didn't come. We did a lot of tunes from the first three albums mixed with newer songs, and we ended the show with "Soul Sacrifice."

I remember that whole project—the CD and the documentary and the tour—gave me more confidence in taking charge and having opinions about things beyond just the music. And I learned to have more and more confidence after the tour with Wayne—in many ways, I think the anniversary and tour helped to give birth to a whole new Carlos. The old Carlos was a nice guy who left a lot of things for other people to do and didn't want to know about them. "I'll just play the guitar, and you go take care of that." The new Carlos didn't want to be a control freak, but he decided there were things that he needed to be more hands-on about. It was that simple.

When your eyes are open, inspiration can come from anywhere. Here's one example. I'm a huge fan of Anthony Quinn. Some people think he's Greek, but he's actually Mexican. He's my favorite actor. I liked him in *Zorba the Greek* because of the advice he gives to the white guy: it's a very important part of the movie. Zorba tells the man he needs some madness—because how else can he cut the rope and be free? Anthony Quinn was crazy—good crazy. I've seen his sculptures. And I know Miles, and the two of them had a profound mutual admiration for each other.

In '75, when I was reading Sri Chinmoy's books or other spiritual stuff, I was more interested in Anthony Quinn's book *The Original Sin,* the first autobiography I ever read. He wrote about driving in Hollywood with a little kid in the passenger seat who did nothing but rag on him, telling him that he wasn't worth anything, that he was nothing but a Mexican monkey playing plastic games, like all the people in Hollywood.

Of course that kid was part of himself—it was his guilt trying to put him in his place. We all have that same guy inside. There ain't nobody who's going to put you down more than you. But there's a difference between being brutally honest and just being brutal. It really was a therapeutic book for me, because it connected with the same ideas and philosophy I was reading elsewhere. Anthony Quinn was asking the same questions—how to evolve and not make the same mistakes everybody around you is making. How to develop a bona fide spiritual discipline, with or without a guru.

He also wrote that he didn't want to go to church because he didn't want to apologize for being a human being. Whoa—*Original Sin.* I got it. Just what I had been thinking.

At the end of 1988, I was watching Quinn in *Barabbas,* in which his character is in prison and gets out because Jesus took his place on the cross, and in my head I kept hearing "You need to play San Quentin." I was thinking, "What?"

"You need to play San Quentin—that's the message of this movie."

"This movie I've seen so many times?"

"Play San Quentin."

I used to be able to see the prison from one of my first homes in Marin County. By '88 I was living just a mile away. Having kids and a family makes you think about what you have and other people don't and about the freedom you have to find your purpose and fulfill it. Those days there weren't that many people wanting to play prisons—B. B. had played San Quentin a few years before, and I heard that only black prisoners went. I also knew about Johnny Cash playing Folsom State Prison—everybody did. My level of confidence was very high, having just done the tour with Wayne, and the guys in the Santana reunion band were gracious enough to be crazy enough to go do it with me.

I put that concert together myself—I arranged a meeting with the warden, Dan Vasquez, a Mexican dude. He said, "Let me get this straight. You want to do a concert in San Quentin? You need to come and walk the yard with me so you can see what you're getting into." I said, "Okay." So even before I signed a contract to perform there I had to sign a waiver saying that if I got caught in any kind of trouble—if I were held hostage, for example—my family and I wouldn't hold the prison responsible for whatever happened.

Then I stepped outside the offices, and we walked to the prison gates. I had guards with me, and as we stepped through and the gates slammed shut, the sound felt like a chunk of ice running down my spine. The first thing I saw were four guards, all with shotguns, walking a black prisoner somewhere. He was shuffling along in chains, and he had more hate in his eyes than I've ever seen in a human being. Then one of the guards with me said, "Look up at the ceiling," and it was pretty high, but it was full of holes from shotgun blasts. "Those are from warning shots. Normally we have to shoot only one time up there—they know that the next time we'll shoot them."

We got to the yard, where everybody was doing things like lifting weights and playing basketball—whites, blacks, Latinos, Native Americans—and people started to recognize me. "Hey, 'Tana, is that you? What you doin' in here, man? Hey, Carlos, what you doin'?" One guy got my attention. "Carlos, I just tried to cross the mountains from Mexico, and the next thing I knew they put me in here." He was just a misplaced soul trying to get in the country, and he wound up in San Quentin. The warden said, "I see you're connected with everybody here, man."

We did two concerts outside in the yard—one for the hard-core criminals and one for the lifers. We did the set we were doing for the reunion tour but included some special songs that you'd think of doing in a prison: Bob Dylan's "I Shall Be Released," Michael Jackson's "Smooth Criminal," the Temptations' "Cloud Nine." We knew this was going to be a tough audience because we needed to reach blacks and whites and because maybe this wasn't any one person's music anymore. You can't buy enthusiasm in San Quentin.

At first they were all just checking us out. By the second song they started to loosen up. I could see the energy changing in their postures and faces. By the third song it felt like they were thinking, "Hey—these guys can bring it." By the fourth song they started to let the music in and smile and forget for a moment where they were. I mean, when I first walked in there I could smell the fear and the controlling of emotions, how bottled up everything was. How they could just explode. I could smell their skin, the clothes they were wearing, even their thinking.

There's a photo from that show in San Quentin that's on the wall in my office. I'm playing, and you can see some very hard-core prisoners on one side. You can zero in on them and see that they were hearing the music. I didn't say much in those concerts—I let the music carry the message: this is required listening to help you not be a victim or a prisoner of your self, to help you change your mind about things and change your destiny. The message is the same inside prison walls or on the outside.

*   *   *

In a funny way, my life has always been local—everything that happens comes from where I am. John Lee Hooker was living in the Bay Area at this time. He was the Dalai Lama of boogie. Shoot, he should have been the pope of boogie as far as I'm concerned. We got to know each other. A lot of times we'd be playing, and he'd say, "Carlos, let's take it to the street," and I'd say, "No, John, let's take it to the back alley," and he'd say, "Why stop there? Let's go to the swamp." I miss him so much.

A John Lee boogie pulls people in as strongly as gravity holds them to this planet. He is the sound of deepness in the blues—his influence permeates everything. You can hear him in Jimi Hendrix's "Voodoo Child (Slight Return)" or in Canned Heat's boogies. That's nothing but John Lee Hooker. When you hear the Doors, that's a combination of John Lee and John Coltrane. That's what they do; that's the music they love.

The first time I heard John Lee, of course, was in Tijuana—on records and on the radio. As I said, there were three guys that had a lot of deep roots in their blues—Lightnin' Hopkins, Jimmy Reed, and John Lee Hooker. Lightnin' lived in Texas, and Jimmy Reed was probably the most viral when I was listening to the blues in Mexico, but he was long gone by the end of the '80s. He made Vee-Jay Records a lot of money.

In '89 John Lee was local to the Bay Area. He was living not far from me, in San Carlos, which is near Palo Alto. We met a few times and talked, and at some point he actually invited me to his house for his birthday, which was the first time I really hung out with him. I brought a beautiful guitar to give him.

When I walked in, I saw that everyone was watching the Dodgers on TV, because that's John Lee's favorite team. He was eating fried chicken and Junior Mints. No kidding—Junior Mints. He had two women on the left and two on the right, and they were putting the mints into his hands, which were softer than an old sofa. I stepped up and said, "Hi, John. Happy birthday, man. I brought you this guitar, and I wrote a song for you."

"Oh, yeah?"

"It sounds like the Doors doing blues, but I took it back from them and I'm returning it to you and I'm calling it 'The Healer.'"

John Lee chuckled. He had a slight stutter that was very endearing. "L-L-Let me hear it."

I started playing, and I made it up right on the spot—I knew how he did the blues, how he played and sang. "Blues a healer all over the world..." He took the song, and when he recorded it, he added to it in his own way. I said, "Okay, we've got to go to the studio with this, but I just want you to come at one or two tomorrow afternoon, because I don't want you to be there all day, man. I just want you to come in and just lay it. I'm going to work with the engineer—get the microphones ready, get the band to the right tempo. You just show up."

"Okay, C-C-Carlos."

When John Lee showed up we were ready. I got the band warmed up—Chepito, Ndugu, CT, and Armando—no bass, because Alphonso didn't make that gig. John Lee and Armando were checking each other out like two dogs slowly circling each other—they were the two senior guys there, and you could really tell that Armando needed to know who this new older guy was. He was looking at him slowly, all the way from his feet up to his hat. Just sizing him up. John Lee knew it, but he just sat there, tuning his guitar, chuckling to himself.

Armando threw down the first card. "Hey, man, you ever heard of the Rhumboogie?" He was talking about one of the old, old clubs on the black music circuit in Chicago, opened by the boxer Joe Louis back before I was even born. John Lee said, "Yeah, m-m-man. I heard of the Rhumboogie." Armando had his hands on his waist like, "I got you now." He said, "Well, I played there with Slim Gaillard."

"Yeah? I opened up there for D-D-Duke Ellington."

I saw what was going on and stepped in. "Armando, this is Mr. John Lee Hooker. Mr. Hooker, Mr. Armando Peraza."

We did "The Healer" in one take, and the engineer said, "Want to try it again?"

John Lee shook his head. "What for?"

I thought about it and said, "Would you mind going back in the booth, and when I point at you, would you be so gracious as to give us your signature—those mmm, mmm's?" John Lee chuckled again. "Yeah, I can do that." I said okay. That was the only thing he overdubbed that day—"Mmm, mmm, mmm."

"The Healer" helped bring John Lee back for his last ten years. He had a bestselling album and a music video—everything he deserved. We started to hang out more and play together. I would see him in concert, too. He had a keyboard player for many years—Deacon Jones—who used to get up onstage and say, "Hey! You people in the front—you might need to get back a little bit, because the grease up here is hot. John Lee's about to come out!" I have so many stories like that as well as stories about John Lee calling me—sometimes during the day, but, like Miles did, mostly late at night.

I remember John Lee opening for Santana in Concord, California, and we had finished our sound check and he'd been waiting for me on the side of the stage. We were done, and he started talking to me while we walked away. The soundman came running up. "Mr. Hooker, we need you to do a sound check, too."

"I don't need no sound check."

"But we have to find out how you sound."

John Lee kept walking. "I already know what I sound like." End of discussion.

One time there was an outdoor blues festival in San Francisco, and I went to support my heroes—Buddy Guy, Otis Rush, and others. The crew came running up to me, saying, "John Lee's on stage, and he called out to you to come over and join him." They'd already set up my amp, so I went over, and he was up there by himself, looking great, as he always did, in a suit and a hat. His guitar was on his knee. As soon as he saw me, he said, "Ladies and gentlemen, a good friend of mine—Carlos Santana. Come on, man."

It was a beautiful day, and from the stage I could see the sky and birds and the Golden Gate Bridge, and all the blues lovers in the audience. I held on to that image and closed my eyes and joined him onstage—just he and I. It was like playing along with a preacher on Sunday morning—I waited for my time to step in, but while he was singing I could hear his voice telling me to start playing. I opened my eyes, and we were together in a groove, playing off each other. I heard his voice inside again, telling me to keep playing, so I closed my eyes and kept going. When I finished there was huge applause—people were freaking out. I looked around, but no John Lee!

I played a little more and thanked the people and went backstage, where John Lee was talking with a young girl. He looked up with that smile he had. "Hey, man, y-y-you did pretty good out there."

"Yeah, but why did you leave me, man?"

"W-W-Well, I was done."

I've always known where my heart is in music, but I really liked some new bands and guitarists that were coming up at the time. Vernon Reid reminded me a little of Sonny Sharrock and Jimi. His band, Living Colour, was from New York City and was one of the first all-black rock bands. Vernon's a strong, funky player—fun to play with live. Vernon is a monster freak and has a beautiful heart. He and David Sancious both have quietness in their faces and a lot of wisdom, and, like me, both are into Sonny Sharrock.

Vernon played on *Spirits Dancing in the Flesh,* the Santana album released in 1990. I think about that album, and I hear the balance of Curtis Mayfield and John Coltrane and Jimi Hendrix doing gospel songs, singing God's praises, and rocking out. Prayer and passion. Alice Coltrane gave us permission to use John's voice on one song. It was nicely recorded, but I still needed to feel raw emotion—I'd rather hear mistakes, you know what I mean?

There is nothing about singing to God and Jesus that should be whiny. The song should come from your heart and deep inside, not just from your mouth. An album about God has to be very honest and raw. A person who's a little out of tune but totally for real is better than someone who's trying too hard or being phony.

I wanted to work with a singer like Tramaine Hawkins, because with spiritual music I have to be very selective: sometimes people can get a little plastic when they praise Jesus. I won't mention any names because I don't want to hurt any feelings, but there's a difference between whining and soul. When I hear Mavis Staples, Gladys Knight, Nina Simone, and Etta James, I hear a huge difference between them and singers from the other side of town, where the girls whine too much—black or white. They might be in tune, but it's not real.

Tramaine came out of San Francisco and was with the Edwin Hawkins Singers for a while; she was perfect for *Spirits*. When I was doing that album I also got to meet Benny Rietveld, who was with Miles at the time. Alphonso was gone, so Benny ended up playing bass on the album and has been with me since '91. He is now the band's musical director. I've come to know and love Benny.

I had just started thinking about the album in '90, and Wayne told me about the songwriter Paolo Rustichelli, who played synthesizers and was recording with Miles and Herbie and who had written a song for me. I ended up playing on Rustichelli's album *Mystic Man*—with Miles on some tracks! Paolo gave me the song "Full Moon" to record, which I was working on when I found out that Benny was coming over. Meanwhile Benny heard we were auditioning bass players. We met, and he asked, "Hey, can I try out?" I looked hard at him. "You're still with Miles, right? You can play with us, but you got to tell him." I didn't want any tension.

Of course you know what happened—Benny didn't tell him, but Miles found out he recorded on my new album, *and* he heard we talked about Benny auditioning. I was at the Paramount in Oakland, where I had just given Miles a bunch of flowers and a gift for winning the Grammy Lifetime Achievement Award. After the show, I was getting ready to leave and was in the parking lot with my friend Tony Kilbert when John Bingham, who played percussion in Miles's band, came to tell me Miles wanted to see me backstage. "Sure, I'll be right there." So I went back inside to his dressing room. "Hey, Miles."

"Close the door."

Uh-oh.

"Thank you for the flowers; thank you for the gift."

"You're welcome, Miles."

"What's going on with Benny?"

"I don't know what's going on with him. He's in your band." Benny had to do his own talking. Miles let me slide. The next thing I knew, Benny did tell him, and he joined the band and played on the album *Spirits Dancing in the Flesh.*

Spirits came out in 1990, but by that time Columbia and CBS had become Sony Music, and they didn't know what to do with that album or the ones before it, many of which were not available anymore. I remember thinking just before *Supernatural* came out that I wish the record company would rerelease some of those albums, because they were so great—*Freedom, Blues for Salvador, Spirits Dancing in the Flesh.* I had that in mind a few years later, when I got a chance to put together *Multi-Dimensional Warrior,* the compilation of Santana music from the late '70s and '80s.

Spirits was the end of Santana's relationship with Columbia, CBS, and Sony Music. They put a guy named Donnie Ienner in charge, and I couldn't work with him. He wanted to work with me, but I was more in charge of the business side of Santana than I had been before, and I felt the same thing I think Miles felt when it was time for him to leave Columbia in 1986. Miles couldn't work with the top guy at his part of the label, and if you feel that way, why stay? I remember my last conversation with Donnie—I listened to what he had to say and responded by saying something about how dealing with the situation was like "artists versus suits," and it didn't get much better after that. I felt Santana needed to be somewhere else, and first we started to go with Warner Bros., then we ended up signing with Davitt Sigerson at Polydor.

The year 1991 was not easy—it felt like the spiritual training wheels were off. My pillars weren't there anymore. My angels were leaving. It was very difficult. It made me grow up in another kind of way, as if God were telling me, "You're on your own now."

It all happened in one month. Santana was playing in Syracuse the day Miles died in California — September 28. Wayne called and told me that night. He said he had seen Miles playing that summer at the Hollywood Bowl. "He played 'Happy Birthday' for me, and in the middle of the song he looked at me and I saw a fatigue in his face that I had never seen before. Fatigue from many, many years back."

I had seen Miles sick before, but I wasn't expecting him to die. I got on the elevator with Benny and said, "Benny, Miles just passed."

"No!"

We both looked at the floor, and I don't remember much else. When someone like Miles or Armando leaves, there's a vacuum, and you can feel the energy level go down. That's the best way I can describe it.

The next morning I got up at five to take a plane so that I could attend Stella's first-grade graduation. I was still numb. That night we played at Ben & Jerry's One World, One Heart festival in Golden Gate Park. I sat in with the Caribbean Allstars, and we did "In a Silent Way" as a tribute.

I hadn't seen Miles much in the previous year. I had sent him flowers in the hospital when I had heard he was sick, and he called to thank me. "This means so much, Carlos," he had said. "What are you doing now?" I told him what I always said: "Learning and having fun, Miles."

"You're always going to be doing that — that's the kind of mind you have."

That was the last thing Miles ever said to me, and I wish more people could have known that side of him. His autobiography had come out the year before, and when I read it I thought he could have been more supported by the people who wrote it with him; they could have given him more honor. I thought they were overselling the Prince of Darkness bit. Not everything that came out of his mouth had to be written down. I'd rather read endearing things about him and other musicians. I like romance — I'm a romantic through and through.

Like an elephant, Miles remembered things. That time in '81

when he came by the Savoy and we hung out all night, I had told him when we were backstage that the world would be grateful enough to him even if he never played another note. I said, "We just want you to be healthy and happy." He said, "What's that?" like it was a strange thing to wish on somebody. I immediately said, "Miles, you're not one of those people who aren't happy unless they're miserable, are you?" He just stopped and looked at me. A whole year later I played a big rock-and-tennis event in Forest Hills, Queens — John McEnroe and Vitas Gerulaitis and Todd Rundgren and Joe Cocker and bassist Jamaaladeen Tacuma and the jazz drummer Max Roach were all there. We finished playing, and I was getting ready to leave when I heard someone call me. "Carlos! Hey, Carlos!"

It was Max Roach. "I need to talk to you, Carlos." He looked serious. He said, "Miles came to see me. What did you say to him?"

Man, I had to run the videotape back a long way to remember our last conversation — it was that long night that started backstage at the Savoy. I thought about it, and two things came to my mind. First was the story Miles told in his book from way back in the early '50s, when Max put some money in his coat pocket when he had been strung out on the street. Miles said that was what had shamed him into getting off heroin.

The second thing I thought about was the look he gave me when I asked him about only being happy when he was miserable. I had called Miles on his stuff that night, and I told Max the story. He listened to me and said, "I want you to know it's working — he's starting to look different."

Who was Miles Davis? What made him do what he did? He maintained a vicious, ferocious pursuit of excellence no matter what he was doing or with whom — black, white, or any other color. As Tony Williams told me, "Before there were Black Panthers or black power or any kind of revolution, Miles wasn't taking any shit from white or black people." He had the fire and the fearlessness. But whether he was happy in the end is another thing.

If you look at advertising and movies and magazines, you'll see that what they tell you is that success comes and then you're happy. Here's how to be happy: wear this, eat that, get this, get that. The truth is the other way around. I think what screams out loudest about anyone's success is whether that person is actually, truly happy.

A few weeks after Miles's memorial I was home and the phone rang in the morning and Deborah answered it. "No! No, no, no!" She started crying right away. "Bill is gone!" I said, "Gone where?" Then I got it, and that was it, man. For at least two months I was numb. Two of my closest friends — gone. Suddenly Miles was not there to call late at night and tell me when to duck. Bill is not there with a clipboard. Now I would have to do it all inwardly.

The last time I saw Bill was the month before at the Greek Theatre in Berkeley. We had done so many shows together by then — it was an incredible evening. I remember being backstage after the concert, holding Jelli, who was just two years old. She was looking up at me with expression of joy on her face, speechless. During the show, the energy had never dropped. Every song felt as if it had been just the right length and had segued perfectly into the next. The audience was a mix of white, black, Mexican, Filipino — a rainbow crowd. They were on their feet from the start of the show. Like Jelli, I didn't know what to say. People were all around us — everyone was happy. Just perfect vibes.

Bill came over with his clipboard and looked at me. I waited. He slowly pulled off a page and turned it around to show me. It was blank. "Come on, man. Really? Wow, thank you, Bill."

"Thank *you*." Then he walked away.

CHAPTER 21

My dad, José Santana, and me at the Bullring by the Sea,
Tijuana, March 21, 1992.

When I became a dad, I let my kids know I love them all the time. And
naturally I would think about music and my obsessions and my kids. Of
course I knew I wouldn't be disappointed if Salvador, Stella, or Jelli
chose music for a career—we'd have more to talk about. But they could
have done anything they wanted and I'd still have been proud of their
life choices. The only thing that would have made me disappointed
would have been if they had let stuff get in the way of achieving what
they want to do. Our family is a no-excuses family. Our children are
responsible for their own quality of thoughts so that they can choose to
turn them into actions and deeds and create their own lives.

It takes strength, man, to know when to let go of your kids — really, really let them go and trust them with the one who made them in the first place. One time in the mid-'90s, when Sal was a teenager, I needed to talk to him. I had been on the road for five weeks and had just come home. I understand that for kids between the ages of twelve and twenty-two, parents are the most uncool people ever. Right then Sal needed to play that out. I was thinking, "The kids'll get over it, as I did, and then they'll realize that their parents are exceptional." But back then I was feeling a separation between father and son.

"Salvador?"

"Whattup?" That was his thing to say then — "Whattup?"

"Son, I've noticed lately that it's your duty to contradict whatever I say. It seems to be a real 24-7 job, you know?" He kept looking at me. "But look outside: it's an incredible day — the sky is blue, the weather's warm. We can't argue about that, right? Would you consider taking the day off with me and just sitting on top of Mount Tamalpais and looking at the hawks and the eagles and getting quiet?"

He surprised me a little, because he only thought about it a few seconds. "That sounds good." We went up there and took our time, lay back, and looked up at the birds floating on the updrafts, and I didn't say a word. In fifteen minutes he opened up, telling me stuff about himself and his girlfriend and school and the way people treat him because he's a Santana and the fact that people are always asking him for money. It was a challenge to sit there and listen, just listen. I had answers and ideas to tell him. But I tried to look at him and see him as his friends and teachers do, and I saw that he was starting to figure things out on his own. He was always well behaved and respectful — he still is.

I'll give you an example. We were on tour together in 2005 — Santana and the Salvador Santana Band — and we were in San Antonio. Someone knocked on my dressing-room door. "Who is it?"

"It's me, Dad. Salvador."

"Son, you don't have to knock. Come on in."

"Dad, I need to ask you something." I put my guitar down. "Can I get a bottle of water from your cooler? We ran out in our room." I mean, he really does that. My heart just burst open.

"Sal, you can have anything, man, my heart included. Anything."

"Uh, okay, Dad. Thanks—have a great show."

I still embarrass him, I know. But I'm not changing, and neither is he. "How you feeling, Salvador?"

"Thanks for asking, Dad. I'm feeling good."

You know, I want to be like him when I grow up.

In 1997 Prince called me to tell me he was playing in San Jose and asked me whether I wanted to come by the show and jam and just hang out. Did I? I love Prince. When I got there, he said, "Come here; I want to show you something." Okay—what? Maybe a new guitar? He took me to a room backstage and opened the door, and his whole band was in there, watching a video. Prince was smiling. "They can tell you: every time before we go onstage, man, I play *Sacred Fire*. I tell them that this is what I want them to bring." I looked at the band and thought, "Great—here's another whole band that I'm telling what to do."

It was an honor to be shown that by Prince—especially because *Sacred Fire: Live in Mexico* was as personal and special to me as *Havana Moon* was. It was a live video, and there was also a live album—*Sacred Fire: Live in South America*—that all came out together, the first time I did that sort of coordinated package—a tour, an album, and a video.

Sacred Fire came out in '93, and the tour came from *Milagro*— my first album for Polydor the year before. There's no doubt about it—there is a certain amount of spiritual confidence in *Sacred Fire*. My going to Mexico and playing there is a little like Bob Dylan going to play in Jerusalem. These are your people. You better bring it. In fact, I take a lot of pride in saying that Santana has never dropped the ball in Mexico City, New York, Tokyo, Sydney, Paris, Rome, London, Moscow—or any of the big cities. Yes, we have dropped the ball in other places because we're human and we're fallible, not because we planned to. Whenever it's a major gig, I just take a deep breath and I say, "May all the angels really come forth and help me with this one."

Milagro was a good-bye letter written especially for Bill and Miles. It opened with Bill's voice introducing us as he always did—"From my heart, Santana!"—then followed with "Milagro," which means "miracle," because that's what those guys were and what each of us is. That song used a line from Bob Marley's "Work." "Somewhere in Heaven" was the next tune, and it began with Martin Luther King Jr. speaking about the promised land. I didn't know exactly where my angels were, but I knew Bill and Miles would still be calling and connecting, giving advice and spiritual blessings. I asked my old friend Larry Graham to sing on the album, and he came up with "Right On." I put on "Saja" as the intro—that came from a very rare album called *Aquarius* and was written by the saxophonist Joe Roccisano. When I heard that song it sounded so much like something Santana would do if we had worked with Cal Tjader. I added that "Shadow of Your Smile" feel, then it slips into a soulful *guajira*.

I still like Marvin Gaye's words, like "For those of us who tend the sick and heed the people's cries / Let me say to you: Right on!" They have a strong message. I think it conveys the same message that's in Santana's music—it's what I thought still needed to be heard in the '90s. Still today.

I remember that after Larry's first take, he asked me, "What do you think?"

I said, "Larry, you're going around the block—you need to get inside the sheets."

He laughed. "Okay! Got it." The next take was it. Everyone knows about Larry's bass playing, but he's an incredible singer, too—at that same session, he did this amazing vocal warm-up. He went to the piano and played the entire keyboard, from the lowest to the highest key, and matched every note with his voice.

Another great Santana lineup came together on that album—I had CT, Raul, Benny, and Alex, plus we added Karl Perazzo, who had played congas and timbales with Sheila E. and Cal Tjader; Tony Lindsay, who had been singing around the Bay Area and had a nice, clear R & B voice; and Walfredo Reyes Jr., who's from Cuba and played drums with David Lindley and Jackson Browne before he came to us. I also had a horn section that included Bill Ortiz on trumpet. Bill, Tony, Benny, and Karl are all still with Santana today. That pairing of Raul and Karl was especially nice and flexible— they respect the clave. They honor it: they know exactly where it is, as Armando did, but they're not fixated with it.

The *Milagro* tour was going to Mexico, and my brother Jorge had already come along and played on a number of legs, so the idea of family was in the air. The plan was to shoot and record our Mexican dates: my father would come down to help open the show in Tijuana; César Rosas from Los Lobos and Larry Graham would play, too. I remember we took a flight to San Diego from wherever we were before, and the weather was really bad. It got so bad we thought the plane was going to go down. It started shaking a lot, then suddenly it dropped, and the coffee mugs the flight attendants were rolling down the aisle all hit the ceiling. One flight attendant ran to her seat, and I could see her crossing herself. The plane dropped again, and a little girl who was sitting near me started screaming—and laughing. "Whee! Do it again! Do it again!" Everybody started laughing, and that got us all relaxed. Then the shaking stopped.

In Tijuana, the local promoter called the concert a *regresa a casa*—a "homecoming." They put the name on posters, and they got permission to use the city's Bullring by the Sea. I think you could say that was really a turning point for me, when I became fully positive about and supportive of my Mexican self. It was a lot easier to go to Autlán, because so few people remembered me there. But in Tijuana a lot of people still knew me, and the whole town knew about my beginnings there on Avenida Revolución, though I didn't have time to visit the old bars or clubs—and El Convoy was gone. We drove down the road, and in some ways it looked like it probably hadn't changed that much. There were different names, different clubs, new places to dance, and not so much live music, but being in Tijuana was definitely like a homecoming.

We did two nights in the bullring, and the concert went on and on. It started with my father singing and playing with a band of local mariachis; then Pato Banton played, because reggae was really getting popular in Mexico then; then Larry Graham went on; and finally Santana played—with my brother Jorge and even Javier Bátiz gracing us by coming up and jamming. It was footage and music from that concert and other cities on that tour that became the DVD *Sacred Fire*. We also decided to shoot some black-and-white stuff in Tijuana, and we used that in the video for "Right On," which was the lead single from *Milagro*—that's the Tijuana bullring you see me playing in. Those shots of people crossing the border at night? That wasn't staged—that was real.

There's a tape that I found of that concert years afterward. I finally sat down with it and listened to it, starting at the beginning and going all the way through to the end. It was significant for me because that was the first time I heard my dad validate my music. At the end of his mariachi set, he spoke to me backstage. He was speaking a lot more than he usually did. "You know, Carlos, I heard your music many times on the radio, and I've seen you play, and there's something very distinguishable about what you do. When I hear 'Batuka' or 'Ain't got nobody that I can depend on'—*that's* Santana."

I had never heard my dad say anything like that. I didn't even know that he knew the names of any Santana songs, much less the lyrics. He knew the melodies. We had gotten so big so fast that I never got to see how my dad's feelings about my music had changed. Anyway, he never did say much. He honored me by allowing me to become what he had been. It was like I became him, but on a vaster scale, and that was enough for him to stop telling me what to do and what not to do.

I got a chance to tell my dad what I had been holding inside me for many years. In '93 the whole family got together for two weeks in Hawaii—it was all my brothers and sisters and their kids, plus my ex-wife's parents and my parents. I said, "Hey, Dad, let's take a break from all this—let the kids blow off some steam."

We started walking, and I said, "You know, I've been wanting to tell you something."

"What is it?"

"I need to tell you how proud I am of you for taking care of all of us with that violin. I know you had to travel without knowing how much money you were going to get. We never missed a meal. I wanted to thank you." He just looked at me. It felt good, like the look between any father and son that says, "We're interconnected." I could see validation not just for himself but for his father and my son, too.

I didn't know he was only going to be around another five years. I still get choked up when I hear the tape from that bullring in Tijuana.

Playing in Tijuana was very difficult because of the local government and politics and the corruption that we had to deal with, but the guys at Bill Graham's company—Bill Graham Presents, or BGP—get the thanks for making that happen.

But let's just say I'm not a huge fan of what happened to BGP after Bill died. I think a few of the people who took over were the ones who would tell Bill what he wanted to hear, and they didn't share his vision or his priorities or his commitment to music and the music community. I used to tell Bill flat-out that he'd never find out I was speaking about him behind his back because I didn't mind saying whatever I had to say to his face. I wouldn't kiss his ass, like some people who worked for him—but some of them talked horribly about him. I don't think Bill had taken care of that side of his business before he died, because there had been no reason to—of course he hadn't been planning on leaving that soon. Today some of Santana's business is still in BGP's hands—they own the memorabilia site Wolfgang's Vault, for example, and you can find Santana posters and T-shirts there. We've learned to do business together, but I still feel like part of what Bill created was sold down the river.

Bill used to describe himself as "a sentimental slob." I'm not that way. I learned that even if you have a sentimental attachment to some people, in this business it's sometimes better not to have too many emotional ties. Then if you need to dismiss someone who isn't helping things along or who can't keep up while you're moving forward, it's okay. I know there are a lot of people who I have carried and kept with me when I should have let them go because they weren't bringing in any vitality or adding anything to the energy or vision of the organization. It's never easy—but in 1995, when I finally started my own management company, it was time to start looking at things that way.

We had started to handle all Santana management in '88, and for a while Bill Graham had been like an overseer, with Ray Etzler as manager. We were still sharing office space with BGP. Then Bill died, Ray left, and Barry Siegel, who was our accountant, came in as business manager and worked with Deborah. She and I—and later my sister-in-law, Kitsaun—all became part of our own management company and learned a collective lesson about being more hands-on with the business, talking with lawyers and accountants, signing our own checks. Deborah was always in and out of the office, questioning whether things could be done better or cheaper. Her years running the restaurant with Kitsaun helped.

Kitsaun King was already a very important part of our family. She was working for United Airlines when we started Santana Management. During the '90s she eventually became a full-time part of our musical family. She could be tough—over the years we butted heads about some band issues—but her instincts were usually right, and I never doubted her loyalty or her absolute determination to do what was best for Santana. I offer my condolences to anyone who was foolish enough to attempt to put me down or say anything bad about Santana in her presence. Auntie Kitsaun did not tolerate that.

In '95 we found some office and warehouse space in San Rafael. Before that we were all over the place—renting storage space and rehearsal rooms when we needed them. So we came up with the idea of bringing everything all together under one roof. Deborah was the one who had the vision and intention to make that happen, and soon we had set up our own company. We got some of our favorite people from BGP—such as Rita Gentry and Marcia Sult Godinez, both very capable and easy to work with—because we wanted some familiar faces. I will be the first to say that working for me is no picnic. In fact I don't need anybody to work for me—I do my own work, thank you. But if you say we're working together toward a common goal, and that this is my role and this is your role, then yes, you should be working for me.

The funny thing is that even though we were taking better care of our business, I think that during those first years of having our own management company Santana was quieter in the studio than we had ever been in our history. We went almost seven years with no new Santana recordings, from '93, when we recorded the concerts in Mexico and South America for the *Sacred Fire* project, to '99, when I started to work on the songs for *Supernatural*. It wasn't that there was a creative or musical problem. I never doubt myself with that kind of thing—I don't get writer's block. I know the music will come through me. It just felt like there was no need. I didn't feel like recording. And we didn't stop playing live—our touring schedule was busy.

I'd rather do nothing than make an album just to keep a music company happy. Also, Davitt Sigerson was gone from Polydor, so they moved us over to Island Records, where Chris Blackwell was in charge. Part of the new deal was that I got my own label, which I called Guts and Grace. There were four albums that came out on it—two by Paolo Rustichelli, one called *Santana Brothers*—that was Jorge and I and our nephew Carlos Hernandez, who plays guitar and is a solid songwriter—and one called *Sacred Sources: Live Forever*. That album compiled live recordings by Jimi Hendrix, Marvin Gaye, Bob Marley, Stevie Ray Vaughan, and Coltrane, all message givers. It was a challenge to get all the parties to agree—all the estates and their lawyers—but it was worth it to release a lot of the rare music in my collection that maybe would never have gotten out otherwise.

Guts and Grace isn't around anymore, but the good thing that came out of it is that I learned for myself that anybody can have a record label, but if you can't get the music into stores or on the Internet and accessible to the public it's like having a car without tires or gasoline. You need to have serious juice backing you up at the company you're part of. Today, of course, it's all different, with online sites and MP3s, but back then we didn't know that the whole system of music stores and physical formats was going to change.

I felt bad because I didn't have enough juice on my own to push Island to take care of my releases. It seemed like Chris Blackwell wasn't all that hands-on by that time. In my eyes, Island had done some great things by bringing out Bob Marley and reggae music and all that African music on Mango Records, but by the end of the '90s I think Chris would agree that nobody at Island was really present.

Managing your own career is not easy at the start—there's a lot of stuff we didn't know. We met with lawyers and accountants and other businesspeople to find out how we could get more money from old recordings and the group's images and album covers and the name Santana. We started to study how other bands handled their business—Dave Matthews, the Grateful Dead, and Metallica helped us and showed us what they did. We started to ask the same questions other bands did—how can we use our money to help people directly instead of paying taxes that only end up supporting the Pentagon? We learned that everything in life is a process of learning.

In 1998 through Santana Management we set up the Milagro Foundation to help empower children and teenagers in crisis. That's still the mission of the foundation. At the start, Deborah and Kitsaun helped manage it. Then we found Shelley Brown, who had been principal at Salvador's elementary school in San Rafael. Her experience dealing with a public school, making it work for a rainbow of children, and basically holding them all together—black, white, Asian, and Latino—made us think she was the right person. She's been amazing. Now it's Shelley, Ruthie Moutafian, my sister Maria, and a full staff taking care of it. Since the foundation began, we've given away almost six million dollars to support youth in all parts of the world.

Why the name Milagro? Because I think life is about making miracles happen—that no matter how much money we give, the most valuable gift we can offer young people is to help them go outside the norms of belief, empowering them to believe that their dreams are not impossible and that they can allow the voice of divinity to take over their lives. If we can teach people to shoot three-pointers in basketball and how to have a healthful diet, we can also teach children in crisis to be happy for just fifteen minutes a day—then an hour, then the whole day—and that's a miracle. If we can get people to stop criticizing each other—and themselves—and see the bright side of life, that's a miracle. The foundation is about raising consciousness and awakening divinity at an early, vulnerable age.

It's really the same message I tell audiences—you can make every day the best day of your life, starting with today. I think that's the greatest miracle you can give yourself, and it's not up to anybody but you. You can make it happen, starting right now.

Milagro started close to home, giving money to an organization that helps runaways who come through Larkin Street in San Francisco—where the bus station is. This organization gets to the kids before the drugs and pimps do, giving them a place to sleep and wash and get themselves together so they can figure out their next steps. We also support a community center in Marin City, where the staff teaches children how to grow plants—and we started sponsoring young musicians.

Another thing the foundation does is encourage programs that get kids away from inner cities even if just for a day—out into nature, to see trees and breathe fresh air. We've helped get young people out of Oakland and up to the redwoods, where the trees are like huge cathedrals that hide you from the rest of the world and look like they've been there so long you can't measure them with time. Can you imagine how that looks to a child who's never seen anything but streets and buildings and concrete? We're not just raising consciousness—this is more like rearranging it.

Milagro is in Mexico now, too. In border towns such as Tijuana and Juarez, there are a lot of kids who are in crisis, surviving on the streets, and living in tunnels at night. They're hungry, so they snort a lot of glue to take their mind off the hunger. We are trying to connect with them to save them from that kind of existence. In Autlán there's now a health clinic and community center called Santuario de Luz—Sanctuary of Light—that Milagro helped found in 2005 with Dr. Martin Sandoval Gomez, and it's really had an incredible impact on the town. The clinic provides ambulance service and modern facilities that Autlán has never had before. I visited in 2006, and they honored me. People came from various towns around Jalisco to meet me and tell me how their lives were affected by what we were doing with Dr. Martin. Hearing that felt better than receiving any number of Grammy Awards.

I think it's important to understand that the Milagro Foundation started before we released *Supernatural*—it wasn't something that came from asking ourselves, "What can we do with all this money?" It started from, "How can we share what we have?" It really goes back long before Milagro, to my mom and her powerful energy of sharing. She would tell us kids, "Everything tastes better when you share it." And then she'd put ice cream or tacos or frijoles in front of us. Milagro is about providing food for the soul and the spirit, and just like real food, it tastes better when you share it with those who are in need.

Remember the charitable couple from Saint Louis—David and Thelma Steward—who said something that blew my mind: "It's a blessing to be a blessing"? That's right. It's a blessing to be blessed with the resources and the Rolodex to help lots of people and make it work. It's a community of giving that I became a part of, and I can't be fooled by my own ego saying, "Look how special I am and what I'm doing." I have to be open to meeting and supporting other people doing the same work.

Andre Agassi and Steffi Graf started a school in Las Vegas in the middle of the ghetto, and it has almost a 100 percent graduation rate. Some casino owners give money to the school, and there is a benefit concert every year that supports it—I've performed at the concert, as have Tony Bennett and Elton John. There should be schools like that in every city: if there were, I know you'd be able to see the benefits for the people living around them in just a few years. There's a saying I'd like to see again and again—here it comes: Consciousness can be profitable.

I'm high knowing that there is a confederation of hope—Bill Gates, Paul Allen, Matt Damon, Sean Penn, Danny Glover, Bono, Elton John, Angelina Jolie, Morgan Freeman, Ashley Judd, George Clooney, Bruce Springsteen, the Dalai Lama, Archbishop Desmond Tutu, and many others. They are all in line together doing what they really believe in. If only we had the opportunity to bring it all together and implement programs and schools and facilities that can help instill the mechanics of equality, fairness, and justice.

I'm also high that sometimes my phone rings and it's Harry Belafonte. I don't think anyone today has the same spiritual clarity and moral compass that he does—definitely no one has had it as long as he has. He was working against apartheid before Nelson Mandela went to prison, and then he fought to get Mandela released until it finally happened. He is a pillar of our community, a person upon whom people psychologically and morally depend to be present 100 percent and to not be any less than his light.

The first time we spoke I called him Mr. Belafonte, and he told me not to look up to him that way. "You're one of us—we stand equal." I told him I thought I was still getting there, but I could have melted right then when he said that. We talk a lot, and I think part of the reason we got close so fast is because we both carry a flame for freedom and stand up strong in our words and beliefs. The people who produced the Kennedy Center Honors event were thinking of asking Harry to introduce me at the ceremony in 2013, and I spoke with him about it. Harry said, "First I want you to look at a speech on YouTube." It was the one he gave at the NAACP dinner honoring Jamie Foxx and others, and he spoke up about gun control and racism: "The river of blood that washes the streets of our nation flows mostly from the bodies of our black children."

It was true what Harry said, and I was honored that he agreed to introduce me in the end. My friend Hal Miller gave me advice: he said that I was going to Washington to be honored by the nation and that this was not the time or place to go to war. "Enjoy and savor the experience," he said. He suggested that I ask Harry to tone it down a bit, too. I told Harry, "Let's take off the war paint." Harry said, "All right—but not all of it."

You can watch Harry's introduction at the Kennedy Center Honors online—including what he said about me and controlling Mexican immigration. He decided to go for the laughs, but he still got his message across. I love his spirit and what he did that night. I'm very proud to call him a friend, and we've done a lot of work together, especially in supporting South Africa.

I think sharing and supporting are always about equality and justice. They are blessings—not something to be sold or kept away from people. If that's being political, that's okay. Mr. Belafonte—I mean, Harry—can't be the only one speaking out.

I was once working with the actor Morgan Freeman against an anti-immigration law in Atlanta, and he said most people don't understand that when politicians pass laws like that, they prevent people from contributing to the community and making it better for everybody. He was right—for society to grow, it must change. Growth means change, and it should be the same for everybody.

At the White House for the Kennedy Center Honors I was talking about this with Shirley MacLaine, and suddenly she stopped me. "What did you just say?" I said, "Patriotism is prehistoric." She nodded her head. "Is that expression yours?"

I think what I was saying resonated with Shirley because she's a forward-thinking person. I mean, we do need to upgrade the software in our brains and start looking at our planet from the aerial view. Even though you may not ever travel outside your hometown or even your neighborhood, you still are living here in a world that is all connected. It's there for you to know and realize and hear—the Universal Tone, the sound vibration that reminds us that distance and separation are all an illusion.

To this day I detest anyone who tries to indoctrinate others into hating people because they are different and trying to get ahead and uplift themselves. I detest it as much as I did when some Mexicans were trying to get me to hate gringos. That's what they tried to tell me in Tijuana, and I didn't buy into that lie, either. We're all people. The other stuff—like flags, borders, third world, first world—that's all illusion. I like the idea of one global family under a single flag: a sun and a silhouette of a woman, a man, a little girl, and a little boy. All this other stuff keeps us stuck in the same place we were ten thousand years ago: Neanderthals fighting over some damn hill.

Any father can see himself in his little girl or boy. I think each of my children inherited a part of me, and then it got amplified. I also think each one of them—Salvador, Stella, and Jelli—have supreme conviction, like their grandmother Josefina. Sal is about respect and spiritual commitment. Jelli is political, the fighter for rights. She knows history and works in the Santana office with the archives. Stella always has something strong to say—she's okay with the spotlight.

We used to call Stella CNN because she was always the first one jumping up to tell me everything when I came home. She'd be sucking her thumb, scratching her eyebrow, and talking: "And then you know what happened?" I would say, "No, but I'm sure you're going tell me." And then we'd hear about it in full detail. Stella was the one, if she thought she smelled any grass being smoked, who'd threaten, "I'm going to tell Mom!"

Stella's my Josefina—the one who's going to test you—more than Jelli and much more than Salvador. She's also so like me in her feelings about school and church. Once I got a phone call from a teacher at the Catholic prep school that Stella was going to at the time. "I'm sorry, Mr. Santana, we seem to have a problem with Stella. As you know, we are a Catholic high school, and we teach Bible study. Today we were reading about Eve being made from Adam's rib, and right out loud Stella started arguing about the passage—saying things like, 'You guys don't believe this stuff, do you?'"

That's my girl. Then the administrators asked me to come in to the school about this one morning, and even though I usually am up late, I got myself there at 7:30 a.m. We didn't really talk that much about Stella, but they showed me around the school for forty-five minutes, and then I knew what was coming. They showed me a space where they hoped to build a new gym, and would it be possible to do a few concerts to raise some money? Or maybe I could donate the money?

I was driving back home and was in the middle of the Golden Gate Bridge when I got a call from Stella. "Dad, what did you tell them?" She was asking about her argument over the Bible—she didn't know about the fund-raising pitch. I told her I had the same answer to both things we discussed—no, I wasn't going to reprimand her for questioning their beliefs, and when they asked for a donation I said, "Thank you for taking the time to show me the school. I have two questions—you do get tuition from all the students here, right? Also, I saw a huge photo of the pope when I came into the school. The Catholic Church is worth billions—can you ask him?" The principal said that for some reason or another they'd had an official divorce from the Vatican. I said, "Didn't you get any alimony?"

The way I'd summarize Stella is that she was born to be the center of attention in the way she looks and holds herself, but at the same time she wants to be invisible. I'll tease her and ask her how she can make that incognito thing work. She'll just raise her hand and hold it to my face—"Talk to the hand." I'm always learning new ways of communicating from my kids.

Jelli is the hippie of the family, the one who wants to help save the world. She called me the other day, and she was so excited—"I'm with Angela Davis!" She was at a lecture, and they had just met. Later Jelli told me that Angela had told her something that really stayed with her, something about having had more courage when she was young. I said, "Hmm. What do you think about that, Jelli?"

Jelli's deep-rooted and no-nonsense. She's a deep thinker, and she has a way with words. She loves Dolores Huerta. She also got arrested for trespassing last year at a protest in honor of Trayvon Martin. She got handcuffed, and we had to bail her out. I don't know if she'll do it again, because that was pretty intense, and you don't want that on your record. But Jelli is Jelli.

When Jelli graduated from junior high school, all the students had to speak and quote somebody, and she got up and said: "I'm the one that's got to die when it's time for me to die so let me live my life the way I want to." I remember thinking, "Dang!" She was quoting Jimi Hendrix. Jelli's going to be a tough cookie. I remember looking in her eyes when she was born and thinking, "This one is really going to be intense—she has a different kind of thrust about her. She has the capacity to make a worldwide impact with whatever it is that she decides to be and do." She hasn't let me down yet.

My kids, when they come into a room, they bring the light with them. When I talk to them individually or collectively, they aspire, as we all do, to make this world a better place to live. I love them for that.

In the late '90s, my dad began to play music less and less often. He still liked to walk and had never learned to drive a car. He also liked to listen to his music on cassettes. I think one of the best gifts I ever gave him was a Walkman—he would walk back and forth, listen to his music, and then transcribe the songs onto paper. I would visit my dad, and we'd sit on the sofa together. He'd reach out to hold my hand, and his hands were just like John Lee Hooker's—incredibly soft. He used to touch my fingers and say nothing. That's how we communicated at the end. José died on November 1, 1998.

When the end came I was by his bedside, watching and waiting, as everything started to shut down. The spirit stayed strong while the body got weaker and weaker. I went through that with my dad, then with my mom in 2009, and just this year—2014—with Armando. They all started to look like babies after they're born: wrinkled and nearly hairless. They were filled with a light that got brighter and brighter. I wasn't afraid, and I didn't cry—it was time for each of them. I sat with them and held their hands and told them it was all right for them to move on if they wanted to. Everything would be okay here.

I've seen a lot of people crying. The only times I cried were at memorial services for Bill Graham and Tony Williams, maybe because their deaths were unexpected. I don't remember crying for my mom or my dad—I think because I had a chance to say everything I wanted to say to them. When it's my time to leave I pray that I have the strength to accept that all the things I had—my body, my skills, my brain, and my imagination—were borrowed from God. When he wants them back I'll say, "Thanks, man, for letting me have fun with all this, because I really did."

The last time I saw my dad clearly and closely was in a dream I had around a year and a half after he died. He was on a mountain, wearing his favorite blue jacket. I was in a car with my brother Jorge. "There's Dad! Stop the car!" I ran up to him, and he was looking away, at a river that was bright and sparkly, like it was made of diamonds.

"Dad!" I really grabbed him because if I didn't, I thought I might wake up and lose him. He turned around, and I could smell his scent. I felt his skin next to mine. Before I woke up, he looked at me and said, "He's calling me. I need to go to him now. I need to tell you that I didn't understand a lot of things that you did or said, but I want you to know that I do understand now why you are the way you are."

CHAPTER 22

I'm not a big fan of awards shows, whether I'm watching them or in them—all the performers are going for the big bang, the big moment when they get to bring down the house. Too many times you can feel that desperation—"This is it, man. I got to take it to the top!" It's the same kind of desperation felt by those guys who get to sing the national anthem, which is so difficult to sing because it's such a strange song. I was watching an NBA game sometime in the '90s, and I remember a guy who was dressed in a red suit and was a sports star who was not known for his singing at all who got up there and said, "Are you all

ready?" like he was going to knock it over the fence. I was thinking that was a pretty cocky thing to say, but now you'd better bring it like Caruso, my friend.

I knew he was in trouble from the first note, because he started much too high—I was thinking he'd need an express elevator to get to the "rockets' red glare," you know? I believe if you're going to go for the moment it should be the same moment you try to hit every night—success comes from lots of practice and supreme confidence in knowing who you are.

I've gotten better at playing awards nights and TV shows and knowing what to say when I'm asked to say a few words. I like it best when the band gets to play—I'm proud that Santana will bring it in one take, no matter when the red light goes on. We always know what we're doing and what we're going to sound like.

I also like some moments when it's not Santana—it's Carlos with somebody else, such as the time I got to play "Black Magic Woman" with Peter Green when they inducted Fleetwood Mac into the Rock and Roll Hall of Fame in 1998. I was proud Santana got in the year before, but that was also when I gave them hell for not already having Ritchie Valens in there. I mean, what's rock and roll without "La Bamba"? Rock and roll doesn't mean white and popular—it means forever relevant. Ritchie was finally inducted in 2000.

I'll tell you one of my all-time favorite moments. In 2004 I was being honored with a Latin Grammy Person of the Year award in Los Angeles. It was the usual scene—famous people in tuxedos and long dresses getting out of limos; lots of speeches and ovations. Quincy Jones and Salma Hayek presented me with the award, and before I even started talking someone yelled, "That's my brother!" It was Jorge. The way he said that out loud and straight from the heart was so endearing I almost lost it.

Please don't ask me to walk the red carpet. I did it for Deborah when her book came out—and I would do it anytime for Cindy. But most times when I show up to these kinds of awards shows, I go through the kitchen and greet the cooks and waiters and dishwashers. I still remember the feeling of my fingers in that warm greasy water and my hands getting all wrinkly.

And don't ask me to sing the national anthem. I get invitations all *the time to play it on the guitar; all I can do is try to play it as well as Jimi did. That guy who sang it at the NBA game? Clive introduced me to him one time at a* Supernatural *party—he was standing there with the saxophonist Kenny G. I didn't laugh or smile, but I was going crazy telling my brain not to think about what I felt about smooth jazz and that performance at the basketball game. My inner voice said, "Just don't go there, man."*

I n 1997 I started to have a feeling that I was pregnant with something new—I had a new album inside me, and it was going to be something special. At that time I was going to call it *Serpents and Doves,* and it was going to consist of singles—the kind of songs that grab you immediately, something powerful with a message that can uplift and teach. It was time for some new music for the new millennium.

That year I was asked to speak in a documentary about Clive Davis and his philanthropy. I hadn't seen or talked to Clive in more than twenty years at that point, but I knew that since CBS let him go in '73 he had started his own record company called Arista and he'd had hits with people like Barry Manilow and Whitney Houston and Aretha Franklin. I also had heard about his philanthropic work because of what we were doing with the Milagro Foundation—we were all in the same world.

I said I'd be happy to say a few words about Clive. "I'm going to tell the truth: the guy is really important to the music world and the well-being of people, too." The producers sent a crew with a camera, and when Clive saw the interview I did he called me up. "Hey, Clive, how are you, man?"

"Carlos—thank you for what you said. What's going on—what are you doing now?"

It was a good question. I hadn't made a new Santana album in more than four years. "I'm trying to get out of my contract with Island Records. I owe them two more albums."

"Well, as soon as you're out of it, call me."

By this time, Island was just part of the big salad at PolyGram, and it felt like Chris Blackwell was on his way out, so I was going to be stuck there in limbo with nobody. Chris heard I wasn't happy, so he came to see Santana play in London, and he knew that the group was kicking booty as much as we ever did. Then he flew out to Sausalito to meet with me. We met at a restaurant called Horizons. He was going to try to convince me to stay. I remember he had to take a phone call, and when he came back he was complaining that he was having trouble with the new configuration at the record company. "They won't spend the money to make sure I have good phone communication with my people."

I was thinking, "Dang! What kind of message is that? Now he's going to try and convince me to stay?" I didn't want to take any more of his time or mine, so I jumped in.

"Chris, I respect you, so I want to be really up front with you. I have deep admiration for everything that you've done with Bob Marley and Steve Winwood and Baaba Maal and so many other musicians from Africa, Haiti, and around the world. To me you're an ally and you're an artist. But I know I have a really good album coming—I can feel it right here in my belly. It's really important that I don't give it to a label that's going to let it sit in the back of some warehouse and end up being a tax deduction that nobody is going to hear.

"From one artist to another, let me go."

Chris looked at me, and he looked at the ceiling for a while. He could see I wasn't going to change my mind. Finally he said, "Carlos, tell your lawyer to call my lawyer. You're free." Just like that. He could have asked me to pay for the albums I still owed him or charged that amount against *Supernatural* when it came out—but he didn't. He let me go with no strings attached, in a way that had a lot of integrity. For that I'll be forever grateful to him—you could say that the first person responsible for creating *Supernatural* was Chris Blackwell.

The other initiator who brought me together with Clive and must get credit for making *Supernatural* happen is Deborah. Once

I was free from Island, she was the one who said, "Okay, now you have to get back with Clive. It could be a good opportunity for you to hook up with him again and maybe get back on the radio."

Radio? I remember wondering whether that was still around and whether it mattered anymore. It had been so long since Santana had any music on the radio. There was part of me that was thinking, "I just don't have the wherewithal to understand radio now." Not that I really did in the beginning, either.

I resisted calling Clive at first, because our last interaction had been way back in 1973, and Clive hadn't been happy with the direction of Santana at the time. I knew that to work with Clive now would mean more than just discussing a song or two and then saying, "See you later — I'll send you the album when we're finished." But Deborah told me to hear what Clive had to say. She was the key to us getting back together. She helped me get out of my own way when an angel was trying to help me.

I called Clive and invited him to come hear Santana at Radio City Music Hall. I stopped the show at one point and acknowledged him from the stage. "Ladies and gentlemen, we have in the house someone who, like Bill Graham, is an architect of this music. Without him it would have been really difficult for you to know who Janis Joplin, Sly Stone, and Simon and Garfunkel are — and a lot of other bands, too, including this one here. His name is Mr. Clive Davis." It felt good to do that: it was the first time I had the chance to publicly acknowledge him that way. The audience gave him a standing ovation.

We talked after the concert. There really were only two questions: did we want to work together? And if so, how would we do it? Clive said something I liked — he was very direct, and he used a very spiritual word. "Do you have the willingness? Do you have the willingness to discipline yourself and get in the ring with me, to work together when I start calling everybody in my Rolodex? Will you trust me?"

He explained that he wasn't into doing just another Santana album — he wanted hits. Anyone who has worked with him knows that Clive Davis only has one thing on his mind—it has to be number one on the radio every time. The message was that he would be involved from top to bottom—picking out songs, suggesting things in the studio, and deciding on the promotion strategy.

Clive told me something else. Even before we got together, he'd spoken to a bunch of musicians he was working with and asked them, "Would you be interested in working with Carlos Santana? Do you want to write with him?" I was surprised, because I was thinking he might have gone to some classic rock people—people from my generation. In '95, we had done a tour with Jeff Beck that was great, and Santana—the original lineup—had been inducted into the Rock and Roll Hall of Fame in '97. I was thinking old school, but Clive said, "Yeah, Lauryn Hill from the Fugees, Rob Thomas from Matchbox Twenty, Dave Matthews, Eagle-Eye Cherry—all those incredible artists and musicians, they want to work with you." I knew the names and some of their music, and I liked this idea.

"They want to bring it to me, help get Santana back on the radio? Okay, then—let's do this." We signed with Arista.

Later, Clive told me that what persuaded him to do the project was that when he started making phone calls to see who'd be interested, everybody said yes. "I'm not lying—everybody. I knew I was going to do something with you, because no matter who I went to, the answer was yes."

I was excited, because I had already started recording. Some of the songs on *Supernatural* I'd been wanting to record even before we talked. You can guess which ones. They sound like typical Santana, the kind my dad would have picked out: "(Da Le) Yaleo" and "Africa Bamba." Clive got more involved with the sessions over time because of the collaborations and because of who he is and how he works—he can be hands-on, with supreme dedication to details such as song form and the match between musicians and producers. I had worked on collaborations before, but this was a Santana album that would have different groups and different producers on each track, depending on the style and direction of each song. That was a new thing for us.

I was blessed at the time with an amazing band—CT was with me, as were Benny and Rodney Holmes, who is a superb drummer with really incredible energy, a killer-diller. It was an honor to create *Supernatural* with him and some of the other people in Santana, as well as with the many other musicians who came in for each track.

I have to stop and focus on Rodney and some other drummers for a moment. Rodney is one of those musicians who is the whole package: he's smart and can listen and react, and he has the right combination of chops and musicality. I first saw him play in a New York City club—I noticed that the pianist Cecil Taylor was there and went crazy just checking him out. Wayne Shorter called him Rodney Podney and put him in his band in 1996.

I'm particular about drummers. I make no apologies for that, because I've known for a long time that for Santana to be Santana we need a drummer with a nice fat groove and fearless drive—and the ability to listen and learn, to get into the music and make it spark. Just before Rodney we had Horacio "El Negro" Hernandez, who brought a strong Cuban feel, and a few years after Rodney, Dennis Chambers came into the band. Dennis is maybe the best power-groove drummer on the planet right now—such a serious pocket. He's an institution unto himself—just mention his name and most drummers will get down on their knees to pay respect. Dennis was with Santana longer than any drummer—I think he intimidated some of the guys in the band at first because of his reputation, but as they got to know him they realized that he loves to joke and is very easy to hang with. Funny thing is that I met Dennis when he was playing with John McLaughlin in the '90s. Right in front of John he said, "So when are you going to call me?"

That was one of the most important signatures of Santana through the years—a flexible drummer with a serious pocket and powerful drive, and two percussionists who can play anything and make it all happen together. We kept that sound for *Supernatural*.

Clive would call me. "I have a song for you. I'm coming over." Or he'd say, "Wyclef Jean has something he wants you to hear." Wyclef showed up and sang the song right there in the studio. He came in and walked up to me and put his face close to mine. It was like he was reading a musical score in my eyes—the next thing he was showing us the words to "Maria Maria" just as if he knew all about my family watching *West Side Story* and what that movie meant to Mexicans like us.

Clive could really get into the details. One time in the studio we were recording a tune, and he went right up to one of the singers. "Make me feel it. Make me feel it *now,* do you hear me?" His veins were popping out. I was like, "Oh, damn." I didn't know this side of Clive—I never saw it back in 1973! But he was right—that's the same thing I ask for from singers: don't be selling something, offer your heart. It impressed me that Clive could hear the difference. The singer looked at me like, "What's going on?" I was thinking, "You should have brought it in the first place, man."

The sessions were fun because they were all different. New people were coming into the band, such as "Gentleman" Jeff Cressman on the trombone, and I was getting to meet more musicians than I usually would. There were two I got to know really well and I'm still very close to—Rob Thomas and Dave Matthews. They're both people who are very present with their music and their spirit, and they're dedicated to both the spiritual and the outer realms. They want to make this world beautiful, and I think Clive knew that about them when he put us together.

The last two songs that we made for the album were "The Calling"—the blues workout with Eric Clapton—and "El Farol," which has a melody that Sal helped write and is really a testament of the love that my son and my father had for each other.

By the time we started recording, I had a name for this album: *Mumbo Jumbo*. I liked it because there really was a Mumbo Jumbo—an African king. We even had the artwork ready for the cover—a painting called *Mumbo Jumbo* by the artist Michael Rios, who designed many of the T-shirts I like to wear.

But when we were down to the last song, Clive told me, "You know, Carlos, I'm going to have to respectfully disagree with you. Most people think that 'mumbo jumbo' is a negative thing, like magic words that aren't really magic, which is not what you want. Also, I think the press would have a field day with that name, and not in a complimentary way." I said, "But Mumbo Jumbo was a real dude, you know—he was historic, and he healed people." Clive said, "Yeah, okay, but...well, whatever it is, we need to go to press pretty soon."

We came up with *Supernatural*, which has two meanings—"mystical" and "*extra* natural." I was definitely okay with the invisible realm and with being very authentic. Plus it did bring to mind Peter Green and his instrumental "The Supernatural"—that's a tune I still love. So okay, Clive—call it *Supernatural*, then.

Clive called a meeting when the album was done to get the troops ready, and he wanted me there. I was in his office with all the soldiers and warriors who were going to push the album— promotion people, marketing people, publicists. Clive played the whole album, and they gave me a standing ovation. I said that I was really grateful to Clive and to each of them because I knew that was the first time we were working together. Then I talked about the music. I said I tried to make sure that each note I played was as genuine and as fresh and as dangerous as a first French kiss in the backseat of a car—as fresh as the eternal now.

Suddenly Clive said, "Hey, Carlos—I'm very sorry for interrupting, but you just said something that I think says exactly what I feel about this album. Everyone knows you have a long history, but that's not what is most special about this music. It's so new and different, just like you were saying, and that's what people need to know. We've got to work on it like it's your first time making music." I was thinking the same thing Bill Graham said: "Didn't I just say that?"

Clive and I were really on the same page with *Supernatural*, all the way. He made sure that the world knew *Supernatural* was coming soon, in June of 1999, with magazine ads and billboards in Manhattan and Las Vegas. We were on tour that summer with Dave Matthews, and I remember Dave was always talking about how much support we were getting from Arista, and he was being very supportive too.

Dave really believed in the music—he came onstage one night

in Philadelphia and introduced us, and we played "Love of My Life" together, and the audience loved it. We had written that one together—he came up with the words, and I got the opening part from a Brahms melody I had heard on the radio. After I went to Tower Records and sang it for the sales guy in the classical department, he recognized it right away. I got the CD, and Dave and I built the song around it.

I loved the way Dave shared his audience with me—talking to them about the music we had just made and opening his heart about how he felt. That was what I try to do with my own audience—putting stretch marks in their brains, opening some ears. That was the first time I really felt that this new music was going to be big—when the audience loved it. Just a few days after that Philadelphia show we were playing at the Meadowlands arena in New Jersey, and Dave looked up and saw an airplane pulling a gigantic banner that said THIS IS THE SUMMER OF SANTANA. He said, "Clive really likes you, man. You guys got it going."

Clive had been saying that even before the album came out: "Carlos, this isn't going to be just one or two million sold. This is going to really, really be something." Then the music came out, and "Smooth" started slowly, but pretty soon it took off like a rocket. *Supernatural* starting selling hundreds of thousands of copies a week, and Clive would call me wherever I was and give me the updated sales numbers. I was in a taxi one time, and he was on the phone saying, "Carlos, they're playing your music *everywhere*."

I was having trouble hearing him. "I know, Clive—it's on the cab's radio right now."

It went crazy, just crazy. Then "Maria Maria" came out, and it pushed sales to another level—even higher—and it just never came down.

The Santana lineup on the first *Supernatural* tours was on fire—we had CT, Benny, Rodney, and Karl, plus the horn section with Bill Ortiz and Jeff Cressman on trumpet and trombone. Because of them we were able to do some melodies from one of my favorite Miles albums—his sound track to the 1958 film *Elevator to the Gallows.* We also had René Martinez, who is a classical and flamenco guitarist who actually was our guitar tech, but he played with such dignity and elegance that we gave him a feature spot just before we did "Maria Maria," and he'd bring the house down.

We crossed paths with Sting in Germany in 2000 at a few festivals, and he was scheduled to go on after us, but the first time he heard us, it was obvious he was impressed. Sting told me this in my dressing room one night when I was having a beer with my friend Hal Miller, who can be a real funny guy sometimes. "Carlos, who the hell is that drummer?"

"That's Rodney Holmes from New York. He played with Wayne Shorter and the Brecker Brothers."

"He's amazing!" Sting said. "And who the hell is that guitarist?"

"Oh, that's René Martinez, my guitar tech."

Sting got quiet for a second. "Wait: he's your tech? Unbelievable."

Like clockwork, Hal stepped in and said, "Yeah. Wait till you hear the drum tech sit in—his name is Elvin."

Sting just started laughing, and then we all did. That really was an incredible lineup, and I'm proud that many of them are still playing with Santana.

It's really hard to describe how it feels when something hits that big, all around the world, and you're in the middle of it. It's like being that cork floating on a big ocean wave—how much am I controlling, and how much is controlling me? Every day the ego games have to be checked, and you have to find your balance again.

In February of 2000, Clive told me that *Supernatural* had been nominated for ten Grammy Awards. Deborah started calling me a new name even before we got to the show. "So, Mr. Grammy, how many do you think you'll win?" The kids were like, "Yeah, Dad, how many?" I was feeling that I'd be lucky and happy with one. That's why, when I won the first one during the event that takes place in the afternoon, I thanked everyone I could—Clive, Deborah, my father and mother and the kids. When I won the next one,

CARLOS SANTANA

I was thanking my siblings and the musicians and songwriters. By the time of the evening event, which was on TV, I felt like one of those dogs playing fetch with a Frisbee, and it became something to laugh about: winners in other categories, such as classical music and country, started thanking me for not doing an album in their genres.

The whole thing was a blur, really. The two things that I was most proud of were playing "Smooth" onstage, with Rob Thomas singing and Rodney Holmes bringing everything he had. I hit that first note, and everyone in the whole place jumped to their feet. My other favorite moment was when Lauryn Hill and my old friend Bob Dylan presented the Album of the Year award—that was the eighth and last Grammy that *Supernatural* won. They opened the envelope, and all Bob did was point to me—no words. I got up to accept it, and suddenly it was clear what I had to say.

"Music is the vehicle for the magic of healing, and the music of *Supernatural* was assigned and designed to bring unity and harmony." I thanked the two personal pillars who first came to mind: John Coltrane and John Lee Hooker.

I have so many thank-yous to give, and a big one is to Deborah for helping me see the anger that was still inside me when I first went public in 2000 about being a victim of molestation. I hate that word—*victim*. I'm not someone who would walk into a room and say, "Hi, I'm the guy who was molested." *Survivor* is better.

It used to piss me off, what had happened to me in Tijuana, and it pissed me off that I didn't have a support system to protect me. At the same time, why didn't I say something about the abuse myself? So it was anger and guilt and blame, spinning one to the other to the next, and it felt like a ball and chain. Even when I didn't know what to call it, I knew I wanted a higher level of consciousness because I could tell that low consciousness is always dragging a ball and chain.

I think all people have something from the past, some pain or suffering that they must deal with, a negative energy that they need to transform and direct toward a place and time where it's not hurtful to themselves or anyone around them. You have to heal yourself, and one thing I've learned in all my years on this planet is that if you want to heal something, you can't do it in the dark. You have to bring it into the light.

That was when the angel Metatron said to me that it's a must— I had to speak publicly about my past.

Metatron is the archangel whom I spoke about in all my interviews that year, the one who had promised to put my music on the radio and make it heard more widely than it had ever been heard before. "We kept our promise," he told me. "We've given you what we said we would. Now we're going to ask something from you."

To explain it further, Metatron is an archangel, the celestial form of the Jewish patriarch Enoch, who appears in many books. I had been introduced to him in '95, when I found *The Book of Knowledge: The Keys of Enoch,* which at first went *whoosh!*—right over my head. But the closer I studied it, the more I realized that in many ways it was a companion to *The Urantia Book* and continued what I now call a velocity to luminosity—understanding how the physical and spiritual planes, the visible and invisible, are interconnected in so many ways and how certain books can attain a divine synchronicity.

J. J. Hurtak is the author of *The Book of Knowledge: The Keys of Enoch* and a metaphysical historian and multidimensional archaeologist. I met him and his wife, Desiree, around the time of *Supernatural,* and they've become for me thought adjusters and enlightenment accelerators—like Jerry and Diane, Wayne, and Herbie. J. J. created a video of symbolic imagery, light, and color that corresponds to and almost dances with some prayer music by Alice Coltrane when I played them at the same time. That realization led me to introduce the two of them and suggest they work together. The result was an amazing album called *The Sacred Language of Ascension,* which combines Turiya's melodies and organ playing with lyrics and chanting in English, Hebrew, Hindi, and Aramaic and which will, I hope, be released soon.

Back to Metatron—after *The Book of Knowledge: The Keys of*

Enoch, I found *The Revelations of the Metatron,* in which Metatron takes center stage, and after studying that book I found that he would sometimes speak to me when I meditated. One night when I was in London doing promotional stuff for *Supernatural*—TV shows and interviews—Metatron spoke and said, "Now that you're on the radio, you have to remind everyone they have the capacity to make their lives a masterpiece of joy." But there was another thing.

"Then we want you to reveal that you were abused sexually, because there're a lot of people walking around with that same kind of wound. Invite them to look in the mirror and say, 'I am not what happened to me.'"

I resisted. I had to battle myself, because I knew my parents, my kids, and all my sisters and brothers were going to see whatever interviews I did. The *Supernatural* album was the biggest thing that year, so the spotlight was on me. It was time to get out of obscurity and go back into the mainstream—but I told myself, "No; I won't do this."

The angels didn't back down—Metatron required selflessness. There was an interview in *Rolling Stone* and one with Charlie Rose coming up. I didn't want to do it in either interview; I didn't want to do it at all. I didn't sleep for nights thinking about that. Then I did it in *Rolling Stone:* I told the world about what happened to me when I was in Tijuana. No dirty details—just the plain fact that I had been molested as a child and that I am still with purity and innocence.

It's my inner voice—everyone has it. I had it at the Tic Tock, even in Tijuana. It stayed with me. If you don't hear that voice you're like a boat without a rudder. You learn to trust it. When I chanted or when it was quiet and late, I could hear it and would write down what it said. I told *Rolling Stone* about Metatron, too. "My reality is that God speaks to you every day...you got the candles, you got the incense, and you've been chanting, and all of a sudden you hear this voice: *Now, write this down.*"

Supernatural did so well and helped bring in so many new fans that all Santana albums were selling again, including the first album and even *Caravanserai*. *Abraxas* was a hit again—on CD. Young people were checking out our history, our whole catalog. Because of Bill Graham and the "all future formats" clause he had included, we were earning money on those albums at the same rate as when they first came out.

Santana used to travel sometimes in business-class seats and sometimes in economy and sometimes we stayed in motels. After *Supernatural* we were flying first class and staying at really amazing hotels. We started doing business as a partner with other businesses—helping to make their products, not just giving product endorsements. Our first partnership was with the Brown Shoe Company. We created a whole line of shoes under the name Carlos. Now we also make hats and tequila through these same kinds of relationships.

Our deal with Arista had to be redone, because they had gotten us cheap for *Supernatural* and they wanted to be sure they had our next album. The usual way that big record companies followed up a megaplatinum album was to give the musicians a big bonus, which really was an advance that had to be paid back in the end. But if the next album didn't do as well, then the musicians would be stuck owing money until they had another hit. That's what happened with Prince and Warner Bros.

Deborah came up with another idea, and we told our lawyer, "Let's ask for a nonrecoupable bonus—so it's really a bonus, not an advance that we have to earn back." It would be a lot less, but we didn't mind. "Let's see what they offer," we said. Arista made a nice offer, and that's why *Shaman* came out on Arista. Real money is when you don't have to pay it back.

The album changed our live shows, too. Our set lists were changing more and more back to songs. We pulled away from jams, and Chester and I didn't write as much as before. CT stayed with us until 2009, but I think his desire to leave started with the *Supernatural* tours and the changes we were going through. After *Supernatural*, we pursued some albums that came out of the same idea, working with a lot of artists who brought their hearts so graciously to the collaborations—from Michelle Branch and Macy Gray to Los Lonely Boys and Big Boi and Mary J. Blige and all the others.

Everyone wanted Santana on all the TV and awards shows and we were trying to accommodate everyone and it was getting crazy. We even had trouble getting to *The Tonight Show*, so when we finally were able to get to Los Angeles with enough time we scheduled two tapings in one week. It was fun, and I remember Jay Leno was so gracious—he came up to me after we were done to tell me how grateful he was that we had been cooperative, and if there was anything he could do for me I should just let him know.

I knew exactly what I wanted. "Jay, you know I'm a huge fan of Rodney Dangerfield." He'd been on *The Tonight Show* many times, since back in the Johnny Carson days, so I asked Jay if he could get me some of those recorded appearances to watch while we're on the road.

The next day my office got an overnight package containing some DVDs—three hours' worth of Rodney Dangerfield on *The Tonight Show*, from the '60s up to his most recent appearance. He told some of his funniest jokes on that show. Man, I still watch those DVDs—I think my favorite parts are when Rodney would say something that pushed the limits of mainstream TV, and Jay would say something like, "There goes the show!" and Rodney would remind him, "It's okay, it's eleven thirty at night." I love that kind of back-and-forth—Johnny or Jay reacting to him but really just egging him on.

In the summer of 2000 we did *Supernatural* live in Pasadena—all the songs with all the singers—and Arista shot it for home video. They asked me who else I wanted on the show, and I told them right away—Wayne Shorter. He hadn't been on the album, and he was the one who didn't fit into the picture, but I knew Arista had to say yes. Wayne and I decided to play "Love Song from *Apache*," which Coleman Hawkins recorded and which I had played in '94 in Montreux with Joe Henderson.

Wayne played a solo on the tune during rehearsal that caught everyone's ears—everything went into slow motion, and the last note sounded like a falling star. You can hear it on one of the bonus tracks on the DVD. I felt so grateful to be able to do that concert, because everybody who played on *Supernatural* came and brought their best. But Wayne, he's that bright angel on top of the Christmas tree. Here's what he said that night about *Supernatural:* "This kind of album that reaches so many people is not even about the music. This is about social gathering and common knowledge of humans."

I was thinking, "That's exactly right. Woodstock was a gathering, and *Supernatural* is one, too. That's the hope we should have every time we make an album or do a show: I'm playing tonight, and this won't just be about the music—it's a gathering."

Supernatural happened because I didn't step in my own way. I had the willingness to trust Clive, and he got on the phone with everyone and made it happen. For years, everywhere I went I heard Santana—radio stations, shopping malls, movies. The strange thing is that Arista fired Clive not long after *Supernatural* and put L. A. Reid in charge. The deal for *Shaman* was done with him.

Supernatural's biggest impact was on my schedule. The longest time I spent on the road with Santana was from the summer of '99 through 2000, and it required a lot of energy. I found myself doing five to ten times more interviews than I had done for any album in the past. We'd play, we'd travel, and I'd get up in the morning for yet another press conference. I know this is part of the job—it always was. I'm just saying that it was more intense than it ever had been before, and it required me to be present and convincing at a lot of radio stations and to talk about the making of the album again and again. People are curious—they want to know things about their favorite music, and you want to give it to them, but it can take a toll.

The good thing was that Santana is a band that has always been strong and ready for the road, so when *Supernatural* hit, we could handle all the dates that came to us. We weren't coming out of retirement or anything like that. But the tours were longer than five weeks sometimes, so we had to suspend the Santana family rule for a while. At the end of 2000 I made a promise to cool things down for at least a year—we didn't even start recording again for around six months.

Meanwhile, people—a lot of corporations—started dangling obscene amounts of money in front of us just to travel and play just one set. "We'll pay all the hotels, all the air travel, and you get paid two and a half million dollars for forty-five minutes."

No, no, no. I said, "There is no Santana right now—none." I know the expression that you should strike while the iron is hot, but I unplugged the iron. I had to stop. There were problems with my being away so long, and I wanted to keep the family from falling apart. It made me realize that love should not be for sale.

I did an interview with a newspaper in Australia recently, and the interviewer asked me why I was one of the few survivors of the Woodstock family. I said that I had learned to listen to my inner voice, and my voice told me that it was going to help me so that I would not overdose on myself—so that I wouldn't OD on me. Too many people who aren't here today OD'd on themselves.

Then I told him, "When you come to my house, man, there's no Santana there. It's just Carlos."

"What?"

"Yeah, there're no Santana photos or posters or gold records in the house. I need to separate the person from the personality." I still have to remind myself to do that. Sometimes it's as Miles said in the liner notes for *Sketches of Spain:* "I'm going to call myself on the phone one day and tell myself to shut up."

Around the time that *Supernatural* came out, this was our domestic rhythm: we were living in San Rafael in a nice house with a hill in front and beautiful hedges and flowers. There was an A-frame building nearby that I called the Electric Church, which was a term I got from Jimi Hendrix. That's where I kept my musical life, where I got phone calls about work and hung out at night when I wanted to play music or listen to recordings or watch basketball or boxing. It was where I kept all my guitars, a Hammond and a Fender organ, drums, congas, and other percussion instruments. It had a special place for my records and audio and video collections. When friends such as Hal Miller and Rashiki would visit, they'd stay in the Church—it had guest bedrooms and a kitchen, too—and I'd come by around ten and we'd make plans for the day or they'd just run errands with me. In the '90s I loved to drive out to Sal's school to pick him up, even after it wasn't cool anymore for me to do that.

About a hundred yards from where we lived was a house we built for Jo and SK, Deborah's parents. My mom and siblings weren't too far away in the Bay Area, so the kids really got to know their family. Our house was all about Deborah and the kids—no Santana stuff. When Jelli and I started hanging out a lot, we'd especially love to watch *MADtv*. I'd tape the episodes, then she'd come over to the Electric Church and laugh till she was rolling on the floor. But if the show got into anything that was too grown-up I'd tell her to cover her ears. Then she'd laugh even harder.

All the kids got into playing music for a while. They studied piano with Marcia Miget, and I used to take all three of them to their lessons. Marcia calls herself a river rat from Saint Louis—she knew all about her city's musical history, including Clark Terry and Miles Davis and Chuck Berry. She taught Sal and Jelli piano, and Stella studied alto sax. I'm happy that I never missed any of their "graduation recitals." I remember Sal doing a great job with "Blue Monk" and Stella playing a Pharoah Sanders ballad with beautiful tone and flow. Only Sal stayed with music, which is absolutely fine. I like the idea that all three of them have known what it feels like to hold an instrument in their hands and make music. Marcia was like a Santana family member for a while—she runs her own school now in San Rafael called Miraflores Academie.

We had a big German shepherd named Jacob—Jacobee, the

kids called him. Sometimes he would get under the fence and go running around the neighborhood and Deborah would call me. "Hey, your dog got out again, and the Smiths want you to get him before he eats their cat, okay?" I'd put down the guitar and stop watching the TV. "Wait: who are the Smiths?" Then I'd go get Jacob.

I loved watching that dog when he was doing the things that made him jump and run around, his tongue hanging out as he was trying to catch up with his breathing. One time I took Jacob and the kids to Stinson Beach, around a half hour away from our house, and the dog found a dead seagull in the sand. It was like he just found a gourmet meal—he jumped on it and bit at it and started rolling in it, man. He needed to get that nasty stink on him.

I was thinking, "Damn. How much do you have to love something to throw your whole body into it like that?" You want it so bad you want to wear its smell. I started to think about how that happens in music—how some musicians go for it, get into a song, and squeeze their bodies in between the notes.

One time Jaco Pastorius and I were playing with some jazz cats at a special session, and the other musicians asked him what he wanted to play. He smiled at me, then said, "Fannie Mae," which is an old jukebox song by Buster Brown—not the kid who lived in a shoe but a blues singer of the 1950s and '60s. The tune is a simple blues with a shuffle. The other musicians either didn't know it or didn't want to play it, but Jaco started it off and got into it just as Jacob got into the seagull on the beach. He was just so into the feel and heart of that song. I kept thinking, "That's the kind of spirit and conviction I want to have in Santana."

I got the kids to jump into the ocean so Jacob could run after them and wash off that seagull funk. It's really something to watch someone be himself.

CHAPTER 23

(L to R) Salvador, Angelica, Deborah,
Stella, and me, 1998.

In 1998, Santana had just gotten into the Rock and Roll Hall of Fame, and in some people's books that meant that our best work had already been done—as a friend said, "You got the stature, now it's out to pasture." You know what Supernatural *was like? It was like getting into the Baseball Hall of Fame, then coming out of retirement and taking your team all the way to the World Series. Retirement? Not yet.*

I've spoken a lot about the phone ringing and hearing Miles or Bill Graham or John Lee on the other end and feeling like that was validation. After Supernatural, *if I had an idea for a special concert or a benefit, or even if I just wanted to give praise to someone, it felt like I could pick up the phone and call anyone. And people called me back. It could be someone at* HBO *or* MTV *or* Rolling Stone. *Or it could be someone in Hollywood.*

It could be Plácido Domingo — we asked him to sing on Shaman, *and he did it in one take. He finished the tune like a bullfighter who had just dealt with the devil and won. I wish I could do a whole album just with him. That cat is brutally good.*

In fact, there's a lot I wanted to do, and now I have — including albums like Guitar Heaven *and* Corazón. *I want to do an album called* Sangre, *which honors my dad, and record it with my children, Cindy, and my sister-in-law Tracy, who's a great singer and songwriter — I call her Sil. And we are working on* Santana IV, *which will finally reunite the guys who are available from the original lineup — Shrieve, Carabello, Rolie, and Schon — and a few guys from Santana today. When we've talked about this there's a different tone in our voices, like everybody is yearning to visit it once more. We've actually rehearsed a few times, and the chemistry was immediately there — a sacredness and a natural chemistry. Maybe we can tour this band together with Journey — each band playing separately, then getting together at the end. I have to give credit to Neal for initiating and diligently pursuing this idea and making me think, "Okay, maybe we can all get back together, jump on our horses, and ride — not into the sunset, but into a new sunrise."*

I can take a deep breath now and say that it's a good time to be alive, because there are very few obstructions and it's not a struggle anymore to manifest music that brings a lot of people together. One of the best compliments I ever received was from the bassist Dave Holland. We met backstage at the Hollywood Bowl one time with Wayne, Herbie, the great Indian percussionist Zakir Hussain, Cindy, and others. Dave said he needed to tell me something, as if he'd been holding on to it for a while. He said, "Every time I've heard your music or seen you in any configuration you always achieve commonality with all people — young

*and old, black, white, and brown." I have a lot of respect for Dave and
for what he had done with Miles and on his own afterward. I was hum-
bled.* "Thank you, man. That means a lot."

*I love creating music that connects as many people as possible, not
only to each other but also to their own divinity. My thing is to use what
I have to try to open hearts and minds and to help people crystallize
their own existence, reach a deeper awareness, and find their real purpose in life. That's it. That's the alpha and the omega.*

When we finally got back into the studio in 2001, the pressure was on to follow *Supernatural* with something that
was just as big. We started working on *Shaman,* and we
had one tune that I knew was going to be as big as anything that
had come before it. "The Game of Love" was not just a great song —
we had invited Tina Turner to sing on it, and what she had done
made it incredible. Unfortunately we couldn't release it at the time,
and then Michelle Branch did a great job with the song, giving it a
different feel, and it became a hit. Still, I'm glad that we were able
to include Tina's version on the *Ultimate Santana* collection in
2007, so people can know why I feel that way about the song.

While we were making that album I'd be in the studio every
day, and it was taxing my brain because I'd be concentrating so
much on each song — getting the mix right and getting all the
parts together. I would get home late and go straight to the Electric
Church. I was still getting late-night calls from John Lee Hooker,
and once I surprised him and called him on his birthday, and he
said, "Man, when I hear your voice, it's like eating a great big piece
of chocolate c-c-cake!" I told him, "Man, it's *your* birthday, and I feel
like you're giving *me* the present."

I came home one night and was so tired that I went straight to
bed instead of going to the Church to wind down. I woke up the
next morning, and the phone rang — someone was calling to tell
me that John Lee had passed the night before. I was numb. I needed
to be alone and let the feelings go through me, to hold a guitar. I

went to the Church and saw the answering machine. I had one message—it was from John Lee, from the night before. "C-C-Carlos. I just wanted to hear your voice, and I wanted to say that I *loves* God, and I *loves* peoples." He hung up, and that was it.

My philosophy is that being conscious means knowing that you are a creator. Yes, there's the supreme creator, but he gave you free will so that you can be the creator of the movie that is your life. Be that creator—work with what you are given.

Around 2003 I went back to Autlán, and this time it was with my whole family—all my brothers and sisters, and my mom in a wheelchair. She was in her glory, because everybody who remembered her made a beeline to her so that they could hold her hand. "Oh, Josefina! We missed you—*te hemos echado mucho de menos.*"

I was there because the town had put up a statue of me— *Supernatural* Carlos, not young, hippie Carlos. I remember I thought it was too big—my hands were huge, and the guitar was not any model that I knew. Maybe it was a one-of-a-kind original.

This was an opportunity to acknowledge and celebrate myself and share who I am with others, but it was also an opportunity not to OD on myself. I still feel like I'm learning to receive and smile and be gracious.

So when I was asked what I thought of the statue, I made a joke about pigeons using it for target practice, and people started cracking up.

On that trip I was overwhelmed with memories of my dad when we were in Autlán and I was very young—riding close to him on the bicycle and smelling that Spanish soap. I was thinking about how it felt to know that he had different eyes for me. But this time I felt proud of it and was not uncomfortable about it anymore.

At one point it suddenly dawned on me that my dad was missing from our group and I just started sobbing. I had no idea that was coming. It was like something had been accumulating since he had died until it had to burst, and I had to excuse myself. I went to the bathroom, and my eyes were all red. I remember I was pouring water on my face when my brother Tony came in and said, *"Está bien?"*

"Yeah, man. I'll be right out."

"Qué pasa?"

"I can't stop thinking that Dad's not here. I'm sorry I didn't do this kind of event earlier."

"No, Carlos, *está aquí*—he's here." The town officials had just put up a big picture of José, and some mariachis came out and started playing music, and there he was.

The town of Autlán put the whole thing together—the statue, the mariachi music, everything. I wasn't involved. The guitar in the statue got stolen a little later because it was just attached, not built in—but it was as big as a sofa, and I guess the thief thought, "How can I hide this thing?" They found it later in a ditch and put it back so that I wouldn't just be playing air guitar.

In 2005 Santana played Mexico City for more than one hundred thousand people in the country's biggest outdoor plaza—Zócalo. I wanted to give the crowd as much of the old Santana as I did of *Supernatural*. To me it felt like Santana and Mexico never got a chance to really get to know each other, so I wanted to show them the full story of the band. We started sounding like Sun Ra—Sun Ra and Jimi Hendrix. People were looking at each other—*"Donde* 'Maria Maria'?" It was a nice break from the stiff *Supernatural* set lists. It was almost like a collective LSD thing, watching the musicians stretching and having fun and playing like kids again. Then we played songs from *Supernatural,* and people were freaking out by then. I found out that in Mexico, when they claim you, they *really* claim you.

These days my set lists are still like that—open and flexible, respecting the different Santanas—from *Abraxas* to *Supernatural* and now welcome to *Corazón.*

By 2003, the Milagro Foundation was five years old, and Deborah and I were constantly looking for ways to utilize energy and to give hope and spiritual support to people. The greatest support anyone can give is to remind people that they're significant and that they have value, that they're a beam of light no matter what they have or don't have. Real philanthropy isn't about pushing money—it's about moving light, and it doesn't matter how many zeros you have to the right in your bank account as long as you have a 1 on the left.

That year Deborah put together a party in our home for Archbishop Desmond Tutu and Artists for a New South Africa to deal with the AIDS crisis that was happening in their country. I had first heard Archbishop Tutu talking on *Larry King Live* around 1983, and he said something really amazing then. He was talking about apartheid and the way the brutal South African government had its knee on the throat of black South Africans, but what was really happening was that black South Africans were looking up at the oppressors and saying, "Join us in our victory—celebrate with us. We've already won." I was like, "Wait a minute: what did he just say?" I heard a song right there.

Twenty years later apartheid was gone, and the African National Congress—no longer a terrorist organization—was running the country. We were dedicating all the profits from the entire Santana tour that summer to ANSA to support organizations fighting AIDS. Governor Brown came to our house with other dignitaries, and Santana played, then Sal played. The archbishop spoke, and everyone donated money to help cover his travel costs. It was maybe the best example of being able to bring together everything I had—my music and shows, my family, my friends and contacts—to help accomplish something that had to be done.

Billy Cosby's wife, Camille, was the connection to ANSA—Deborah and Camille are old friends, and Camille had produced a documentary on the AIDS crisis. When I saw the movie, I said, "Damn. This situation is about as real and desperate as things can be." It was a cycle of neglect that was just getting started and could be stopped with the right medicine and compassion in the right places. Camille's documentary convinced me that the problem would go on for a long time if something wasn't done right away.

In August we were able to present the organization with more than two million dollars, and we stayed in touch with ANSA and Archbishop Tutu. Three years later, in September of 2006, Deborah and I hosted a special event in Beverly Hills to help celebrate the archbishop's seventy-fifth birthday and to talk about the lives that had been saved and what had been done to stop the epidemic. A month later, we went to visit South Africa along with a group of friends, including Samuel L. Jackson, to see what had been done.

I can tell you about meeting Nelson Mandela and other stuff that I will always treasure. But what I will never forget were two things: the first was seeing around fifty people do a traditional dance, way, way out in the rural country, where they didn't have any electricity or running water. As they were dancing, one of them would step out and throw his leg above his head and slam it back on the ground at the same moment as the rest of them were clapping and singing and hitting on the 1. I remember Sal saying, "Not a flam," and he was right. "I know how they're doing that and why it's so tight and synchronized."

Samuel Jackson said, "How, Sal?"

"Two things—it's in their history, in their DNA. It's not last week's beat. And no TVs or other things like that, so no distractions."

The other thing I remember from that trip was going to a clinic and seeing the real faces of AIDS—the people who had been dying but were then recovering. But it wasn't just the sickness—it was the extreme poverty, despair, and sadness. That's what I really felt. I remember that when Deborah, Jelli, Sal, and I were helping to hand out boxes of supplies to the families of AIDS patients, one old lady had been sitting there for a long time by herself, lost in her thoughts, wearing a blank, faraway look. When we came to her, she looked up at Deborah, then at me and Salvador, and slowly became more present. Then she realized that the box of flour, sugar, and canned foods we were holding was for her, and suddenly she started crying.

It's a memory I will never be able to get out of my head. Just thinking about it now still gives me chills—some of us cannot know how lucky we are in this world until we meet someone who has been through devastation and seen what hell looks like. You can't help but think about what we have in this country, and I believe too many people think that opportunity is something you get and then keep to yourself. How did you get it in the first place? You had to take it from someone who didn't want to share it—so now everybody has to do that?

America takes what it wants and says that's the right thing to do without looking at the consequences. But all those justifications come from fear and prejudice. We might like to think that we have God on our side, but if you start with fear, it can only lead to negative justifications and lost opportunities. There's no consciousness in that, nothing divine. Look at all the disasters that have happened recently, such as 9/11, Hurricane Katrina, and Hurricane Sandy. Even then we had trouble getting it together and helping each other. On the government's part, there was more fear—about people taking too much and about who should pay the bill—than there was an effort to do the right thing and help out.

What we need is to be free from fear and prejudice. That's a blessing everyone can use.

In 2006 a few things happened one after the other, even before we went to South Africa. Deborah came out with her book, *Space Between the Stars,* which spoke about her life and our family history and brought many things about us into the light. I supported her and did interviews with her to promote it—that's when I walked the red carpet with her to help celebrate her honesty in writing it.

A few months later, in the middle of summer, her mother passed away. SK was already gone, and I knew Deborah would need some time to heal. At that time we were in the middle of so many things—a worldwide tour as well as the ANSA trip to South Africa coming up.

I had just spoken to Jo a few weeks before—she had called the house one night, and I answered. "Hi, Mom. How you doing? Let me get Deborah." She said, "I'm doing fine, darling—actually, I want to talk to you. I've never said this, but I wanted to tell you that ever since the first day Deborah brought you to our home, you brought me a quality of peace of mind, because I knew that you would always take care of her and protect her."

Deborah and I had been together almost thirty-four years by then. I think the examples of both sets of parents played a role in the way we handled our marriage. They helped us to be wise and not get caught up in little stuff. They also taught us the importance of constant maintenance—paying attention to the inner romance and honoring each other's feelings—because unconditional love comes first before our individual stuff.

Through 2006, Deborah was as busy as I was—taking care of the family, promoting her book, and overseeing Santana Management. As she later told me, I was the one who came up with the ideas and visions for projects, and she was the nuts-and-bolts person: "I'm the one dealing with the agents and lawyers and accountants. I'm watching over everything—the business and the royalties and the houses"—by then we had a house in Maui—"and it's just too much now."

This was in February of 2007, and I remember it very clearly. We were in the house in San Rafael, and I was playing guitar when Deborah came in and started telling me how she was feeling. "Your world is crushing me." That's how she described it. "I need to find myself and do my own thing. I need to take care of me now, because I feel like I'm disappearing in your world."

I said, "Damn, Deborah, what can I do?" and she told me, "You're not doing anything wrong. It's just the way things have come to be. I need to do something for myself now, because I'm sinking under all these duties—taking care of the kids, the business, your family, and my family. I need time away for at least six months. I need you not to call or contact me. I'll be at the office once a week to take care of stuff, but please don't be there when I am."

I did not see this coming, not at all. It was totally out of the blue for me. We had decided to put Santana on hold for most of 2007— no tours or albums, just a few shows—so I was thinking this would be our time together. Deborah could tell I wasn't expecting this. She said, "I know this is a surprise. Why don't you go to Hawaii for a week and see your friend Tony Kilbert, and let's you and I think about things?" So I went to Hawaii.

I was only there a few days with all these thoughts in my head, going through these dimensions of pain and frustration, not knowing what was really happening, when one night a storm came that was brutally loud. It hit the house, and everything was shaking without mercy. I was by myself, facing all these fears, wondering whether any of the windows would break, and when it was finally over and the sun came out the next day I felt so good to be outside and alive that the fear of facing what could really be going on with Deborah was lifted. So I called her that morning and said, "Hey, what's going on?" She said, "I told you: please don't call me for a while." I had to ask, so I did. "Are we getting a divorce?" The tone in her voice changed right away. "Well, do you need to know that now?"

I thought to myself, "Damn." I had not heard that tone many times at all—it sounded like something she had been holding inside for a long time. There was part of me that wanted to say that she always had help in the house and with the kids and that she had people in the office to help her. I had been wanting to say this even before I left for Hawaii, but thought she might not be ready to hear that then, so I didn't say anything. Now I was thinking, "Wait: you knew who I was and what I did before you married me—the music and the touring and the commitments."

By then I could see it didn't matter. For a few days I was hoping that there was still a chance things would get better right away, that Deborah would change her mind about the six-month idea. Even during the following few months I kept hoping that this was just a trial thing. I did what she asked and stayed away and hung out with my friends, who did their best to keep up my spirits. "This is about her, like she told you," my friends would say. "So don't make it about you, man." Still, my mind would not stop going around and around, asking, "What does that mean? What went wrong? Why can't she live with me anymore? Why is it so unbearable? Why, why, why?"

When I got back home, Deborah had moved out, and all the kids were away at school or living their lives, and that was the worst—the darkest night of the soul. Things got really intense—I remember it was a beautiful summer, and I would get up in the morning and the sun was shining and there was an incredible smell of flowers when I'd come into the kitchen, but there was nobody there to enjoy it with, no one to share it with. Things were getting really, really intense. The whole house started to feel like a coffin, and I was the only one in it.

I had my brothers and sisters, who were constantly calling me and checking on me. I had my friends, whom I'd get together with even though I knew I wasn't always good company. I had old friends, such as Quincy Jones, calling. I had one friend who told me it was time to get on a plane with him and go to a place in Brazil, because he had some girls he knew I had to meet. "All you need is some..." I told him, "Thanks, but no thanks. I need that like I need a hole in my head, man."

I remember my mom's reaction was, "What did you do to her? What did you do to Deborah that she would do this?" I said, "Mom, why don't you ask her?" I had enough to deal with just keeping my brain from torturing me, from taking on all that guilt and shame.

It was a few months later, when Deborah and I were talking on the phone, that she said she wanted to talk about what we needed to do now that our marriage was over. That was the first time she used those words. I said, "So you're going to pull the trigger?" She didn't say yes or no, just, "We're going to need to do this, and go through this procedure, and..." I remember asking, "Where are we with love—do you still have any feelings for me?" She said, "Well, I don't need to tell you that." I just said, "Okay."

I never really got a clear "I don't feel anything anymore" or "I'm not in love with you," and what made it more difficult, I think, is that we never really fought or argued or let our emotions go.

But that was when I finally told myself it was over, period— when it's broken, it's broken. We were talking about stuff we needed to figure out so we wouldn't have to do the whole thing through lawyers, and I kept hearing a voice inside saying, "Just ease up on this. Don't fight, don't resist, don't argue, and don't bargain. This is not about money for you, and it never has been. Give her what she wants."

The kids knew about the divorce before anyone else did. They had known about Deborah moving out and getting her own place, and they all had their own way of dealing with it. From the start I told them that I'd be calling and texting them just as much as before, no matter how they felt, and if necessary I was ready to wait for them to get to a point where they could ask me anything they wanted and I would answer as honestly as I could. Even when things were getting bad and I was feeling depressed and angry, my plan was just to believe that anyone can make each day the best day of his or her life, even though it might be in another configuration. I always believed that was the best way to show your kids anything, really—by example rather than by talking.

In a way it was good that they were not around and were doing their own things. Salvador came around a lot to check up on me, and he was like the Switzerland of the situation—very neutral and not taking sides, just wanting to be there for both his mother and his father. It's not that the girls weren't that way, too, it's just that Sal was older and more able to demonstrate wisdom and compassion and fairness. That really affected me and helped a lot. He had really gotten into Keith Jarrett at the time, and he'd come over and play piano and just transport me. Keith was already one of my favorite pianists of all time, and he could be the spiritual deliverer of such romantic, raw, beautiful melodies. There's something very therapeutic and healing about them.

I remember driving through Napa by myself around this time when Keith's version of "It's All in the Game" came on. Suddenly I started sobbing and had to pull over. Whatever I had been going to do wasn't important anymore, so I turned the car around and went home to spend some time alone, look for some inner guidance, and heal some more.

*   *   *

Divorce is a very personal thing, and I had no experience dealing with something like that in public. Talking about stuff that happened to me years ago was one thing, but talking about personal things going on right then—things that can get the TMZ treatment so easily—was another. No one wants to feed that machine. I had the feeling that somehow Deborah and I had earned enough respect from newspapers and TV programs to keep them away during this period—they didn't feel the need to get in our faces about it. I also think we both consciously made a commitment to take the high road for the sake of our kids and our families. When it was finally announced that we had broken up because of irreconcilable differences, I took a long, deep breath. I consider it a blessing that it didn't get played out in the media.

Through the end of 2007 time moved very, very slowly. I was still in recovery, man—it was all a blur of pain. I was doing a lot more inner work, doing what Wayne Shorter likes to call inner gardening—pulling out the weeds. I was reading a lot, just to keep my brain from torturing me with guilt and shame and all that ego stuff, and was finding wisdom in a lot of different books. In one magazine, *Sedona Journal of Emergence,* I found a line from a Persian poem: "The sun will never say to the earth, 'You owe me.'" Can you imagine benevolence or light that is more supreme?

One night around Thanksgiving I lit a candle and started reaching out for help, and that inner voice came back again, saying, "I'm right next to you: isn't that enough? You need to let go of Deborah and your kids. They're fine—I got them, and they're okay. Take care of yourself."

That was around the time I got in touch with author Marianne Williamson. She and I first spoke just before Deborah left, and by the end of that summer, after we were separated, something told me to reach out and see if Marianne could help me. It was like I was scuba diving into a big lake of pain, and I really needed lessons on how to breathe again. She listened to me and heard something in my voice, and right away she referred me to Jerry Jampolsky and Diane Cirincione, who are married and live in Sausalito. Jerry and Diane are therapists who use the book *A Course in Miracles* in their work. They also run a network of counseling centers that help people by giving lessons in spirituality and transformation.

I went to visit Jerry and Diane at their house, and they really saved my life. I remember that the first time we sat down together Jerry asked me to define myself—separate from my siblings and family and friends. I said I saw myself as the one puppy that gets away from the rest of the litter because he's distracted by something to play with, such as a slipper, and then goes from playing with it to tearing it apart with his teeth—*grrrr.*

Jerry said that was pretty interesting. Then he said, "But why don't you see yourself first as a child of God?" It was such a revelation to me, the way he opened my eyes to how far I had drifted away from the path of divinity, especially after the breakup with Deborah. He also opened my eyes to how much I was fighting and struggling with everything, both within myself and within the situation. I said to myself that it had been a long time since I looked at anything from that perspective. Other people may have said something like that to me, but when Jerry said it things really shifted for me, and I began to heal with honesty and an energy I didn't have before. I got back onto the track I had been on before—holding my wholesomeness together.

We began to talk almost every day, reading *A Course in Miracles* over the phone, which became a source of inspiration and guidance, with Jerry and Diane's coaching. We still do it—I think we are on our fourth or fifth reading of the book. They call me every morning between seven thirty and eight, whether I'm at home or on the road, which is amazing to me because sometimes my morning will be the middle of the night in Sausalito! We read the lesson of the day together, lessons that I apply to whatever is going on in my life. It was Jerry and Diane who were finally able to get me past my anger about being molested when I was in Tijuana and forgive the man who did that to me. They asked me to imagine him in front of me, and turn him into a six-year-old child with a divine light shining behind him. I looked at him, forgave him, and sent him into the light, releasing both him and myself from the past. Finally, I could breathe—it felt like that chapter of my life was over.

Jerry and Diane helped me to get to the other side after Deborah left. Meeting them gave me another chance to see that in my life it's always been about recognizing the angels who appear when I need them the most. I was able to get back to the point where I could wake up and be happy with myself. I'm sure that one of the reasons Deborah and I came apart was because it had to be tiring for her to start the day with someone who couldn't accept himself and was creating distance between himself and the rest of the world. Who knows for sure?

It was painful that first year and a half, but life continued. At the start it was especially difficult because Santana was taking a break from the road. I did a few sessions—Smokey Robinson called me and asked me to play on a song called "Please Don't Take Your Love," which I did two versions of, and he took the best from both. In 2008 Santana was back on the road, and that helped me to stop thinking about the past, to be present and to get back into my usual swing.

Seven years later I am now at a point where everything that's left from my life with Deborah, her parents, and my former sister-in-law, Kitsaun, is beauty and blessings. I'm now in a place where I can sincerely give my best to Deborah and say thank you for everything. I can honor her and all that we had and at the same time embrace what has come after—the way I grew and changed and then received Cindy, my love and my wife. I have never been happier in my life than at this moment.

Everything that happened in 2006 and 2007—ANSA and Archbishop Tutu and Deborah—came to mind in 2014, when I went to play in South Africa for the first time. I had visited the country but never played there, and it was incredible. I think the first time playing in South Africa has to be amazing for any musician, especially those who went through the days of apartheid and boycotts and discovering all the great artists who came from there, including Hugh Masekela and Ladysmith Black Mambazo.

I called Archbishop Tutu and asked if we could get together—well, my assistant, Chad, did. We were playing in Cape Town, where the archbishop lives and is building a center for his spiritual foundation; it's one of the most beautiful cities I've ever seen. He invited us to his home, and after we spoke for a little while, I reminded him of something he said recently—that if heaven discriminates against homosexuals he didn't want to go there. I also mentioned that two months after he said that, the pope himself said the same thing, which shows that the archbishop really knows how to use words so people wake up and get the message.

I embrace knowing that his message is for all people and that he's still talking about things that need correcting—he didn't clock out after apartheid was over. It's like what Martin Luther King Jr. said about no man being free until we are all free.

The night before I visited the archbishop, Stella had texted me a photo of my ex-wife, Deborah, meeting the Dalai Lama, and I loved seeing that we were still both on the same path, even if we weren't on it together. I was thinking, "What are the chances of this happening at the same time—that Deborah and I would each meet two of the world's most inspiring spiritual leaders?" Then suddenly I had a vision.

I started to think of who would be able to channel all this energy. What if we could get Archbishop Tutu and the Dalai Lama and the pope and top leaders from the Jewish and Muslim worlds together on a plane? They could travel to places such as Ukraine and Syria and Venezuela—and to places that CNN doesn't even talk about—bringing light into the darkness and dismantling the hate that's starting there before it builds up into wars. I would come along with Santana and we would play, and I'd help recruit other headline groups to join in, too, so that we make world news and can stop the carnage before it has time to happen.

I mentioned this idea to the archbishop and asked if he could imagine doing this and helping us by reaching out to other leaders, such as the pope. His eyes went wide, then he became modest and said, "But why would they listen to me?" That's when my friend Hal Miller, who was with us, stepped in and said what he needed to hear: "Because when you speak, the world listens."

The archbishop smiled, and when we left he asked me to stay in touch about the idea. I know — it's a dream, naive and audacious. But that's the kind of audacity I want to live with. I have faith in the principles of John Lennon and John Coltrane, Jesus and Martin Luther King Jr. I have faith in those who believe with all their being that it's never too late to fix this planet.

CHAPTER 24

Releasing the past: Cindy and me on our wedding day in
Maui, December 19, 2010.

*I was in Sweden recently. It was my birthday, and I was shaving, and in
my eyes in the mirror I could see my parents. "Hi, Mom," I said. "Hi,
Dad." Both of them are gone, but they're still with me and still with each
other. I still get a lot of strength from the loyalty they had to each other.
I remember the way they looked at each other across the room at their
fiftieth anniversary party: the rest of us could have been chopped liver.
That stuff was still there, even after all that went on between them. You
can ask any of us kids—my sisters or my brothers. I don't think any of*

us can remember my parents smooching and hugging. But Mom did get
pregnant eleven times.

One time I walked in on Mom and Dad. I was seventeen, and we
were living in the Mission District. It was after school, and I was in a
hurry to get to my job at the Tic Tock. I opened the door, and they were
in bed. They gave me a look that said, "Not now." I quickly closed the
door, and suddenly everything went in slow motion. Of course! They do
that—there has to be intimacy. I walked out feeling like there was a
warm blanket over me. There is nothing that makes you feel more secure
than seeing your parents in love with each other. Then the whole world
is cool. That's the foundation I wish every child could have and the kind
of love that I hoped to have in my life—a relationship that will endure
and feel like it did on the first day, even on my last.

Around two years after my divorce, I finally took a deep breath and
told myself, "Okay, let's get to the new day. I have no doubt that God
will send someone my way, because I have got to have a queen." I have
all these achievements and a big house and I travel and stay in wonder-
ful hotels—I still receive a lot of blessings and honors. I enjoy abun-
dance and incredible beauty. But it's incomplete unless I have a queen
to share it with.

I n 2009 I was in Las Vegas, and it was a Sunday night. I got a call
that my mom had fallen down and was in the hospital in a coma.
I chartered a flight, and the whole family got together at her bedside. Everybody took turns sitting next to her, whispering in her ear
and saying what we needed to say. "Mom, it's Carlos again. I'm
holding your hand, and I want you to know that I remember everything you told me. I remember you saying that everything I have
belongs to God—my guitar, my music, my sound, my body, my
breath. It's all just borrowed, and when he wants it back, I must
open my hand and give it to him. Remember you said, that, Mom?"

My mom had talked with me about dying a few months
before—she asked, "Are you afraid of death?" I said, "Absolutely

not." She thought about it and said, "Me, neither. But some people die before they're done because they're already petrified by it. They give death too much power."

I asked everyone to hold hands, including Mom's, and form a big circle. Then I said, "Mom, we are all here, and we give you permission to go if you want to go." A few minutes later, she left.

I know lots of people and have lots of friends and relatives, but I have very few *friend* friends—people with whom I share a deep, sincere level of closeness. That's not a complaint. Those few friends are what I call my spiritual support system—they know me and my heart sometimes better than I know myself. The key word is *trust*—I trust them to see things I may not see, and I've learned to pay attention and listen to what they tell me.

After the divorce, I really came to lean on my best friends, and they did not let me down. It's important for me to acknowledge their presence in my life and the fact that they've opened me up to all kinds of fun possibilities with dignity and benevolence and funkiness, depending on their nature—they're all so different.

Gary Rashid—Rashiki, as Armando decided to call him—I've known the longest. He started working with Bill Graham in '73, which meant he was around Santana a lot, and at that point he was just starting to really listen to music and find his way around. By '79 he was one of my best friends and was checking out Little Walter and Slim Harpo and John Coltrane, hearing things in the music I had turned him on to that I had never picked up on. I loved watching him develop to the point where he was teaching me. To this day, when I'm in the Bay Area, one of the most enjoyable things I can do is get into the car with Gary and take an hour's drive along the coast and just listen to Miles.

There's something else about Gary that I embrace: he has a purity and innocence about him—he's childlike, not childish, and he's never callous or overly opinionated. I know I can be like a lion sometimes and roar. He's also like a dove, and I need that around me. And he's a killer tennis player, and nice enough to let me win sometimes.

Tony Kilbert—Brother TK, as I call him—is my anchor in Hawaii. We can hang together at the beach, and he'll snorkel for hours and hours. That's his meditation. He's a tall, good-looking guy who was one of the golden-voiced radio DJs in the Bay Area when we first met in the '70s. I remember the care he put into his questions when he interviewed me. I think his interview with Bob Marley from around the same time should be required listening for any journalist because of the respect and awareness that TK put into it. You can feel how Bob just opens up his heart to him.

TK had a good life and was living in San Rafael, but then most of his family—his mother and aunts—passed away within a five-year period, and he decided to step away from the career stuff and move to Maui. He still works with music and teaches, and he gets involved in fighting for causes that support the natural integrity of the islands and rights of local people. I admire the way he follows his inner voice. We love the same musicians, the same music, and the same life principles.

Hal Miller is my buddy who lives in Albany. He was a doo-wop singer and a drummer, and he's originally from New York City. He saw and heard both Coltrane and Miles playing around town—I love it when he talks about growing up at a time when he got to see these legends and others. I met Hal in the 1980s, and these days he's one of the world's leading jazz video collectors. He has such a dry sense of humor that you can't light a match around him or things will all go up in smoke. Actually I think the word is *irreverent*—nothing is too sacred or holy for him. One time Dennis Chambers got all emotional over the music we were playing and got up from the drum kit for a minute, which was the first time I'd ever seen him do that. Later we were talking, and Hal said, "Oh, that's not the first time I've seen Dennis crying. The last time was when he came home after a tour and walked in the house and said, 'Honey, I'm home,' only to find me sitting in his living room in his favorite chair and wearing his robe!" Man, we were all on the floor after that, including Dennis. Hal comes up with those one-liners and pops people with them all the time.

That's one of the reasons I like to have Hal come on the road with Santana. Sometimes he'll sit in on congas, but he also knows our history and all the musicians personally. He can hear the band with precision and elegance from year to year. I love his ears and the way he finds the words to describe what is working with our music and what can be better. One thing, though — Hal does not hang with anything too spiritual or metaphysical. If the conversation gets too cosmic, he'll say he needs to leave the room, and that's okay. I know his spirit, and that's good enough for me.

One more best friend I have to mention is Chad Wilson, my first security guy, who came to Santana around the time of *Supernatural,* when everything exploded and got so big. He's from Ohio, and I remember the first time we went to Paris and had a day off, we were walking around, and he was like Dorothy out of Kansas, just frozen when he saw the Arc de Triomphe for the first time. Then he'd snap back, like he needed to be alert, and I was looking at his eyes and laughing. "Go ahead, man. Eat it all up — I'll watch out for us."

Chad's been amazing to watch. At first he was a Metallica fan — which I am, too — but now he'll put on *Kind of Blue* and really get into it. Like Rashiki, he came a long way, and he had to be the band's punching bag for a while but he caught on in so many ways. By being around us, he realized that there are many dimensions to expansion, and he's allowed himself to grow fearlessly.

Chad does much more than security now. He's my personal assistant, companion, and part of the family — he's godfather to Jelli. The funny thing is it took me around six months to be able to say his name right — my mom never could, so she just called him Ramón. When he came with me to visit her she'd say, *"Oye Ramón, quieres unos chiles rellenos?"* — you want some chiles rellenos? And that was it — he's been hooked on Mexican food and he's been Ramón ever since.

They say that if you go swimming in the sea and get wiped out by a big wave and you're all confused, the thing to do is find the light and swim toward it. When I kept going up and down after my divorce, the strength and gentleness that Chad, Rashiki, TK, and Hal all showed me kept me from going the wrong way and getting lost in myself. I learned to recognize how fortunate I am to have these friends, and their constancy and their strength of character, around me. From them I learned to take words of advice even when I may not have wanted to hear them.

If you had asked me about Las Vegas even a few years before I started playing there regularly, in 2009, the only thing I would have thought about it was that it was home to the Rat Pack and was a place for square people hanging in lounges. Later came performers such as Donnie Osmond, Wayne Newton, and Tom Jones. I would never have equated Las Vegas with the music of John Lee Hooker. The first time we played there was in 1969, with the Grateful Dead, and it was scary because you could feel what people who lived there thought about long-haired people—they weren't letting hippies get anywhere near the casinos back then. It was a place to do a one-nighter and then get the hell out.

But things have changed in Las Vegas, and most of the people visiting there grew up with Santana—it's their music. That's the thing: I didn't realize that people who would come to hear us play in Las Vegas didn't necessarily live there. They would come from all over the world. Also, when we play there now it's not like the old days, when you were nothing but background music that people could talk and drink over. Now we're the main attraction, and what better place to deliver a dose of a spiritual virus that people can bring home with them along with the T-shirts and caps and whatever they win in the casinos? I really find no more of a barrier to what I'm doing onstage with Las Vegas audiences than I do anywhere else.

The Las Vegas thing for Santana started in 2009 at the Hard Rock Hotel, and by 2011 the House of Blues offered us a deal to do our show there. The House of Blues honors us by presenting us in a way that is not shallow or synthetic—the facilities and technical people are professional, and they give us the kind of promotional support that the top acts in Las Vegas get. The same was true of the Hard Rock Hotel. The audiences are able to get up close, and I like that. In some ways it's better than the stadiums and arenas because I can hear it if they want to get intense or request songs—I can know how they're feeling.

When we moved to the House of Blues, we realized that the city could work not only as a headquarters for the band but also that it made sense for me to start living there. There were a number of reasons—we could save money by not being on the road all the time and not having to pay travel costs. The Mandalay Bay casino, which is in business with the House of Blues, provides hotel rooms and meals and airfare to get us there. Also, as a Nevada resident, I'd be paying a lot less tax than I did in California. The point again is not just about saving money but, as with the Milagro Foundation, to control where the money goes so that it doesn't just feed the government but invests in real people and real institutions that can be of service to humanity in general.

The person who discovered this and made it all happen is Michael Vrionis, who's now my manager. After the divorce, when the position of CEO of all of Santana's business needed to be filled, Michael was able to step in and not be overwhelmed by the job. I knew his plan was a good one, because our lawyers and accountants immediately called me to say that I had lucked out—that this idea would save us a lot of money. Michael's a veteran of the business world and speaks that language really well. He's also married to my sister Maria, and together they make a really great team and keep Santana's standards high. In 2011 we reformed the group's management, based it in Las Vegas, and called it Universal Tone. In the end it's not just a monetary thing. Michael's been very good at maintaining relationships: he's constantly staying in touch and keeping things strong with the main people at HBO and Sony Music—even with Clive Davis. In 2012 he helped start Starfaith, our new label, which the Santana album *Shape Shifter* came out on.

*   *   *

Today Santana is blessed with musicians who bring conviction and consistency. Benny Rietveld's still our musical director and bassist, and his featured solos—like his blowing on John Lennon's "Imagine"—are a big part of our shows. Karl Perazzo has been with Santana the longest, and his power and grace is our link to that incredible San Francisco Latin scene—he played with Sheila E. and even Prince for a while. I love turning around and facing him when we trade riffs on guitar and timbales. Bill Ortiz and Jeff Cressman make up the Santana horn section and also come up out of that incredible Bay Area jazz tradition. Bill's recorded an excellent album playing trumpet over hip-hop tracks, and Jeff's expressive solos on anything with a Caribbean flavor remind me of great ska trombonists like Don Drummond. Andy Vargas and Tony Lindsay are the voices of Santana, and between them they cover the full range of flavors—from gospel and gutbucket to clear and smooth—and they help hold up the energy, since they're always right up front, on the edge of the stage.

Now we also have Tommy Anthony, who came to us from Gloria Estefan's band and is a triple threat—a singer with a high, clear voice; a great rhythm guitarist with an amazing vocabulary of rock chords; and he's one of Miami's best guitar soloists. And we have David K. Mathews on keyboards, who was with Tower of Power and Etta James before us. He's become imperative to the band because he's got knowledge of everything from Otis Spann and McCoy Tyner to Randy Weston and Eddie Palmieri. He also has tattoos depicting piano legends Fats Waller and James Booker.

The two newest members are Paoli Mejias Ramos on congas and José Pepe Jiménez on drums. They both have Puerto Rican roots and have brought their own authenticity and commitment, which gives the music a new feel but keeps us in a band situation—it's not just me up front with guys playing parts and wearing the Santana jacket. I'd rather hear us taking chances and trying out new songs and having a bad performance than have an okay performance that just rubber-stamps all the old hits.

Before every Santana concert I still meditate for fifteen to twenty minutes, and anyone in the band is welcome to join me— it's not required, but just about everyone comes by and joins the circle at least once in a while. I tell them, "Nothing is mandatory except you being one hundred percent present and playing your ass off onstage." After meditating, I'll have a pre-show huddle to talk about the show and go over new tunes or new segues or a new part of a song that keeps the show fresh and moving. We might try out something that came to mind because of something somebody said or something I heard on my iPod. We were in Monaco recently, and I decided we should try an O'Jays song I know, "I Love Music"—which has words about coming together and helping each other out and has great gospel energy. A perfect message for a hoity-toity dinner theater in that part of the world, right? Maybe we should have done "Rich Get Richer." Anyway, we worked on it through sound check and backstage before the show. We only did it once, but it was worth it.

There's a lot of money in Vegas—a *lot*. I know that's not news to anyone. For me, there's a feeling of possibility in that desert atmosphere—a crystallization of intent that could reach people in all parts of the world—which is something you don't feel in other places. It's like the difference between millions and billions. It's not difficult there to meet with people like the head of Mandalay Bay or other performers and spread ideas about how to put some of this money to work and really make a difference. It's starting to happen—just look at Andre Agassi and Steffi Graf's foundation and what they're doing right there with kids and schools in Las Vegas.

One night not long ago, my lawyer, John Branca, Michael, Cindy, and I had dinner with some top casino executives and their wives, and they were asking about Santana and how we keep it fresh and hit with so much energy after all this time. I told them, but then I said, "Look, man, I'm happy to answer these questions, but I need for you to know two things from my heart. The first is that consciousness can be very profitable. The second one is this: here in Las Vegas you have the means and money and the talent to get together and create a nightly talk-and-music TV show that would beat anything that comes out of New York or Los Angeles. Just find the right host, someone who can be funny and who's not predictable and who can get the right message across about how we can all best serve the planet."

They looked at me like they were wondering just how serious I was, and they saw I was very serious. After a moment I said, "There's nothing that's not possible when you have supreme determination and undeterred vision."

I miss certain things about the West Coast, but it's just a ninety-minute flight to get back there, and I have learned to love Las Vegas and share it with Cindy, the new queen of my heart—watching the sunrise and the sunset together, so beautiful in the desert, meditating, exercising, playing guitar, listening to my favorite music, then eating with her at a really great restaurant, where I've gotten to know the chef and the people working there. Then my favorite thing—waking up the next day with Cindy, who is so soft—not only her skin but her mind and her heart—and then starting it all over again.

In February of 2010 Salvador had come out with a new record and had a party in Los Angeles. Deborah was there and came to greet me when I arrived and gave me a courtesy hug. I could tell the kids were all watching. The next day I flew back to Las Vegas and received a card from her saying that it was nice to see me. I called her and thanked her for the card. We were still working out how to handle ourselves with each other, but our priority was to do what was best for our kids—to be open and positive and respectful.

At that point two things happened: I consciously let go of feeling guilty about Deborah, both emotionally and psychologically, and I quit smoking—really quit smoking this time, not part-time.

I continued with the inner work, but it was different, like a huge door was opening to a room that had been closed for a long time. When I stepped into the room I could hear a voice saying, "Take a deep breath, clean up the place, brush your teeth, open the door, open your heart, and be vulnerable again." I took a deep breath, and the air was refreshing and tasted different in my lungs. Then I heard, "Now invite your queen."

The first time Cindy Blackman and I met nothing really happened. I wish I could say it did, but we were both in different places in our lives, and part of the joy in life is not having everything handed to you all at once. Only when you look back do you see how the story makes sense. It was 2002, and she was playing drums with Lenny Kravitz, and we were all at a rock festival in Germany. Dennis Chambers had been telling me, "Man, wait till you see this lady play. She's killer." So I stuck around to see Lenny's show, and maybe it was the two songs I heard, but I didn't hear what he was talking about. I was thinking, "Okay, hmm. When is she going to play?" What she was doing was basically holding the beat steady, as if she were holding a tray for somebody—the music didn't want to let her go. But the next night was a revelation. Cindy took some great solos and played some crazy fills. That's when I knew she really could play.

The more I have listened the more I have changed my perception of Lenny and his music. I have to thank him from the center of my heart, because he made it possible for me to know that Cindy existed. A few years later, Cindy's sister Tracy, who's a singer and guitarist, saw me eating at a restaurant in the Bay Area called Comforts. Suddenly there was a woman with beautiful red hair and freckles standing next to me, and with supreme confidence she said, "You're Carlos Santana." I said, "Hello," and I was thinking she wanted me to sign something or take a photo. But instead she had one message to give me. "You need to meet my sister—she plays drums." And of course I recognized the name when she told me. I said, "Okay, I'm very grateful."

It still didn't mean anything to me—Cupid hadn't shot any

arrows yet. Then in May, we played a private show for a German electronics company in Orlando, and Dennis couldn't make it because he had been booked with someone else. I heard a voice say, "Call Cindy."

"Cindy?"

"Remember Cindy Blackman, who played with Lenny?" So I asked my production manager to do that, and we had already confirmed her when Rashiki and I got around to downloading some of her albums and listening to them while driving around. I was going, "Uh-oh. That's not the same person I heard that time in Germany!"

Cindy was playing music on a different level from what I expected—improvising and setting up highly evolved grooves—and she had people like Patrice Rushen and Buster Williams playing with her. I could tell she had a lot of Tony Williams and some Elvin Jones in her music collection—later I got to know that she had learned a lot from hanging out with Art Blakey. She left a voice mail on my phone to talk about the music for the show. I called her back, and we went over the set list, then I went into my story about hitting the "wah," which I tell every new person who comes into the band.

This goes back to something I saw in Africa when we played there in 1971—a circle of six or seven women who started chanting together, going "Hey ya na na na..." faster and faster, their voices chanting different parts, until they brought it all together at the same moment with a huge *"Wah!!"* It was amazing—all that energy at once. After that I started noticing the "wah" in Buddy Rich's and James Brown's and Duke Ellington's and Tito Puente's music, and that each has his own way of hitting the "wah"—or the 1. But the band cannot hit it too hard or go over the top—they need to visit it just enough, at the right time, to give it a collective consciousness.

We were getting ready to do the sound check in Florida a day before the Orlando show when I noticed Cindy walking slowly to the stage through the house, and she smiled and waved. She had come down to check out the band before she played with us, and she was carrying something with her. She was dressed very plain Jane, like she was going to yoga class—plain but funky, with no makeup, which for me can be ten times more magnetic than glamour. She listened to the band, and I kept watching her out of the corner of my eye. There was a spirit in her that I could feel. I knew she was very excited to be there and play with us, which is exactly what I hope any musician will bring.

We met backstage after the sound check, and she presented me with a book—the catalog of a Miles Davis exhibition in Montreal. So I reached into the shoulder bag I always have with me and gave her my iPod, which was filled with every bit of Miles music I had collected over the years, much of it very hard to find. She went back to her hotel room, listened to the iPod, and found Paolo Rustichelli's "Capri," a beautiful melody with Miles playing on it. It's such a beautiful melody that, looking back on it now, I'm almost sure she wanted to marry me on the spot. I'm kidding, but really with music like that I don't think she stood a chance.

We did the show together in Orlando, and it went great, and she killed it. She knew all the parts, and her drumming reminded me of a hummingbird or an angry bee. Cindy has great time, but she's not just a timekeeper; she isn't about finding the pocket and just parking it. Then the rest is kind of personal, but I will say this—we got together and talked for hours, and I found myself showing her what we were doing with Santana, the Milagro Foundation, and a website called Architects of a New Dawn, which has some of my favorite videos. I realize now that what I was doing was trying to show her who I am personally, who I am outside of that Santana guitar guy.

The next day Cindy told me she had to leave for a gig with a Native American rock guitarist and singer: "I'm going to Santa Fe to play with Micki Free and his band." I didn't try to hide my disappointment. "Really? Why do you have to—" I couldn't believe I heard myself saying that to another musician. "Why don't you just stick around?"

"No, really—I have to make this gig."

So Cindy left, and I grabbed Chad and said, "We need to go to Disney World."

"Disney World? What for?" I didn't have time to explain the whole thing to him, but somehow Cindy and I had gotten to talking about Mickey and Minnie Mouse the night before, so told him, "I got to find those Minnie Mouse ears with glitter so I can send them to Cindy." We walked around for two hours to every store in that place—and there were a lot of them. The sales clerks kept sending us "that way" and "over there," but most of them didn't know what we were talking about. Chad was ready to have them custom-made. Just before we gave up I found two salesladies who said, "Oh, you mean the ones for little girls? Those are the only ones with glitter. Here you go."

I relaxed and had them specially wrapped and brought them home with me—somehow I had a feeling that once I gave them to Cindy, something really remarkable was going to happen. And it did.

I am a resident of Nevada, but I also have a house high up in the hills in Tiburon, with an incredible view of the North Bay and the Golden Gate Bridge. I invited Cindy to come visit me there when we were both off the road in June, and she accepted. I remember watching how she walked into my home, with a smooth gait like a panther's, looking all around her. The house has big windows, and the day could not have been more beautiful, with the sun shining through and the sky and the bay each an incredible shade of blue. She came up to me and gave me what I call a kitchen hug—not just because of where it took place but also because it was long and tender and filled with a pledge of domestic devotion. It was sealed right there—and then I put the Minnie Mouse ears on her. Man, it was like being seventeen and in high school again and feeling in one moment all the passion and emotion that you think you'll ever feel in your life. Well, more like fourteen and junior high.

We sat down, and I remember holding her hands and looking into her eyes and then hearing my own voice saying very softly, "Cindy, would you be my wife?" She was like a little girl. Her eyes sparkled and opened wide, and she said yes.

CARLOS SANTANA

Of course I had to ask her father, Daddy Dude—that's what I
call him—for his permission. Since I asked Cindy to come along
with Santana that summer and sit in with us every night, we waited
a few weeks until the tour brought us to Chicago, where he lived.
We went out to a soul food restaurant, and I waited for his answer.
He looked at me, then he looked at Cindy for a long time and said,
"I don't think I've ever seen her more happy, Carlos."

The next night I couldn't keep it inside me any longer. Cindy's
dad and his lady were at the concert, along with Buddy Guy's wife
and Otis Rush's wife, too. It all felt like family. After Cindy sat in
and took a drum solo on "Corazón Espinado," I went up to the
microphone and took the chance and in front of the audience at the
First Midwest Bank Amphitheater in Tinley Park, Illinois, I asked
her one more time to be my wife. Her answer was the same as it
was the first time.

Cindy traveled with Santana through the end of 2010, sitting in
almost every night—in fact, that's never stopped happening. She'll
come out on tour with us or sit in at the House of Blues in Las
Vegas even while she continues to make her own music happen—
including her Tony Williams Lifetime tribute band, with Vernon
Reid, organist John Medeski, and bassist Jack Bruce. At home I'll
watch her play drums—I mean really play—and look at her face,
and I'll say to myself, "This is what she was born to do with or without me," and that's absolutely okay. I feel sorry for anyone who
would try to put himself between someone like her and what she
loves, saying, "It's either me or the music." Excuse me? Well, you
know how I feel about that.

I love confidence in women, and I really need it in my woman.
Cindy has a quiet confidence that comes from not having to prove
anything to anyone. It's a blessing to be with someone who is just
comfortable in her own skin.

Besides being a lover and a friend, she is patient and compassionate and attentive—she's always asking if I'm keeping myself
hydrated, which is important in a place like Las Vegas. If she brings

THE UNIVERSAL TONE

along one bottle of water for a drive, she'll always have a second one for me. I took her to her first professional basketball game, and now I've got her cheering for the Golden State Warriors and she's got me into some Chicago teams. Now I've got a partner when I go up against basketball fans like Hal Miller and Chad Wilson, who always want to gang up on me and bet against me. I'll tell them what we think about the Heat or the Spurs, and they'll go off saying something like, "Oh, now it's 'Cindy and I'!"

Yes, that's right. Cindy is one of the boys—I mean, she came up hanging with Art Blakey & the Jazz Messengers and Tony Williams and hearing all the guy talk and laughing and not getting all bent out of shape. Like any couple, we are still learning to communicate. We do it by phone and text and, when I come home, by words and touch.

There's that saying again: you don't necessarily attract what you want or what you need, you attract who you are. It didn't surprise me to learn that Cindy studied kabbalah and is deeply spiritual. When I first spoke to her of things like angels and the invisible realm, it was as if we were just picking up a conversation that we had started a long time ago. When I told Jerry and Diane, they said, "You know, Cindy is a creation of your spirit. You created her, and she created you. You both prayed for each other, and you both did the inner work. Cindy is also here to help you clean your inner closet." I said, "Inner closet?" Jerry told me that I needed to pull open all the drawers and bring out all my compulsions, my embarrassments, my fantasies, and get past the guilt, shame, judgments, and fears.

Now Cindy and I aspire together; we share the desire for divinity. Cindy and I read together every day to recharge our belief and to reinforce our hope, trust, and faith so that when we need to we have the strength to clear our paths and move our egos out of the way. Together we write poems and spiritual messages that we post on Facebook and share with all. Together we wrote the following poem, "I Am the Universal Tone," on July 8, 2011:

I am the universal tone
That gives birth to inspiration, vision, motivation and aspiration.
You are the beat that's in touch with the pulse of all hearts.
We are the vessels that channel God's Light & Love.
All and every thing in God's kingdom is a harbinger of His essence
Sweet harmony, solid oneness, gracious grace, divine and beauty
Is what and who we are when we are conscious of being in the center
    of our heart
And when we are in perfect harmonic flow with our Creator and the
    universe
We remain open to receiving his light and to channel it out to ALL
    that exists.
Smile and let the light shine through and elevate, transform,
    illumine all and everyone
With the joy, peace, light, love of your spirit.
Be happy and love-filled in your supreme divinity.

Four years later I'm grateful—really, really grateful. I still can't believe that out of everyone in this world God picked a partner so compatible with my energy and my principles and put her in front of me. As Wayne says, it takes courage to be happy, and right now I believe I am the happiest person on this planet. My most treasured possession right now is a new guitar that my wife commissioned from Paul Reed Smith and gave to me when we were married on December 19, 2010, in Hawaii. Written on the back between the tuning knobs are the words: THE FIRST TIME EVER, EVERYTHING. ETERNALLY YOURS, CINDY.

Our wedding included everyone who is important to us—our families and best friends, my kids, and Jerry and Diane, who spoke and asked for a moment of silence so we could all behold each other without the distraction of words or thoughts. Herbie and Wayne were there, too, and honored us with their presence and their music—they played "Afro Blue" and "Stella by Starlight." Before the ceremony I asked Sal whether he was okay with what I was doing, and what he said still makes me wonder how he achieved such a high level of spiritual awareness. He asked if Cindy and I, as part of the ceremony, would fill a wooden bowl with rainwater and wash each other's hands to symbolize the forgiveness of all things from our pasts—that we were starting fresh and clean. We did that, then Cindy read her vows from her iPhone and I read from my iPad, and then we danced to Ronald Isley's recording of Burt Bacharach's "The Look of Love."

The second time I walked the red carpet was with Cindy, in December of 2013, for the screening of the HBO special of our concert in Guadalajara. That was her first time—she looked amazing, and I couldn't stop checking her out. I'm constantly looking at Cindy anyway: her nose is so beautiful, her lips and her hair are incredible, and her heart brings it all together perfectly for me. When it came time to stop for the photographers that night, she forgot to look at the cameras, as you're supposed to, and instead she was checking *me* out. I remember that we laughed about it, then Cindy got a little serious and said, "But can you see the way I'm looking at you?" Man, I could feel tears of joy coming, so I had to quickly say what I was thinking right then, the only words that came to me in that moment.

"Oh, yes. *Yes.*"

AFTERWORD

Hoy y Mañana

Archbishop Desmond Tutu and me, February 24, 2014.

When we played live at the Montreux Jazz Festival in 1988 with Wayne Shorter, Wayne said in an interview, "I look for books that never end." I love that idea. This book is like that—there's much more to come, and yet it lives in the holy instant, a sanctuary from worrying about the future or being stuck in the past. Nobody's insane if he's 100 percent present in the now, you know?

In my life, the now that's still being written has always included three parts—my music, the spiritual realm, and the domestic rhythm.

I said this before, and I'll say it again: in my family, even after the divorce, there remains nothing but blessings and beauty. I am grateful to Deborah for our years together and for our three beautiful children. I am so proud of them—they've never been in any trouble, and each has a natural feeling for staying in the groove with elegance and integrity. I can see members of my family reflected in each of them and I can see that they all come from a long river of music: my father was a musician, and his father was a *músico municipal,* as was his father before him. On their mother's side, SK was the original King of R & B, playing blues and ballads before B. B., Albert, or Freddie ever did. Through Sal, Stella, and Jelli, the river keeps rolling.

While working on this book I kept thinking about my kids. "What will they think when they read it?" I know they're going to say that I was honest, raw, and compassionate, and that's enough for me.

I have learned from my kids how to be a dad—when to speak and when not to speak. From Santana, in the musical realm, I learned how to be a leader in a band. Even before Santana, I figured out that sometimes somebody has to step up and say something, and if nobody does, then I'll have to be the one to be the chef in the kitchen. I learned that a leader is not hesitant to speak up and say, "The potatoes are still raw, and they're too hard. Let them cook some more."

Santana came about because I would hear a new musician such as Michael Shrieve or Chepito or Neal Schon and think, "Hmm. He could work well with the band we have now," and that is still true today. There's always room for growth and change. Santana in 2014 is not what it was in '68, '73, or '89. It is not meant to be the same. I believe that is the Santana signature—the one thing that has stayed the same in our music is a consistency of higher and higher presentation.

I believe that's why the music of Santana stays vital and strong. I also believe that our music reminds people that they don't have to wait for heaven to arrive; it's already here. It has the power to inspire, to transport, and to change people, even on a physical level. I get letters and e-mails and online posts from fans saying that a concert helped them heal in ways that they needed but never expected. In the past year alone I've heard from people in Dayton and Spokane who've said that our music has reached their souls and transformed their bodies. It is all ignited and connected by sound, so when I speak about my musical life and the spiritual realm, you must understand that they cannot be separated. Sound assaults your senses and bombards your molecules, and your body knows that no matter what the mind is thinking the connection is always there.

More than a walk down memory lane, this book is meant to bring all the stories in my life to light so people can see that there's always room for growth and enlightenment. By "enlightenment" I mean lightening up—having fun with your life. Even when my life was totally in balance, when the domestic, musical, and spiritual were all manifested at the highest levels—even at Woodstock and at the Grammy Awards—I had a hard time accepting myself and seeing myself the way others saw me. But now I can do that, and I'll relax and lighten up. I'll be brushing my teeth or combing my hair, and all of sudden I'll yell out, "Damn!" Cindy will come in and go, "What happened—you okay?" I'll keep looking in the mirror and say, "Man, that's one handsome Mexican. No wonder you chased me all over the place." She'll look at me and just shake her head.

I am now sixty-seven years young, and I feel great—I have loads of energy. My typical day starts early and goes late into the night. I believe that my years of maintaining a strict vegetarian diet, even though I now eat meat, helped my body in the long run. I still am picky about my meals: I try not to overeat, and I eat salads when I can. I enjoy a beer or glass of wine, but I'm not a big drinker. I exercise daily, too. I'm happy to say that my eyes and ears don't need any help, and everything else that needs to function—as a musician and as a man—is working just fine, thank you very much.

Wayne and I have spoken about what happens if we ever come to a time when certain things are taken away from us, when our fingers don't want to work anymore, and he said he wasn't worried. "Creative people will always find a way to create." I take a lot of comfort in that and thank God every day that my fingers can hold a guitar and work the strings and hit the notes that can transform and inspire. If a time ever comes when my fingers can't do that anymore, I'll just be grateful that there was a time when they could.

If my abilities leave me I think I might just start a tiny little church in Hawaii. I'll call it the Church of the Holy Choice, because that's what everyone has—a choice. It'll be different from most churches, because the only thing required will be for you to make an inner commitment to attaining a tangible change within yourself, to take responsibility for yourself and stop being a bitter victim. You have to be like a dog shaking off water, shaking off all that stuff that you shouldn't be carrying around.

I see the church as having pews and being open to the outside world, and it will have vibrant, vital music, the primary part of which will be the rhythm. It can be local music, but it will have to have congas to put away the false notion that drums and percussion are the instruments of the devil. I will speak, and there will be chanting, and even if I can still play I'll put the guitar down and keep it to one side for special events. When the time comes that part of my life will be dedicated to presenting what the Holy Ghost wants me to present.

I've been on this beautiful planet since July 20, 1947, and I have never, ever prayed or asked anything from Satan, Lucifer, devils, or any other dark force. I believe in angels, archangels, thought adjusters, sentient beings, benevolent spirits, and family members who have passed on and are still here to guide me and protect me. I still read and meditate and do what I can to strengthen my belief muscles, just as going to the gym develops my other muscles. Some people might think that once you start discovering godly things and go down the path to enlightenment you have to lose your appetite for the world, and that's just not true. That's not how I've lived my life, and that's not going to change.

I believe there is a supreme being, a supreme creator, and whether it's Jesus, Buddha, Krishna, or Allah, it's as John Coltrane said: "All paths lead to God." Divinity has many names but only one destination. God is all harmony—not just one chord or one note. To say that one of them is the only one, and that everyone who worships another is wrong and going to hell, is mummified and petrified thinking.

I don't want to go to heaven if it's selective. And there's another thing I pray for — I only want to go to heaven if they have congas up there.

My book started with a parade — it ends on an island.

I think about islands a lot. Sometimes interviewers want to know what music or other things I'd take with me to a deserted place. I usually tell them Miles Davis's *Sketches of Spain,* my guitar, and a copy of *A Course in Miracles.* At the end of 2013 I was pretty much ready to move to an island: we went from the Kennedy Center Honors straight to Mexico to film the HBO special, and we were finishing *Corazón* around the same time.

That's still a dream I have — to be able to cash in all the chips and move to someplace like Hawaii the way it was a hundred years ago. There are still places like that around the world, where you can escape and hide out and coexist with nature; where the sky is your roof, the ocean is your bathtub, and it's always the right temperature. If you feel hungry, you can just pull a papaya or a coconut or a mango right out of a tree.

I used to tell myself, "Wow, what an incredible existence that would be." Now I hear a voice that says, "Don't kid yourself, man. You'd be bored to death in two hours."

The part of my life that's exhausting is the dichotomy between having all this energy and feeling that I really do need to find out how to relax and slow down the touring and the planning so that I can catch up with myself and get a better look at what's up ahead. Being with Cindy has helped me with that; I have consciously made a commitment to get off the road and stop doing the Santana thing from time to time, to get away from the craziness. Now, as ever, I'm all about the holy instant, the state of grace that I always try to attain and maintain, ready everywhere and in every way to receive the Universal Tone.

Acknowledgments

There were a number of people who were supremely instrumental in assisting me in presenting this book. Ashley Kahn brought his writing skills and his consciousness to capture my voice and take the moments and memories and erect them into a building that feels like home to me and is an open invitation for anyone to learn and discover and experience a forever joy. Hal Miller sat and traveled with me, recording my stories and preserving the details and names and dates, and kept an overview of it all to make sure it was on a high road and maintained a balance of the different parts of my life—the domestic, the music, and the tried-and-true funky street psychology. I am grateful to the team that made this all possible—my book agent, Jillian Manus; public relations manager Michael Jensen; and Michael Pietsch and John Parsley at Little, Brown. They all believed in this book from the very beginning. My heart goes out to my two old friends from high school, Michael Carabello and Linda Houston, for sharing what they remembered about us back in my earliest days in America. I'm eternally grateful to my sister Maria and her husband, Michael Vrionis, for looking over my shoulder during all this, and to my wife, Cindy, for reading through every word and being at the center of my inner and outer support systems.

With Santana, I am now the head of a fast-rolling train, and I'm responsible for many things that happen as we keep moving—concerts and recordings and products and now this book. Even if my A-Team of music and production professionals were not directly involved with the words on these pages, they are all in here in spirit. I like to remind them that if people don't notice anything of what they do or their combination of experience, daring, and sheer focus, that's because they're doing a perfect job. I must give thanks to this team for their divine dedication and mention them by name.

Skip Rickert, our tour manager, formerly worked with Stevie Ray Vaughan throughout his whole career and also with major acts like Barbra Streisand, Guns N' Roses, ZZ Top, and the Backstreet Boys. He makes sure the road is as clear as possible and has expanded our touring world by introducing us to new venues in Africa, India, and Europe. Assistant tour manager Libby "Mr. Thousand Rainbows" Fabro works with a quiet and efficient elegance and intention, always trying to make life on the road as comfortable and predictable as possible. Our production manager, Michael "Hoss" Keifer, takes care of everything we need onstage no matter the country or the situation and oversees the technical guys, making sure all the sound, lights, and video are at the same high level of presentation as the music. The Santana crew is the envy of many other touring bands—I've heard this again and again over the years—and a big reason for this is Hoss. Chris "Stubby" McNair does almost anything a stage tech can be asked to do and gets it done immediately—he's Mr. Super Dependable, the guy responsible for maintaining and securing our equipment all year round. My guitar tech, Ed Adair, has been with Santana since the 1980s, and between the two of them I know every instrument's going to be ready to grab and play. No matter where the gig is, Ed's the one guy I know who will always be right by my side keeping everything in tune. I know that the Santana sound is going to hit the audience in the best way possible because of our sound engineers—Rob Mailman in the house and Brian Montgomery onstage. They are super important in making sure Santana is supremely present and powerful in consistency, every night. Bob Higgins is the director in charge of our in-concert videos, which we added to our show after *Supernatural*. He does a great job of connecting the visuals with the spiritual center and rhythm of each song, including putting the audience themselves into the show.

The people at Universal Tone Management have been with Santana for decades now and are loyal and invaluable. I must thank Adam Fells, who's been with us since before *Supernatural* and started out on the road and now touches almost everything we do. He's our day-to-day, get-things-done man who knows the Santana history almost better than anyone. Rita Gentry, our link to Bill Graham and our incredible make-it-happen resource, knows how to deal with any challenge or any person. Micki Alboff's been our office manager for over twelve years—she has the amazing talent of knowing exactly what's happening with everything we're doing at any time. My daughter Jelli runs the Santana archives and is doing a valuable job preserving the band's history. There are many others in the office, and I cannot see how Santana or I could do what we do without them—all the concerts, the recordings, the business, and the travel. Even this book.

Finally, I am eternally grateful for the fans of Santana—so many of them have become family. After all these years on the road, they are the ones who still excite me and make me eager to get to sound check and rehearse new songs and show them that Santana still has it. I know many of them by name—like Kristin, Phillipine, Lisa, and Natalie, the four girls I first met in Vienna in 1989 and who've grown up with Santana's music, faithfully coming out to hear us every year, and who are now adult women with families of their own. And Sara, the woman in Montreux who always gets up and dances so beautifully, as long as we're playing a *guajira,* so we make sure we do that every time we are there.

I dedicated this book to my mom, but I could not have done that or had the stories to tell without the fans who have supported Santana since our beginning days in San Francisco and who are now everywhere around the world. Their supreme love and steady support is why we continue to do what we do—this book stands in appreciation of them.

Ashley Kahn would like to personally amplify the gratitude expressed to John Parsley, Michael Jensen, Jillian Manus, and Michael and Maria Vrionis, and include thanks to his literary agent, Dave Dunton at Harvey Klinger, Inc., as well as to Adam Fells, Chad Wilson, Cynthia Colonna, Abigail Royle, Sonny Schneidau, Laurent Masson, and especially Hal Miller—his sparring partner on this literary and spiritual journey. He reserves his deepest appreciation for Carlos himself, with thanks for the opportunity to listen, to learn, and to know what it's like to be unafraid to dream of the infinite.

Photograph Credits

Introduction: © Santana Archives
Chapter 1: © Santana Archives
Chapter 2: © Santana Archives
Chapter 3: © Santana Archives
Chapter 4: © Harry Crosby / University of California, San Diego
Chapter 5: © Santana Archives
Chapter 6: © Santana Archives
Chapter 7: © Jim Marshall Photography LLC
Chapter 8: © Michael Ochs Archives / Getty Images
Chapter 9: © Bill Eppridge / Time Life Pictures / Getty Images
Chapter 10: © Sony Music Entertainment
Chapter 11: © The Estate of David Gahr / Getty Images
Chapter 12: © Michael Ochs Archives / Getty Images
Chapter 13: © Sony Music Entertainment
Chapter 14: © Michael Ochs Archives / Getty Images
Chapter 15: © Michael Ochs Archives / Getty Images
Chapter 16: © Jim Marshall Photography LLC
Chapter 17: © Sony Music Entertainment
Chapter 18: © Ebet Roberts
Chapter 19: © Santana Archives
Chapter 20: © Ken Friedman

PHOTOGRAPH CREDITS

Index